An Introduction to Civil Wars

*To my grandfather Fernand Joseph DeRouen Sr. (1898–1981)
and my son Fernand Jacques DeRouen*

An Introduction to Civil Wars

Karl DeRouen, Jr.
University of Alabama

Los Angeles | London | New Delhi
Singapore | Washington DC

Los Angeles | London | New Delhi
Singapore | Washington DC

FOR INFORMATION:

CQ Press

An Imprint of SAGE Publications, Inc.

2455 Teller Road

Thousand Oaks, California 91320

E-mail: order@sagepub.com

SAGE Publications Ltd.

1 Oliver's Yard

55 City Road

London EC1Y 1SP

United Kingdom

SAGE Publications India Pvt. Ltd.

B 1/I 1 Mohan Cooperative Industrial Area

Mathura Road, New Delhi 110 044

India

SAGE Publications Asia-Pacific Pte. Ltd.

3 Church Street

#10-04 Samsung Hub

Singapore 049483

Printed in the United States of America

Library of Congress Cataloging-in-Publication Data

DeRouen, Karl R., 1962-
An Introduction to civil wars / Karl DeRouen, Jr., University of Alabama.

pages cm
Includes bibliographical references and index.

ISBN 978-1-4522-4432-7 (pbk. : alk. paper)
1. Civil war. 2. Conflict management. 3. Peace-building.
4. Intervention (International law) I. Title.

U21.2.D338 2015
303.6′4—dc23   2014011890

This book is printed on acid-free paper.

Acquisitions Editor: Sarah Calabi

Editorial Assistant: Davia Grant

Production Editor: Kelly DeRosa

Copy Editor: Patrice Sutton

Typesetter: C&M Digitals (P) Ltd.

Proofreader: Alison Syring

Indexer: Mary Mortensen

Cover Designer: Michael Dubowe

Marketing Manager: Amy Whitaker

MIX
Paper from
responsible sources
FSC® C014174

14 15 16 17 18 10 9 8 7 6 5 4 3 2 1

CONTENTS

LIST OF FEATURES

Boxes

Figures

Maps

Tables

C ivil war is the most prevalent form of organized armed violence, affecting millions of people worldwide every year. According to the Uppsala University's Uppsala Conflict Data Program, as of 2012 there were 31 active civil or internationalized civil wars—and one active interstate war (see http://www.pcr.uu.se/research/ucdp/). Scholars are well aware of the vast body of literature on the topic as well. It is therefore surprising that there are few books on civil war that are appropriate for student readers who are approaching it for the first time. This volume provides students with a systematic, comprehensive overview of the topic by covering civil war patterns, types, causes, costs (human and economic), outcomes, peace agreements, and duration; terrorism and intervention in the context of civil war; conflict management; and post-conflict issues, such as peacebuilding.

This book is appropriate for undergraduate and graduate course adoption, researchers, and the policy-making community. The book will find its greatest use in courses on civil war, conflict management, international security and conflict, and international relations. Because of its broad coverage of the literature, it will be of special utility for classes requiring research and writing assignments. There, students can make use of the book's Appendix materials (the UCDP's list of civil wars) and the comprehensive bibliography as well. Especially useful for upper-level undergraduate and graduate courses on civil wars, conflict management, and international conflict, I also include a list of suggested readings for each chapter.

A special feature of the book is its focus on conflict management. Each chapter has a section that links conflict management (which encompasses activities like negotiation, mediation, conflict prevention, peace agreements, peacebuilding, and peacekeeping operations that are designed to ameliorate, resolve, and even prevent future conflict) to the main subject of the chapter. For example, I discuss how war termination type has implications for the duration of the peace. War type (war over control of government and territorial wars) is also expected to impact war duration and intractability. This theme helps tie the book together and puts the scholarly literature directly into conversation with the practitioner and policy-making community. The book has an empirical orientation, so readers will be able to compare features of civil war and understand trends. To this end, relevant data are presented graphically and in tables throughout the text and important datasets are identified. The Appendix also includes a list of civil wars since World War II and the names of the rebel groups fighting in each one.

The book is organized so that, after a brief introduction that provides an overview of the subject, readers are first presented with what scholars think is the most urgent issue: the costs of civil war. To establish the importance of studying civil war, that chapter (Chapter 2) covers costs, such as casualties, economic problems, human displacement, lost educational opportunities, crime, and environmental degradation. Chapter 3 considers the dynamics of civil war including types (wars over government, such as coups and revolutions and wars over territory), trends, tactics, and counterinsurgency strategies.

Chapter 4 covers the causes of civil war. Topics include the greed versus grievance debate, democracy, globalization, environmental causes, ethno-religious factors, and rebel opportunity. Chapter 5 focuses on natural resources and civil war. The relevant sections in this chapter are the resource curse, the role of resources such as oil, timber, and gems in war onset. Civil war termination and post-conflict issues are covered in Chapter 6. Specific topics include outcome trends, peace agreements, international intervention involving mediation and peace agreement assistance, peacebuilding, humanitarian law, and statebuilding. International intervention is the subject of Chapter 7. Here, I further discuss the role of third-party mediation, the United Nations, and peace agreements. Chapter 8 covers terrorism in civil wars. The chapter begins with the incidence of terrorism and civil war terrorism; the targets, tactics, and means of terrorists; violence against civilians; spoilers of peace processes; the role of Islam; and case studies on Iraq and Afghanistan where terrorism in the civil war context has been rampant. The final chapter is the Conclusion in which the book is summarized in the context of the conflict management theme.

Feature boxes are incorporated throughout the text to explore certain topics like critical data resources and watershed events in further detail. For instance, in Chapter 4, we look at the Minorities at Risk Data Project, and in Chapter 3, we discuss the Arab Spring uprising in the context of failing regimes. Because the book is empirically focused, I naturally included many maps, tables, and figures to help illustrate critical trends in civil wars, and I have also included a handful of photos to help make the subject matter more immediate to readers.

ACKNOWLEDGMENTS

I owe great debts of gratitude to Paul Bellamy and Sugu Narayanan. Both played major roles in the writing of the first draft, and Paul was instrumental in helping me to revise that draft. Charisse Kiino of SAGE was a great supporter of the project and offered valuable comments and support throughout. Elise Frasier was instrumental in editing the first draft, Patrice Sutton did a great job copyediting, and the final product is much better for their efforts. I would also like to thank the reviewers of the manuscript proposal for their insights and suggestions: Roy Licklider, Rutgers University; Caroline Hartzell, Gettysburg College; Bethany Lacina, University of Rochester; Doug Lemke, Pennsylvania State University; Artyom Tonoyan, Baylor University; and Shadrack W. Nasong'o, Rhodes College.

Many of the insights and ideas contained herein are drawn from research funded by the Folke Bernadotte Academy of Sweden, the Marsden Fund of the Royal Society of New Zealand, and the British Academy.

MAP 1.1
Civil Wars Worldwide, 1946–2011

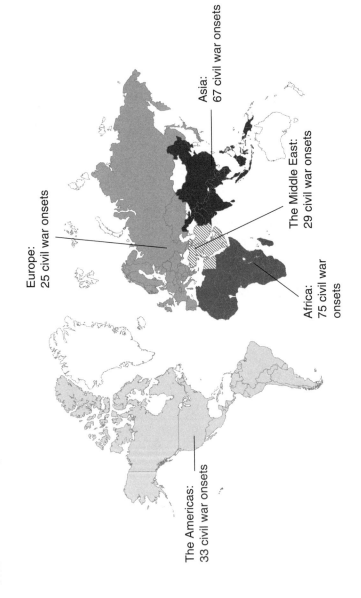

Europe:
25 civil war onsets

Asia:
67 civil war onsets

The Middle East:
29 civil war onsets

Africa:
75 civil war
onsets

The Americas:
33 civil war onsets

Sources: Gleditsch et al. (2002); Themnér and Wallensteen (2012).

CHAPTER 1

Introduction

Civil war is a global phenomenon with profound social and political consequences. From 1946 to 2011, a total of 102 countries—about half of the entire world's states—experienced civil wars. During that 60-year period, Africa witnessed the most with 40 of its more than 50 countries experiencing civil wars. In the Americas, 20 countries experienced civil war, Asia saw 18, Europe 13, and the Middle East 11 (Gleditsch et al. 2002; Themnér and Wallensteen 2012).

Civil wars are not only widespread; they also occur more frequently than wars between states. In 2000, a report from the UN Secretary General concluded that while interstate wars had been declining for some time, since the 1990s, most wars have been mainly internal. Indeed, former UN Secretary General Kofi Annan identified freedom from armed conflict as a UN priority, pointing to the fact that intrastate wars are brutally violent, claim millions of lives, and prey on ethnic and religious differences (United Nations [UN] 2000:43).

Loss of human life is certainly the most significant cost of civil war. The UN report showed that from 1990 to 2000, civil wars claimed more than 5 million lives worldwide, including countless civilians and children. According to one leading research organization, the Peace Research Institute Oslo (PRIO), there were approximately 350,000 civil war battle-related deaths in Europe and the Middle East between 1946 and 2008, and during the same period, African civil wars produced more than 1.2 million battle-related casualties. The most alarming statistic comes from Asia, which lost more than 3.1 million battle-related lives in brutal civil wars especially in Vietnam, Sri Lanka, India, and China (Harbom and Wallensteen 2009; Lacina and Gleditsch 2005).

Adding to the loss of life are other tragic factors that affect victims of civil wars. As noted in the UN report,

Women are becoming especially vulnerable to violence and sexual exploitation. Children are being taken away from parents, ending up as forced laborers and forced to become child soldiers.

Civilian populations are used as covers for the operations of rebel movements. In other cases, civilians face brutalities and become targets of genocides. (United Nations 2000:46)

Another of the profound international consequences of civil wars is human displacement in the form of refugees and internally displaced persons (IDPs) or people who have not crossed international borders to avoid violence but instead remain within their country's borders. At the beginning of 2013 there were over 15 million refugees in the world—most of whom had been displaced by civil conflict (UN High Commissioner for Refugees [UNHCR] 2014b). Between 1999 and 2004, there were 500,000 displaced from the war in Aceh, Indonesia, alone (Czaika and Kis-Katos 2009), and in a more extreme and short-term example, over 2.5 million people have been internally displaced in Syria since 2011 (UNHCR 2014a). In the past, governments and international organizations have more or less ignored the issue of displacement, but in recent years, partly because of UN and other international pressure, there have been greater efforts to address refugee needs.

International forces have also been mobilized to hold those accountable for crimes committed during civil wars: For instance, in April 2012, the UN-sponsored Special Court for Sierra Leone convicted former warlord and President of Liberia Charles Taylor (pictured in the photo on page 3) for crimes, such as mass murders, sex slavery, and using child soldiers (ABC News 2012). Still, the scale, frequency, and severity of civil wars warrants sustained attention and research to understand its many dimensions.

THEME OF THE BOOK

This book focuses on the central factors that explain civil war, including defining what scholars mean by civil war, who the major actors are, why civil wars start, how they are fought, the costs in life and livelihood, what explains their duration, how they end, and what makes them recur. At the end of each chapter, I return to conflict management, the theme of the book. The features of civil war discussed in this book have relevance for conflict management. For example, an understanding of the causes of civil war can help inform conflict prevention. Knowing the determinants of duration can help shape policies to shorten wars, and knowledge of war recurrence and civil war-related terrorism can help shape better peace agreements that are more likely to hold. Each of these features forms the basis of the chapters, but here in the Introduction, we will start with the basics: an overview of theoretical approaches to war in general and civil war in particular and discussion of the key terms and concepts involved in its empirical study.

Conflict management, as the term is applied here, refers to a set of practices, encompassing negotiation, mediation, conflict prevention, peace agreements, "peacebuilding," and peacekeeping operations that are designed to ameliorate, resolve, and even prevent future conflict. While each of these processes is discussed in detail in the relevant chapters, I can describe each of these processes in general terms.

Negotiations are talks between disputants or between a disputant and an outside negotiator. The goal of negotiations might be a cease-fire or peace agreement. Mediation is similar with the exception that the mediator shares information between the disputants either directly (in same room) or indirectly (separate locations). Conflict prevention takes place before a crisis situation escalates to armed violence. Peace agreements are documents containing provisions designed to stem the violence and lead the country toward stable peace. The provisions often address grievances, reconciliation, and power sharing. Agreements are often preceded by mediation and/or negotiations. It should also be mentioned that as peace talks near the agreement stage, they can trigger spoilers who see the process as a threat to their interests. Spoilers sometimes carry out terrorism to disrupt the peace process.

Peacebuilding is a process that occurs after the violence has ended. It is often preceded by a peace agreement. Peacebuilding often entails building democratic institutions so that peace is consolidated (see Doyle and Sambanis 2000). Peacekeeping operations (typically under the auspices of the United Nations) are also active after the violence has stopped. As such, they are also sometimes part

Charles Taylor

Former President of Liberia, Charles Taylor, seated during his trial in the Special Court for Sierra Leone (SCSL) in the Netherlands.

Credit: UN Photo/SCSL/AP Pool/Peter DeJong

of the peacebuilding process. Peacekeeping troops and trained civilians have many roles, such as maintaining law and order, assisting with new constitutions and elections, and, in many cases, patrolling to deter a recurrence of the civil war.

THE BASICS OF CIVIL WAR

There are several basic features of civil war that must first be considered before proceeding on to more advanced topics. These features include the definition of civil war, human costs of civil war, the disputants, and types of civil wars. They form the basic tool kit needed to analyze more advanced topics covered later in the chapter such as onset, duration, termination, and recurrence of civil war.

Definitions of Civil War

Researchers have long drawn a distinction between wars that occur between states, namely, interstate wars, and civil wars that take place between parties within the boundaries of a state. However, there are differences in the various ways that civil war is defined according to empirical standards, and the student of civil war must appreciate the fact that small changes in definitions can give rise to large differences in research discoveries. Indeed, as it will be noted later in the chapter, one of the reasons for varying opinions on what causes civil wars lies with differences in classification as indicated in Table 1.1. Notice that all of the definitions are based on two specific criteria: the number of deaths and the identity of the disputants.

Number of Deaths

I begin with a definition of armed conflict:

> Armed conflict is a contested incompatibility that concerns government or territory or both, where the use of armed force between two parties results in at least 25 battle-related deaths. Of these two parties, at least one has to be the government of a state. (Themnér and Wallensteen 2011:532)

While definitions vary, civil war is a type of armed conflict. Of the five major sources of data on civil wars, four define a civil war as a conflict causing 1,000 deaths, though distribution of those deaths across time varies. The Uppsala Conflict Data Program (UCDP), however, provides a benchmark of 25 battle-related deaths per year, which are classified as "civil conflicts." Conflicts involving over 1,000 deaths are "civil wars."

Each of these can be considered civil war, though some researchers may prefer to focus only on one definition over the other. In this book, all intrastate conflicts with at least 25 battle deaths in a calendar year are considered a civil war.

TABLE 1.1
Comparing Different Definitions of Civil War

Source of Definition	Sides to Conflict	Deaths	Remarks
Correlates of War (COW) project	Central government and an insurgent force	1,000/year	Insurgent must be capable of inflicting on government army at least 5% of fatalities it sustained
Doyle and Sambanis (2000)	Government versus organized, capable rebel group	1,000 overall, and in at least one of the war years	Occurs within internationally recognized country; both parties will live together after the war
Fearon and Laitin (2003a)	Country versus nonstate group	1,000 overall, with at least 100/year, and at least 100 for both sides	Fighting is over government takeover or a region, or fighting to change government policies
State Failure Project	Government and a political challenger	1,000 overall and at least 100 in any one war year	Each side must possess at least 1,000 soldiers
Uppsala Conflict Data Program and Peace Research Institute of Oslo (Themnér and Wallensteen 2013)	Of the two parties, one must be the government, fighting an organized, armed, nonstate group	At least 25 battle-related per year in low-intensity civil conflict; 1,000 in civil war	Fighting is over government, territory, or both

If we follow UCDP's definition of civil conflict, then there were 36 active conflicts in 2009 and 30 active conflicts in 2010 (Themnér and Wallensteen 2011). In contrast, using the higher threshold of 1,000 battle-related deaths gives only six civil wars in 2009 and four in 2010. The value or virtue of using the lower threshold is that many low-intensity civil wars are utilized in the analysis. It is important that these wars not be ignored because even though they might be minor in terms of deaths, they can still have a devastating impact on human displacement, democratization, economic growth, and foreign investment.

The UCDP dataset work is highlighted in Box 1.1.

BOX 1.1 Key Civil War Datasets

Since the 1970s, the Peace and Conflict Research Department at Uppsala University, Sweden, has kept track of armed conflicts worldwide through the UCDP. The department compiles on an annual basis every account of civil war, and it produces a comprehensive publication. In collaboration with the Center for the Study of Civil War at PRIO, a detailed, comprehensive dataset covering armed conflicts from 1946 to the present has been maintained. These data are typically referred to as UCDP/PRIO Armed Conflict Data (ACD), and they also reflect interstate conflict. The data are employed in quantitative research, meaning statistical techniques are used in a scientific process aimed at analyzing civil war onset, duration, and outcome. The ACD data list all the parties that have been engaged in war, the location of the conflict, years of the war, the intensity of the war, and the type of war, among others factors.

Over time, the Armed Conflict Data continue to be refined, and revisions are published in subsequent issues of *Journal of Peace Research*. The UCDP Conflict Encyclopedia website is the broadest UCDP publication as it covers conflicts since 1975 and includes a large number of variables relevant for conflict analysis. Thus, there is a dataset with data from 1946 on a limited number of variables and a database with information from 1975 on many variables and containing detailed conflict descriptions (UCDP 2014a).

Wars are classified according to three different categories. A civil war may be of the general type (internal armed conflict) or one that has involved other countries (internationalized internal armed conflict) or perhaps one in which the government of a country fights the rebel group outside the boundary of that country (extra-systemic armed conflict). A more detailed discussion of this is found in Chapter 3.

To be considered a civil war, UCDP/PRIO uses a relatively low threshold of 25 battle-related deaths per year. The "incompatibility" of the war describes whether the war is over a disputed territory (war over control of a territory) or over the control of government (war over control of government) or both. Most civil wars happen over one of these issues and not both. The data are available to the public at the UCDP website (http://www.pcr.uu.se/research/UCDP/) at no cost. It should be noted that the UCDP also maintains an extensive catalog of datasets on other aspects of armed conflict, such as peace agreements, war termination, and civil war onsets.

The Correlates of War (COW) project maintains datasets comprising various information on civil and interstate wars. Founded by the late Professor J. David Singer of University of Michigan in 1963 and later joined by Professor

Melvin Small, the project maintains data for wars back to 1816. The COW project has data on both interstate and civil wars. A clear difference exists between UCDP/PRIO and COW in terms of what constitutes armed conflict. The COW requires interstate and intrastate to have at least 1,000 battle deaths per year. Some scholars prefer to focus on major wars and some scholars prefer studying a wider range of civil wars from very minor to major. In addition to data on war, the COW houses data on the power of countries as judged by factors such as military and economic power, energy consumption, iron and steel production, and population size. Other times, series information held by the COW includes data on bilateral trade between countries, state membership in intergovernmental organizations, and alliance data. In fact, the COW project was the first major foray into the use of scientific methods in the study of international relations. The data are available to the public online at the COW website, www.correlatesofwar.org (at no cost).

Parties to Conflict: Governments and Rebel Groups

UCDP/PRIO defines a government as the party at that time which is in control of the country's capital (Gleditsch et al. 2002). A government is an organized bureaucracy—elected or unelected—that manages the affairs of state. Governments comprise institutions that make policies for citizens to follow, and its functions include rule making, service delivery, adjudication, and national security. In contrast, rebels usually do not have institutions or provide service delivery. However, in some cases, rebels create and control a de facto state (e.g., the Tamil Tigers in northern Sri Lanka). UCDP/PRIO data and definitions are employed in this text because of their widespread usage in research and their reputation for accuracy.

A key aspect of defining civil war is recognizing what constitutes a rebel group. Whether they use sticks and stones, grenades and machine guns, or the latest weapons, rebel groups and organized criminal groups employ weapons to fight their enemies. They both have a clear leadership with some sort of an organizational structure. Key differences exist between the two, however. For example, a rebel group may or may not be motivated by profits. Although a group may be fighting the government because of discrimination or barriers to progress, Collier and Hoeffler (1999, 2001) view rebel leaders as generating profits from war for self-gain and maintenance of the group. On the other hand, an organized criminal group's goal is always profit (Saab and Taylor 2009:457). Though they fight against government troops and police, the violent drug gangs of Mexico are not considered rebels as they have no formal political agenda, goal to secede, exact political change policy, or government takeover plan. For the purposes of this book, the UCDP/PRIO definitions and data (e.g., onset, duration, battle deaths, termination type, peace agreements) are utilized to the fullest extent possible because of their international reputation for being comprehensive and accurate.

Governments and rebels may enter into armed conflict for a number of reasons. Two of the main schools of thought here are the grievance and greed models. The former represents a traditional line of reasoning that rebels start civil wars because they have suffered some deprivation at the hands of the government or another ethnic or religious group. This model has been challenged by other scholars who argue that some rebels do not fight because of grievance but rather because they are prospering in war through the exploitation of lootable resources, such as diamonds, drugs, or gold. Working under the auspices of the World Bank, the economist Paul Collier was the leading proponent of this greed perspective at the turn of the century. His findings and methods have been challenged in the last few years (see Fearon 2005). We must be careful not to overgeneralize, but political scientists tend to privilege political explanations for the onset of civil war over economic motivations. For at least some economists, the situation is reversed. The latest trend in the greed-grievance divide is toward the conclusion that lootable resources have a role in prolonging war rather than causing them. Oil, however, has been linked to onset.

Types of Civil War

Borrowing from the UCDP/PRIO methodology, this text breaks civil wars into three major classifications: wars over control of government, wars over territory (secessionist/autonomy wars), and internationalized civil wars. While some scholars may differ in their categorization of war types, this grouping captures the overarching differences. As I describe below, there are several subcategories.

Control Over Government. Wars over control of government involve rebels aiming to topple and replace the government. Examples include the Russian, Cuban, and Chinese revolutions. In each case, the rebels fought to completely sweep away the old regime and redirect government toward a highly centralized socialist system (in the case of Cuba, the socialist nature of the revolution did not become apparent for a few years). All elements of government were replaced as a result of these wars. In the Cuban and Chinese cases, many voluntarily left the country in the years before and after the revolutionaries came to power.

The grievance explanation argues that rebels cannot tolerate a government anymore because it is inefficient, practices discrimination, or imposes restrictions and barriers on minorities, so they initiate a civil war. Grievances can be caused by, among other factors, rural-urban differences in service delivery or subsidies, differences in income levels and class differences, or unfair treatment of ethnic groups. Of course, in some cases, grievances can combine and reinforce each other.

Ideology, sometimes related to grievances, also plays a role in wars over government. During the Cold War, there were numerous wars involving government takeover. This was because the Cold War divided the world into two distinct ideological groups, communism and capitalist democracy. Both the Soviet Union and the United States lent support to government or rebel leaders with the aim of either converting the country toward their ideology or at least in order to gain influence. For example, the Vietnam War indirectly pitted the Soviets (backing the Communists in the North) against the U.S.-backed South. The situation was similar in the Korean War. Several Cold War-era wars fell into this classification. In large part, wars over control of government were caused by Western colonization, which resulted in inefficient and incompetent institutions that endured decades or centuries of external domination.

Islamic takeover of government is another common cause of governmental conflicts. In the Middle East, these conflicts can be related to the Sunni-Shi'ite religious divide. The 1979 Iranian revolution is a clear example. The post-9/11 conflict in Iraq provides another example. The Sunnis controlled politics during the Saddam Hussein regime, and the Shi'ite majority was envious of this. After the American invasion of Iraq, a power-sharing arrangement between the Sunnis and Shi'ites was established. The "Arab Spring" (referring to the uprisings in the Middle East/North Africa region in 2011 and 2012) added to the list of wars over the control of government in the Middle East and North Africa. Each of the rebellions in the Arab Spring was aimed at government control. The grievance model best explains the Arab Spring.

The Arab Spring began in December 2010 in Tunisia when street vendor Mohamed Bouazizi set himself ablaze (he died weeks later) to protest harsh treatment by a government official. His action came to represent divisions within Tunisian society as Bouazizi was very poor and struggled to make it in a country with very high unemployment. His protest led quickly to mass uprisings in Tunisia that became so large the president fled the country. Events in Tunisia were not confined to that country. By January 2011, protests broke out in Egypt, Yemen, Morocco, and Oman. Uprisings began in Libya that resulted in the ouster of the Gaddafi government. In March, protests began in Syria that eventually resulted in a bloody civil war that persists to this writing (British Broadcasting Corporation [BBC] 2012a). The Arab Spring uprisings manifested differently in each country, but one main organizing theme was a desire for change in the autocratic nature of the regional governments.

The long-term effects of the Arab Spring are not yet apparent. While the uprisings have not led to immediate democratization and incipient institutions of freedom of press and speech, they have at least given people in the region an outlet for venting their frustration with regimes that hold on to power for years or even decades and harbor little dissent. The relevance of the Arab Spring to this text is that it directly led to civil wars over control of government in Libya and Syria.

In contrast, the greed explanation argues that the capture of government is about the control of resources. In this model, rebels' greed is the motivation for war, and they fight to exploit diamonds, gold, timber, or other valuable resources. The rebels may also be motivated to fight because of the potential to profit from the sale of illicit drugs. Greed issues can be very prominent if the state has valuable natural resources. For example, leaders in oil-exporting states stand to gain personally over the awarding of oil leases.

The National Union for the Total Independence of Angola (UNITA) rebels in Angola were thought to be on the verge of being militarily defeated after American support dried up with the Cold War's end. UNITA rebels were able to regroup and even thrive despite the loss of U.S. support in large part because they were able to substitute profits from illicit diamond sales for several years in the 1990s. For its part, the government of Angola sustained its army through oil-lease revenues.

It is important to note that the resources did not cause the war but rather were used to prolong it. The question of whether resource exploitation actually leads to war or if it simply prolongs it is taken up further in Chapter 5.

Secessionist/Autonomy-Seeking Wars. Secessionist-based wars are fought between governments, which are found at the "center" of the country where power is based and a large part of the population resides. Rebels are typically concentrated ethno-religious groups, based in the periphery. Since these groups reside a considerable distance away from the core, they have ample opportunity to mobilize or raise armies. A perfect example of this is Indonesia. There are roughly 9,000 scattered islands in Indonesia. Jakarta, the capital city, simply cannot monitor all activities taking place across all of these islands. Northern Ireland's location is so far from London that there was no way the core could completely control Catholics in Northern Ireland. These rebel groups are ethnically different, such as the Tamils in Sri Lanka who live in the North and Northeast, speak a different language, and practice Hinduism (though some Tamils are Muslims), versus the Sinhalese who live in most other parts of Sri Lanka and are Buddhist. In Indonesia, the Acehnese living far from the center speak a different language than the majority Javanese-speaking Indonesians. People in East Timor in the periphery of Indonesia also speak a different language and practice Catholicism whereas the Javanese are

Muslims. Differences between the core and the periphery may also be seen in Spain (Basques versus Spaniards), the Philippines (Moro-Muslims versus Catholic Filipinos), India (numerous secessionist groups in the Northeast who do not practice Hinduism, the majority religion in India), and the bulk of the sub-Saharan African conflicts involving Christian-Muslim or tribal divides. The list goes on.

It is more likely for distinct groups concentrated in the periphery to have greater disgust with the government and a keen desire to secede than groups in the center. When these groups are poorer than the majority of the country, there is a further reason to secede, even if secession hurts economically. The poor peripheral group chooses self-rule to try and better their lives economically. This may be a reason why secessionist conflicts are the most intractable and the most severe type of conflict (Walter 2003).

The government of an ethnically divided country realizes the impact of geography and ethnic differences. Some governments then decide to reduce the periphery's power to alleviate the chance of war. In doing so, these governments cause exactly the opposite of what was originally desired. One measure is to inject majority group members into the periphery to minimize the influence of the upstart ethnic or religious group. This process is known as transmigration and has been done in the Philippines, Bangladesh, Sri Lanka, Indonesia, India, the Soviet Union, Botswana, and Argentina.

Transmigration can make grievances even more severe as the incoming group competes for land (leading to deforestation in some cases) and jobs in the region to which they move. The peripheral group sees the migrants as intruders and the government sponsorship of the transmigration as a threat to their cultural and/ or religious identity. Tensions increase further when the government extends senior civil service and political positions to the migrant group. This leads to conflict between the migrants and the original group that can extend into civil war against the state. These "sons-of-the-soil" insurgencies have elements of greed but are mainly grievance-related (see Fearon 2004; Fearon and Laitin 2011).

The case of the sons-of-the-soil war in Aceh, Indonesia, is illustrative as there were resource, ethnic, religious, and transmigration issues at work. The Aceh region is on the northern tip of the island of Sumatra. The capital and population hub of Indonesia is Jakarta, located on the island of Java. The separation by water allowed Aceh to retain much of its historical identity at the expense of an incipient sense of national identity. This distinct history included a more conservative brand of Islam.

Large natural gas deposits off the coast of Aceh led to grievances in the 1970s as Acehnese were disenchanted by having to share resource revenues with the rest of the country. Revenue sharing from a resource considered "theirs" was especially problematic as Indonesia is a fragmented state comprising thousands of islands separated by great distance. The sense of identity caused Acehnese to question why they were forced to share resource wealth with ethnically different people (e.g., Javanese) on distant islands in the far-flung country. To make matters worse, it appeared that governmental investment in Aceh was not commensurate to its contribution to the central treasury. These animosities and differences led the newly formed Free Aceh Movement (GAM) to declare independence in 1976. The secessionist civil war between GAM and the government of Indonesia lasted from 1976 to 2005 with periods of low or no activity interspersed.

Another pattern surrounding territorial conflicts has to do with natural resources. Resources, such as oil, seem to be concentrated in the peripheries of countries. Scholars know that these peripheries contain a different ethno-religious group than the core. The people of the peripheries consider these abundant resources as theirs or as partly theirs. The core, however, claims that they belong to all citizens of the country and typically do not distribute gains made from the resources to the peripheries fairly. Collier et al. (2003) showed that resource-related conflicts are usually territorial. A comprehensive discussion of natural resources and their connection to civil war will be presented in Chapter 5.

While many territorial conflicts are caused by grievances (Kreuzer 2005; Krippendorff 1979) and changing policies of the core (as in Sri Lanka), one important pattern surrounding such conflicts is the historical discourse. Rebel leaders operating from the outer regions (peripheries) commonly cite history as a reason for their struggle. A history of the region having been independent in ancient history or before the colonial masters took over creates a sense of the need to return to independence among citizens in the peripherals (Kearney 1987–1988:568). Sometimes, the periphery refers to its inclusion in the country as illegal (Baruah 2003:323, 330). The leadership of the Patani United Liberation Organization (PULO) rebel group in Thailand, the Moro Islamic Liberation Front (MILF) and Moro National Liberation Front (MNLF) rebel groups in the Philippines, and GAM in Aceh, Indonesia, all claim that their peripheral regions were historically sovereign lands and their inclusion in their respective countries was illegal. That is why in the sons-of-the-soil conflicts, any attempt to inject migrants into the outer regions is considered a violation of independence by the people in the periphery.

Secessionist wars are centered on ethnic, religious, cultural, or linguistic grievances. Sometimes, two or more of these dimensions make up the grievances. Difference in economic levels between the core and the periphery can exacerbate existing ethno-religious grievances. Past history can also explain secessionist wars. Kearney (1987–1988:568) argued that a previously independent territory that had been conquered by a colonial power and then forced that territory to be a part of a newly independent state can stir up secessionist sentiment. The inclusion of the disputed territory within the newly independent state will be considered illegal by the peripheral (outer region) population (Baruah 2003:323, 330).

Resources found in the peripheries provide an opportunity for greed-based secessionist civil wars. Examples of this are the Angolan and Democratic Republic of Congo wars in Africa. Collier et al. (2003) argued that resource-related conflicts are usually territorial.

The American Civil War (1861–1865) was a secessionist war. While the issue of slavery was an important cause of the war, other factors were at play as well. Southern states believed that they had the right to nullify federal laws such as those on tariffs the South considered illegal. The South also did not share the same economic interests with the Northern states. Most of the Northern cities were urban and highly populated, hence more suitable for manufacturing, shipping, and fishing endeavors. The Southern cities were smaller and the region more agrarian based. Slave labor was an important aspect of the economy. If slavery were to be abolished, Southern states' economies would go to shambles. Finally, the election of Abraham Lincoln, an antislavery proponent, also contributed to the war. Although the South had resounding victories in the early stages of the war, the North eventually prevailed. The war's casualties exceeded 500,000.

Burma and India are particularly prone to secessionist wars. These two countries have had and are still experiencing numerous wars where various groups are attempting to split from the motherland. In Burma, Islamic groups in Arakan, Christians in Kachin, and minority ethnic groups in various other parts of the country are fighting the Burmese government for independence. Animist and Christians in Nagaland, Christians in Tripura, Muslims in Kashmir, and tribal and minority ethnic groups in Manipur have been fighting against the Hindu-majority India since before the end of the Cold War.

Internationalized Civil Wars. Civil wars can become internationalized when a second state intervenes in a civil war, for example, the United States' involvement in aiding South Vietnam in the Vietnam War. What was an extra-systemic war that started in 1957 between colonial-power France and the Union of the Populations of Cameroon (UPC) rebel group in Cameroon transformed into an internationalized civil war after Cameroon received independence from France in 1960. In 1990, Zaire sided with the government of Rwanda against the Rwandan Patriotic Front (FPR) in one of modern history's worst ethnic conflicts.

Nine of 30 civil wars in 2010 were internationalized civil wars, the most cases of this type of war since the end of World War II (Themnér and Wallensteen 2011). All but one (Afghanistan) of the internationalized civil wars in 2010 were in the Middle East/North Africa region. The recent Arab Spring uprisings in 2011 and 2012 have seen outside interventions. Outside forces intervened in Libya and

Syria. Even though foreign intervention did not directly occur in Egypt and Tunisia, the United States had strong indirect presence in these two countries especially in support of the rebels.

Most internationalized wars do not begin as such. There is usually a period of fighting where domestic parties sort it out themselves. For instance, the war between French colonizers and Cameroonian rebels (UPC), which broke out in 1957 and which took tens of thousands of lives, transformed into an internationalized civil war after Cameroon received independence from France in 1960. As mentioned, Zaire intervened in 1990 on behalf of Rwanda in the latter's fight against the Rwandan Patriotic Front.

There are patterns scholars notice in explaining the onset of internationalized civil wars. Ideology can play a role. This was most common during the Cold War. The civil war in Angola (1975–2002) had Cold War-induced third-party intervention.

Regan (2000) writes that potential third-party interveners use a rational (cost-benefit) decision process before sending troops. Such intervention could be perceived as an embarrassing mistake if the intervening side loses (Pearson 1974). Foreign powers might intervene in civil wars to help an ally, for humanitarian reasons, to protect domestic multinational corporations (MNCs), and to protect embassies and military installations overseas. Other considerations include the potential for success, the duration of the war to that point, and domestic public opinion. States are more likely to intervene in wars with serious humanitarian problems (for example, a large number of refugees or human rights violations) (Regan 2000).

There are several other less common forms of war. Some are related to the types described above.

An extra-systemic war takes place between a rebel group and a government outside of the government's homeland territory (Gleditsch et al. 2002). A recent example is the United States fighting Iraqi insurgents in Iraq after 9/11. Colonial wars are wars fought between locals and their colonial masters. Such wars were very common during the pre-World War II era. Throughout history, the world has seen numerous such wars (Gandhi's independence struggle in India, the Dien Bien Phu battle of Vietnamese against French rule, the American war of independence, Algerian independence war against France, and multiple Latin American independence wars and African independence movements). Irredentist wars are those in which the group that staged the rebellion aims to unite its territory with a neighboring country. The rebels wish to separate from the motherland in order to be a part of the neighboring country. Typically, this type of war happens when the rebel territory's population shares more characteristics (usually ethno-religious) with the neighbor than with its own motherland.

Another category is sometimes mentioned though it is not clearly a type of civil war. Since the end of the Cold War, more and more attention has centered upon nonstate wars—wars between or among nonstate groups. Examples include ethno-religious groups fighting each other in nonstate wars: Hausa versus Igbo in Nigeria, Hindus versus Muslims in India, Catholics versus Protestants in the United Kingdom, and Sunnis versus Shias in the Middle East.

The focus of this text is civil wars between government and rebels. I specifically focus on the first three war types: wars over government control, secessionist/ autonomy-seeking wars, and internationalized wars.

CIVIL WAR ONSET

In general, scholars explore the onset, duration, and outcome of civil war. It is not surprising that scholars often study the onset, or outbreak, of civil war because, to put it simply, researchers want to understand why civil wars begin. The researcher isolates the different factors that either separately or collectively caused war to break out that year. For example, Fearon and Laitin (2003a) identify 127 civil war onsets between 1945 and 1999. The UCDP data report 229 onsets between 1946 and 2011 (Gleditsch et al. 2002; Themnér and Wallensteen 2012). These UCDP onsets include wars that recur after a peace spell of at least five years. The Appendix at the end of this volume contains a list of civil wars from 1946 to 2009.

Interesting patterns emerge when we break down civil war onset and civil war incidence (observations) according to the different regions of the world as indicated below. Onset of civil war refers to the outbreak of a war between two parties. If there is a 5-year (other durations can be used depending on preference) break in the war and it reignites, this recurrence is considered a new onset. From 1946 to 2011, Europe experienced 25 onsets, the Middle East 29, the Americas 33, Asia 67, and Africa 75 (Gleditsch et al. 2002; Themnér and Wallensteen 2012). Clearly, Asia and Africa experienced the greatest number of onsets. This is likely linked to high ethnic and religious diversity exaggerated in some cases by border people ignoring each of these features and variations in government type ranging from democracy to authoritarian military regimes.

Scholars and policy makers do not always agree on the causes of the onset of civil war. Though this will be covered in greater detail in Chapter 4, briefly, the scientific study of causes of civil war is divided between the following explanations:

1. *Civil war is a result of citizens' frustration arising out of continuously or continu-ally having been discriminated against, barriers or restrictions to their progress or prac-tices, and/or the inability to channel complaints to authorities.* As mentioned, this is

commonly referred to as the grievance argument. The line of reasoning here is that rebel groups arise out of group deprivation.

An overreliance on natural resources, such as oil, can be linked to grievance-related civil war (see Ross 2004). For example, a corrupt regime in a developing state that exports oil might enrich itself with money from multinational oil companies at the expense of a legitimate taxation relationship with its people. In such a situation, the regime does not need to worry about keeping the people happy because it does not rely on the people for taxes. Nigeria arguably provides a case in point here.

2. *Civil war is a result of greed and the desire for private gain.* This theory treats rebellion as a business enterprise, where rebel leaders seek gains from the war. Greed basically follows a rational choice calculation of choosing the choice that maximizes benefit to cost. The profit from resources can be used to entice recruits.

3. *Wars result from opportunities.* This theoretical perspective explains war from a state capacity ("weak state") standpoint. Stronger governments are more prepared to control uprisings and thwart rebel recruitment. States with capacity also have a monopoly on the use of violence in all of their territory. There are no regions where rebels can organize with impunity. High-capacity states are more likely to meet the basic needs of the citizens. In weak states, rebels recognize the opportunity to organize and start a war (Fearon and Laitin 2003a:76).

Some wars do not fit neatly into only one category. Further, there are other models that are used to explain the causes of civil war. For instance, there are at least five models (see Chapter 4) that explain why ethno-religious wars happen.

THE DURATION OF CIVIL WARS

The length of civil wars varies. Some last for only days whereas others go on for decades. Twenty-five percent of civil wars last longer than five years and 8 percent of civil wars last longer than twenty years (Cunningham 2006). This brief section provides an overview of duration. Some revolutions and coups are quite short while other wars can last decades. The rebels of South Moluccas fought a war against Indonesia that lasted only a few months in 1950. The Karen National Union, on the other hand, has been fighting against the government of Myanmar since 1948. Most coups last only a very brief time. A military coup in Argentina in 1963 lasted 4 days. Long wars might have a relatively low rate of death but can still have devastating impacts on human displacement, disease, and development. War duration is an all-important consideration because of the devastation involved.

For the purposes of measuring duration, an incidence (observation) of civil war counts every single year a civil war takes place including the outbreak year. For example, the Israel-Palestinian civil war broke out in 1949 but continues today. The onset of this war was in 1949 whereas its incidence was recorded for every single year there was war including 1949. Hence, the data will contain many more incidences (observations) of wars than onsets.

Across all world regions, there were 1,337 years of civil wars between 1946 and 2011. During this period, Africa had 443 civil wars years, Asia had 420, the Middle East had 215, the Americas had 173, and Europe had only 86. The same trend is observed for both the pre- and post-Cold War eras with Asia and Africa having the most civil war years in both eras. For both eras, Europe and the Americas had the least number of civil wars (Gleditsch et al. 2002; Themnér and Wallensteen 2012). These low numbers are likely linked to the presence of stable democracy, strong economies in the case of North America and Western Europe, and religious, language, and ethnic similarities in much of Latin America.

Type of War and Duration

Some war types are, on average, longer than others. Fearon (2004) links insurgency strategy to duration. Coups and revolutions seek quick tipping points so that outright victory is achieved. The strategy of peripheral wars—usually with an ethnic component—is to seek dominance to win more favorable terms at the bargaining table. Peripheral wars do not necessarily depend on military victory in order to realize important political goals.

Coup organizers do not set up rebel armies ready and willing to fight many years from a base in the countryside. Coups are fought by members of the government (often the military) who set out to quickly take the reins of power. Coup leaders do not set out to engage the government's army in protracted battle. This is not to say that coups cannot be followed by new coups carried out by different individuals.

Peripheral, territorial wars tend to endure and are unlikely to end conclusively with peace agreements or military victories. Fearon (2004) reasons that a lack of credible commitment on the part of the government leads the rebels not to trust any sort of autonomy deal the government might offer. This means the rebels do not consider the government as a credible partner in negotiations. In other words, the rebels feel the government will renege or not follow through on any commitment it makes. When the rebels are doing well vis-à-vis the government, the latter will offer generous concessions. However, the rebels will expect the government to break these promises as the rebel advantages dwindle.

The government would prefer military victory to an autonomy deal, but it is difficult for the government to end a territorial war militarily as the peripheral group can use the local terrain to its advantage and can blend into the civilian population. In addition, because the rebels do not threaten the control of the central government, the government does not feel compelled to pay the high economic and political costs a military victory would invoke. Another obstacle for the government is that ethnic rebels operating in the periphery often use guerrilla tactics. Examples of these peripheral secessionist wars include several of the wars in Myanmar and the Aceh war in Indonesia. These conflicts are sometimes called sons-of-the soil wars. Fearon also notes that rebel access to contraband resources will further prolong these wars.

Wars over control of government, on the other hand, rely on a tipping effect and typically do not last as long (Fearon 2004). Wars designed to take central government usually involve a large, well-armed rebel army if they are to have a chance at victory. In these wars, the stakes are high because the central government is directly threatened. The government is likely to go all out to defeat the rebels as quickly as possible. Subsequently, on average, these wars are shorter. There are exceptions to this rule, such as the war between Fuerzas Armadas Revolucionarias de Colombia (FARC) and the government of Colombia that has waged for decades. This is due, in part, to the FARC sale of coca.

Coups are a very brief type of war (some may not even consider these civil wars) as they are generally even more extreme examples of all-or-nothing affairs than wars over government. The hallmark of the coup is that it is carried out by elements from within the current government. Often, the military takes the reins of power. If the coup planners do not achieve a quick victory, there is a high probability the government will kill, exile, or imprison them (see Fearon 2004).

Lootable Resources and War Duration

Certain commodities of value can make for longer wars. The illegal exploitation of resources (sometimes called contraband, black market, or lootable goods) can provide finances to rebels that can be used to pay for food, weapons, recruits, and other miscellaneous supplies (see Buhaug, Gates, and Lujala 2009). Some, most notably Paul Collier, argue that profit from the lootable goods is another mechanism that keeps the war going. Lootable natural resources are effective because they do not rely on legitimate markets that might otherwise preclude profits going to rebels.

Lootable resources potentially prolong the war both because rebels are making money to pay for their operations and because in some cases they are making a profit. However, scholars have arrived at different findings regarding the specific linkages. Humphreys (2005) argued that civil wars relating to natural resources last longer. Regan and Norton (2005) arrived at the same conclusion for diamonds. However, Ross (2006) could not prove that diamonds had any bearing on the length of conflicts. Lujala, Gleditsch, and Gilmore (2005) found that secondary diamond production lengthens ethno-religious civil wars and primary diamond production shortened ethno-religious civil wars. Fearon (2004) reported gems, such as secondary diamonds, made sons-of-the-soil civil wars last longer.

Diamonds are an especially useful form of contraband possessing a high value to weight ratio and until recently were fairly easy to sell on the black market. Some forms of alluvial diamonds require very little capital investment as rebels can just wade through rivers and scoop up sediment in their search for diamonds. Diamonds were successfully exploited by UNITA rebels in Angola after the Cold War ended and the United States and South Africa withdrew their support. The international community cracked down on this mechanism through the so-called Kimberley (because talks began in Kimberley, South Africa, in 2000) Process that makes it harder to sell conflict diamonds.

Drugs and black market timber are other forms of lootable goods. The previously mentioned use of drugs by FARC rebels in Colombia and timber by various rebels in Myanmar are prime examples here. The sale of drugs by rebels requires a certain amount of secure territory that is stable enough to grow and/or process the goods. The exploitation of black market timber requires only a few trucks and chainsaws. Each of these commodities has extended wars.

It is important to note that while lootable goods play a key role in duration, they are not as clearly linked to the onset of the war. One possible exception to this finding is that the war in Aceh can be partially traced back to grievances linked to large natural gas deposits in the region. The local population felt ownership of the resource on their land and was not satisfied about sharing the revenue with the rest of the country.

While Collier and company, Fearon, and others argue that lootable commodities lengthen war, it is also possible that contraband can work against the rebels to shorten war. Weinstein (2005) observes that contraband resources in rebel areas might actually undermine the recruitment of dedicated rebels. This is because rebels drawn to contraband-fueled wars might only be interested in short-term financial gain and not the wider cause. When contraband is lacking, these short-sighted opportunists stay away and more dedicated fighters are recruited.

Spoilers and War Duration

Not all actors favor peace processes. Stephen Stedman (2000) identified another factor that can prolong war: the presence of spoilers both inside and outside a peace process. He defines spoilers as parties who see the peace process as a threat to their power or worldview. As a result, spoilers will often turn to violence to derail the peace process. Acts of violence during a peace process will understandably generate obstacles to the peace process. Spoilers undermine the peace process because they feel it will threaten their interests or power (Stedman 1997). This may also help explain why mediation sometimes leads to increases in rebel terrorism.

The Real Irish Republican Army was a spoiler group that broke away from the Provisional Irish Republican Army in protest of the peace process.

Foreign Intervention and War Duration

Third parties can impact civil war duration. Surprisingly, interventions tend to lengthen civil wars. Regan (2000) mentions that out of the 190 civil wars that had foreign involvements, only 57 ended. Elbadawi and Sambanis (2000) agree with Regan's findings that interventions make civil wars longer. This is a point to note for intergovernmental organizations and states that usually intervene (e.g., United States, France, and United Kingdom). As Balch-Lindsay and Enterline (2000) pointed out, it is useful to determine how duration of war is affected by which side the intervener takes. Just as Regan (2000), they found that foreign interventions increase duration whichever side the intervener takes. However, if a foreign power stages military action against the government, the war may be expected to be shorter. A military attack causes the government's power to be significantly reduced and forces it to cede to either the rebel's or the foreign power's demands as was witnessed in the North Atlantic Treaty Organization (NATO) attacks on Serbia in the Kosovo war in the 1990s.

UN intervention can be a curse for both government and rebels in a narrow sense. The United Nations makes it harder for either the government or the rebels to win. On the other hand, UN involvement reduces the time taken to strike a truce or a peace treaty (DeRouen and Sobek 2004).

Other Factors Affecting Duration

Civil wars last longer in countries with high ethno-religious fractionalization. This may be attributed to strong ethno-religious bonds that exist in ethnic or religious rebel groups. Rebel group cohesion makes it difficult for the government to practice the divide-and-rule strategy. Hence, a quick victory for the government or government ability to force the rebel group to the negotiation table becomes more difficult, and the result is a long war (Collier, Hoeffler, and Soderbom 2004). This explains in part why separatist wars last longer (Balch-Lindsay and Enterline 2000). Most territorial claims are based on the ethno-religious basis, for instance, in Sri Lanka, Northern Ireland, the Philippines, Sudan, and Turkey. Studies (e.g., Elbadawi and Sambanis 2000) have shown that the ethno-religious variable may be impacting the length of wars in a more complicated manner. Civil war duration increases with increasing ethno-religious fractionalization but becomes shorter after fractionalization peaks in a curvilinear relationship. This is to say that countries with very high and very low fractionalizations will experience shorter wars.

DeRouen and Sobek (2004) assess the impact of state capacity on duration, using two measures of state capacity: the first, bureaucratic quality measured by effectiveness, independence, and stability of the bureaucracy; and second, military size. In our study, we report a bigger military contributes to decreasing the length of wars.

An interesting point to consider is the dynamics at play in the early stages of a civil war. About half or more of all civil wars end within the first year (Balch-Lindsay and Enterline 2000). If allowed to continue, however, the rebel group benefits from the continued war. Time is the rebels' ally especially in non-ethno-religious wars in states with low ethno-religious fractionalization with rough terrains. Crushing the rebel group within the first few months or as early as possible is a strategy the government needs to employ. This is because the likelihood of rebel victory increases with time (DeRouen and Sobek 2004). The ease of crushing a rebellion is easier in autocratic countries. Because of this, civil wars tend to be shorter in autocratic states (Elbadawi and Sambanis 2000).

OUTCOME AND TERMINATION OF CIVIL WARS

Rebels and governments are faced with challenging questions during the course of wars. The decision to continue, give up, or call for a settlement lingers through the course of the war. Such decisions are constrained by various factors.

There are three possible ways a war can end: government victory, rebel victory, or negotiated settlement. Of course, in many years, war does not terminate and simply continues. When one party predicts an obvious victory (by calculating probability of victory), it will continue fighting until it wins the war without considering settlement.

The probability of victory is not the only factor predicting how wars end. Mason, Weingarten, and Fett (1999) report an array of factors determining the outcome of civil war—duration of war, battle deaths, foreign intervention, type of war, and state capacity. As previously stated, the longer the war, the more beneficial it is for rebels (see DeRouen and Sobek 2004). The majority of wars in which the government has won were short wars (50 percent in the first year and most of them within the first 5 years). There is an interesting difference between the Mason, Weingarten, and Fett study compared to the others because researchers of this study also found that 56 percent of rebel victories occurred within the first year of war. Nevertheless, the striking statistics on government victory previously noted suggest that quickly crushing the rebels is a worthwhile strategy if the government aims to be victorious.

Brandt et al. (2008) similarly reported government victories are usually in shorter wars and rebel victories in longer ones. They, however, did not find government victories in the early stages of the war, instead finding that they happen between the fourth and the eighth year. Mason, Weingarten, and Fett (1999) showed that after 5 years pass, there is a high likelihood that rebels will force the government to the negotiating table. They showed that government is, however, more likely to win in ethno-religious conflicts. This is bad news for ethno-religious rebels. Because the chance of a rebel victory is slim in ethno-religious conflict (as was also found by DeRouen and Sobek 2004), their best bet therefore would be to secure negotiations. War weariness increases the likelihood that parties to war will be more accepting to third-party negotiations. Hence, negotiated settlements are more likely in long wars with foreign interventions.

This is not the case for shorter wars. The war-weariness explanation also explains why when cost of war increases (measured in number of battle deaths), the outcome is more likely to be a negotiated settlement as found by Brandt et al. (2008). This idea applies only to the government. An increase in battle deaths increases the chance of a rebel victory. This may be attributed to shifting sympathies toward the rebel side from the masses. For the government to balance this, it needs to increase state capacity via an increase in military size (Mason, Weingarten, and Fett 1999). As previously stated, it may be a good idea to employ different measures of state capacity when studying duration and outcome of war. State capacity measured by the quality of bureaucracy surprisingly has no effect on the chance of a government victory but greatly curtails the chance of rebel victory (DeRouen and Sobek 2004). Weak or corrupted governments help pave a way for rebel victory (Brandt et al. 2008).

The pattern of civil war terminations seems to favor the government. There is a 64 percent chance that the government will win a civil war. Instead of hoping for a victory, the rebel group should rather aspire to force the government to negotiate. This is because 31 percent of the time, wars end in settlements leaving very little chance for rebel victory (DeRouen and Sobek 2004). Past experiences of rebels changing their stance from a total independence claim to agreement to autonomy (for instance, the MILF, PULO, and GAM in Asia) bear witness to this.

CIVIL WAR RECURRENCE

Often wars end only to start up again a few years later. The war fought between the Democratic Forces of Casamance Movement, Senegal (MFDC) rebels of the Casamance region and the government of Senegal recurred four times after the first episode in 1990. Recurrence can be defined as the renewal of fighting after a period of peace. This section summarizes the major factors impacting recurrence.

War Type

Whereas several scholars note that ethnic-secessionist wars are more intractable than wars over government, there is not a wealth of empirical evidence showing these wars are more likely to recur. One exception is Wucherpfennig (2008) who theorizes that recurrence probability goes up in secessionist wars. Prior wars, he argues, lock in the positions of each side. After a war episode, the ethnic rebel's view of its cause as legitimate gets stronger, and the government's position as unwilling to compromise is cemented.

Outcome of the Previous War

DeRouen and Bercovitch (2008) model the duration of peace after civil war. This is inherently the same as modeling the recurrence of civil war because if the peace ends, the implication is that the war has recurred. In our research, we find military victories tend to make peace more enduring because one side is completely vanquished as a fighting force. According to Quinn, Mason, and Gurses (2007), however, civil wars are less likely to recur when rebels win or if there is a peace agreement accompanied by peacekeepers. It is important to note that these two studies used different data.

Walter (2004) diverges from the argument that the previous war's outcome is a critical explanation of recurrence. As discussed, she posits instead that opportunity costs as measured by quality of life and access to democratic institutions will shape the ability of the rebels to recruit. If the economy is growing, the country allows political participation, and rebels will be less likely to join the fight.

Nature of the State at War's End

All things considered, democracy will promote peaceful conflict management practices (see Greig 2005). Democratic regimes should be more able to establish the appropriate peacebuilding institutions. Democratic regimes are more amenable to peaceful resolution of disputes (see DeRouen and Goldfinch 2005; Dixon 1994). Hartzell, Hoddie, and Rothchild (2001) find that democracy lengthens the duration of civil war negotiated settlement as these forms of government are best suited to accommodate competing interests and weaken the threat of defections.

The capacity of the state at war's end will also be an important determinant of recurrence. As mentioned, if the economy is solid, it is harder to recruit rebels (Walter 2004). Higher levels of development could also signal greater chance for a peace agreement to obtain and thus a decreased chance of recurrence. DeRouen et al. (2010) provide case study evidence that state capacity is a critical ingredient of peace agreement implementation. A state needs a certain amount of capacity to implement the peace. Such implementation often includes disarming and reintegrating former rebels, democratizing, holding elections, or establishing an independent judiciary. If the government lacks capacity to implement reforms, the rebels might grow impatient and renew fighting.

Quinn et al. (2007) also find that higher levels of development at war's end reduce the probability of recurrence. It is likely that greater state capacity raises the opportunity costs for rebels. In other words, rebels incur a cost by foregoing an economic opportunity that could well be offered in a prosperous state. This would be expected to undercut rebel recruitment and motivation to fight.

Rebel Recruitment

For a rebel movement to sustain itself to the extent needed to renew a war, it needs a renewable supply of recruits who are willing and capable. Walter's (2004) empirical results lead her to conclude that recruitment of rebels is a function of opportunity costs as measured by quality of life and access to political participation. If the economy is growing and there is some level of democracy, it will be harder to recruit rebels. It stands to reason that if conditions during a war allow potential rebels to freely voice their opinions and/or have a reasonably good chance of finding work in the licit economy, it will be harder for rebels to recruit for a renewed war. In short, the better the state is doing, the harder it is for rebels to recruit and the lower the probability of a recurrence.

Peacekeeping Operations and Military Intervention

Peacekeeping operations are specifically designed to make recurrence less likely. Specifically, peacekeepers typically take up positions between former combatants to lower the probability that one side will take aggressive action against the other. Accordingly, it is important that as researchers we control for their effects lest we attribute too much credit to mediation. Doyle and Sambanis (2000) report the virtues of peacekeeping as an enhancement for local capacity at war's end.

Some wars such as those in Lebanon and Cambodia experienced third-party military intervention. On one hand, these wars should be more likely to be mediated because of the complicating nature of third-party military involvement. This involvement provides a context that would draw in mediators. On the other hand, it could make the party on whose behalf the intervention occurs less likely to agree to mediation. During the Cold War, the civil war in Angola was internationalized with the presence of South African and Cuban troops and significant aid from the superpowers. Mediation becomes less likely in such a situation as actors see their prospects enhanced by the presence of armed foreign allies.

Duration and Death: The Costs of War

The cost of war can be measured in terms of duration and deaths. Toft (2009) finds death rate and total deaths have opposite effects on recurrence. Total death reduces the probability while the average rate increases the probability of the war restarting. It is plausible that a high rate can be more closely linked to an urgent need to resolution.

In general, the costlier the war, the more likely it will be mediated. Greig (2005) reports that the longer the war, the more likely it will be mediated. As noted by Bercovitch and Gartner (2006), deadlier wars attract the attention of mediators. In general, the prospects for mediation should increase with war duration.

As above, deaths and duration each represent a component of the costs of war. The question is whether high costs make recurrence more or less likely. Quinn et al. (2007) argue that war-related deaths should help the postwar peace because these deaths make recruiting more difficult by discouraging fighters and diminishing the recruiting pool. They also note that high casualty rates also cause each side to doubt its ability to win in any case of renewed fighting.

Walter (2004), however, suggests that high-casualty rates could undermine the peace if the government indiscriminately kills great numbers of civilians as part of its retaliation against rebels: Popular support for the insurgency may well grow, and the rebels might be more likely to start fighting again as they attract new and committed recruits. Toft (2009) also finds that death rates have a positive effect on recurrence probability.

The duration of the previous war, on the other hand, is expected to make recurrence less likely. Long wars should increase the chance of mediation and/or negotiated settlements as information is revealed to fighters pertaining to what they are likely to face if the war recurs and on the level of resolve of the other side (Quinn et al. 2007). Doyle and Sambanis (2000) also argue that longer wars result in battle fatigue. The longer a civil war that preceded it lasts, the lower the probability of recurrence as the weaker side reaches a point where it knows it cannot prevail on the battlefield (Walter 2004). In other words, the longer the war, the more information will be available to each side in terms of the adversary's power and resolve. A long-lasting civil war might give some actors the opportunity to learn that they do not have sufficient resources to pursue a war. Thus, they will be unwilling to initiate another war.

The war's end begins a spell of peace. The duration of these spells after the war can help determine if a lasting peace will take hold. The duration of peace after a civil war has been shown to have a negative impact on recurrence (see DeRouen and Bercovitch 2008). In other words if peace has lasted 20 years after a war has ended, the probability of war in a future year is quite low. There was a civil war in Costa Rica in 1948, but the probability of this war recurring is virtually zero after 64 years. On the other hand, the probability of a war recurring on two or three years after ending is relatively higher as a stable peace might not have taken hold.

The duration of the war can also be considered a cost of war and as such has relevance for recurrence. If a long war has been fought and ended with government victory or negotiated settlement and the rebels are contemplating renewing the fight, the memory of the long war will be on their minds. The rebels will likely recall the costs and war weariness from the long war that they did not win. On the whole, a long war should lower the probability of recurrence (see DeRouen and Bercovitch 2008). A note of caution is that many long wars are relatively low in intensity (rate of deaths), so the rebel cost of fighting is not exceptionally high. From this perspective, a long, low-intensity war might well recur after ending. Very long but low-intensity ethnic wars in Burma match this scenario.

On the whole, we expect that costliness lowers the probability of recurrence. This could be seen as a result of what Zartman calls a "hurting stalemate" (Zartman 1989). The longer and more deadly the previous civil war, the more stable the subsequent peace because belligerents value peace over the uncertainty of another long and/or deadly war.

CIVIL WAR PATTERNS

Figure 1.1 reports data on armed conflict from Themnér and Wallensteen (2011). One very noticeable trend is that there are many more civil wars than interstate wars since World War II. The general trend is an increase in the number of countries experiencing civil war. The number of civil wars also followed an increasing trend.

There was a spike in the number of civil wars and percentage of countries experiencing war in the early 1990s. This is in large part due to wars that broke out as the Cold War ended. This includes wars in Yugoslavia and the Union of Soviet Socialist Republics (USSR).

The End of the Cold War and Its Effect on Civil War

The Cold War was a period of intense rivalry between the two greatest military powers, the United States and the USSR. The United States was the leader of the democratic world while the USSR controlled Communist states.

The collapse of the Soviet Union left a power vacuum in the newly independent republics. This opened the door to violent power struggles. The fall of the USSR also began the unraveling of communist control in Yugoslavia. Communism had been a key force that united the various ethnicities and religions of the republic.

FIGURE 1.1
Number of Armed Conflicts by Type, 1946–2010

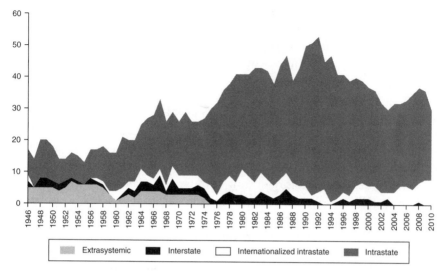

Source: Lotta Themnér and Peter Wallensteen (2011:526). Reprinted with permission.

Huntington's (1993) "clash of civilizations" framework argues that the end of the Cold War will unleash more conflict. He predicted wars will erupt because of cultural differences between such groups as Christians and Muslims. He argues ethnic, religious, cultural, and linguistic differences threaten international and intrastate stability more than economic competition between and within states (Huntington 1993, 1996). These forces had been more or less held in check during the Cold War. Chapter 4 describes this in greater detail.

There was great emphasis on the effects of democratization within states after the fall of communism. Interest centered upon the effects of freedom on intrastate stability. One finding was that war was more likely in the middle range of political freedom (e.g., Hegre et al. 2001; Reynal-Querol 2002; Sambanis 2001). This situation was common in countries emerging from communism. In these mid-range polities (also called anocracies), citizens will have grievances and a new ability to mobilize collectively. This may even result in armed opposition. In a fully democratic state, citizens have all the freedoms they need including the freedom to criticize leaders and vote them out. There is little need to fight. In the other end of the scale, in very autocratic states, any attempt to mobilize will be crushed. The experiences of Yugoslavia, the former constituents of the USSR (including Russia), Yemen, and Congo each fall within this category.

CONCLUSION

From death, disease, displacement, sexual crimes, child soldiers, torture, economic problems, and terrorism, civil wars cause multiple miseries. The United Nations estimates that over 5 million people died because of civil wars in the 10 years following the end of the Cold War. Between 1946 and 2011, there were approximately 229 civil war onsets. Three main explanations for onset were put forward in this Introduction. The greed perspective posits that rebels are profit-seeking opportunists. Dissecting war from this particular angle therefore puts pressure on governments to tackle the problem of how to prevent selfish rebel leaders from raising a rebel army based on illicit gains from natural resources. Here, rebel leaders treat rebellion as a business. The second perspective is the grievance perspective. Here, rebel leaders raise an army because of various grievances held by themselves and their followers. Grievance may be political in nature or economic, social, and cultural and ethnic. A common grievance is that the government restricts minorities from equal participation or that it fails to provide equal opportunities. Additionally, grievance may be about restriction of their religious or cultural practices. A third perspective is the capacity and opportunity model.

This book is an overview of civil war using the UCDP/PRIO definition of civil war as the basis of the analysis. The features of civil war covered in Chapter 1 include the definition of civil war; relevant civil war datasets; types of civil war; causes of onset, duration, outcome, and termination; and patterns of onset and recurrence of civil war. These features provide a foundation for the remainder of the book. The recurring theme of the book is conflict management. As appropriate, the book discusses conflict management in the context of each of these features. A thorough understanding of these features will inform conflict management. In turn, the discussion of conflict management can shed light on civil war.

SUGGESTED READING

Collier, Paul, V. L. Elliot, H. Hegre, A. Hoeffler, M. R. Querol, and N. Sambanis. 2003. *Breaking the Conflict Trap: Civil War and Development Policy*. Washington, DC: World Bank and Oxford University Press.

DeRouen, Karl R., Jr. and Uk Heo, eds. 2007. *Civil Wars of the World—Major Conflicts Since World War II*. Santa Barbara, CA: ABC-CLIO.

Doyle, Michael W. and Nicholas Sambanis. 2000. "International Peacebuilding: A Theoretical and Quantitative Analysis." *American Political Science Review* 94(4):779–801.

Doyle, Michael W. and Nicholas Sambanis. 2006. *Making War & Building Peace: United Nations Peace Operations.* Princeton, NJ: Princeton University Press.

Fearon, James D. 2004. "Why Do Some Civil Wars Last so Much Longer Than Others?" *Journal of Peace Research* 41(3):275–301.

Fearon, James D. and David D. Laitin. 2003a. "Ethnicity, Insurgency, and Civil War." *American Political Science Review* 97(1):75–90.

Gleditsch, Nils Petter, Peter Wallensteen, Mikael Eriksson, Margareta Sollenberg, and Havard Strand. 2002. "Armed Conflict 1946–2001: A New Dataset." *Journal of Peace Research* 39(5):615–637.

Newman, Edward and Karl DeRouen, eds. 2014. *Routledge Handbook of Civil War.* London, UK: Routledge Press.

Themnér, Lotta and Peter Wallensteen. 2013. "Armed Conflict, 1946–2012." *Journal of Peace Research* 50(4):509–521.

CHAPTER 2

Costs of Civil War

The devastating nature of civil war is graphically illustrated by the wide range of costs they inflict on societies. War-torn Somalia is one of the most dangerous places in the world, and certainly one of the least stable (Fund for Peace 2013). It is the worst ranked Failed State on the Failed States Index and has dominated this position in recent years (see Chapter 6). There is a lack of effective national governance with an economy and infrastructure seriously degraded by the many years of conflict. Accompanying this are starvation and high mortality rates, lawlessness, environmental degradation, and the mass displacement of people. Other countries rated highly on the index, and thus, typically experiencing lost physical control of their territory or a monopoly on the legitimate use of force, are Sudan and the Democratic Republic of the Congo (DRC). Here, lawlessness and human suffering are again widespread, while the inability to provide reasonable public services is clearly evident (Fund for Peace 2013).

In the sections that follow, we will look at each of the major types of costs of civil war—human casualties, displacement, economic costs, increased crime, and costs to education and environment—in turn. We address the most palpable cost—casualties in the form of loss of life and infliction of injuries, particularly among unprotected civilians during civil wars—through the use of casualty data and identification of major conflicts. Casualties are caused by various features of civil wars, such as the indiscriminate use of modern firepower and the collapse of health and sanitation systems along with the subsequent spread of disease. It is important to note that casualties continue to be sustained after a conflict has ceased as it takes time to rebuild, and deadly remnants, such as land mines, claim lives.

Beyond the casualties, we look at how people are displaced from their homes by fighting and at the fear of death and the social, economic, and political consequences that follow from displacement. The forced abandonment of homes and possessions, along with the likely loss of local work and social networks, makes such people vulnerable to violence and disease. Overall living conditions are worsened by the severe economic problems often associated with civil wars, such as the loss of productivity and undermining of good governance. People also face an increased risk of their human rights being violated with the break-down of law and order that frequently accompanies civil war. Similarly, education is often seriously disrupted as children are unable to attend schools, and education systems suffer. This in turn has a detrimental effect on future opportunities and the ability to generate an income. Finally, the wider natural environment does not escape the destructive impact of civil wars and ultimately can cause major problems for people and societies.

A word about context: Though civil war has a long history, our focus in this chapter is on the post-World War II (WWII) era. Civil strife that had been "interrupted" by WWII resumed and increased after 1945 in countries like India and China and started anew elsewhere, inflicting costs on societies against the background of the Cold War. This has meant that civil wars often involved fighting between forces identified as Communist or non-Communist. In turn, the United States and the Soviet Union frequently became involved in these conflicts, increasing the threat of escalation and increased casualties. This blight was felt throughout the world but particularly in some regions such as developing Asia. Although major international changes occurred in the late 1980s and early 1990s with the Cold War's conclusion, many countries continued to experience the devastating consequences of civil wars. Indeed, the former Soviet bloc especially suffered in the 1990s, although most of the conflicts were short (Bellamy 2007a:2; World Bank 2003:112–115). During the late 20th century, many countries also moved toward democracy from authoritarian regimes, which led to a change in the type of regime that battled insurgencies (Bellamy 2007a:2–3). Again though, as we will see, the deadly consequences of civil wars on lives and livelihoods remained all too evident.

CASUALTIES

The appalling loss of life and widespread sustaining of serious injuries represent the most graphic cost of civil wars. Researchers looking at civil wars focus on how to measure the severity of conflict in terms of casualties, who is most vulnerable, why some conflicts are more likely to produce casualties than others, and what strategies and instruments make civil conflicts so deadly, as well as the long-term effects of civil war on human casualties.

Who Gets Injured or Dies?

Casualties are especially prevalent among civilians and the vulnerable, such as women, children (who are frequently recruited as fighters), and the elderly. Apart from being unarmed and unable to defend themselves, large civilian populations inhabit cities and urban areas, which are strategically important. Warring factions often strongly contest control over such areas, directly threatening civilians. Furthermore, battle lines are commonly nonexistent or poorly defined with fighting throughout the country, thus, denying civilians of safe havens. This is graphically illustrated by the conflict in the former Yugoslavia during the 1990s. Here, the July 1995 fall of Srebrenica and its environs to Bosnian Serb forces "made a mockery of the international community's professed commitment to safeguard regions it declared to be 'safe areas' and placed under United Nations protection" (Human Rights Watch 1995:1). The massacre that followed has been termed the worst atrocity in post-WWII Europe; an estimated 7,000 to 8,000 Muslim men were killed by Serb soldiers (BBC 2005b). Indeed, civilians can be specifically targeted. Research suggests that violence against civilians is motivated by military objectives. For instance, a government might displace large parts of the civilian population (this is covered later) to reduce the fighting efficiency of rebel groups, as they cannot hide as easily and then obtain less support (Azam and Hoeffler 2002:461).

What Contributes to the Number of Casualties in Conflict?

Certain factors make some civil wars more deadly than others. Further research indicates that democracy, rather than economic development or state military strength, most strongly correlates with fewer deaths. Religious heterogeneity does not necessarily explain the military severity of internal violence, and ethnic homogeneity might be related to more deadly conflicts. The role of democracy in reducing deaths might be influenced by various factors. Democratic leaders under public pressure to avoid bloodshed at home and abroad may tend to grant concessions when faced with a major insurgency. Similarly, democratic governments can be unwilling to use the harshest measures against rebels or to inflict great collateral loss of life among civilians. They may be constrained by institutional checks on their powers (such as courts to prosecute war crimes) or public pressure arising from sympathy with insurgents or bystanders. Democracies might also be better equipped to co-opt, contain, and negotiate with insurgents than are other governments. Democracies allow for power rotation and public participation in policy formation and provide for checks on the center, such as an independent judiciary or federalism. These institutions are available to incorporate insurgents as additional players in a peaceful political contest (Lacina 2006:276, 282–283).

There is debate over measuring casualties but statistics are widely available. This debate includes how casualties are most effectively measured. For instance, some surveyors during wars in specific countries try to estimate mortality on the basis of household deaths; study analysts attempt to calculate mortality from

censuses using demographic techniques comparing the age distribution of a pre-
and postwar population; and practitioners of passive surveillance methods use
information from eyewitness and media reports or statistics from mortuaries,
gravesites, and health facilities (Obermeyer, Murray, and Gakidou 2008). The
Human Security Report Project (HSRP) has studied the impact of civil war. The
HSRP and the Uppsala Conflict Data Programs are two very useful conflict data
sources and are summarized in Box 1.1 (see Chapter 1). The HSRP analysis of
state-based conflicts (recall the battle-related deaths data given in Chapter 1 are
from the UCDP/PRIO) shows the average number of battle deaths per year from
international and intrastate conflict. Reported battle deaths per state-based
armed conflict ranged from 84,018 in 1950 to 357 in 2005 (see Figure 2.1).
Intrastate deaths peaked in 1947 at 40,029 and fell to a low of 357 before increasing to 763 in 2008 (Human Security Report Project [HSRP] 2011b:22–23). *Battle
deaths* are those reported and codable directly resulting from combat between

FIGURE 2.1

*Reported Battle Deaths per State-Based Armed Conflict:
International Conflicts Versus Intrastate Conflicts, 1946–2008*

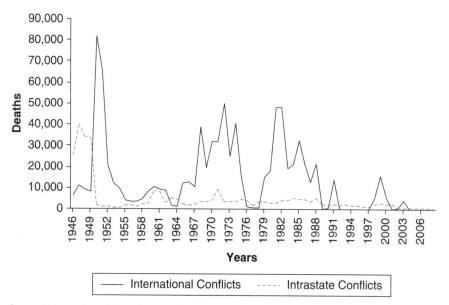

Source: Data are from Human Security Report Project. 2011. Human Security Report 2009/2010: The
Causes of Peace and The Shrinking Costs of War. New York: Oxford University Press.

warring parties in a conflict. The majority of battle deaths will be combatants; however, deaths of civilians caught in the cross fire are also included.

Civil wars involving external military support are particularly deadly, with deaths on average being higher than for those without such involvement. Over a 20-year period between 1989 and 2009, HSRP recorded approximately 31,571 deaths in internationalized civil wars, peaking at 7,187 in 1997 due largely to the fighting witnessed in the Democratic Republic of Congo and the Republic of Congo that year. To place these data in perspective, those civil wars that were *not* internationalized claimed approximately 14,260 lives over the same two decades, making them about half as deadly (HSRP 2012a:161, figure 5.8).

Over the nearer term, the most costly conflicts active during 2011 in terms of casualties were as follows: Afghanistan, the war between the government and Taliban or "students" (7,184 deaths); Pakistan, the war between the government and Taliban Movement of Pakistan (2,599); Somalia, the war between the government and Al-Shabab (1,917); and Libya, the war between the government and National Transitional Council (1,600) (Stockholm International Peace Research Institute [SIPRI] 2013b:43–45). There were 4,804 U.S. and coalition deaths in Iraq (U.S. troops completed their withdrawal in December 2011) and 3,412 deaths in Afghanistan by early January 2014 (Cable News Network [CNN] 2014). The formal end of conflicts does not necessarily mean that they do not continue to claim casualties. The Iraq Body Count, a nongovernmental organization with a public database that includes deaths caused by U.S.-led coalition forces and paramilitary or criminal attacks by others, estimated that as of August 20, 2013, there had been at least 119,973 civilian deaths since U.S.-led coalition forces entered Iraq in 2003 (Iraq Body Count 2014).

The devastating consequences of civil war on human life are magnified by the indiscriminate use of modern weapons. The firepower of weapons has increased significantly since WWII and is often used to devastating effect, especially in urban areas where numerous civilians live. Moreover, these weapons are widely available. According to SIPRI data, world military expenditure in 2012 was an estimated $1,756 billion. This represented 2.5 percent of global gross domestic product (GDP), or $249 for each person in the world. The total was lower in real terms than in 2011, the first fall since 1998, but the total was higher than in any year between the end of World War II and 2010. The United States, China, Russia, and the United Kingdom were the largest spenders (SIPRI 2013c:134). The impact of modern weapons is illustrated by the war-ravaged former Yugoslavia during the 1990s. Much of the fighting occurred in urban areas and involved heavy weaponry, such as artillery and tanks. Sarajevo, the Bosnian capital, was under siege from 1992 to 1995. Over 44 months, more than 10,000 people reportedly died during daily shelling and sniping attacks in Sarajevo (BBC 2005b).

Serbia was then bombed by the 1999 North Atlantic Treaty Organization (NATO) Operation Allied Force. Some 500 Yugoslav civilians were killed in the bombing (Human Rights Watch 2000).

Syria has witnessed an uprising since March 2011 during which the regime has been internationally condemned for using heavy weaponry against civilians. By August 2012, an estimated 17,000 people, mostly civilians, had died since the uprising started, many killed by regime forces (UN News Centre 2012). The UN High Commissioner for Human Rights Navi Pillay in January 2013 commented that casualties were "truly shocking" and attributed the toll to the international community's inaction: "Collectively we have fiddled at the edges while Syria burns." Pillay further said, "While many details remain unclear, there can be no justification for the massive scale of the killing highlighted by this analysis" (CNN 2013b:para. 9). The United Nations in December 2013 referred to well over 100,000 deaths. The embattled regime has reportedly used missiles against its opponents and "barrel bombs," oil drums filled with explosives and shrapnel dropped by aircraft (BBC 2013e; UN News Centre 2013).

No less deadly are common lighter and low-tech weapons. Although poorly equipped and organized armies may have relatively little capacity to cause high numbers of battle deaths, and a limited will to engage other factions, they can still cause numerous casualties. In a very poor nation with weak state structures, it may not require strong military capacity to destroy the infrastructure of health and human security, hence, causing a humanitarian disaster (Lacina and Gleditsch 2005:159–160). An estimated 60 to 90 percent of all direct conflict victims are killed with firearms (Religions for Peace 2010:4). Similarly, many of the Rwandan deaths during the 1994 conflict were caused by machetes. Despite the modern weaponry of coalition forces, rocket-propelled grenades, bombs, and improvised explosive devices have also inflicted high losses among both civilians and military combatants in Iraq and Afghanistan. Other countries facing such indiscriminate weapons include Pakistan and Syria. In Pakistan, an estimated 606 people were killed in 2011 by suicide attacks (Khan 2012). In March 2013, Iran, North Korea, and Syria blocked what would have been the first treaty to regulate international trade in conventional arms. The draft would require states to ensure that conventional weapons were not transferred across borders if they were to be used in human rights abuses (BBC 2013b).

The indiscriminate use of cluster bombs has received extensive coverage. After many years of civilian casualties resulting from such munitions, Israel's 2006 massive use of cluster bombs in southern Lebanon encouraged the international community to act with groups including Human Rights Watch, an independent organization dedicated to internationally defending and protecting human rights, and various governments working together. This led to the Convention on

Cluster Munitions, adopted on May 30, 2008. The convention prohibits cluster munitions and requires their clearance and assistance to victims. As of September 2013, a total of 113 nations had joined the convention. These include numerous former users, producers, and stockpilers of the bombs, along with countries suffering from the remains of these deadly weapons. However, many countries have not signed the convention, and the weapon continues to be used in civil wars. For instance, since mid-2012, Human Rights Watch and others have reported on civilian casualties caused by the Syrian regime using air-dropped cluster bombs. In early 2013, there were also reports that the regime had used ground-based cluster munitions (Cluster Munition Coalition 2013; CNN 2013a; Human Rights Watch 2013b).

Casualties After Conflict

The "winners" of conflict often inflict additional casualties upon the populations they ostensibly now govern. Groups that use violence to seize power are likely to be willing and capable of widespread violence if they believe their power is threatened and if they can take extreme measures against perceived threats. Illustrative of this are the brutal force used by the Myanmar, or Burmese, regime against protesting monks in September 2007; Libyan leader Muammar Gaddafi during his 2011 struggle to retain power; and the ongoing violence used by Syrian President Bashar al-Assad. Moreover, victorious groups might employ force to ensure that their goals and ideals come to fruition, which may be extreme themselves. The resultant social and economic disruption can cause widespread hardships, as witnessed in Cambodia under the Khmer Rouge from 1975 to 1979 (Bellamy 2005:17–20).

The devastating consequences of civil wars remain long after the fighting has subsided or concluded with higher mortality rates. The World Health Organization estimates that 269,000 people died in 1999 from the direct and immediate effects of civil and international wars. However, one study found that perhaps another 15 million lives were lost indirectly during 1999 to death and disability. These resulted from various diseases in war-torn countries and their neighbors caused by the lingering effects of civil wars from 1991 to 1997. In the long-term, the most frequent civil war victims were women and children (Ghobarah, Huth, and Russett 2004:870, 880). According to another study, during a 5-year civil war (the average length of a civil war is approximately seven years), infant mortality increased by 13 percent, and remained 11 percent higher than the baseline in the initial 5 years of postwar peace (World Bank 2003:23–24, 93).

Long-term threats to life vary. Civil wars greatly raise the subsequent risk of death and disability from numerous infectious diseases, including malaria, tuberculosis, and other infectious respiratory diseases. Evidence also indicates that civil wars may increase the risk of death and disability through the breakdown of norms and practices of social order, with increases in homicide, transportation accidents, and other injuries (Ghobarah et al. 2004:881). While men tend to suffer higher mortality immediately, women in the long-term experience as much mortality because of the war's lingering effects. These often cause widespread homelessness, forced migration, and economic recession that negatively impact mortality. Such effects are reinforced by war damage on health-related facilities and infrastructure, along with the death or fleeing of medical professionals. The destruction of road and rail links hinders the transportation of the sick and wounded together with medicine, while the pollution of water and sewerage system breakdown helps spread disease. This is especially problematic given war, and war preparations often reduce resources available for health investment and countering health threats (Li and Wen 2005: 471–474). Furthermore, long-term war trauma and psychological distress, including fear and hopelessness, are detrimental to daily life.

Livelihoods are additionally threatened by deadly remnants of war. Unexploded ordnance and cluster munitions often take lives and cause injuries, particularly among civilians, while land mines are especially menacing. The frequent use of mines, along with the difficulty of clearing them and their indiscriminate harm to people and livestock, enhances their threat. The estimated number of people killed or injured by mines annually declined from around 20,000 in 1999 to just over 4,000 in 2010. However, in 2011, there was more reported use of land mines by government forces than during any year since 2004 (International Campaign to Ban Landmines, no date). Those who survive encounters with mines are often maimed, an inability to work threatening them with a life of poverty and their ostracizing from society. More generally, mined transport links and destroyed bridges are significant obstacles to postwar recovery. Such damage hampers the harnessing of valuable natural resources and reconstruction efforts. Minefields also prevent the use of land suitable for agriculture and resettlement, especially those surrounding major population centers.

DISPLACEMENT

Many people try to flee the death and destruction of civil wars. The UN High Commissioner for Refugees (UNHCR) characterizes people who have fled across interstate borders as refugees and those who have been displaced from homes but have relocated within their state's borders as internally displaced peoples (IDPs). Research suggests that the violent behavior of governments and dissidents (and their interaction) are the primary determinants of forced migration flows, and high levels of dissident violence might be the strongest indicator. Large refugee diasporas, high wages, and the absence of genocide in neighboring countries each can encourage refugee flows relative to IDP flows (Moore and Shellman 2004:742, 2006:619). The forcible displacement of people due to war and persecution is a major challenge facing the international community. According to the UNHCR, at the end of 2012, some 45.2 million people worldwide, including some 15.4 million refugees, were forcibly displaced due to conflict and persecution, generalized violence, and/or human rights violations. An estimated 7.6 million people were newly displaced due to conflict or persecution, including 1.1 million new refugees—the highest number of new arrivals in a single year since 1999. Another 6.5 million people were newly displaced within the borders of their countries, the second highest figure of the past 10 years (UN High Commissioner for Refugees [UNHCR]. 2013).

Those displaced often carry minimal possessions and must survive with these, at least until they find new homes or shelter at refugee camps. The UNHCR expressed concern for 35.8 million refugees at the end of 2012 (UNHCR 2013:6).

Tent Camp in Jordan

The Za'atri refugee camp near Mafraq, Jordan, on the border with Syria. The Za'atri tent camp houses hosts tens of thousands of Syrians who have been displaced by conflict.

Credit: UN Photo/Mark Garten

Refugees are unlikely to receive adequate assistance from a weakened state, and they are vulnerable to attack and disease. Their plight is worsened by the trauma of witnessing death and destruction, as has been reported of Syrians fleeing their regime's repression to Jordan (BBC 2012e). Nor do camps often provide adequate care, food, and shelter to an influx of refugees. With inadequate support, infectious diseases can rapidly spread, as in Kenyan and Ethiopian camps during 2011 where poor conditions were exacerbated by heavy rains and accompanying risks of waterborne diseases (UNHCR 2011b). Refugees who flee abroad and are not in camps can experience major problems too. Many cannot afford accommodation or access local support systems because of their legal status and language barriers. In turn, they are vulnerable to exploitation and abuse. Moreover, refugees returning to their homes face challenges, as in Sudan where many found it difficult to readjust and went back to their new dwellings (McLaughlin and Selva 2004).

Refugees and displaced populations can increase the risk of subsequent conflict in host and origin countries. Refugees may expand rebel social networks and, although the vast majority does not directly engage in violence, refugee flows may facilitate the transnational spread of arms, combatants, and ideologies conducive to conflict. They also alter the state's ethnic composition, and can exacerbate economic competition (Salehyan and Gleditsch 2006:335). Resentment can develop against refugees (this is noted later), while disputes may arise between countries experiencing mass refugee inflows and the home countries of refugees. Refugee-receiving states can intervene with force to prevent further inflows, while refugee-sending countries can violate borders to pursue dissidents (Salehyan 2007:1).

ECONOMIC COSTS

The economic costs of civil wars are often severe. During a civil war, government military spending is typically about 5.2 percent of GDP compared to 3.3 percent in societies with otherwise similar characteristics but a history of domestic peace (Collier and Hoeffler 2004b:19). Moreover, as a society at war diverts some of its resources from productive activities to destruction, there is a double loss: the loss of resources that contributed to pre-conflict production and the loss from the damage inflicted (World Bank 2003:13). Skills are lost with people fleeing and dying, and the damage to the country's infrastructure and environment seriously hinders economic development and activity. The loss of reliable electricity supplies cuts productivity, and damaged transport systems restrict both the inflow of resources and the outflow of products. The uncertainty surrounding civil war discourages investment. Indeed, factions can target foreign investment, as in the

MAP 2.1
Displacement Worldwide, 2012

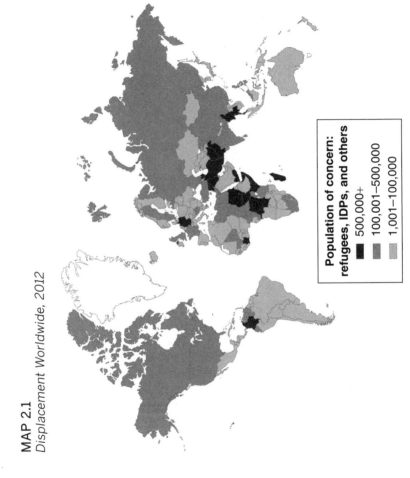

Population of concern: refugees, IDPs, and others

- 500,000+
- 100,001–500,000
- 1,001–100,000

Source: Data are from United Nations High Commissioner for Refugees, Overview. Persons of Concern to UNHCR. http://popstats.unhcr.org/PSQ_POC.aspx.

Philippines where the New People's Army has targeted overseas mining interests to gather protection money, weapons, and equipment along with support from antimining communities (Greenwood 2012:56). Civil war costs can also heighten economic instability as people try to stockpile goods and inflation reduces the value of money (Bellamy 2007a:11).

Costs are illustrated by the economic performances of countries experiencing them. The longer and more destructive the war, the greater the negative impact on economic growth (Kang and Meernik 2005:101). A World Bank study estimated that during civil war, countries generally grow around 2.2 percent more slowly than during peace. Hence, after a typical civil war of 7 years' duration, incomes would be approximately 15 percent lower than had there been no war (assuming steady growth as a default). This implies the incidence of absolute poverty increased by about 30 percent. The cumulative loss of income during the war would be equal to approximately 60 percent of a year's GDP. In another study, researchers analyzed the economic impact of civil wars, utilizing data from 18 countries affected by such conflict. For 14 countries whose average growth rates of GDP per capita could be calculated, the average annual growth rate was –3.3 percent. Macroeconomic indicators worsened with fighting too. In all 18 economies, the external debt increased as a percentage of GDP; in 15 countries, per capita income fell; in 13 countries, food production declined; and in 12 countries, export growth dropped (World Bank 2003:17). In the aftermath of war, especially when a stable peace emerges, GDP per capita can gradually increase, but investment rates may lag (Chen, Loayza, and Reynal-Querol 2007:11–13). Moreover, post-conflict governments often respond to a greater risk of civil war by continuing high military expenditure. This can actually significantly increase the likelihood of further conflict (Collier and Hoeffler 2004b:20).

Good governance is undermined with the breakdown of law and serious economic problems. This in turn creates opportunities for economic mismanagement and corruption. Transparency International, a global civil society organization fighting corruption, annually publishes a corruption perceptions index measuring the perceived level of public sector corruption. In its 2013 index, the least corrupt countries were not experiencing major armed conflicts, contrasting those most corrupt. The worst corruption perceptions were found in countries including conflict-torn Somalia, Afghanistan, Iraq, and Sudan. Contrasting this, the least corrupt perceptions existed in peaceful countries with Denmark, New Zealand, and Finland all ranked best (Transparency International 2013).

Fighting factions are likely to violate laws and to seek by any means necessary the resources needed for achieving victory. Poorly policed borders encourage cross-border trafficking, feed the informal economy, weaken the legitimate economy, and erode customs revenues and hence the state's ability to provide public services or pay public servants. Fragile public institutions motivate petty corruption as unpaid or underpaid civil servants try to survive. Finally, international relief, development, and peacekeeping personnel, with their large operating and aid budgets, create opportunities for corruption (Boucher et al. 2007:9). Such problems hinder development, increase living costs, and ultimately might cause discontent and further conflict. Contrasting this, research suggests a well-financed and administratively competent government can contribute to fewer civil wars (Fearon and Laitin 2003a:88).

A civil war's economic impact goes beyond the host country. As countries are closely interlinked by the global economy, when war affects the economy in one country, it frequently affects others, especially neighbors. The impact's magnitude is shaped by the nature of the country's economy. Fighting in a country with a large economy and strategic resources, such as oil, is more likely to have a larger impact on the global economy than war in a country with a small, resource-restricted economy. War can have a particularly damaging impact on the economies of neighboring countries. This impact can include reduced investment and the disruption of trade. Fighting in Mozambique doubled Malawi's international transport costs and an economic decline occurred. Likewise, the DRC war closed the river route to the sea for the Central African Republic (Bellamy 2007a:11–12; World Bank 2003:35). Civil wars can have a significant negative influence on short-term growth within the country and its neighbors (Murdoch and Sandler 2002). According to the World Bank, having a neighbor at war reduces a country's annual growth by around 0.5 percent (World Bank 2003:35). Economic growth rates may be adversely affected for various reasons. For instance, war is likely to discourage investment. Trade obstacles caused by fighting are especially challenging for landlocked countries (World Bank 2003:35).

The regional impact of war is magnified by additional demands placed on economies. The flight of refugees can strain the economies of neighboring countries experiencing their influx. According to the World Bank, large-scale and protracted refugee influxes can have macroeconomic impacts on the host country's economy. Some of these impacts are associated with increased but uncompensated public expenditures related to the care and maintenance of the refugee population. Refugees may compete with local citizens for scarce resources like water, housing, food, and medical services. Their presence increases demands for education, health services, infrastructure, and sometimes natural resources. For example, Syrian refugees have placed an increasing strain on neighboring governments and host communities (Cordesman 2013). However, refugees can make positive contributions. These include bringing to host countries their skills, knowledge, and trading opportunities and their access to transnational resources, such as remittances and social networks (World Bank 2010:7–9). Likewise, refugees can undertake unpopular work (UNHCR 2011c). Furthermore, threat perceptions and the perceived need for defence expenditure can increase in countries near wars. Encouraged by anxiety that fighting could spread, there is a heightened risk of regional instability, and border disputes might arise as warring factions seek to use border areas as sanctuaries. Military expenditure during 2011–2012 increased the most in the Asia and Oceania region, which had 13 state-based conflicts active in 2011 (SIPRI 2013c:47, 131).

CRIME AND VIOLENCE

Numerous deaths and injuries result from war crimes. Human rights are often violated during civil wars as social mores against such crimes are weakened along with general law and order. These developments provide opportunities for historical animosities to surface, for leaders to exploit tensions, and for factions to take revenge for perceived historical injustices. This can initiate a cycle of violence as factional violence against each other leads to retaliation. In turn, violence increases the level of hatred and the risk of war crimes. Human rights might be systematically violated too, as terror and brutality are employed to achieve dominance and guarantee a population's compliance. Furthermore, the breakdown of law and order can provide the opportunity for numerous violations to occur untroubled by the fear of punishment. The International Criminal Court (ICC) has been established to help end this impunity and gross violations of international humanitarian law. This court, an independent international organization, is governed by the Rome Statute that entered into force during 2002 (International Criminal Court [ICC], 2013b). Other courts, such as the International Criminal Tribunal for the former Yugoslavia, focus on war crimes during specific conflicts. The statute of the ICC defines war crimes as, inter alia, "serious violations of the laws and customs applicable in international armed conflict," and "serious violations of the laws and customs applicable in an armed conflict not of an international character" (Red Cross 2013:para. 2).

The HSRP research uses the term *one-sided violence* to describe campaigns of organized violence directed against unarmed civilians incapable of fighting back. From 1989 to 2002, the number of such campaigns increased by some 70 percent. However, after campaigns peaked in 2002 and again in 2004, they declined to 26 in 2008 (HSRP 2011a:177). More recent SIPRI data are also available. The SIPRI has defined this violence as the use of armed force by the government of a state or by a formally organized group against unorganized civilians that cause at least

25 deaths. A state or group that killed 25 or more unarmed civilians during a year was registered as a "one-sided actor." A total of 130 actors were recorded as carrying out one-sided violence in 2002–2011 including 23 active in 2011. This compared with a peak of 47 during 2002 (SIPRI 2005–2013, *Yearbook* 2013:55). Deaths from one-sided violence from 1989 to 2009 totaled approximately 676,340, and ranged from a peak of 504,084 in 1994 to a low of 3,294 in 2008 (HSRP 2012a, figure 8.2). Nonstate actors were the most frequent cause of one-sided violence, representing 13 of the 23 one-sided actors in 2011. One-sided actors were most common in Africa (10 in 2011), followed by Asia and Oceania (7), the Middle East (4), the Americas (1), and Europe (1) (SIPRI 2005–2013, *Yearbook* 2013:55).

The conflict in Rwanda during the 1990s provides graphic evidence of the atrocities that can occur. Here extremist Hutu militia and elements of the Rwandan military undertook the systematic massacre of Tutsis. Approximately 800,000 Tutsis and moderate Hutus were killed (Bellamy 2007b:6). This was the deadliest post-World War II period of organized violence experienced by any country (HSRP 2011b:112). Rates of genocide and politicide (genocide victims are identified by communal characteristics, such as ethnicity, whereas politicide victims ideologically oppose the government or dominant group) can be effective and consistent predictors of future disability and death rates following civil war (Hoddie and Smith 2009:177, 192).

The human rights of females are particularly threatened during civil wars. The incidence of rape rises with law and order collapsing, and power is held by those holding weapons, often young, poorly educated males using alcohol and other drugs. Violence can occur with ill discipline, but may also be employed as another tool to gain the population's submission. Such violence is illustrated by conflict in the Democratic Republic of the Congo (DRC) where widespread and sometimes systematic rapes of women and girls occurred. Many suffered gang rapes or were used as sex slaves, while the rape of men and boys was reported too. Women suffering injuries or illnesses caused by rape were frequently denied medical care and abandoned by their husbands and excluded by their communities because of prejudice. With such violence, the risk of infection with HIV/AIDS and other sexually transmitted diseases increases. Indeed, it has been estimated that HIV was prevalent among 60 percent of military forces in the region (Amnesty International 2005; Human Rights Watch 2002:2–3).

However, recent HSRP research on sexual violence against adults and children in wartime provides findings that differ from many commonly quoted. The research suggests that the mainstream narrative exaggerates the prevalence of combatant-perpetrated sexual violence, while largely ignoring the much more pervasive domestic sexual violence perpetrated during wartime by family members and acquaintances. The narrative also largely ignores the impact of wartime sexual violence against males. This is despite its being substantially greater than generally believed. Finally, much research fails to acknowledge female perpetration of sexual violence (HSRP 2012b:2, 5, 20).

Human trafficking involves a disproportionate number of women too, both as victims and as culprits. This involves the recruitment, transport, transfer, harboring, or receipt of a person by means including threats, force, coercion, abduction, fraud, and deception for the purpose of exploitation. It often occurs from less developed countries, where people are more likely to experience conflicts, to more developed countries with victims at any one time conservatively numbering an estimated 2.5 million (UN Office on Drugs and Crime 2013). Research indicates that immediately before and during conflict, trafficking is primarily related to the recruitment and use of child soldiers and women associated with the fighting forces (WAFF). Immediately following conflict, most child soldiers and WAFF victims are released and try to reintegrate back into civilian society. As peacekeepers enter a country, prostitution often increases. The post-conflict phase also sees human trafficking increase because of weak state institutions.

The demand for weapons and breakdown of law and order facilitate the illegal trafficking of weapons. This in turn helps arm factions along with fueling civil wars and can escalate fighting along with criminal activities as evident by widespread piracy along the coast of Somalia. According to the United Nations, illicit weapons have fuelled wars in Central Africa (Voice of America 2010). For instance, arms traffickers supplied weapons to Angola throughout its 27-year civil war despite a UN-imposed arms embargo. Traffickers included Arcadi Gaydamak, Jean-Christophe Mitterrand, the son of former French President François Mitterrand, and Viktor Bout, a high-profile arms trafficker incarcerated in the United States (Marques de Morais 2009). In Africa, limited national and regional capacity, porous borders, and the spillover effects of conflicts in the region have impeded effective small arms control. Thus, illicit weapons are common, exacerbating intercommunal violence, increasing cross border crime, and threatening ongoing peace and national reconciliation processes. Weapons are frequently recycled from country to country, and their ownership is transferred among fighters, security forces, and war profiteers (Religions for Peace 2010:4).

The production of illegal drugs is similarly facilitated by civil war. Fighting, poor governance, and widespread poverty can create territory outside the control of a recognized government, in which illegal activities, such as drug cultivation, can develop. This cultivation or control of the illegal drug industry frequently provides a vital revenue stream for factions. Cultivation can also become an income source for people with economic options reduced by war or who reside in areas controlled by guerrilla and criminal groups. An estimated 95 percent of the global production of opium occurs in countries experiencing civil wars (World Bank 2003:41). In Afghanistan, the deeply embedded opium economy not only finances armed opposition groups but also brings profits to most major local politico-military actors, including those loyal to the government, alongside criminal trafficking networks (see SIPRI 2014). The link between conflict and illegal drugs is further shown by Colombia. Colombian intelligence sources have estimated that 40 percent of its total cocaine exports are controlled by paramilitaries and their allies in the narcotics underworld. Similarly, U.S. Secretary of State Hillary Clinton in September 2010 said that Mexican drug-related violence increasingly had the characteristics of an insurgency (BBC 2010).

EDUCATION

As with females, children are another particularly vulnerable group. There is some debate over the exact impact of conflict on education, some recent research suggesting that education outcomes actually *improve* on average during wartime at approximately the same rate as the average nonconflict country (though from a lower baseline). HSRP research has confirmed that conflict-affected countries generally have substantially lower educational outcomes than nonconflict countries, but it challenges the widely held notion that this is *because* of war. It indicates that educational outcomes were also low, or lower, during the previous periods of peace. According to the HSRP, these educational outcomes could thus not have been caused by warfare (HSRP 2012b:10, 11, 108). Despite this research, it is clear that civil wars can have significant and long-term detrimental effects on educational attainment, in turn impacting upon health outcomes and labor market opportunities for future generations.

A particularly troubling occurrence during civil wars is the loss of educational opportunities when children as young as 8 years of age are recruited as fighters, messengers, porters, and cooks and for forced sexual services by warring factions. Some are abducted or forcibly recruited; others are driven to join by poverty, abuse, and discrimination, or to avenge violence against them and their families. Children are viewed by factions as a readily available supply of recruits easily trainable and indoctrinated, who require no pay, and eat less food than adults. They are especially vulnerable when separated from their families or orphaned. It is estimated that some 300,000 boys and girls under the age of 18 years are involved in conflicts worldwide (UN Children's Fund, no date; UN, no date-c).

Apart from their recruitment, children often face a degraded educational system. Reduced government expenditure on education is probable during civil wars. This can be due to direct economic costs, such as military costs, and indirect costs. These include the loss of revenue resulting from negative developments like reduced tourism and foreign investment. The effect on expenditure continues after the civil war ends given the destruction of schools, general loss of government revenue, and casualties. Furthermore, school enrollment is likely to decline with the physical destruction of schools, school closures due to safety risks, and the deaths of students and educators (Lai and Thyne 2007:278–279). Schools, their staffs, and students can be specifically targeted by armies and rebel groups alike. As war adversely affects household income and well-being, children may be forced to work rather than attend school. Even if they can combine work and school, they face low nutritional levels and tiredness that reduce educational outcomes. Displaced children are particularly vulnerable to being denied access to education due to the poor conditions of refugee camps, discrimination, lack of documents, and high costs (UN Educational, Scientific and Cultural Organization [UNESCO] 2011b:16–18). Indeed, too little education, unequal access to education, and the wrong type of education can make societies more prone to armed conflict. For instance, when many young people are denied access to decent quality basic education, the resultant poverty, unemployment, and prevailing sense of hopelessness can act as strong recruiting agents for factions. Similarly, unequal access can generate grievances and a sense of injustice (UNESCO 2011a:60).

ENVIRONMENT

The natural environment within which people reside and interact provides an essential basis for their lives. This is because ecosystems provide key inputs for human communities: the production of food, raw materials, and energy; and recycling of wastes back into resources. The destructive impact of civil wars is not restricted to human life but includes the natural environment and ecosystems. Indeed, the natural environment can be targeted as groups try to expose their enemies by destroying any natural cover and restricting their sources of food, for instance, by contaminating fresh water supplies. Such destruction presents serious long-term problems. In line with this impact, the United Nations during 2001 declared November 6 "International Day for Preventing the Exploitation of the Environment in War and Armed Conflict" (Patrick 2011:para. 1).

A key indicator for the health of the environment is biodiversity. This reflects the number, variety, and variability of living organisms and how these differ according to location and change over time. Biodiversity is vital in all ecosystems and is the basis of the benefits provided by ecosystems to people. The loss of biodiversity through civil wars has direct and indirect negative consequences on eight major factors. The first four are food security (biodiversity often increases the adaptability of communities to change); vulnerability (ecosystems often become less resilient and stable as species are lost); health (a balanced diet requires diverse foods); and energy security (wood fuel provides over half the energy used in developing countries, and thus, major problems can arise from shortages). The other factors are clean water (the loss of forests and watersheds reduces water quality and availability); social relations and cultural identity (many cultures attach values to ecosystems or their components); freedom of lifestyle choice (the loss of species and ecosystems often means reduced choices); and finally, basic materials (biodiversity provides people with goods vital for their livelihoods) (UN Environment Program 2010).

The impact of conflict on the environment and biodiversity is wide-ranging. Wildlife is often killed or driven from its natural habitat, rivers and soils are polluted, and natural land formations destroyed. The migration paths of pelicans and endangered Siberian cranes cross through eastern Afghanistan—a region that became a war zone filled with the noise of helicopters, jets, and exploding shells. As a result, the World Wildlife Fund reported the number of birds safely surviving the migration south had fallen by 85 percent (Smith 2002). Environmental protection is rarely a priority in conflict-ravaged countries with natural resources recklessly exploited. For instance, in Somalia, the absence of law and order has facilitated unsustainable fishing in its coastal waters (Peace Pledge Union, no date). The pollution of water hinders the resettlement of areas after conflicts and important activities such as agriculture, and the death of wildlife both removes a source of livelihood and can upset delicate ecosystems, and the removal of natural cover increases the threat of soil erosion and flooding. Cooking fuel is very limited in most humanitarian emergencies; thus, women and children are forced to forage for firewood on their own, which can have a devastating impact on the environment. For example, refugees fleeing the Rwandan genocide in the 1990s collected an estimated 1,200 tons of firewood each day, causing permanent deforestation in Tanzania and other host countries. Years of collecting firewood and shelter material by both displaced and host communities in Darfur has also taken a major toll on the environment, with minimal or no trees remaining in vast areas of the region. To find firewood, women and children are forced to travel ever-greater distances, making them increasingly vulnerable to attack (Patrick 2011).

The negative impact of civil war on the natural environment is further shown by the consequences of frequently used land mines. When mines do explode, in addition to causing serious injury and death to humans, domestic animals, and wildlife, they shatter soil systems, destroy plant life, and disrupt water flows, accelerating ecosystem disruption.

Data on the number of animals killed by land mines is limited and highly biased toward domesticated animals with little known about the impacts suffered by wild populations. However, animals regularly harmed included brown bears in Croatia, while in Rwanda, the mountain gorilla, one of the most endangered apes, has been threatened by land mines and fighting (Berhe 2007:7; Rutagarama 2001). With regard to domesticated animals, a 1995 study of 206 communities in Afghanistan, Bosnia, Cambodia, and Mozambique reported that more than 57,000 animals were killed by mines (Andersson, da Sousa, and Paredes 1995:718; Berhe 2007:7).

Mines further accelerate environmental damage through forcing populations to live in marginal and fragile environments to avoid minefields, in turn speeding the depletion of biological diversity. Interactions between natural disasters and buried land mines cause additional serious problems. For example, the flooding in Mozambique during 1999 and 2000 is feared to have displaced hundreds of thousands of land mines left from the civil war. Moves to locate and remove the mines were thus hindered (Leaning 2000:1159).

CONFLICT MANAGEMENT IMPLICATIONS

The costs of war are inextricably tied to conflict management—particularly in terms of civil war recurrence. Costs measured in terms of casualties and human displacement can cut two ways. Many deaths might lead to deep-seated hatred, making war recurrence more likely should there be a break in the fighting. Animosity built up over years or even decades of fighting makes reconciliation difficult. On the other hand, high death tolls can lead to war weariness and a mutually hurting stalemate in which the sides are ready for peace because they each realize there is no end in sight and there is little to be gained from further fighting (Zartman 2001). High costs can also attract offers of mediation, which can help guide the disputants toward a cease-fire and even a comprehensive peace accord.

The education and economic costs of civil war can also have an impact on recurrence. If the economy is in shambles for years after a civil war, opportunity costs for rebels pondering whether to restart an armed struggle are lower. That is, with the economy disrupted, rebels have no cost imposed by missing out on employment in the licit economy. A similar argument can be said about education. If education is disrupted through funding or infrastructure damage, opportunity costs associated with restarting the war are lowered.

These cost-based arguments point to the need for directly and quickly addressing economic and educational opportunities in peace agreements and the subsequent peacebuilding process. Crime and low-level violence also make the job of peacebuilding more difficult as these can be evidence that the nation has not truly healed in the wake of a civil war.

The bottom line is that taken together, excessive costs seem to lead to higher probability of civil war recurrence. If peacebuilding is to truly take hold, the potential effects of costs must inform the peace process. Otherwise, a vicious pattern of civil war may be difficult to avoid.

CONCLUSION

Civil wars pose a major threat to both individuals and societies in general because their costs are often wide-ranging and devastating regardless of where they occur and why they started. The chapter has outlined some of these major costs associated with civil wars, starting at the graphic and widespread loss of life. As shown by international data on conflicts and by ongoing conflicts in countries such as Afghanistan, Pakistan, Somalia, and Iraq, casualties are often high. Moreover, these casualties are especially prevalent among those that are most vulnerable, namely, civilian women, children, and the elderly. Casualties are caused by numerous factors that include the indiscriminate use of weapons that do not have to be sophisticated to kill and maim, and the violence of fighting factions. Casualties continue to be sustained long after the fighting has subsided or concluded with higher mortality rates. These rates are often recorded against the background of serious social and health hazards arising from chaos and the destruction of vital infrastructure and the remnants of fighting such as mines. Moreover, those that flee the carnage are likely to become refugees with minimal possessions who then face serious challenges and struggle to survive. These all pose significant and costly long-term challenges in countries that can least afford them.

Lives and livelihoods are further threatened by the disastrous economic impact of civil wars. Resources are used for fighting rather than productive activities, the economy is hit by the destruction of infrastructure important for the normal functioning of societies, and productivity is degraded as skills are lost through people dying or fleeing. The impact is worsened by companies unlikely to invest in countries experiencing conflict and the overall decline of law and order eroding good governance practices. The economic impact of civil war is not restricted to the conflict-ravaged country as others, especially those near the fighting, are likely to face extra economic burdens. Such burdens can range from the diversion of resources to address the arrival of refugees, and a greater emphasis placed on defense, through to the disruption of trade.

War crimes cause additional suffering. Human rights are often violated during civil wars as general law and order breaks down. Of particular concern is the cycle of violence that can emerge as factions commit violence against each other that in turn provokes their response. Human rights may also be systematically violated, as terror and brutality are used to win dominance and force the population's compliance. Moreover, a breakdown of law and order can provide the opportunity for widespread violations to occur unhindered without fear of punishment. Females are especially vulnerable to crimes including rape and human trafficking. However, recent research indicates that wartime sexual violence against males has been significantly underestimated. The violence against vulnerable groups is facilitated by ill discipline among fighting groups, but such violence may be employed systematically as another tool to gain the population's submission. The intensity of conflict is likely to increase with weapon trafficking helping to arm factions and revenue generated from illegal activities, such as the production of illegal drugs.

Finally, the negative long-term impact of civil wars is enhanced by their detrimental effects on educational attainment and the natural environment. The loss of educational opportunities often associated with conflict impacts upon the health outcomes and career opportunities of future generations. Nor is the destructive impact of civil wars restricted to human life but rather encompasses the natural environment and ecosystems. Indeed, the natural environment can be targeted by fighting factions, and environmental protection is rarely a priority in conflict-ravaged countries. Ultimately, the magnitude and diversity of civil war costs make it vital to better understand them and to try and prevent such wars from occurring, or at least enhance the ability to establish peace.

SUGGESTED READING

Chen, Siyan, Norman V. Loayza, and Martha Reynal-Querol. 2007. "The Aftermath of Civil War." *World Bank Policy Research Working Paper 4190.* Washington, DC: World Bank.

Collier, Paul, V. L. Elliot, H. Hegre, A. Hoeffler, M. R. Querol, and N. Sambanis. 2003. *Breaking the Conflict Trap: Civil War and Development Policy.* Washington, DC: World Bank and Oxford University Press.

Ghobarah, Hazem Adam, Paul Huth, and Bruce Russett. 2004. "The Post-War Public Health Effects of Civil Conflict." *Social Science & Medicine* 59:869–884.

Human Security Report Project. 2011. "Reported Battle Deaths per State-Based Armed Conflict: International Conflicts versus Intrastate Conflicts, 1946–2008." *Human Security Report 2009/2010: The Causes of Peace and the Shrinking Costs of War.* New York: Oxford University Press.

Human Security Report Project. 2012. *Human Security Report 2012: Sexual Violence, Education and War: Beyond the Mainstream Narrative.* Vancouver, Canada: Human Security Press.

Kang, Seonjou and James Meernik. 2005. "Civil War Destruction and the Prospects for Economic Growth." *Journal of Politics* 67(1):88–109.

Lacina, Bethany and Nils Petter Gleditsch. 2005. "Monitoring Trends in Global Combat: A New Dataset of Battle Deaths." *European Journal of Population* 21(2–3):145–166.

CHAPTER 3

Civil War Dynamics

Scholars place types of civil conflict into three categories, each with distinctive patterns. The core features of these major types of civil wars are their frequency, type, and tactics. Taken together, these features of civil war, and the accompanying factors such as duration, types of termination, and probability of recurrence, compose civil war "dynamics." These dynamics deserve particular attention as scholars seek to prevent, or at least reduce, the likelihood of civil war occurrence or recurrence. These dynamics must be understood in order to have a comprehensive understanding of civil war.

The first category of civil war is wars fought over control of government. Revolutions and coups are the two main examples of this type. Significant revolutions that have removed regimes have occurred in Russia, France, China, Mexico, Nicaragua, and Cuba. There have also been many coups, although their frequency has generally declined. This is likely correlated with the rise in the number of democratic governments since the end of World War II with an additional jump after the Cold War.

A second major category of civil war is secessionist/autonomy-seeking. A signature feature of secessionist wars is the promotion of a separate ethnic or other identity of a group of people in a particular area and their explicit demand for a separate or autonomous territory. Various conditions are associated with the violent escalation of ethnic conflict, and these include events weakening a regime and a single ethnic group dominating policy making without accommodating others. Conflict itself might occur between members of a minority ethnic group concentrated in a particular region that perceives itself as the indigenous "sons of the soil," and relatively recent, ethnically distinct migrants to this region from other parts of the same country. This conflict occurs with competition and disputes over scarce resources, such as natural resources and work. Violence associated with sons-of-the-soil wars often begins as communal conflict but can escalate to civil war if the state intervenes to forcefully support the migrants (see Fearon 2004). Secessionist/autonomy-seeking wars are generally longer than other civil wars but less costly in terms of casualties.

A third type of civil war is internationalized. Here, a second state becomes active in the fighting. External actors can become involved in civil wars in various ways. They might deploy their own forces or indirectly help to finance and equip those they support. Regardless of the nature of this involvement, the level and intensity of violence frequently increases as warring factions become stronger, particularly if there is direct intervention on their behalf. External involvement might be encouraged by actors who believe that they will benefit from the ongoing conflict and who support the goals of a particular faction in the belief its victory will promote their own interests. There have been many post-WWII internationalized conflicts, and these were especially common during the Cold War (for more information about the Cold War, see Box 3.1). During this period, such involvement was used as a tool by the superpowers and their allies to promote rival strategic interests. More recently, eight internationalized civil wars occurred in 2012 (see Table 3.1).

To place these types of conflict dynamics into context, we will also look at recent trends in civil war as we look more closely at each type of war. At the end of the chapter, we will look at another type of civil war dynamic as we discuss insurgency and counterinsurgency tactics. This is useful as civil wars, and thus the societies experiencing them, are shaped largely by the tactics used by those fighting (i.e., the rebels often use insurgency tactics and governments employ counterinsurgency techniques). Moreover, the continuation and outcome of the conflicts are influenced by the success of these tactics.

BOX 3.1 The Cold War

The term *Cold War* is frequently used to describe the period of rivalry and confrontation between the superpowers—the United States (and its allies) and the Soviet Union (and allies)—from WWII's conclusion to thawing relations in the late 1980s. Writer George Orwell used the term, and Bernard M. Baruch, an advisor to U.S. President Harry S. Truman, during April 1947 said, "Let us not be deceived—we are today in the midst of a cold war. Our enemies are to be found abroad and at home." Baruch himself credited the phrase to Herbert B. Swope, the former *New York World* editor, and that same year the writer and journalist Walter Lippmann used the words.

There is debate over the Cold War's exact duration. Some scholars identify its origins as predating 1945, but the period's initial years are commonly associated with the immediate post-WWII period. The 1962 Cuban missile crisis is generally viewed as the period's most dangerous event, the super-powers coming close to nuclear hostilities. Tensions continued during the following decades but began to ease after 1985 when Mikhail Gorbachev took power in the Soviet Union. During the late 1980s, Soviet domination over Eastern Europe declined, as symbolized by the Berlin Wall falling in 1989. Two years later, the Soviet Union collapsed.

There are different interpretations of the Cold War, its origins, and why it ended. Factors commonly linked with the period include the continuation of great power rivalry for domination and strategic advantage; misperceptions over motives causing the WWII alliance that defeated fascism (an authoritarian right-wing ideology) to splinter and encourage an arms race; events largely promoted by those benefiting from them, such as the military-industrial complex; and an ideologically driven conflict between capitalism and communism, or between democracy and totalitarianism (a political system whereby the state seeks total power over society and attempts to control all aspects of public and private life) (Bellamy 2011a:261–263). Despite the Cold War's end, some tensions associated with the period continue, such as those between North Korea and the international community. Indeed, these tensions have been called the "last Cold War," and the future remains uncertain (Bellamy 2010; Bellamy 2011c; and Bellamy 2012). This is particularly the case given the North's pursuit of nuclear weapons, a pursuit that has been globally condemned with three nuclear tests by early 2014. U.S.-Russian relations have also been increasingly tense since Vladimir Putin's domination of Russia from 2000, such as over Ukraine.

CIVIL WAR TYPES AND TRENDS

UCDP data provide a useful overview of armed conflicts. The data distinguish between three types of armed conflicts: interstate, intrastate (civil war), and internationalized intrastate. Interstate conflicts are fought between two or more state governments, while intrastate conflicts are between a state government and one or more rebel groups. Internationalized intrastate conflicts are those intrastate conflicts where one or both sides receive troop support from an external state. Overall, in recent years, the total number of conflicts has been increasing, though the total figure for 2012 was the same as in 2002 and down from 2011. Conflicts peaked at 37 in 2008 and 2011, while only 30 occurred in 2003. Civil wars and internationalized civil wars dominated the 2002–2012 period, representing about

97 percent of wars in 2012 (see Table 3.1). Civil wars over governmental power are more common (18 of the 31 civil wars), and more costly than those over territory (see Tables 3.2 and 3.3). Indeed, the civil war over governmental power in Syria caused the highest number of fatalities in 2012. Battle-related deaths were estimated to be over 15,000 (Themnér and Wallensteen 2013:518).

Wars Over Control of Government

Civil wars over governmental power, whether over the type of political system or a change of central government or its composition, have been more common than those over territory (interstate control of territory, secession or autonomy). UCDP data indicate that during 2012, there were 32 armed conflicts with all but one (conflict between Sudan and South Sudan over their common border) intrastate. The highest number of civil wars occurred in Africa (12), followed by Asia (10), the Middle East (five), the Americas (two), and Europe (two). Eighteen of these were over government with Africa suffering the most (nine), followed by Asia (four) (Themnér and Wallensteen 2013:510, 517–519). Civil wars over governmental power were more costly in fatalities than those over territory (see Tables 3.2 and 3.3).

TABLE 3.1
Interstate, Civil War, and Internationalized Civil War Conflicts, 2002–2012

Year	Interstate	Civil War	Internationalized Civil War	Total
2002	1	28	3	32
2003	2	26	2	30
2004	-	28	4	32
2005	-	26	6	32
2006	-	27	6	33
2007	-	30	5	35
2008	1	30	6	37
2009	-	28	8	36
2010	-	22	9	31
2011	1	27	9	37
2012	1	23	8	32

Sources: Data are from SIPRI (2013:47); UCDP (2014b).

TABLE 3.2

Five Most Costly Civil Wars Over Control of Government in 2012

Location	Year Started[a]	Opposition Organizations	Best Estimate of Deaths in 2012
Syria (Middle East)	2011	Free Syrian Army; and Support Front for the People of Syria	15,055
Afghanistan	1978	Taliban ("Students")	7,442
Pakistan	2008	Movement of the Taliban in Pakistan	2,705
Somalia	2006	Al-Shabaab ("The Youth")	2,620
Yemen	2009	Al-Qaeda in the Arabian Peninsula	2,321

Source: Data compiled from Appendix of Themnér and Wallensteen (2013:517–519).

[a] This year indicates when the armed conflict reached 25 battle-related deaths for the first time. If a conflict has been inactive for more than 10 years, or if there has been a complete change in the opposition side, the start refers to the onset of the conflict's latest phase.

Revolutions

A second type of civil war is the revolution, which has changed governments through force for hundreds of years. They require our attention given their diverse nature and enormous impact on both the host country and international community and often provide the context, and indeed sometimes the trigger, for major civil wars.

Early cases include Greek city-state governments changing from aristocracies and tyrannies in the 3rd to 6th centuries BC, and the revolutionary founding of the Roman Republic during the 6th century BC. During the 16th-century European Renaissance, the Italians introduced the word *revolution* (in Italian "revoluziones") to describe the alternating victories of popular and aristocratic factions fighting for control of Italian states, which became republics or duchies (territory ruled by a duke or duchess). In the mid-17th century, the philosopher Thomas Hobbes used the English word *revolution* to describe the power transferral from England's King Charles I to Oliver Cromwell's Puritan Parliament and, after Cromwell's death, back to Charles's son, King Charles II. In these cases, revolution meant the transferral of power and a recasting of government from one party and government type to another. According to Goldstone, this change was not necessarily permanent or progressive as power could be seized again by a previously defeated group (1993:730).

During the 18th and 19th centuries, views of what constituted a revolution changed. Influenced by the 1789 French Revolution, many believed that society would progress toward greater fairness and productivity and revolutions were needed to destroy obsolete and unfair social orders. Thus, a perception arose that revolutions were progressive and necessary permanent social transformations rather than cyclical governmental crises. This view was strengthened by Karl Marx and Frederick Engels in *The Communist Manifesto* (1848). Here, it was argued that throughout history, revolutions were linked to inevitable economic progress. These would ultimately lead to workers overthrowing capitalists, the development of a superior production system, and a long-term period of utopia (a community or society with very desirable or perfect attributes). This view was powerful by the later 19th century and through most of the following century, often in its Marxist form. However, Goldstone notes that the progressive utopian view of revolutions did not necessarily conform to the reality of revolutions. This is especially shown by the graphic hardships and many casualties of the 1917 Russian and 1949 Chinese revolutions that did not achieve utopian societies. By the start of the 21st century, the utopian view of revolutions was challenged by those who believed they were neither necessary nor progressive but rather were costly and often tragic symbols of governmental crises (Goldstone 1993:730).

Today, more recent scholars such as Skocpol (1979) define revolutions in less ideological terms, as rapid, basic transformations of a society's state and class structures that are accompanied and in part undertaken by class revolts from below. Goldstone et al. (2010:191) refer to revolutions as one of the most common types of civil war, though Fearon (2004) identified only three of 128 civil wars from 1945 to 1999 as popular revolutions. These involved at their outset mass demonstrations in the capital city in favor of deposing the governing regime. The median war duration in these cases, along with coup-related wars noted later, was 2.1 years and median number killed 4,000 (Fearon 2004:280).

Common factors have been identified to explain 20th-century revolutions. According to Goldstone (1993), four major factors largely account for these revolutions: weak states, conflicting elites, rapid population growth, and erratic international intervention. With regard to weak states, those recently established or economically struggling frequently experience revolutions, and in the 20th century, they became more common. Likewise, with much greater international trade, investment, foreign aid, and military support, the potential for conflict among the states' elite significantly increased. Rapid population growth can strengthen pressures on weak states and conflicting elites too. This can be through contributing to poverty, resource exhaustion, strains on state services, and increasing competition for power and status. Finally, state governments lacking a stable international balance of power and stable policies cannot count on international support to stay in power. Indeed, challengers to their power might actually be supported. In many states, one or more of these conditions can arise without causing a revolution; where all the factors appear simultaneously, the likely outcome is a revolution. No one ideology motivated 20th-century revolutions, but with all these factors present, a revolutionary ideology emerged. This ideology combined elements of nationalism and utopianism (the belief in a perfect and ideal society) along with whatever widely held indigenous beliefs could be used to oppose the existing regime's ideology (Goldstone 1993:731–732). The role of people in rebellions against regimes can vary from neutrality and noninvolvement to active participation in an armed insurrection or full-time guerrilla unit (Petersen 2001).

Beyond the theory of revolutions, it is useful to briefly outline major revolutionary turmoil of the 20th century and early years of the 21st century, especially that associated with civil wars. The exact nature of revolutions can vary, but their goal is essentially the same, the seizure of power through force and the most common type of civil war. Furthermore, the factors that can increase the likelihood of a revolution all can contribute to the instability from which civil wars might arise. The February and October 1917 Russian revolutions set the scene for a costly civil war. The Communist revolution was an all-out attempt to seize control of government and turn it down a Marxist path.

The February revolution occurred against a background of disastrous World War I (WWI) military defeats, serious economic problems, such as food shortages, and discontent with Czar Alexander Nicholas II's rule. These combined to encourage widespread unrest that led to his abdication and the replacement of Czarism with a provisional government. Bolshevik Party leader Vladimir Lenin argued that the Bolsheviks should not be content with this *bourgeois* (middle class) revolution but should seize power for the *proletariat* (working class) and poor peasants (Lenin 1917). Consequently, the Bolsheviks seized power in the October revolution. A civil war then started in 1918 between the Bolsheviks (the Reds) and groups ranging from monarchists and liberals to moderate socialists (the Whites). In addition, former allies during WWI, such as Britain, France, Japan, and the United States, supported the Whites. The conflict destroyed much of Russia's industry and agricultural sectors with a resultant famine. Ultimately, the Red Army was victorious, the Soviet Union emerging in 1922, and its support for Communist revolutions internationally caused significant tension during the Cold War (Gall and Gall 1999:489; Teed 1992:405).

The October 1949 Chinese revolution witnessed the victory of the Chinese Communist Party and establishment of the People's Republic of China after a costly civil war. Chinese interest in communism was encouraged by the October Russian revolution, and the Party's first congress was held in 1921. Mao Zedong (commonly known as Mao), who increasingly dominated the Party and would govern China from 1949 to 1976, rejected the Marxist orthodoxy that capitalism was a vital prerequisite for socialism. Mao believed that the peasantry and countryside were more important than the industrial proletariat and city in revolutions. Conflict with the government nationalist forces started in 1927 with the Communist guerrilla campaign against their better-equipped opponents. As Japanese aggression increasingly threatened China in the late 1930s, an uneasy truce developed between both groups. However, conflict again broke out with Japan's surrender in August 1945, and the morale of government forces declined with successful Communist attacks. This, along with economic problems and the government's corruption, facilitated the Communist victory in 1949. After achieving victory, a policy of permanent revolution developed with the population's mobilization aimed at swiftly modernizing China and its transformation from socialism to communism. Particularly symbolic of this were the Great Leap Forward (1958–1960) to modernize China and the Cultural Revolution (1966–1976) to defeat a perceived move away from socialism toward capitalism. Both of these caused significant upheaval (Joseph 2001:188; Teed 1992:91).

Many other dramatic seizures of power have occurred internationally. Following a guerrilla campaign, Fidel Castro and Ernesto "Che" Guevara seized power in Cuba during 1959. Major reforms such as the creation of a centrally planned economy were undertaken, and revolutions were promoted abroad. Here, Guevara played a leading role with his treatise promoting revolutionary guerrilla warfare against dictatorships and his active role in such conflict, as in Bolivia (his *foco* strategy is outlined later). Although he was captured in battle and later executed in 1967 during this campaign, his call for youth to revolt and promise of victory through revolution encouraged many, particularly in South America, to revolt, and he still inspires many revolutionary groups (Knight 2001:185; Davies Jr. 2001:344). Another major revolution occurred in Iran with unrest over the unpopular and corrupt royal dictatorship, leading to Ayatollah Ruhollah Khomeini's 1979 seizure of power. An Islamic republic was established and inspired other Middle Eastern groups to seek power (Hooglund 2001:467). The Soviet Union's decline sparked revolutions against Communist regimes during the late 1980s and early 1990s in Eastern and Central Europe. These ranged from Czechoslovakia's peaceful Velvet Revolution to Romania's violent revolution and civil war that followed the disintegration of Yugoslavia.

These three revolutions are similar in that they each set out to completely change the form, structure, and ideology of government. The revolutionaries cast aside old power structures, undercut the principles of private property and capitalism, and

Che Guevara

A hand-painted mural in Old Havana, Cuba, shows Che Guevara's portrait over the Cuban flag.

Credit: The Carol M. Highsmith Archive, Library of Congress, Prints and Photographs Division.

instituted strong and authoritarian central governments. These revolutions had lofty goals and in this sense represented all-or-nothing ventures. If a revolution is not won and a tipping point not reached in the first few years, the chances of success begin to decline.

More recently, Arab uprisings (the "Arab Awakening") started in late 2010 and ultimately led to the 2011 overthrow of autocratic regimes in Egypt and Libya that have been described as revolutions. These uprisings are looked at in greater detail in Box 3.2. According to the International Institute for Strategic Studies (IISS), these uprisings occurred against a background of social and economic conditions that made the region "ripe for upheaval." Increasing food prices has been identified as one "catalyst" with social networks an "accelerator." However, widespread corruption and long-entrenched autocratic regimes meant that the region's young, educated populations not only sought more jobs and better economic conditions, but also wanted greater democracy and openness. The uprisings started with the Tunisian fruit seller Mohamed Bouazizi setting himself on fire in December 2010 to protest against his treatment by officials. The resultant protests led to President Zine al-Abidine Ben Ali's resignation after 23 years in power. Protests then occurred in other countries such as Algeria, Egypt, and Libya (International Institute for Strategic

Studies [IISS] 2011:ii-v). Syrian protestors against President Bashar al-Assad were encouraged by these developments, but violence dramatically escalated. Indeed, in July 2012, the International Committee of the Red Cross said that with widespread fighting, the country was essentially experiencing a civil war (BBC 2012c). As noted in the previous chapter, the death toll from this fighting has been horrendous. Various regimes fell from power (see Box 3.2) while other regional countries, such as Morocco, Algeria, and Jordan, have promised reform (BBC 2012a).

BOX 3.2   Fallen Regimes During the Arab Spring Uprisings 2010–2011

Egypt: President Hosni Mubarak resigned in February 2011 after 23 years in power. He was given a life prison sentence in June 2012 for failing to stop the killing of protesters in the previous year's revolution. However, this sentence was overturned in January 2013, and a retrial was ordered.

Libya: After 42 years in power, Colonel Muammar Gaddafi lost power when rebels took the capital Tripoli in August 2011. Gaddafi and his family escaped, but he was captured and killed on the outskirts of Sirte during October 2011.

Tunisia: President Zine al-Abidine Ben Ali resigned during January 2011 and went into exile in Saudi Arabia. He had held power for 23 years. In June 2012, he was sentenced in absentia to life in jail for the killing of protesters, having already received a sentence of 35 years in jail during June 2011.

Yemen: Following a November 2011 agreement, President Ali Abdullah Saleh formally ceded power to his vice president in February 2012 after holding power for 33 years.

Coups

Coups are another common form of civil war that involves seizing control of the central government. Powell and Thyne (2011) defined a *coup d'état* (a French expression meaning a "stroke of state," or a "blow to the state") using four features. First, the target of a coup is the state's primary leader. Second, coup perpetrators are any elite part of the state apparatus. These can include noncivilian military and security service members, or government civilian members. The third feature relates to tactics used to overthrow the leader. Here, the activity is illegal but not necessarily violent (therefore, not all coups are civil wars). Finally, the coup attempt needs to be overt with a visible movement to claim power. More specifically, if the perpetrators seize and hold power for at least 7 days, the coup has been successful. This approach is useful as it does not solely focus on military attempts to seize power, distinguishes coups from other forms of antiregime activity together with those where foreigners are the primary actors, and avoids unreliable coup reports (Powell and Thyne 2011:250–252). Furthermore, the Powell and Thyne data cover the period 1950 to 2010, thus providing comprehensive information.

Numerous coups have occurred since WWII. Based on Powell and Thyne's dataset, 457 coup attempts occurred from 1950 to 2010, of which 227 (49.7 percent) were successful and 230 (50.3 percent) were unsuccessful (Powell and Thyne 2011:255). Another two coups occurred in 2011 with one successful and the other a failure (see Figure 3.1), and by the start of 2012, two more with the same outcomes had been staged (Powell and Thyne 2012a, b, c, d). Coups from 1950 to 2010 most commonly occurred in Africa (169), and 51.5 percent of these

FIGURE 3.1

Coups, 1950 to 2011: Successful, Failed, and Total Number

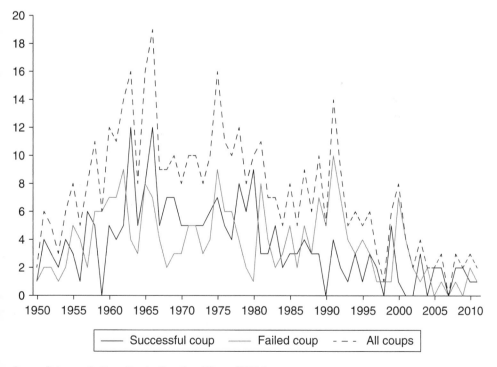

Source: Data supplied to author by Powell and Thyne (2012d).

succeeded. The Americas experienced the second highest number with 145 coups and a success rate of 48.3 percent. Significantly fewer coups occurred in other regions, as the Middle East experienced 72, Asia 59, and Europe 12. The success rates in these regions ranged from 55.9 percent for Asia to 45.8 percent in the Middle East and 33.3 percent in Europe (Powell and Thyne 2011:255). During recent years, coups have occurred in countries such as Madagascar (2010) and Mali (2012), while comparatively peaceful regions have not been exempt from their occurrence. For instance, Fiji experienced its fourth coup in less than 20 years during 2006, this having a negative impact on society (Bellamy 2008). Countries such as Thailand, which experienced its latest coups in 1991 and 2006, have histories of numerous coups.

There has been an overall decline in the frequency of coup attempts. Coup attempts peaked in the mid-1960s followed by an increased frequency in the mid-1970s and early 1990s. Similarly, the number of successful coups declined. Successful coups peaked in the mid to late 1960s and 1970s (see Figure 3.1). Turning to the percentage of coup attempts that resulted in successful regime changes, the mean success rate was 48 percent during the entire period. This rate peaked around 1970 and 1980 before declining until the 21st century. The success rate started to increase again in 2003 with 12 of the 18 (67 percent) coup attempts since then being successful (Powell and Thyne 2011:252, 255–256). As mentioned, one probable explanation for the drop in coups is the concomitant rise in the number of democracies in the world. The longer-term outcomes of coups can vary. Some research indicates that whereas most pre-1990 successful coups installed their leaders durably in power, between 1991 and 2004, this changed with the majority of coups leading to competitive elections in 5 years or less. This has been influenced by international pressure, those countries most dependent on post-Cold War Western aid being the first to embrace competitive elections after a coup (Marinov and Goemans 2012:1–2, 18). However, World Bank research indicates that the risk of civil war is increased by political instability resulting from a history of coups, violent protests, and demonstrations (Bodea and Elbadawi 2007:24).

Various factors can motivate coups. Although Welch Jr. (2001) focuses on coups involving the military, his division of major coup explanations into three broad schools of research provides a useful overview of motivating factors. The first school covers factors internal to armed forces. The military is particularly relevant in the staging of coups as they generally have the capability in terms of weaponry and personnel to seize power, and they have frequently used this ability. Military coups have occurred often in developing countries where militaries are both the defender of the government against external threats and internal rebellions. For instance, in Africa from 1960 to 2001, there were 145 military coup plots that proceeded no further than the plot stage, 109 failed coups, and 82 successful coups (Collier and Hoeffler 2007:9–10). The military's corporate grievances can be influential in prompting them to stage coups. Such grievances can involve their budget, policy autonomy, and possible threats to the military's identity along with personal grievances among officers (Welch 2001:181). Indeed research indicates that in Africa, increasing military spending is an effective way of reducing the threat of a military coup (Collier and Hoeffler 2007:20).

Grievances can also arise outside of the military and motivate other groups to seize power. The second school deals with the environment of the overall political system, primarily the domestic economic, political, and social backgrounds. Ethnic fragmentation, political mobilization, and violence can increase the likelihood of coups. For instance, a power vacuum resulting from a government's collapse or its ineffectiveness, which could be provoked by a major economic or political crisis, can provide coup plotters with an opportunity to act. The final school focuses on the international context where nondomestic factors such as changes in world prices and direct or indirect encouragement by outside groups can be important. To this should be added the actual capacity to stage a coup. The available coup forces, their cohesion and mood, along with presence of capable coup leaders are important here (Welch 2001:181; Henderson and Bellamy 2002:125–126, 129).

Armed conflicts and coups often go hand-in-hand. As noted, SIPRI identified 31 civil wars active during 2012. The most violent conflicts in 2012 occurred in countries sharing a history of coups. Coups can spark civil conflicts by weakening the state, as in Nepal (1960) and Afghanistan (1978) (Powell and Thyne 2011:256–257, appendix tables 1, 2). Fearon, in his study of 128 civil wars already noted, identified 19 coup-related civil wars where conflict occurred between groups seeking control of the state and those led by recent members of the state's central government (2004:280). Coups might also influence the duration of civil wars and thus impact upon the number of casualties. They can lengthen conflicts by encouraging further governmental instability, as shown by Sudan's 1989 coup, or shorten them by bringing more conciliatory leaders to power, as in Colombia during 1953 (Powell and Thyne 2011:256–257).

Secessionist and Autonomy-Seeking Wars

Civil wars can occur as factions seek the secession and autonomy of territory within a state. Whereas wars over control of government seek to take central authority, secessionist wars are fought to break away from the central government.

According to Collier and Hoeffler (2006:38), the secessionist rebels inhabit contiguous territories that can form a unity distinct from the existing political entity. Secessionist groups often require both domestic and international support to defeat resistance from their host governments. Without domestic support, group leaders cannot launch successful insurgencies, and movements with limited support are less likely to succeed than those supported strongly. Insurgencies do not necessarily need numerous fighters, but they do require sufficient popular support to ensure they receive regular supplies of food, shelter, and funding. More importantly, secessionist groups must usually be territorially concentrated. As secessionist movements are founded on territory claims, their leaders need to demonstrate that they enjoy support from inhabitants in their claimed territory to create the popular basis of these demands. Associated with this is the need for a secure territorial base. External support, or at least a lack of resistance, is also important for a successful insurgency (Saideman, Dougherty, and Jenne 2005:611-612).

A major feature of secessionist wars is the promotion of a separate identity of those people in a particular area. This can involve secessionist leaders selecting symbols, myths, practices, and traditions that resonate broadly with their popular base. Three main types of identities that can be used for secessionist bids are territorial, communal, and ideological. A territorial identity is defined as a bond based on common residence within a particular region distinct from the core. This "homeland" identity is vital as secessionists need territory to claim as their own before they can legitimately demand territorial self-determination. The territory's ethnic composition can influence the importance of this identity too. When the territory is dominated by a single ethnic group, a salient territorial identity can be less important for winning the support of its inhabitants (Saideman et al. 2005:612-613). Indeed, secessionist wars generally have an ethnic component, as noted next. Communal identities are "tribal" allegiances that determine membership in politically active groups. Such allegiances are based on descent and can be racial, religious, linguistic, regional, or cultural. These identities differ from territorial identities where membership depends on descent. Finally, ideological identity is based on shared ideological beliefs rather than location or descent (Saideman et al. 2005:614-615). According to Sambanis (2001), identity wars are predominately caused by political grievances.

At the start of the 21st century, 82 percent of all independent states were composed of two or more ethnic groups, which frequently were in disputes either with each other or with the state itself. Although these disputes did not necessarily lead to war, they often did, as shown by the Balkans, Rwanda, and Timor-Leste (Toft 2001:1). There are different views on the causes of ethnic violence, but two major approaches are the symbolist political theory and rational choice theory. The first theory is based on a social-psychological view that emphases the importance of intangible concerns, such as a group's emotional state, when characterizing motivation behind ethnic violence. Extreme acts of ethnic violence are caused by factors including group myths that justify hostility and fears of group extinction (Kaufman 2006b:45–86). For instance, Kaufman (2006b:70) wrote that the 1994 Rwandan genocide was motivated by "an exceptionally hostile" Hutu mythology against the Tutsi. Advocates of the rational choice theory believe that ethnicity is a construct of the elite utilized by them to help maintain power and manipulate the masses. Ultimately, elites format ethnic violence to generate political support, which then encourages more antagonistic identities and additional violence. Hence, in Rwanda preexisting ethnic divisions were used as "scapegoats" for the problems facing the country and to further incite a need for greater government control (Jean 2006:5–6).

Sons-of-the-Soil Wars. Some territorial wars have unique features. Sons-of-the-soil wars are an example of territorial wars with an ethnic component. These wars pit indigenous groups concentrated in a peripheral region against migrants. The indigenous groups perceive themselves as "sons of the soil" (see Fearon 2004:283). This type of conflict occurs with competition and disputes over scarce resources, such as natural resources and work (Fearon and Laitin 2011). These findings are in line with Petersen's (2002) research on Central and Eastern European ethnic struggles where ethnic animosity was most frequently inflamed by resentment arising from sudden changes in ethnic status hierarchies. This can occur when individuals of a losing ethnicity feel these changes are unjust and intolerable and an opportunity arises to try and regain a higher status level (Petersen 2002).

Violence associated with sons-of-the-soil wars often begins as communal conflict, but it escalates to civil war levels if state forces intervene to support the migrants. The wars have been particularly common in Asian countries, including China, India, and Myanmar. As migration often occurs gradually and continuously, and the sons-of-the-soil are normally a small, weak group compared to the center, the duration of the wars is generally longer than other wars with an estimated median length of 15.1 years. This is over twice the median length of other civil wars (Fearon and Laitin 2011). The length of these wars stresses the need for effective conflict resolution techniques, such as the designing of credible guarantees on the terms of a negotiated settlement between factions (Walter 1999:129). However, the wars generally cause fewer casualties (an average of 33,254 deaths) compared to other civil wars (138,534 deaths) with rebels focusing their efforts on a region rather than seeking to capture the capital (Fearon and Laitin 2011).

As already noted, civil wars over territory are less common than those over the government. In 2012, there were 13 civil wars fought over territory, and the highest number occurred in Asia (six) and Africa (three). In 2012, the five most costly wars over territory caused significantly fewer deaths than those over government (see Table 3.3). Furthermore, territory is often associated with ethnic conflicts given its importance to both ethnic groups and states. Ethnic groups often view territory as closely linked to their identity, meaning that control over it ensures a secure identity. With regard to states, territorial control is directly associated with their physical survival (Toft 2001:3).

Internationalized Civil Wars

Civil wars are internationalized when external actors become actively involved. External actors can become involved in civil wars with the deployment of their own forces or indirectly by helping to finance and equip those they support. Regardless of the involvement's nature, the level and intensity of violence often increases as warring factions become stronger, particularly if there is direct intervention on their behalf (as noted in Chapter 2). This involvement might be encouraged by external actors who benefit from the ongoing conflict and who support the goals of a particular faction in the belief its victory will promote their own interests.

There have been many post-WWII internationalized conflicts, and military intervention has been a focus of much research (Regan, Frank, and Aydin

TABLE 3.3
Five Most Costly Civil Wars Over Territory in 2012

Location	Year Started[a]	Opposition Organizations	Best Estimate of Deaths in 2012
Turkey	1984	Partiya Karkeran Kurdistan (Kurdistan Workers' Party)	811
Myanmar	2011	Kachin Independence Organization	702
Russia	2007	Forces of the Caucasus Emirate	516
India	1989	Kashmir insurgents	141
Thailand	2003	Patani insurgents	132

Source: Data compiled from Themnér and Wallensteen, Appendix 1 (2013:517–519).

[a]The year the armed conflict reached 25 battle-related deaths for the first time. If a conflict has been inactive for more than 10 years, or if there has been a complete change in the opposition side, the start refers to the onset of the conflict's latest phase.

Vietnamese Refugees

Following a Viet Cong attack on their village, Vietnam War refugees ride a U.S. Air Force helicopter to a safe area near Saigon in March 1966.

Credit: United States Information Agency

2009:135). For instance, Regan (2000) examined the involvement of foreign powers in civil wars, and his work on interventions to end conflict is noted in Chapter 7. Of the 165 civil wars identified by Harbom and Wallensteen (2005) from 1946 to 2004, 36 (or about one-fifth) involved troops from an external state, most often a neighboring state. Furthermore, such involvement has occurred more recently, and this is described in greater depth (see Figure 3.2). The number of these conflicts was particularly high from 1975 to 1982, the number peaking at eight in 1979 before declining during the 1980s to zero in 1991. There was an average of just over three conflicts annually from 1992 to 2001 (Harbom and Wallensteen 2005:627–628). During three conflicts, former colonial powers, including the United Kingdom and France, intervened in their former colonies, and there have been moves by regional powers to assert or increase their influence. This was evident in 2000 and 2001 when Russian troops were involved in Uzbekistan and Libyan forces in the Central African Republic (Harbom and Wallensteen 2005:627–628).

External involvement frequently occurred during the Cold War. During this period, it was often used as a proxy tool (hence, the term *proxy war*) by the super-powers and their allies to promote rival strategic interests. Seven conflicts were particularly associated with these years: Afghanistan 1979–1988, Angola 1975–1989, Cambodia 1970–1989, Cuba 1961, Ethiopia (Ogaden) 1975–1983, Laos 1963–1973, and South Korea 1948–1950 (Harbom and Wallensteen 2005:628). The Vietnam War also illustrates the dynamic nature of internationalized conflicts. This war started as a civil war in 1960 between the South Vietnamese Government and the National Liberation Front (or the Viet Cong) before becoming an internationalized civil war with the deployment of U.S. advisers in 1961. However, the conflict was fundamentally altered in 1965 when the United States began bombing North Vietnam, and that year the first combat forces arrived. At this point, the conflict transitioned from a civil to interstate war as the United States and its ally South Vietnam fought against North Vietnam. External involvement continued during the Cold War's final years and its aftermath (see Figure 3.2). Neighboring countries remained frequent external actors. Indeed,

FIGURE 3.2
Internationalized Civil Wars, 1946–2004

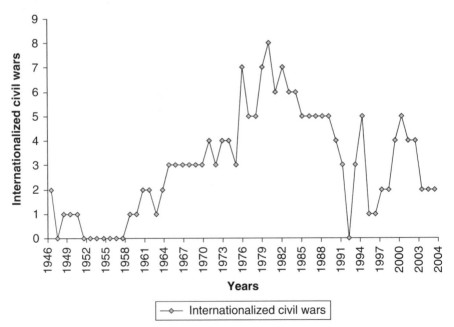

Source: Data from Harbom and Wallensteen (2005:628).

only neighbors were identified as interveners in internationalized conflicts from 1989 to 1998 (Harbom and Wallensteen 2005:627–628).

There were nine internationalized civil wars active in both 2010 and 2011, the highest annual numbers from 2005 to 2011. Although this number fell slightly to eight during 2012, it remained significantly higher than the lowest number of five in 2007 (see Figure 3.3). These conflicts were in Afghanistan, Azerbaijan, Central African Republic, Democratic Republic of the Congo, Rwanda, Somalia, and Yemen (Themnér and Wallensteen 2013:510). Note that several of these are linked to the U.S.-led global war on terrorism.

Internationalized wars are costly, as graphically shown by casualties in Afghanistan and Iraq (Afghanistan's conflict is examined in greater depth shortly). With regard to the external states contributing troops, this support often is for the government party in the countries experiencing conflict, and the United States is frequently involved (SIPRI 2005–2013, *Yearbook* 2011:73–76). However, external states have been supporting Syrian insurgents. Saudi Arabia and Qatar, with U.S. and Turkish facilitation, have reportedly been arming and funding the opposition. Furthermore, as noted in Chapter 1, direct external

FIGURE 3.3
Internationalized Civil Wars, 2005–2012

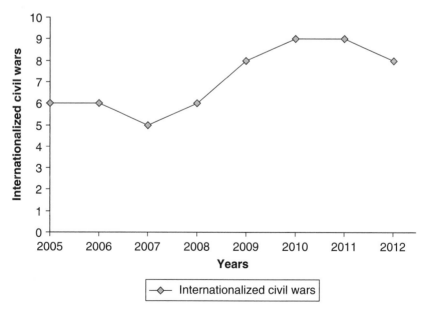

Source: Data from SIPRI (*Yearbook* 2013:47); UCDP (2014b).

involvement occurred in late 2013 to destroy the regime's chemical weapons after their earlier use in Ghouta.

The nature of involvement by external actors has varied. In addition to those internal conflicts at the Cold War's conclusion where external actors deployed troops, as many as 80 of those conflicts involved actors providing support other than troops. Here, the provision of weapons, financial assistance, or the sanctioned use of a neighboring state's territory occurred. With regard to the direction of support, states gave their support to the government side in 56 conflicts and to the insurgents in 57 cases. Neighbors again can play a key role here. For instance, the Nepalese and Indian governments helped each other fight Communist insurgencies, such as through sharing intelligence. In Angola during the 1970s and 1980s, the South African government supported the Angolan government, while Cuba assisted the insurgents. The September 11, 2001 attack on the United States motivated the external deployment of large forces in the global war against terrorism, as in Iraq and Afghanistan. Overall, support for the government's side in a conflict was nearly always provided by other governments (Harbom and Wallensteen 2005:628–629). However, major recent case studies are mixed. An international coalition was involved with the downfall of Libya's Colonel Muammar Gaddafi, while evidence indicates that Iran has actively helped the Syrian regime militarily to fight insurgents, and Russia has provided weapons (BBC 2012d; CNN 2012).

The conflict in Afghanistan clearly shows the potentially major role of external actors. Mohammed Daud Khan took power in a 1973 coup and tried to play off the Soviet Union against Western powers but was overthrown in 1978. After a power struggle, Soviet forces were deployed the following year to support a pro-Communist regime and in 1980 installed Babrak Karmal as leader. However, Communist resistance intensified, with various *mujahideen* (this can be defined as "strugglers" or "people doing jihad") groups fighting pro-Communist and Soviet forces. These groups were supplied with money and arms by countries that opposed the Soviet Union, including the United States and Pakistan. The United States and the Soviet Union finally agreed to end military aid to both sides in 1991, two years after the withdrawal of Soviet forces (Bellamy 2007a:20). Significant forces returned in 2001 with the global fight against terrorism. The International Security Assistance Force (ISAF) was established in 2001 with NATO assuming leadership in 2003. The ISAF's mandate was initially limited to providing security in and around the capital of Kabul, but the United Nations in 2003 extended its mandate to cover all Afghanistan, facilitating the mission's nationwide expansion. In January 2014, the ISAF consisted of 49 states with troop contributions ranging from the United States' 38,000 to New Zealand's two (North Atlantic Treaty Organization [NATO] 2014).

CIVIL WAR TACTICS

Tactics are essentially the plans of war. Rebels and governments have used a variety of civil war tactics. The most general categories of tactics are guerrilla warfare (most commonly used by rebels) and counterinsurgency (used by governments). Within these categories are various subgroupings.

Guerrilla Warfare

Factions staging armed rebellions (or insurgencies) against governments have often used guerrilla warfare. This form of warfare commonly involves small and mobile units that seek to harass, weaken, and demoralize larger military forces. Insurgents do not need to be militarily strong to win; indeed, military strength can backfire if the threat of an insurgent military victory galvanizes government security forces (Connable and Libicki 2010:xvii). Research suggests that the degree of violence used by insurgents against civilians can be influenced by their strength. Weak insurgents can be encouraged to use violence against civilians as a means to acquire necessary resources and to prevent collaboration with the government. However, stronger groups are better equipped to make competitive offers to potential supporters and can have fewer incentives to use violence to acquire support (Wood 2010:612).

Important works on insurgencies include those by Mao and Guevara. Mao in *On Guerrilla Warfare* (1937) wrote that small independent and loyal insurgent groups using mobile military tactics, such as ambushes, could effectively fight larger but less mobile formal militaries. They should attack enemy forces whenever the opportunity arose and where they were most vulnerable, before withdrawing to protect themselves from the superior firepower of their enemies. It was also important for insurgents to win the support of civilians who could assist them (see Zedong 1937). Guevara was a key member of the revolutionaries (the *foco*) who invaded Cuba in 1956 and ultimately seized power 3 years later. The *foco* (Spanish for "focus") is based on cadres of small, rapid-moving paramilitary groups providing a focus for popular discontent against a regime and, thereby, leading a general insurrection. His book *Guerrilla Warfare* (1961) outlined how a small and determined armed group could facilitate a revolution. A revolution was facilitated by the guerrillas winning legitimatization and support for their fight by politicizing the peasantry and further weakening support for an oppressive and corrupt regime (for a brief overview and evaluation of his approach, see Johnson 2006). The support of civilians is vital with insurgents who minimize innocent civilian deaths but maximum government casualties and who are thus more likely to achieve victory than those who indiscriminately kill (Connable and Libicki 2010:xvii).

Such warfare has been practiced throughout history and around the world. There are references to irregular forces in ancient Chinese military writings, the Bible, Roman military history, and medieval accounts of war. The term *guerrilla*, or "little war," was popularized by the hit-and-run attacks of Spanish insurgents fighting Napoleon Bonaparte's 1807 invasion of the Iberian Peninsula. Operations commonly associated with guerrilla war include surprise attacks and ambushes, the destruction of enemy supplies, cutting transportation and communication links, attacks on advance units or stragglers, and targeting political and military leaders along with hostage taking. Historically, guerrilla fighters have operated from rural areas, forests, mountains, and deserts. However, as urban populations grew throughout the world from the 19th century, urban guerrilla warfare became more common. Guerrillas often try to live off the land and win local support, while the provision of sanctuaries by other countries can increase their effectiveness. Examples of such sanctuaries include Greek bases in Albania, Yugoslavia, and Bulgaria (1946-1949) along with Taliban bases in Pakistan during the Soviet occupation of Afghanistan (1979-1989) and more recent war against terrorism since 2001 (Loveman 2001:342-343).

Many conflicts have involved the use of guerrilla warfare. During the 18th and 19th centuries, features of this warfare were evident in the American War of Independence against the British (1775-1783), the Haitian liberation from France (1804), and the independence movements in Spanish America (1810-1825). During the 19th century, the warfare often was initiated in countries where groups sought to resist European colonialism, while the 20th century witnessed both a continuation of this fighting and provides significant examples of regimes facing guerrilla war (Loveman 2001:343). These include the Czarist regime in Russia that ultimately fell during 1917 to revolutionaries and the successful use of such techniques by Chinese Communists leading to China's 1949 revolution, both of which have already been outlined. Since WWII, many civil wars have been fought as insurgencies, particularly where conditions favor such a strategy. These conditions include weak states experiencing significant poverty and instability and with mountainous terrain (Fearon and Laitin 2003a:85; Young 2012:2). Further research indicates that insurgencies are most likely in repressive states with limited resources. Such states are susceptible to dissident challenges, and they increase the likelihood of civil war via repression that erodes popular support and encourages violence (Young 2012:32).

There were 90 post-WWII insurgencies identified in a 2008 study. These included China (1946-1950), Vietnam (1945-1954 and 1960-1975), Northern Ireland (1969-1999), Indonesia/East Timor (1975-1999), Afghanistan (2001), and Iraq (2003) (Jones 2008:2, 135-138). Of particular relevance are tactics employed in current major armed conflicts. Here, tactics used in the most violent major conflict in 2010 (Afghanistan) are briefly outlined. Following the initial success of U.S. and Afghan forces in overthrowing the Taliban regime in 2001, an increasingly violent insurgency developed. A mixed group of insurgents, including the Taliban, the Haqqani network, foreign fighters, local tribes, and criminal organizations, began a sustained campaign to overthrow the Afghan Government (Jones 2008:xi). Insurgents conducted diverse attacks against U.S., coalition, and Afghan security forces, along with civilians. Insurgent tactics included yielding the population centers to U.S. and Afghan forces, operating from rural areas, distributing propaganda to the local population and opposition forces, threatening and intimidating the local population, and conducting armed attacks. Examples of armed attacks included ambushes and raids using small arms, grenades, and improvised explosive devices (IEDs). Taliban forces were deployed in larger numbers over time with targets shifting from "hard" targets like U.S. forces to "soft" targets, such as the Afghan police (Jones 2008:50–52). The insurgents apparently have been significantly helped by external support from states, particularly Pakistan, and various jihadist sources (Jones 2008:53–54, 61). Furthermore, the quality of Afghan forces and governance capacity has been mixed (Jones 2008:85).

Counterinsurgency

The term *counterinsurgency* (often abbreviated to COIN) was invented during the wars of national liberation (1944–1980). It can be described as all measures adopted to defeat an insurgency, these evolving in response to changes in insurgencies themselves (Kilcullen 2006:111–112). Factions staging insurgencies against governments often utilize guerrilla warfare. This commonly involves small and mobile units that aim to harass, weaken, and demoralize larger military forces. As already noted, insurgents do not need to be militarily strong to win. The ongoing conflict in Afghanistan graphically illustrates the various tactics that can be used by insurgents and how difficult it is to develop effective counterinsurgency tactics to fight them. Similarly, there is debate over the effectiveness of common tactics used against insurgents. This is especially shown by the debate over moves by states to kill insurgency leaders with the aim of "decapitating" their factions. Ultimately, the nature and dynamics of civil wars can be complex and variable, making it harder to effectively end them. This further emphasizes the need to prevent their occurrence, or to act swiftly when such conflict ignites.

There have been various successful counterinsurgency campaigns where insurgents are defeated, such as the Philippines defeat of the Huks (1946–1954) and Indonesian defeat of Darul Islam (1948–1962) (Johnston, no date:17). However, the development of an effective response can be time-consuming and demanding.

For instance, effective strategies can require states to initiate broad and fundamental political and economic reforms to address grievances that motivate insurgencies, along with restructuring military and law enforcement agencies to better combat factions. Indeed, states might achieve military victories over insurgents but experience political defeat if members of the public increasingly doubt and then oppose operations. This was experienced by the French in Algeria during the 1950s and a decade later by the United States in South Vietnam. Regimes that use powerful military forces indiscriminately also risk alienating their domestic populations further and ultimately increasing support for the insurgents, as has been noted in Syria ("Al-Assad's Fall" 2012).

The challenge of mounting an effective counterinsurgency campaign is clearly shown by the typical longevity of insurgencies. According to a 2008 analysis of 90 post-WWII insurgencies by Jones (2008), successful counterinsurgency campaigns lasted for an average of 14 years and those unsuccessful for an average of 11 years. Many ended inconclusively too (the termination of civil wars is covered in Chapter 6). Approximately 25 percent of insurgencies won by the government and 11 percent won by insurgents lasted over 20 years. These insurgencies met the following criteria: (a) they involved fighting between agents of (or claimants to) a state and nonstate groups who sought control of a government, took power in a region, or used violence to change government policies; (b) at least 1,000 individuals were killed over the course of the conflict, with a yearly average of at least 100; and (c) at least 100 were killed on both sides (including civilians attacked by rebels) (Jones 2008:10, 14). Two years later, another analysis of 89 insurgencies during the post-WWII period estimated that they lasted approximately 10 years with the government's chances of winning potentially increasing slightly over time (Connable and Libicki 2010:xii).

Jones's study indicated that three key variables can be linked with the success (or failure) of counterinsurgency efforts. First, the capability of government security forces, especially the police, to defeat insurgents and establish law and order is a vital component of any successful counterinsurgency. Insurgents are better able to survive and prosper if the security forces they oppose are relatively weak and lack legitimacy with the public. The police are important as they can be the government's main tool for maintaining domestic security. Second, the government's capacity to effectively rule influences the outcome of counterinsurgencies. The stronger and more competent a government is in distributing services to its population, the better its ability to weaken popular support for insurgents and greater likelihood that it can defeat an insurgency. Finally, the ability of insurgents to obtain external support is correlated with their success. Insurgencies that received support from external states won more than 50 percent of the time, and those with support from nonstate actors and diaspora groups won over 30 percent of the time. However, insurgents with no external support won only 17 percent (Jones 2008:15–16, 18, 21). Likewise, the 2010 study showed that the withdrawal of direct or indirect support by a state typically cripples an insurgency and leads to its defeat. This was often because the cessation of support removed a sanctuary for the fighters. The impact of losing support is shown by the defeat of Greek insurgents after WWII (Connable and Libicki 2010:xiii).

There is debate over the effectiveness of specific components of counterinsurgency strategy. This is especially shown by the debate over moves by states to kill insurgency leaders with the aim of "decapitating" their factions. All insurgent groups have at least formal leaders, commanders, subcommanders, and foot soldiers (Johnston 2008:109). Thus, attempts to defeat insurgencies through killing their leaders have been common. In a study of 168 insurgencies (1803–1999), in 70 (45.2 percent), top insurgent leaders were killed or captured during 155 counterinsurgency campaigns (Johnston, no date:1, 15). More recent examples include the targeting of insurgency leaders by various methods such as the controversial and increasingly frequent use of U.S. flying drones. By May 2012, an estimated 2,000 to 3,000 suspected militants or terrorists outside the battlefield had been killed by these drones (Zenko and Welch 2012). However, civilians have also been killed during such attacks, encouraging resentment toward the United States. Another major instance of "decapitation" is the May 2011 killing of al-Qaeda leader Osama bin Laden in Pakistan by U.S. Special Forces that angered Pakistan.

There has been much speculation over the effectiveness of decapitation with some scholars questioning its usefulness (Johnston, no date:3–4). Conflict continues in both Afghanistan and Iraq, while terrorism remains a global threat. However, the study of insurgencies from 1803 to 1999 suggested that leadership decapitation does work, the importance of leaders to the effectiveness of insurgencies meaning that their removal weakens and disrupts their movements. This at least provides a marginal advantage to counterinsurgents (Johnston 2008:137). Moreover, the death of Osama bin Laden was a major symbolic victory of the United States and was accompanied by the gathering of valuable intelligence material.

CONFLICT MANAGEMENT IMPLICATIONS

War types and tactics are two key categories of civil war dynamics. Like the costs mentioned in the previous chapter, these dynamics closely intertwined with conflict management. Wars over control of government, such as coups or revolutions, are relatively short and tend to end more conclusively than do territorial wars or internationalized civil wars. Wars over territory are typically longer and are more likely to recur.

In part because they are more likely to end in military victory and in part because of a relatively higher probability for political settlement, wars over government have a lower probability of recurrence. Recurrence is even less likely if third-party peacebuilding efforts include verification of rebel disarmament. The UN involvement in Guatemala exemplified this approach.

Fearon (2004) details how territorial sons-of-the-soil wars are particularly intractable as the government will usually not credibly commit to the peace process. This is because the rebels know the government negotiates only when the rebels are doing relatively well. When the situation changes, the rebels expect the government to renege on the previous deal. For this reason, rebels are particularly distrustful of the government as a negotiating partner. This information can prove useful to a third-party mediator who would do well to shore up the lack of credible commitment on the part of the government in a sons-of-the-soil war.

Managing guerrilla wars brings with it challenges. The rebels prefer to fight on their own terms in terms of location, target, and timing, and their losses are often minimal. In turn, they do not inflict high costs. When the costs to fighting are low, the disputants are likely to have very high demands in a peace process (see Wittman 1979). Negotiators and mediators must be prepared for this type of stumbling block.

CONCLUSION

The main types of civil wars are wars over control of government (revolutions and coups), secessionist/autonomy-seeking wars, and internationalized wars. From 2002 to 2012, the number of civil wars peaked at 36 in 2008–2009 and 2011. Of particular concern is the increasing number of such wars that involve external states (i.e., those internationalized). Whereas there were only two in 2002, their number had increased to eight by 2012.

Wars over control of government are often short all-or-nothing affairs. A graphic example of this type is Syria's brutal civil war that started in 2011 and, despite international attempts, shows little indication of being peacefully resolved in the near future. Revolutionaries, or coup-plotters, generally seek to win the reins of power in a swift stroke. They might seek power within the context of a weak state and conflict among the elite. The stakes are quite high in these conflicts as failure generally is disastrous for the rebels. The power of the regime is directly threatened, and therefore, the government will generally take extreme measures to defeat the rebels. Revolutions with major international consequences include those that witnessed the triumph of communism in Russia and China, along with the more recent regime changes resulting from the Arab Spring. These have destabilized the Middle East with wide-ranging repercussions given the region's strategic and economic importance.

A major feature of secessionist wars is the promotion of a separate identity of those people in a particular area. Various conditions are associated with the violent escalation of ethnic conflict. These include events weakening a regime and a single ethnic group dominating policy making without accommodating others. Conflict itself might occur between members of a minority ethnic group concentrated in a particular region that perceives itself as the indigenous sons of the soil and, relatively recent, ethnically distinct migrants to this region from other parts of the same country. This type of conflict occurs with competition and disputes over scarce resources, such as natural resources and work. Violence associated with sons-of-soil wars often begins as communal conflict but escalates to civil war if the state intervenes to forcefully support the migrants. The wars are generally longer than other civil wars, but less costly in terms of casualties.

Civil wars are internationalized when external actors become actively involved. External actors can become involved in civil wars in various ways. They might deploy their own forces or indirectly help to finance and equip those they support. Regardless of the nature of this involvement, the level and intensity of violence frequently increase as warring factions become stronger, particularly if there is direct intervention on their behalf. External involvement might be encouraged by actors believing that they will benefit from the ongoing conflict and who support the goals of a particular faction in the belief its victory will promote their own interests. There have been many post-WWII internationalized conflicts, and these were especially common during the Cold War. During this period, such involvement was used as a tool by the superpowers and their allies to promote rival strategic interests.

Factions staging armed rebellions (or insurgencies) against governments have often used guerrilla warfare. This form of warfare commonly involves small and mobile units that seek to harass, weaken, and demoralize larger military forces. Whether the regime can successfully defeat such warfare is influenced by the capability of its security forces, ability to effectively govern, and whether the insurgents are receiving external support. The Syrian regime's evident willingness to use chemical weapons on its opponents, and indeed innocent civilians, further indicates the brutal nature of the conflict and the unlikelihood of President Bashar al-Assad peacefully ceding power.

SUGGESTED READING

Connable, Ben and Martin C. Libicki. 2010. *How Insurgencies End.* Santa Monica, CA: RAND Corporation.

DeRouen Jr., Karl R. and David Sobek. 2004. "The Dynamics of Civil War Duration and Outcome." *Journal of Peace Research* 41(3):303–320.

Fearon, James D. 2004. "Why Do Some Civil Wars Last So Much Longer Than Others?" *Journal of Peace Research* 41(3):275–301.

Goldstone, Jack A. 1993. "Revolution." In *Oxford Companion to Politics of the World Second Edition*, edited by Joel Krieger (editor in chief). New York: Oxford University Press.

Powell, Jonathan M. and Clayton L Thyne. 2011. "Global Instances of Coups from 1950 to 2010: A New Dataset." *Journal of Peace Research* 48(2):249–259.

Skocpol, Theda. 1979. *States and Social Revolutions: A Comparative Analysis of France, Russia, and China.* Cambridge, UK: Cambridge University Press.

CHAPTER 4

What Causes Civil War?

APPROACHES TO CIVIL WAR ONSET

Chapter 1 highlighted the difficulties associated with arriving at a single definition of civil war. Because of differences among researchers in data selection, control variables, time horizon, measurement of variables, and research design, explanations of the onset of civil war differ. In this chapter, we delve deeper into the question of causes, looking at the factors related to civil war onset: grievances brought on by government restrictions or barriers, level of democracy, ethno-religious fractionalization or polarization, dependence on natural resource exports or lootable commodities, type of government, ease or opportunity of rebellion, and level of development. Some of these factors are connected to citizen complaints; for example, barriers or restrictions and low per capita income while others such as lootable natural resources provide income for rebels. These factors give rise to several leading models and lines of inquiry into civil war onset including greed versus grievance, level of democracy, globalization, environmental degradation, and insurgency, or opportunity, each of which we explore in the first part of the chapter.

The chapter then outlines separately those factors that can cause ethno-religious civil wars. This is because their onset can be based on variables specific to them while still potentially having some overlap with explanations provided by the greed, grievance, and insurgency models. Ethno-religious wars (those conflicts between ethnic groups which have different religions) further require a separate focus as they have been particularly costly in human lives and have threatened regional stability. Such conflicts include the civil wars that engulfed the former Yugoslavia, the Tamil rebellion in Sri Lanka, and Northern Ireland's violence. Many of the conflicts primarily revolve around ethnicity with religion being simply one of the factors that differentiates the ethnic groups involved. Thus, one cannot assume that because fighting ethnic groups have different religions they must be inherently religious. However, in some conflicts religion is the key factor. Relevant conflicts have been identified as the Sudan and Iran's repression of the Bahai minority (Fox 2002: 143).

Greed Versus Grievance

The phrases *greed versus grievance* or *greed and grievance* refers to two major approaches used for evaluating the causes of civil wars. *Greed* is when combatants are motivated by the goal of advancing their own situation and self-enrichment. They perform an informal cost-benefit analysis before deciding if the rewards of fighting justify the associated risks. These motivations are manifested in various ways, including economic gain via control of goods and resources or by enhanced power within a state. *Grievance* involves conflict over issues of identity rather than over economics. Here, fighting motivated by ethnicity, religion, and social class are relevant. For instance, a sons-of-the-soil type conflict might occur. There is debate over the importance of greed or grievances in causing civil wars, though in reality both often influence the development of a civil war to some degree.

Greed. Collier and Hoeffler (2004a) argue that greed—the desire for private gains—is a great incentive for rebel leaders to stage rebellions. However, rebellions are not staged without careful calculations of the possibility of victory, benefits of victory, associated costs, and whether success can come within an expected duration of time (Collier and Hoeffler 1998). This is to say that rebels are very calculating, with the likelihood of civil war going up with expectations of success and a short war (Collier and Hoeffler 1998).

Collier and Hoeffler (2004a) argued that when rebels expect it to bring tangible benefits, the possibility of war increases. This is the case with abundance of resources for potential loot, such as oil, gemstones, and timber. When a country has natural resources, these commodities become a target for rebels looting them and financing the group. The looting of minerals by the National Congress for the Defense of the People (CNDP) and the Democratic Forces for the Liberation of Rwanda (FDLR) rebel groups in the Democratic Republic of Congo illustrates this. Both groups profited from illegal sale of gold and other resources amounting to millions of dollars (UN 2009). The profits from the sale of such resources, along with help from ethno-religious diasporas, may be used to set up and maintain a rebel army. The availability of natural resources increases the worth of the country, referred to by Fearon (2004) as the "prize" of war. The increased worth propels potential rebel leaders to capture the state.

Because the possession of natural resources within a country is linked to a greater likelihood of war, Collier and Hoeffler (2000, 2002a) emphasized the need for countries to diversify their economies.

In addition to the link between resources and greedy rebels, Collier and Hoeffler (2000, 2002a, 2004a) arrived at the following conclusions:

There is no relationship between ethno-religious factors and the likelihood of war except when the country contains a dominant group. Second, the more frequently the country has seen war, the greater the probability of future wars. Third, the size of ethno-religious diaspora has a positive impact on the likelihood of civil war because of expectation of external support. A more expanded discussion about the resource-war issue will be covered in Chapter 5.

Grievances. The grievance model of civil war onset is in more or less direct contrast to the greed model.

All of us have grievances, and some of our complaints occur on a daily basis. Most grievances are either resolved or dissipate over time. Less commonly, grievances over an issue may lead to fighting and even actual war. Grievances connected to civil war form a long list but may be briefly listed as follows:

- Complaints about the division of resources or the economic pie
- Envy of other more successful groups
- Dissatisfaction over the injection into one's territory (usually a government-inspired ruling) of another ethnic group
- Barriers or limits to success—political, economic, ethnic, religious, or cultural-linguistic
- Discrimination
- Territorial claims
- Lack of freedoms, or lack of democracy

Ted Robert Gurr (1970) defines frustration as anything that interrupts one's attempt to fulfill something. The interruption will be countered with aggression. These frustration-aggression and threat-aggression relationships are the basis of Gurr's relative deprivation theory of rebellion. In ethno-religious conflicts, persuasive elites are able to lead the masses into violence (Gurr 1993). Other forms of indirect influences can also convert frustration to collective violence, for example, the rise of a tyrannical leader or a new government policy that sharply discriminates against one group. A few individuals here and there having the same discontent or personal deprivations or discriminations will likely have no effect on the likelihood of violence. However, many individuals having similar frustrations could.

Table 4.1 shows economic differences between the different regions of the world. Although the regional breakdowns by the UCDP and World Bank do not

TABLE 4.1
Regional Poverty and Civil Wars

Poverty by Region (2010)	
Region	Poverty Headcount Ratio at $1.25 a Day (PPP) (% of Population) 2010*
East Asia & Pacific	12.5
Europe & Central Asia	0.7
Latin America & Caribbean	5.5
Middle East & North Africa	2.4
South Asia	31.0
Sub-Saharan Africa	48.5
Civil Wars by Region (2012)	Number of Civil Wars Ongoing
Africa	12
Americas	2
Asia	10
Europe	2
Middle East	5

Sources: World Bank (2013); Themnér and Wallensteen (2013: 517–519).

* Population below $1.25 a day is the percentage of the population living on less than $1.25 a day at 2005 international prices.

exactly correspond, it is evident that civil wars are more common in regions with higher poverty rates, such as Africa and Asia.

Gurr (1993) used the Minorities at Risk (MAR) data to conclude that grievances cause ethno-religious civil war. He writes that elites manipulate the masses by highlighting group differences, perceived discrimination, and territorial issues. Such manipulations can create, heighten, and consolidate grievances and could lead to civil war.

Banton (1983), who agrees with Gurr's instrumental model, which suggests ethno-religious wars are caused by external factors acting upon inequalities that trigger fighting, suggests that manipulation by elites leads to mobilization and is especially likely in ethno-religious situations. This is discussed further below in the section on ethno-religious war.

Relatedly, a famous study carried out in the 1970s and 1980s by Horowitz (1981) arrived at an interesting discovery. Poorer people belonging to a distinct ethno-religious group are likely to favor an independent homeland even if secession seems like a risky proposition. This suggests ethno-religious sentiments might exceed economic or financial calculations, or gain.

BOX 4.1   The Minorities at Risk (MAR) Data

The Minorities at Risk (MAR) project (founded by Ted Robert Gurr) collects data on all politically active ethno-religious groups within countries and groups them into various risk groups by region. The risk is an assessment of the probability a country faces from one or more of the groups becoming violent and/or protesting. In addition, the MAR project analyzes the risk the group faces from government or another party's repression. Groups unlikely to protest or rebel are excluded from the data. There are currently approximately 283 groups identified in the project. There are detailed descriptions of each group's geographic distribution, size, and other factors.

The MAR data are unique in that these describe almost 300 communal groups with distinct cultures and long-standing identities without having an official territory or political status in a comprehensive manner. This is a huge undertaking. Many scholars and policy makers have benefited from the project, which is still maintained at the University of Maryland.

Level of Democracy

As the Cold War ended, research focusing on the effects of democracy on war and peace took a special place in political science research. First postulated by Immanuel Kant hundreds of years ago, a number of scholars quickly began to correlate democracy and peace. Among the pioneers were Rudolph Rummel, Bruce Russett, John Oneal, and William Dixon. Their work argued that democracy acted as a pacifying force reducing the likelihood of conflict between states. Maoz and Russett (1993) attributed this to the norms democratic countries practiced and the structural constraints (e.g., legislative and judicial branches, media, elections, etc.) that preclude a rush to violence. The Russett and Oneal (2001) study clearly supported these premises. The democratic peace considers the peace between countries. The democratic civil peace is built around peace within a country.

Types of Democracy. Regime type has also been linked to civil war onset. Most democratic countries either follow a winner-take-all system (single-member district [SMD]) or a proportional representation (PR) system of elections. In the winner-take-all system, each electoral district is allocated one seat in the legislature. In the PR system, citizens vote for parties, and districts are represented by more than one candidate. Seat allocation in the legislature is based on the share of the percentage of votes received by the parties in the election. Marta Reynal-Querol (2002) reports democratic states with PR systems mitigate potential religious civil war while countries practicing the winner-take-all system better mitigate animist (an animist religion is a traditional form of religion similar to the ones practiced by tribal and primitive societies) wars. In the PR system, there are discussions between different religious groups leading to consensus in seat allocations in elections. Where it would have been impossible for minority religious groups to win seats in a winner-take-all system (because of gerrymandering and other boundary issues), the PR system provides, if not substantial seats, at least the number of seats proportional to the minority group's population.

In general, democratic countries practice norms conducive to discussions between different ethno-religious groups within the country (Maoz and Russett 1993). A democracy reduces the likelihood of onset of civil war because of the availability of channels for grievances to be heard (Gurr 2000). But not all levels of democracy reduce conflict. Actually, the most conflict-prone countries are those that are semidemocratic (anocracies) (Ellingsen 2000; Henderson and Singer 2000).

The arguments that Reynal-Querol provided are more or less in accordance with the grievance perspective that grievance acts as a concrete drive toward war. One restriction of this study is that it basically considered incidence (prevalence) of war rather than onset. Another restriction is that the study analyzes only religious wars.

At any rate, grievances may not explain the path to war. Instead, political factors, such as lack of democracy, explain the path to civil war (Henderson and Singer 2000).

Democracy as a Cause of Civil War. It is interesting to note that democracy promotes peace, but some studies (see Auvinen 1997; Gleditsch et al. 2002; Hegre et al. 2001) report that the democratization process itself can be destabilizing.

According to Hegre et al. (2001), domestic violence is associated with political change where semidemocratic regimes have a significantly higher probability of civil conflict than either democracies or autocracies. While the risk of a civil war is surprisingly equal between a very democractic or a very autocratic country (usually a slim chance in both), countries somewhere in the middle of the two (anocracies or semidemocracies) face the greatest risk.

This does not mean that countries should not democratize. In countries that have more than one ethno-religious group, democracy is still more stable than autocracy. Ethnic and religious relations are more peaceful in the West than in third world countries. This is due to the mitigating effect of democracy (Jalali and Lipset 1992–1993).

It is natural for leaders of a changing state to institute changes as quickly as possible. This can be expected in a democratizing state. Mansfield and Snyder (2005) warn that participants in a country going through transformation should be aware that instituting democratic practices can actually cause violence instead of securing peace, citing examples of countries that rush to hold free elections when the economy has not been improved, the country has not properly stabilized, or institutions are still underdeveloped.

The violent scenario in anocracies is only a short-term phenomenon. Once the country has attained full democracy or is close to that, the chance of a conflict is greatly reduced. Even though the chance of a conflict is slim in an autocratic country, citizens may seize the slightest opportunity available to them to bring about changes. Autocracies are therefore more likely than democracies to become anocracies. Because anocracies are conflict prone, the trick is therefore to become a democracy as fast as possible because the longer the country remains an anocracy, the more challenges it has to face.

There are other arguments linking democracy to civil war. Horowitz (1985) argued that ethno-religious conflicts are more likely in democracies. He attributed this to the election arrangements in ethnically divided states. Because many ethnically divided countries form political parties and contest along ethnic lines, the whole idea of democracy as a tool to mitigate ethno-religious tension is defeated. When a party composed of one ethno-religious group loses an election, strong feelings of being excluded from the policy process arise. This can cause ethno-religious conflict. Thus elections, a main characteristic of democracy designed to foster cooperation, fuel ethnic conflict instead. Horowitz (1985) offers the Lebanese and Sri Lankan policies on ethnic preferences to support his argument. In both countries, government ethnic policies produced grievances which upset democratic arrangements.

Globalization

After the demise of the Soviet Union followed by the fall of communism, former Communist states opened up to foreign investment. As communism lost favor, third world states in Latin America and Asia began to elect or select leaders who were more open to democratic ideals. These leaders (for instance, Rao of India; Deng Xiaoping of China) encouraged foreign investment and trade openness. Even incumbent leaders became more capitalistic (for example, Mahathir

Mohamad of Malaysia; Suharto of Indonesia; Salinas of Mexico). Western industries rushed into these countries because of low taxes, cheap land, and cheap labor. These phenomena gave rise to globalization—the unprecedented spread of capital, ideas, and goods facilitated by technology and democracy.

Globalization can be negative if it leads to inequitable growth, exploitation, or the demise of unique cultures and traditions. Local jobs can also be predominately menial jobs, with managerial and executive-level positions reserved for employees from the home countries of these multinational corporations (MNCs). Additionally, large industries introduced automation, the beginning of an end to human labor. Third world states tend to have higher population growth rates than industrialized ones. The factors mentioned above, coupled with population increases, provide a good mix for rebellion (Mason 2003a).

Yet globalization can also be positive—for example, foreign investment in a poor country that provides jobs and money for educational improvement or schools. Globalization has been shown to increase the wages of local labor while increasing productivity. Western industries practicing the culture of capitalism create competition between the different companies. Competition brings prices down and creates efficiency (Barbieri and Reuveny 2005). Obviously, leaders understand this well and make efforts to enhance economic development because development reduces the likelihood of war, and war is an impediment to progress. War only exacerbates failure of interstate trade and local businesses, causing investors to leave. Therefore, both government and potential rebels generally will consider this relationship carefully before embarking on any violent endeavor (Barbieri and Reuveny 2005). Globalization tends to follow a pattern similar to democratization with countries that are intermediate globalizers potentially prone to civil wars (see Barbieri and Reuveny 2005; Bussman and Schneider 2007). However, countries that followed the world-globalization trend are generally not conflict prone. Interestingly, Bussman and Schneider (2007) found that a globalized country is not prone to conflict, but the movement toward becoming more economically liberal can cause war. The process through which states globalize triggers conflict. This is especially true in sub-Saharan Africa, where scholars have noted that many African states seem unable "to protest in a nonviolent manner against plans to liberalize the economy" (Bussman and Schneider 2007:94).

Automation in the workplace increases unemployment because human labor becomes redundant when machines can perform these functions. Information technology (IT) has made the world smaller. Since the late 20th century, IT has enabled people to communicate with almost anyone anywhere in the world. If the Internet has created effective communication and therefore reduced miscommunications, it has also made mobilization of disgruntled citizens easier

(Mason 2003a:24). In contrast to this, Barbieri and Reuveny (2005) argued that in the less developed countries, Internet has acted as a mitigator of conflict.

Environmental Degradation

There also is an indirect connection between the rate of environmental degradation and the onset of war. Deforestation, land degradation, and the amount of available freshwater are linked to the onset of conflict (Hauge and Ellingsen 1998). When the rate of environmental degradation exceeds the rate those natural resources are replaced, a "recipe" for conflict can emerge. For instance, when a country is unable to replace lost forest or eroded agricultural land, social problems can develop. Lack of arable land or freshwater could force populations to migrate to territories occupied by a different ethno-religious group. For the locals, the migrating group may appear to be intruders, and this could lead to conflict (e.g., as apparent in various ethnic conflicts within northeast India, East Timor, West Papua, and Sri Lanka). Hence, a sons-of-the-soil type conflict might be "ignited." Likewise, increased environmental degradation leading to decreased crop production or ranching can provide an incentive for people whose income depends on the once productive land to rebel against the government. The Bougainville civil war in Papua New Guinea was related to degradation from a huge copper mine.

Hauge and Ellingsen (1998) investigated human-induced land degradation and reported countries suffering from land degradation are more susceptible to conflicts than those that suffer from lack of freshwater and deforestation. Additionally, imagine a scenario when environmental problems are coupled with population growth. This is like a double-jeopardy situation because there is a lack of income-generating land as well as more people to compete for this now scarce resource. Elites are now forced to be partial in the treatment of citizens. Naturally elites will favor their kinfolk or groups favorable to them. This leads to envy due to the unequal treatment of citizens by elites, thus, rebellion by those groups that have been left out (Homer-Dixon 1994).

Recent research explored the connection between climatic conditions and civil war. Nils Petter Gleditsch (2012) assessed research on how climate changes affected the likelihood of civil war. Except for some evidence correlating climate change to intercommunal conflicts, there seems to be no clear connection between climate change and civil war.

Insurgency/Opportunity

The insurgency model of civil war is related to the greed model of civil war. Grossman (1991, 1995, 1999) laid the early groundwork for this economic explanation of war.

The insurgency model is based on rational choice as prospective rebels calculate the prospect of victory by identifying the presence of terrain to hide in and the availability of support from rural population and means of finance. Assuming it is difficult to calculate the probability of victory, prospective rebels will still assess government strength because this allows them to figure out if an uprising would be crushed. The presence of a weak state creates opportunity that further increases the rebel prospects for staging a war.

Fearon and Laitin (2003a) identify a number of factors that can increase a state's vulnerability to insurgency. The first factor is the availability of rough terrain, such as mountains or forests. Rough terrain provides a mean of hiding from government forces. Because potential rebels calculate their chances of victories, their expectation of victory increases with the availability of mountains. This in turn increases the likelihood of civil war. The second factor that increases a state's vulnerability to insurgency is state power. State power is measured by both political and economic power. They report that better equipped and stronger governments are prepared to forestall the emergence of insurgent groups. If the military or police are weak, potential rebels will recognize this, and their expectation of victory increases; therefore, there is a higher chance of rebellion. A country that is unstable also gives potential rebels the impression that it is unable to withstand a rebellion. A poor, low capacity country faces a higher risk of civil war. This includes countries with low per capita incomes and lower levels of economic development. The third factor that drives rebellion is the presence of a supportive rural base. In addition to rough terrain, a solid support from the rural population for the rebel group increases rebel motivation to fight. Villages and farms can act as a source of rebel hideouts. Rural populations provide food, supplies, recruits, and moral support. One of the main reasons Che Guevara's attempt at revolution in Bolivia failed was that the rural base (at least in the area of operation) was not supportive.

ETHNO-RELIGIOUS CIVIL WAR

Ethno-religious wars follow fairly different causal paths. Civil war studies in the 1970s, as in the case of Skocpol and Tilly (not including works by Gurr), centered on non-ethno-religious wars. Conflicts revolving around ethnicity, culture, linguistic, or religion (collectively called ethno-religious conflict) are found the world over, though especially in Asia and sub-Saharan Africa. From the Basque and the Irish conflicts in Europe to the Hutu-Tutsi conflict in Africa to the Mindanao Moro conflict in the Philippines, ethno-religious wars, like any other type of civil war, are caused by a variety of factors. In fact, again, scholars disagree on which are the main culprits causing ethno-religious wars. We cannot expect ethno-religious war to follow the same dynamics as other types of wars or civil war in general. There were 283 politically active ethno-religious groups in the world as of 2005 (Minorities at Risk Project [MAR] 2005). Imagine what the number would be if researchers included all the other groups that are not currently active. It can easily be expected that some or many of these groups may not be able to see eye to eye with another, hence, conflict. An ethno-religious war happens because of economic, cultural, linguistic, religious, or purely ethnic reasons. Skin color, conflicting religious practices, or the fight over scarce resources may be issues dividing the different groups. The majority group may have an issue with a proposal to add a minority language as an official language. The minorities on the other hand could be puzzled as to why the addition of another language to government forms and textbooks is such a big issue. The list goes on.

Ethno-religious conflicts may be associated with both political and economic factors. When there are differences, be they political or economic, when one group receives less than the other, war can erupt. Part of this problem of inequality arose from European or other colonial powers practicing what is called "divide and rule." These colonial powers allowed different groups to control the different sectors; for example, one group controlled the economy while another controlled politics. When the colonial masters left, the control of different sectors by different groups seemed to strike a nice balance of power. However, after some years, the balance was disrupted and civil war erupted because the group that had lost its grip on its portion of the balance began to feel the loss.

The increase in ethno-religious conflict in the post-Cold War era was not a sudden occurrence but a continuance of a trend from before (Fearon and Laitin 2003a; Gurr 1994). The trend was a continuance from the 1960s. Gurr predicted an increase in ethno-religious wars. Ethnically fractionalized countries as well as weak governments, he said, would be the main targets, as occurred in the Soviet Union and Yugoslavia in Europe, and Ethiopia in sub-Saharan Africa (Gurr 1994:364).

Defining Ethnicity and Ethno-Religious War

Ethnic issues underlay many civil wars. Ethnic causes can come in the form of ethnic animosity toward a group migrating into another ethnic region, the desire for an ethnic group to be independent or autonomous, a sense that an ethnic group "owns" a valuable commodity(ies) that occurs in its region, or any combination of these and other ethnic issues. For these reasons, most empirical studies of civil war onset capture some element of ethnic differences within a country.

Ethnicity may be explained based on one's shared history, beliefs, race, religion, language, or homeland (Ellingsen 2000:229). A similar definition refers to ethnicity in terms of some combination of the following: shared nationality, race, culture, language, religion, or affinity toward a territory (MAR 2005). A slightly differing definition mentions the hereditary aspect in which ethnic groups are groups consisting of members who are genetically more closely related to each other than to the members of other groups in a racial, tribal, linguistic, caste, national group, or old religious community manner (Horowitz 1985).

An ethno-religious war is therefore one that is fought based upon one or more of the elements described above.

Periphery Versus Core in Ethno-Religious Conflict

One explanation for the cause of ethno-religious conflict is that under certain conditions, minority groups in peripheral regions begin to make political and/or economic demands. Again, these demands begin as a result of differences in incomes, education levels, or coveted civil service positions of those in the outer (peripheral) regions to the majority group living in the center. The influx of majority members from the center to these outer regions can also result in peripheral grievances (sons-of-the-soil conflicts) because of a feeling of being impinged. Two examples of this type of war have taken place in Indonesia. In East Timor, a former Portuguese colony subsequently invaded by Indonesia, many Muslim Javanese migrated to the predominantly Catholic Timor, and the bitterness that ensued led to a long civil war. Similarly, many Indonesians from outside of the province (whose annexation has also been contested) have migrated to an ethnically and culturally distinct West Papua.

Ethno-Religious Fractionalization and Ethno-Religious War

Countries with some degree of ethno-religious fractionalization—essentially the division of society by ethnicity and religion with the often resultant emergence of conflicting interests—face a higher risk of war because situations arise where minorities feel discriminated against (Thambiah 1989:345–347). This fractionalization can be determined by various measures. Fearon and Laitin (2003a) refer to the Ethno-Linguistic Fractionalization (ELF) index, which gives the probability that two randomly drawn individuals in a country are from different ethno-linguistic groups, and the authors measure the population belonging to the largest ethnic group, using data from sources such as the Central Intelligence Agency's "Factbook" (*The World Factbook*). They also identify the number of distinct languages spoken by groups exceeding 1 percent of the country's population. To measure religious fractionalization, they use a measure analogous to the ELF using data again from the Factbook and other sources (Fearon and Laitin 2003a:78–79).

Examples of grievances relating to differences in incomes, education levels, or coveted civil service positions mentioned above are grievances by the minority Malays (who are mostly Muslims) in a majority Buddhist Thailand, the minority Tamils (who are mostly Hindus) in a majority Buddhist Sri Lanka, the minority Moros (who are mostly Muslims) in a majority Catholic Philippines, and the Bougainvilleans in Papua New Guinea. Examples of countries in which there is a link between high fractionalization and minority dissatisfaction are Malaysia (Chinese and Indian ethnic minorities), Pakistan (Mohajir ethnic minority), blacks in South Africa, the Juhayman movement by the Ikhwan tribe in Saudia Arabia, and again, Sri Lanka. Because outer regions in most countries are occupied by distinct ethno-religious groups and these regions are far away from the center, conditions are favorable for the secessionist type of war. Examples of this are again the Tamils in Sri Lanka; Bengalis in then East Pakistan; Acehnese, West Papuans, and Catholics in Indonesia; again Moros in the Philippines Malays in Thailand; Uighurs in China; Baluchis in Pakistan; Kurds in Turkey and Iraq; Tibetans in China; Kashmiri Muslims, Nagas, and Sikhs in India; and all the different peripheral groups in Myanmar. Ellingsen (2000) found that the share of the largest and second largest ethno-religious group's populations is a key determinant of civil war. Further, she discovered that countries with three or four ethno-religious groups have a higher likelihood of war than countries with one or two groups or countries with five or more groups.

Ethno-Religious Polarization

Recent research is gravitating toward ethnic polarization as an explanation of civil war onset. Polarization measures the distance between one ethnicity, religion, or cultural group from another, for example, how different one group is from another on the basis of ethnicity, religion, or culture. Because it is more precise, religious polarization provides a better explanation of ethno-religious wars than does religious fractionalization. In addition, religious differences seem to be a clearer cause of conflict than linguistic differences (Reynal-Querol 2002). The polarization measure is important especially in regions like sub-Saharan Africa because of the existence of numerous groups, subgroups, tribes, and religious beliefs. Williams (1994) noted that the literature cites four causes of ethno-religious conflict: strong ethnic identities and/or boundaries, grievances, opportunities, and mobilization; these may actually be conveniently classified under one of the five models below.

The Primordial Model. This model is based on the premise that war is caused directly by ethno-religious factors. The primordial model posits that conflict arises from old, enduring differences that have been going on between different religious, ethnic, linguistic, or regional groups. For instance, the Muslim-Christian conflict can be traced back to the crusade war years of the 11th century AD. The model therefore supports the premise that ethno-religious differences and hatred are ancient, based on things that are already present in society through the years such as kinship. Some deep-rooted differences are so ancient that nobody knows exactly when they started. For instance, recent researchers employing a sample of 545 Muslims and Jews found that the indirect grievance-related link between religion and violence is psychological, not economic (Canetti et al. 2010).

Vanhanen (1999) explained how primordialism relates to ethno-religious civil war. Vanhanen called kinship or affinity within one's own group ethnic nepotism. Vanhanen's research enables scholars to answer the question, When people are fighting over resources which are scarce, would they ensure that their own kind will survive versus other kinds, and in extreme cases of resource scarcity, will they ensure that only their own kind will survive? Now, if the group survives, the individual within that group in turn is expected to survive. He argued that ethnic nepotism is alive and well: "Members of the same group support their group members over non-members because they are more related to their group members than to the remainder of the population" (Vanhanen 1999:57).

Primordial forces or grievances alone cannot explain war between groups or why people rebel in ethno-religious wars. Conditions such as the opportunity to set up forces and conditions favorable to rebels must be present before rebellion takes place (Fearon and Laitin 2003a). Let us consider a scenario in which citizens in a country are severely frustrated because of government restrictions on their religious practices. However, if that government is very autocratic, any attempt by citizens to stage a rebellion will be easily crushed. In fact, governments that are restrictive are also usually very authoritative (Nordas 2004).

The primordial model explains ethno-religious conflicts well because it is based on enduring conflicts between the same pairs of rivals through history. Huntington's clash of civilizations theory (discussed in greater detail in a later section) is basically based on primordialism. Gurr (1994) found that there is some indirect link between Huntington's civilizational divisions and ethno-religious civil wars.

A grievance stemming from economic, political, or social frustration can quickly transform into a civil war if old, enduring differences and hatreds are already present in the community. Hall (2003:379) argued that in specifically religious violence, religion may not just be symbolic but a tool for expressing deeply and widely held social expectations. A pioneering quantitative study established that ethno-religious war is caused by political grievances (Sambanis 2001).

The Instrumental Model. The instrumental model is based upon the premise that ethno-religious wars are not caused directly by ethno-religious factors. Instead, war is a result of external forces that highlight inequalities between peoples, instigating them to fight.

External forces may be a group or an individual acting upon self-interest (Carment and Rowlands 1998; Horowitz 1985) or forces trying to politicize nascent sentiments (Williams 1994). In other words, instrumentalists believe that if the government can provide equal opportunities and stop the practice of discrimination, then people will not be subjected to the indoctrination by outside forces that split the population (Hansenclever and Rittberger 2000). Selfish elites or rebel leaders are typically driven by economic gains.

One idea connecting radical Islam to this model posits that in many predominantly Muslim countries, the imams (leaders of mosques) are able to influence Muslim followers into terrorist activities. New migrants from rural areas migrating to cities have very limited sources of contacts in the urban areas. New migrants need help of various sorts upon arriving in the city because of unaccustomed lifestyle. These migrants typically depend on friends and relatives who introduce them to the imam or his representatives. Being new and in need of help, these migrants are easily influenced by anti-Western (some of these rural folks migrate to the city with existing anti-Western ideas) or secular ideas. The imams and their representatives portray themselves as champions of the rural migrants in the city (Mousseau 2011:35–47). When individuals feel they lack something or have been deprived of what should be theirs, they seek external support and will accept instructions from it, and if the external entity, be it an idea, person, or group, advocates violence, these individuals will follow. This is especially true in religious war (Canetti et al. 2010).

It may sound strange, but it is true that at times, elites cause violence between groups by creating new groups or ethno-religious identity (Horowitz 1985). As long as elites successfully manipulate citizens into believing that the identities are in fact intrinsic (that is, primordial), it does not matter if the new identity is genuine or not. After all, identity is something that separates one group or community from the other based on either something obvious (seen) like skin color or unseen like religion. If members of a group strongly believe that they possess a trait that is sharply different from the other group, that could act as a separating line. Elites can use such a difference to spark violence for personal gains.

Collier and Hoeffler's (1998, 2002a) greed model by postulating elites' inducement of rebel soldiers into looting of natural resources and extortion of locals lends itself well to the instrumental model even though the greed model does not particularly emphasize ethno-religious wars.

Samuel Huntington's Clash of Civilizations. Huntington (1996) discounts ideological and economic causes of conflict, arguing instead that post-Cold War conflicts have been based on ethno-religious or cultural bases, which Huntington called civilizational. The theory encompasses both interstate wars and civil wars. He identified seven civilizations that divide the world and between which conflict occurs: Western, Latin American, Islamic, Sinic, Hindu, Orthodox, and Japanese. He foresaw a Sinic-Islamic alliance and a West versus Sinic-Islamic conflict, with the conflict between the West and Islam being more severe. Huntington argued that these civilizational conflicts can occur between countries or within countries. For example, a Muslim country will fight a Western country or a Hindu group will fight an Orthodox group within a country (Huntington 1993:22–49; Huntington 1996).

Other scholars have noted that conflict between countries or within a country may not necessarily be due to the existence of a long-term friction and rivalry between Islam and the West or because of an Islamic threat. They could be because both religions tie religion to their social problems, among other means, instead of enduring and traditional hatreds at play (Halliday 1996).

The Modernization Model. The modernization model is based on the premise that civil war emerges when countries begin to modernize, and special pressure is put on ethnic or religious relations. Modernization produces new industries and businesses and new opportunities for employment, but these opportunities inevitably engender competition for positions and ownerships and can inspire collective action. Contest over increasingly scarce resources, sometimes intense, leads to conflict. Therefore, the model states that when a country modernizes, the likelihood of civil war also increases. As modernization theorists Raymond Taras and Rajat Ganguly put it: "In modern states, particularly those in the middle ranks of economic development, ... modernization leads to rapid social mobilization. ... These states are particularly vulnerable to intense competition and conflict" (Taras and Ganguly 2008:19–20).

They state that modernization destroys traditional elites and elite culture, and when modernization erodes traditional ways, it can cause fear among people. The result is ethnic nationalism among the new urban middle and lower middle classes.

People are able to interact with each other more easily in more modern societies because communication and transportation are easily accessible. Such a condition allows in-group members to mobilize more easily. The opposite of this is that such modern conditions can also allow members of different groups to come together (Taras and Ganguly 2008). The coming together of different groups can possibly cause fear, suspicion, hatred, envy, prejudice, or aversion.

Urdal's (2005) research on the other hand found no connection between a country's intense urbanization and ethno-religious war. Alexseev (2003) states when opposing groups believe that interactions between them will provide economic gain, there will be less hostility. This is true even if the groups previously had negatively preconceived notions about each other.

Normally, in industrializing states, foreign investment flows into the country especially from the West and Japan. Western firms' culture is very oriented toward division of labor. Taras and Ganguly (2008:16) argue that in such an organizational culture, the management and executive jobs are kept among the majority race with minorities given only the unskilled jobs, hence, conflict.

Islamic Militancy and Civil War. The question of the connection between Islam and violence has been studied for a long time. However, this subject gained substantial significance since the September 11, 2001 attack on the New York World Trade Center building. While certain religious wars are confined to civil wars, Islamic violence is more widespread, civil as well as interstate. It is not unusual to hear about violence in the Middle East or about the Kashmir Muslim militants or the Nigerian Muslim-Christian bloodshed. To know how critical Islamic wars are, just look at the world map. Islamic-related wars are currently being fought in Iraq, Afghanistan, India (Kashmir), the Philippines (Mindanao), Indonesia, Lebanon, Thailand (Pattani), and in some sub-Saharan states.

Monica Toft (2007) asserted that between 1940 and 2000, Islamic warring groups far exceeded other religious warring groups. She argues in favor of the instrumentalist position that leaders manipulate religion and people for self-interest and for political survival. Manus Midlarsky (1998) investigated Islam and its relationship to democracy. While concluding that Islam and democracy can actually survive side by side, he also found that "most any government that allows revealed truth to be its guiding ideation tends to be more autocratic" (Midlarsky 1998:493).

In their investigation of this Islamic militancy issue, Fearon and Laitin (2003a) concluded that, in Middle Eastern and North African regions, oil is in fact a cause of war. The size of the Muslim population in a country, however, did not cause war. But they found some evidence connecting the number of young males in a country and war.

A recent quantitative study showed that the variables causing Islamic war are different from what causes other types of wars. Islamic wars have to do with the proportion of Muslims in a state, government restrictions and barriers on her people, and oil (Narayanan 2008).

So could Islamic violence be due to the fact that most Islamic countries are autocratic, such as Saudi Arabia, Iran, and Syria? Or could there be other less apparent factors at work? Why do some Muslims and other religious radicals carry out attacks and murders? The reasons are numerous, ranging from the requirement of religious leaders, duty, and frustration, and could even be economic in nature.

Not all scholars believe that ethno-religious factors have a bearing on the onset or incidence of war. Contrary to findings of most others, Fearon and Laitin did not find any cultural, linguistic, ethnic, or religious linkage to war (see also Henderson and Singer 2000).

CONFLICT MANAGEMENT IMPLICATIONS

This chapter presents an overview of the literature on the causes of civil war. The greed versus grievances debate peaked around the turn of the 21st century. Scholars such as Paul Collier challenged the prevailing wisdom on civil war onset by arguing that rebels were often just in it for the profit.

So the question becomes how can what is currently known about greed and grievances inform civil war prevention. Snyder (2006) has explicated a theory on how a state can avoid resource-related conflict. In particular, he refers to a "political economy of extraction framework" to demonstrate how in some countries lootable resources can lead to violence whereas in others they do not. If governments keep a tight rein on revenue from lootables, they can use this wealth to build state capacity. Such a capacity reduces the opportunity for rebels to organize in the face of weak state institutions. The policy implication of Snyder's framework is that peace agreements should contain provisions that codify that revenue wealth go toward building a strong state with good service delivery, law and order, and effective rule of law.

What we as scholars know about democracies tells us that these countries should not have civil wars as their institutional means for settling grievances. However, there have been long post-WWII (or recently) civil wars in Great Britain, Spain, and India. One problem is that democracies do not seem eager to have their wars mediated. Perhaps this is because of a perception that having an outside entity involved in their affairs would be indicative of failure since democracy is designed to resolve differences peacefully. Mediation of civil wars in Northern

Ireland and Israel are exceptions. New thinking is warranted for mediation to take root in democracies. This is an ever-pressing issue as more countries become democratic.

CONCLUSION

The grave nature of civil wars is clearly shown by the ratio between the frequency of civil wars and international wars since the end of the Cold War. During this era, the majority of wars that took place in the world were civil wars. In 2010, none of the 30 wars that took place in the world were interstate wars.

The chapter presented the correlates of civil war onset. We found that there is no single theory that is able to explain the causes of civil wars definitively. Civil war is a result of a multitude of factors acting under complex conditions and environments explained by various scholarly theories. In general, these theories may be classified under the greed basis of war and the grievance basis. Scholars have used numerous variables that test these two opposing arguments. Some of these variables are GDP per capita, government restrictions or barriers, population size, ethno-religious fractionalization or polarization, whether a country is too dependent on natural resource exports, the type of government, ease of rebellion, and whether the country's status is semidemocratic or not.

The grievance model puts the blame squarely on dissatisfaction; that is, citizens have complaints which lead to collective action which in turn leads to war. The grievance model therefore seems to revolve around marginalized citizens portrayed as victims, with the government and elites portrayed as aggressors. In the greed model, the blame switches to rebel leaders. One point put forward by this model is that economically motivated greedy rebel leaders treat rebellion as a business venture. Leaders thrive on rebellions, make business deals with outside parties, and prolong the war. Economically motivated civil wars are connected to an abundance of natural resources. In other words, such wars are also connected to countries that are quite dependent on natural resource exports to maintain the economy. A third model that falls under neither of the categories above is the rational actor (insurgency) model of civil war. According to this model, potential rebels are not dumb individuals who stage rebellion because of emotions caused by ancestral hatred or acute grievances. Potential rebels study the cost of war and the probability of success. The main factors considered by rebel leaders are the country's ability to crush rebellion and physical bases for rebels to hide. Prospective rebels consider it an opportunity if the country is weak or if it is incapable of responding to rebellion with great force. Opportunity increases the probability of rebellion. The bulk of the literature forms arguments based upon one of the two—greed or grievance. However, Fearon and Laitin's insurgency model has been rapidly gaining acceptance since it was published in 2003.

Research stemming from the three models has given rise to issues about how environmental forces, globalization, resources, economic development, regime type and change, ethno-religious divisions, elite behavior, and population size shape the onset of rebellions.

The pacifying effect of democracy on civil war really depends on how democratic the country is. Many studies have found that regime change has a strong positive relationship to war onset. Similarly, Bussman and Schneider (2007) found that a globalized country is not prone to conflict but the movement toward becoming more economically liberal can cause conflict. Some studies, however, portrayed democracy as a conflict-inducing variable (see Horowitz 1985) and more so in ethno-religious conflicts (see Saideman et al. 2002). This is true also for countries with high population. Countries with high populations tend to be war prone. Among all the variables analyzed in quantitative studies, the consistent factor that reduces the likelihood of war is economic development, measured by GDP per capita of the country. Lack of economic development has a direct impact on conflict-causing grievances. The results for the effect of ethno-religious divisions and ethno-religious problems are mixed. Some studies showed a nonlinear relationship between ethno-religious factors and war, others showed no connection between them. The chapter cites, among others, Homer-Dixon's research on the link between environmental and demographic factors on war. These factors do play a part in inciting rebellions. The case of the Zapatista National Liberation Army (EZLN) rebellion in Mexico was shown to illustrate how ill effects of globalization can bring about war. Technology that MNCs inject into newly globalized states, for instance, the Internet, can have adverse effects. Environmental degradation, a common result of globalization, is yet another correlate of war explaining the higher frequency of civil wars in third world countries than in developed states. Climatic changes in a country, however, have not been shown to have a bearing on conflict, and this may be due to the fact the subject is still in its immature stage.

The chapter continues with a detailed discussion about what causes ethno-religious conflicts as a completely separate discussion. The onset of ethno-religious conflict can uniquely be based on variables specific to it while still within the scope of explanations provided by the greed, grievance, and insurgency models. Five classifications of ethno-religious conflict are presented. The primordial model argues that conflicts have much to do with differences between people of different groups. Hatred is considered to be ancient and enduring. Therefore, it may actually be impossible to mitigate ethno-religious conflicts because of this long-standing rivalry. Kinship plays an important role in determining which side individuals will take in conflict situations. The instrumental model argues that selfish or greedy external forces, be it a group or individuals, have been known to politicize mass sentiments within a country. The "brainwashing" is followed by the pitting of one group with another. Al-Qaeda's strong influence on its members against Western forces in many countries is in a way proof of this. Huntington's the clash of civilizations model posits that civil wars after the end of the Cold War are not a product of ideological or economic reasons but instead are because of cultural or religious differences, which Huntington called civilizational differences. The modernization model portrays a grim picture of modernizing states. Scholars showed that the closer interactions of different groups arising out of modern communication and transportation can lead to conflict. Additionally, modernization creates acute competition for scarce resources, a reason to fight. The section ends with a brief discussion of what causes Islamic conflict.

There is a difference between the causes of the outbreaks of the different types of wars: wars over control of government, over territory, and internationalized wars. Various cases illustrate the differences between them. For instance, the Vietnam War (war over control of government) followed a different pattern of causes than the Moro uprising (secessionist war) in the Philippines. Similarly, internationalized civil wars have causes that are specific to them, as noticed in the internationalized civil wars in sub-Saharan Africa and the recent Arab Spring experience.

SUGGESTED READING

Bussman, Margit and Gerald Schneider. 2007. "When Globalization Discontent Turns Violent: Foreign Economic Liberalization and Internal War." *International Studies Quarterly* 51(1):79–97.

Collier, Paul and Anke Hoeffler. 2004a. "Greed and Grievance in Civil War." *Oxford Economic Papers* 56(4):563–595.

Fearon, James D. and David D. Laitin. 2003a. "Ethnicity, Insurgency, and Civil War." *American Political Science Review* 97(1):75–90.

Gleditsch, Nils Petter. 2012. "Whither the Weather? Climate Change and Conflict." *Journal of Peace Research* 49(1):3–9.

Grossman, Herschel I. 1999. "Kleptocracy and Revolutions." *Oxford Economic Papers* 51:267–283.

Gurr, Ted R. 1970. *Why Men Rebel.* Princeton, NJ: Princeton University Press.

Gurr, Ted R. 1993. *Minorities at Risk: A Global View of Ethnopolitical Conflicts.* Washington, DC: United States Institute of Peace Press.

Gurr, Ted R. 1994. "Peoples against States: Ethnopolitical Conflict and the Changing World System." *International Studies Quarterly* 38(3):347–377.

Gurr, Ted R. 2000. *People versus States: Minorities at Risk in the New Century.* Washington, DC: United States Institute of Peace Press.

Hegre, Håvard, Scott Gates, Nils Petter Gleditsch, and Tanja Ellingsen. 2001. "Toward a Democratic Civil Peace? Democracy, Political Change and Civil War 1816-1992." *American Political Science Review* 95(1):33–48.

Toft, Monica D. 2007. "Getting Religion?: The Puzzling Case of Islam and Civil War." *International Security* 31(4):97–131.

CHAPTER 5

Natural Resources and Civil War

The influence of natural resources on the onset of civil war has been debated for years, and in recent years, these analyses have often relied upon sophisticated statistical modeling. Researchers have looked especially closely at whether and under what conditions there is a link between resources and war, determining which natural resources are the biggest culprits, and uncovering the political, economic, and social mechanisms that link resources and war. For instance, findings show that oil, a non-lootable commodity that requires large amounts of capital to exploit, is more robustly linked to civil war onset than diamonds, drugs, timber, or gold. The international community has also taken some important mitigating steps. For example, the United Nations initiated the Kimberely Process that is designed to prevent civil war combatants from using diamonds to fuel war efforts. Essentially, the process utilizes safeguards to verify the source of diamonds as shipments cross international borders.

This chapter covers the debates that swirl in the literature concerning the role natural resources play in civil war. Specifically, we will consider natural resources and the inherent *resource curse*; three civil war onset models and their linkages to natural resources (greed, state capacity, grievance); and the roles of oil, diamonds, illicit drugs, and timber. The chapter is designed this way to present a comprehensive look at the mechanisms through which resources might potentially impact civil war onset and/or duration.

The civil war onset models mentioned are useful in addressing the natural resource issue. The greed model holds that rebellion is essentially a business enterprise. In this endeavor, lootable resources can be very profitable. The state capacity model contends that rebellion is based on opportunities which are greater when the state lacks capacity to prevent uprisings. A weak state lacks the capacity to prevent states from looting natural resources. The grievance model suggests resources can cause conflict even if the rebels are not exploiting the resource, as in the case of the Panguna Copper Mine in Bougainville, Papua New Guinea. Lately, the pendulum has swung toward more support for the state capacity model, thus confirming political rather than economic explanation of the role natural resources play in civil war.

The chapter also discusses the impact of resources on civil war duration. Insurgents require funding in order to pay for food, weapons, personnel, and other expenses associated with maintaining a rebel force over long periods. For a civil war to occur, intergroup antagonisms and grievances are required, leaders must coordinate and manage recruitment, while resources and supplies are needed to support the movement over time (Walter 2004:375). In line with this, conflicts can be lengthier when the rebels have access to finance from contraband goods like opium or cocaine. For rebels to sustain a long-running war, it helps to have a dependable source of finance and weapons that can be provided by contraband (Fearon 2004:283–284, 297). According to the World Bank, improving the international governance of natural resources, such as diamonds, can reduce the global incidence of civil war. For instance, transparency enhances domestic scrutiny over how such revenues are used. If rebel finances can be curbed and citizens believe that resources are being well used, civil war will be less likely (World Bank 2003:x).

NATURAL RESOURCES AND THE RESOURCE CURSE

Among the world's natural resources are oil, gold, platinum, timber, coltan, and diamonds. These resources are, however, not evenly distributed. For example, the Middle East has abundant oil but South Asia has very little. Sub-Saharan Africa boasts gold and diamond mines. The tropical forests of Southeast Asia contain many hectares of timber.

There are various categories of natural resources. One type of natural resource is mineral. Oil, gold, silver, copper, uranium, iron, bauxite, columbite-tantalite (coltan, which is used in many electronics), and tin fall within this category. Oil, which is sometimes classified together with natural gas, is a fuel mineral. The rest of the minerals are termed non-fuel minerals. Some of these non-fuel minerals qualify as precious minerals, such as gold and silver. Other precious minerals are termed gemstones, for instance, diamonds, rubies, and sapphires. Another category of natural resource is timber. A further category of natural resource is agricultural products. Coffee beans, cocoa beans, cereals, milk, vegetables, sugar cane, fruits, leaves, and even some illegal narcotics are examples of agricultural products. Natural resources are goods that have not been processed—unprocessed timber, gold that has not been processed into bars or coins, cocoa not manufactured into chocolate, unprocessed coffee beans, and narcotics not yet converted to usable illicit drugs. Collectively, natural resources and agricultural products make up primary commodities. Note, however, that most primary commodity data do not include illicit drugs and precious gemstones (Fearon 2005).

Scholars divide resources into lootable and non-lootable types. Lootable resources are resources that are not difficult to extract and relatively easy to sell. Snyder and Bhavnani (2005:565) define *lootable resources* as "high-value goods with low economic barriers to entry." Non-lootable resources are those resources that are not easily extracted and are usually not scattered widely in a country. Lootable resources are more useful for rebels because they are dispersed and easy and cheap to extract. Regan and Norton (2005:328, 329) observe that territory with diamonds and other gemstones and drugs can be controlled by the rebels and are generally easy to transport. Oil (petroleum and gas) are considered non-lootable resources because they are expensive to extract and transport. Timber may be classified as either lootable or non-lootable depending on the geography of the country. In countries that have good forest cover, timber becomes a lootable resource.

Natural resources can be an important source of revenue for countries lucky enough to have them, yet they are usually not a panacea. Natural resources can indeed be a curse in places they flourish, a classic example being Nigeria. This is commonly referred to as the "resource curse." Resource is wealth that awaits tapping and conversion into cash. Under normal circumstances, governments sell their resources and use the proceeds from the sale to provide services to the people of the country. However, many leaders are not interested in being viewed as legitimate and do not feel compelled to govern in a democratic fashion. Leaders such as Iraq's former dictator Saddam Hussein take profits from sales of oil and oil leases and use it to enrich their network of supporters rather than for public goods like schools and medical facilities.

Countries with abundant natural resources, such as oil, often have high poverty rates (e.g., Nigeria, Angola, and Venezuela) and slow economic growth. These countries derive a huge portion of their revenues from the sale of natural resources or mineral leases to multinational companies. They therefore do not need to rely on the masses for tax revenues. As a result, elites neglect citizen grievances because the social contract between leaders and the people is not fully established, as often observed in sub-Saharan African states. This is a potential recipe for civil war, as the state apparatus used to govern the state and maintain relations between the government and the people is weak.

The resource curse can also manifest itself in a very different way. Even after a resource war is over and while parties are working toward peaceful extraction of resources, illegal smuggling can persist. For example, illegal smuggling of diamonds and gold in postwar Sierra Leone drove the price of legal diamonds down (Cooper 2008). Additionally, spoilers of peace are able to channel profits derived from remnants of illegal resource trade to bring back war. Postwar Angola and

Sierra Leone were faced with this situation (Cooper 2002). Thus, at the minimum, resources play an indirect role in civil wars.

RESOURCES AND CONFLICT

Collier and Hoeffler's studies (mentioned in the previous chapter) posit a link between resources and civil war onset. Some scholars who have later dissected that work made indirect links between resources and war. The majority of those other scholars emphasized politics instead of economic greed as a driving force behind resource-related wars. This is an important divergence from Collier and Hoeffler's economic model of war. The literature is also mixed on whether the presence of resources or resource dependence leads to civil war. Most studies revolve around three leading models outlined shortly: the Collier and Hoeffler greed (economic) model, the Fearon and Laitin state capacity (political) model, and the grievance model. Recent research has gravitated toward the state capacity model to explain the relationship between resources and civil war (Ron 2005).

Lujala (2010) asserts that resources are a cause of war, demonstrating the importance of all models—greed, grievance, and state capacity or insurgency—to arrive at a sound explanation of resource-related wars. The argument states that civil wars related to resources are caused by both direct and indirect links. They are caused directly by the rebel leaders' greed along with citizen grievances and the rebel calculation of the probability of victory. The indirect link relates to the structure of resource-rich states. As noted, these normally lack proper political structures, citizen-inclusive tax systems, and a diversified economy. Such an arrangement indirectly fuels war. An additional indirect means to war arises because war-torn and war-prone countries normally face economic and political deterioration, which in turn can cause more wars.

The majority of African civil wars have been resource-related. Algeria, Angola, the DRC, Liberia, Nigeria, and Sierra Leone each experienced resource-related wars. Angola, Nigeria, and Equatorial Guinea possess natural resources that can easily be converted to cash.

After the bloody massacre of Tutsis during the Rwandan civil war, many Tutsis fled to the neighboring DRC. In the 2000s, a Tutsi rebel leader in the DRC, General Laurent Nkunda, staged a rebellion against pro-Hutu groups and indirectly against the government because of the latter's unfriendly policies toward the Tutsis. Nkunda's rebel group, the National Congress for the Defense of the Congolese People (CNDP), and his rival group, the Democratic Forces for the Liberation of Rwanda (FDLR), both reportedly profited from illegally mining and selling resources including gold, cassiterite, coltan, and timber. The FDLR

Rwandan Child Refugees

Child refugees from Rwanda's bitter civil war between the Hutus and Tutsis tribes in Southern Africa carry containers of water atop their heads.

Credit: United States Information Agency, MSGT Rose Reynolds

alone is reported to have probably made millions of dollars annually from the illegal gold trade and several hundred thousand to a million dollars on other minerals including coltan. Moreover, the total amount of illegal gold exports leaving the DRC each year is $1.2 billion (UN 2009). Coltan is essential in the manufacture of electronic devices, such as cell phones, laptops, and video games, and in nuclear reactors. In the DRC, rebel groups backed by Rwanda and Uganda made tens of millions of dollars from coltan mined illegally in the country's war-torn eastern region (Ware 2001). The proceeds of coltan sales are used to finance rebel armies, such as the Rwanda-supported Congolese Democratic Rally (RCD). In just 18 months, the Rwandan army made $250 million from coltan smuggled from the DRC (Delawala 2001).

In July 2010, the United States passed a law that would monitor the flow of minerals from the DRC in an attempt to ensure these minerals did not come from illegal sources (Dagne 2011). The issue of natural resources is so contentious that in addition to war between rivals' forces, infighting has also occurred, for example, within the CNDP over the control of timber (UN 2009). Therefore, it is not surprising that a 2010 United Nations peacekeeping mission report made it clear that one of the mission's central goals was to stop illegal looting of natural resources by rebel groups (UN 2010).

Diamonds are also connected to ethno-religious civil wars. In ethno-religious wars, the mere presence of diamonds (all types of diamonds considered together) had no effect on onset. However, the production of secondary diamonds can trigger ethno-religious wars, while the production of primary diamonds reduces the likelihood of ethno-religious war occurring (Lujala, Gleditsch, and Gilmore 2005). The difference between primary and secondary diamonds is explained in the section on diamonds.

The resource curse is not confined to onsets of conflicts; resource-related conflicts often last longer too. Grievance-based wars cannot be fully understood without understanding their economics. This explains why greed provides convincing explanations for the duration and intensity of resource wars. The effect of greed is sometimes evidenced by the indirect pathway to resource wars that involve outside parties. A greedy foreign state or MNC may lengthen the conflict in the host country (Humphreys 2005). Using the Colombian example, Sanchez, Solimano, and Formisano (2005) confirmed that greed plays a part in resource wars. They wrote that the war in Colombia bred drug-related activities which ultimately extended the conflict.

Table 5.1 matches the different natural resources with the country experiencing civil war. The table also matches the resource that linked the rebel group to the war.

The Greed Model

Scholarly studies on this resource issue were greatly motivated by a series of studies by Collier and Hoeffler (1998, 2000, 2004a), who in Chapter 4 we discussed as the leading advocates of the greed model of civil war in general. Collier and Hoeffler (2000, 2002a) found that the possession of natural resources within a country—in particular the amount of primary commodities in the export sector—is linked to a greater likelihood of war. When potential rebels decide war will bring resource-related benefits, the probability of war increases. This was the case with the looting of diamonds by the Revolutionary United Front (RUF) in Sierra Leone. The profits (typically referred to as rents) from the sale of such resources are used to set up and maintain a rebel army. In the bigger picture, the availability of natural resources increases the worth of the country, which in turn makes capture of the state a tempting idea. In other words, war is a result of greed—the desire for private gain (see Nafziger 2006).

According to Collier and Hoeffler, the effect of resources as a percentage of exports on the probability of civil war is curvilinear. In other words, when a country has very low or very high levels of natural resources, the likelihood of war is lower. Countries with very low levels usually are poor and have low capacity.

TABLE 5.1
Matching Resources to Countries and Rebel Groups

Resource type	Country	Rebel Group
Oil	Angola	MPLA
	Burma	Various groups
	Indonesia	GAM
	Nigeria	Biafran Militia
	Sudan	SPLM/A, JEM, and other South Sudan groups
Drugs	Afghanistan	Taliban, Mujahideen, and various other groups
	Burma	SSA, KIA, UWSA, and various other groups
	Colombia	FARC, AUC
	Laos	Pathet Lao
	Cambodia	Khmer Rouge
	Guatemala	Various groups
	Mexico	Criminal groups (connected to Colombian civil war)
	Sri Lanka	LTTE
Diamonds	Angola	UNITA
	Sierra Leone	RUF
Coltan	DRC	RCD
Timber	Burma	SSA, KIA, PNDF, KIO, and various other groups
	DRC	RCD, CNDP, FDLR
	Indonesia	GAM
	Liberia	Movement for Democracy
	The Philippines	MNLF, MILF

Sources: Lujala (2011); Ross (2004); UCDP (2014a); and U.S. Department of State (2014).

Civil war is likely here. This risk is reduced at high levels because these countries usually have greater capacity and can thus prevent rebellion and generally provide for their citizens (Collier and Hoeffler 2000, 2002a). As mentioned, wealthier countries are also less likely to have civil wars.

The general findings on the resource curse by Collier and Hoeffler led other scholars to pursue the matter more deeply. Greed-related incentives can be linked to resource availability directly and indirectly. The direct connection relates to the increased value of a state that has resources, hence increasing the "prize" of state capture. There is also a direct link between resources and secessionist conflicts. In secessionist conflicts, the presence of resources in the periphery can be a temptation for rebels who desire the revenue for their territory upon independence or autonomy. This dynamic increases the likelihood of secessionist conflicts (Humphreys 2005). The indirect link has been apparent in the war in Colombia. This war began as a grievance-based revolution but has turned into a conflict based on drug profits.

De Soysa (2002) showed that war arising from resource abundance may be evident by three different routes. The first route explains war using the greed argument. Rebel leaders are rational actors. The availability of resources motivates them to resort to looting these resources. If the cost of looting tends to be higher than the benefits derived, they will not stage a rebellion. A country with lootable resources therefore stands a greater chance of being in conflict than one without. The second route by which abundant resource leads to war considers population shifts. As a country's population increases, resources become relatively scarcer. This can cause grievances that lead to conflict especially if wealth is not evenly distributed. The third route considers Islamic militancy. Because many oil-producing countries are Islamic, the conflict may be related to sectarian divides or religious fundamentalism. He reports that oil is the resource most likely to spur conflict (de Soysa 2002).

The greed model received great attention from the late 1990s to the first few years of the 21st century. It was a high-profile model as Collier was affiliated with the World Bank. The United Nations adopted the greed model in dealing with civil wars in Angola, Sierra Leone, and the Democratic Republic of Congo (DRC). While the greed model does not provide a conclusive explanation of war onset (see Fearon 2005 and the next section), resource issues cannot be discounted. Grievance-based wars cannot be fully understood without some attention to the potential economic role of resources. Greed can play a role in the duration of wars if lootable goods are exploited by rebels to sustain their fight.

The State Capacity Model

Fearon and Laitin (2003a) argue that rebellion is more likely if there is opportunity. In the state capacity model, rebels are motivated by the lootability of the resources—in other words, the ability to obtain, process, and sell the resources. The mere presence of resources may not be enough to explain war (Fearon and Laitin

2003a). Prospective rebels calculate the prospect of victory by identifying the presence of favorable physical conditions and local support. They assess government strength as well. A weakened state creates an opportunity for potential rebels to exploit resources and conceal their army.

While each model supports the notion of opportunity as a cause of civil war, the state capacity model does not argue that resource-related wars result from rebel greed. They are a result of weakened states. When a major portion of state revenues come from resource exports, there is no pressing necessity to derive revenues from income tax. The lack of a taxation system means that citizens are no longer "shareholders" in the country. Under this arrangement, elites tend to neglect the masses. Additionally, resource-rich states do not usually have strong political structures. This is because they do not see a need to connect with citizens or to raise revenues from them. In the long term, these countries are politically weakened, facilitating potential rebellions (Humphreys 2005). Humphreys further writes that resource-dependent states need not diversify their economies because revenues raised from commodity exports are used to maintain the economy. These states therefore lack commercial and manufacturing sectors. Where there are factories and commercial offices, interaction is widespread. This is absent in resource-dependent countries, giving rise to the presence of isolated citizen groups lacking interactions between the various groups. Individuals from different cultures and ethnicities do not have the opportunity to understand each other and to learn to cooperate. There is a greater chance for suspicion and misunderstanding between the groups.

The resource curse can also negatively impact upon the rebel group. A country with lootable resources attracts citizens willing to be combatants. However, these potential combatants agree to join the group for selfish financial gain. The group is therefore faced with the question of its long-term survival. Potential combatants may also demand payment in cash or in kind before participating in rebel operations. While it is more difficult to recruit combatants in states without lootable resources, the quality of combatants can be higher compared to those in countries with lootable resources. In nonresource exporting states, individuals often join the group because of common ideological or ethno-religious beliefs. Rewards are reaped later, if at all, when the territory secedes or when the government is toppled (Weinstein 2005). Using Weinstein's micro-level study addressing rebels instead of the state, analysts can expect that the lack of lootable resource endowment should not be an impediment for ethno-religious groups to mobilize. This is not unusual in Islamic civil wars, an issue addressed in the previous chapter.

Fearon (2005) points out methodological problems with Collier and Hoeffler's argument (2004a), stating that it is inaccurate because of the use of onsets of each 5-year period instead of adhering to annual onset of civil war (the 5-year onset obscures annual changes and leads to many missing observations) and because of the exclusion of gemstones and narcotics from their data. The Collier and Hoeffler proxy for lootable resources mainly captures agricultural resources and oil—two commodities unlikely to be readily exploited by rebels as these resources are not normally trafficked illegally and require considerable logistical infrastructure. Disreputable importers are more likely to deal with rebels if the commodity is normally considered illegal (narcotics) or if it is cheaper for them to obtain via the black market (e.g., rough diamonds and gold). Collier and Hoeffler's (2004a) reliance on proxies for their variables raises additional important methodological issues. Fearon (2005) reports that the measure Collier and Hoeffler use does not even take diamonds and other precious stones into account. The grievance model is also not without its weaknesses. Grievances are found in every segment of society and in every country; however, war is very rare. This calls into question the role of grievances in civil war onset.

The Grievance Model

Most studies explain resource wars using either the greed or the state capacity models. On occasion, however, resource wars are based on the grievance argument. The path to resource wars may be explained by the grievance model using the degree of resource abundance, nature of extraction, and allocation. Both medium and high resource-dependent states can experience conflict. Countries with only medium levels of resources are unlikely to generate enough resource rents to be able to evenly distribute economic benefits to all groups. This can cause feelings of envy and anger toward economically well-to-do groups, as in the case of the 1998 massacre of Indonesian Chinese. The highly resource-dependent states face the danger of falling commodity prices that can crush the economy. The more vulnerable groups in the country are usually subjected to the ill effects of such failures. These groups channel their anger toward groups that are unaffected by economic problems. Government neglect of rural citizens' complaints about environmental degradation caused by mining or oil drilling companies can also lead to grievances as in the Bougainville case in Papua New Guinea. Addison, Le Billon, and Murshed (2001:13) observe that the Niger Delta region is an example of conflict arising from grievances about receipt of oil revenue and environmental degradation. Ross (2005) stated that the Aceh civil war in Indonesia broke out not because of greedy rebels looting resources but rather because of the sentiment that natural gas deposits in the region should not have to be shared with the rest of the country.

Table 5.2 provides a breakdown of country dependence on natural resources by region. Notice that sub-Saharan Africa, which has a high prevalence of war, is

TABLE 5.2
*Comparing Natural Resource Exports as
a Share of Total Exports or GDP Across Regions*

Regions	Fuel Exports (% of Merchandise Exports)		Oil Exports (% of GDP)		Total Natural Resources Export (% of GDP)	
	1995	2005	1995	2005	1995	2005
High income countries	6	9	1	1	1	2
All East Asian and Pacific countries	4	6	0	1	1	3
All Latin American and Caribbean countries	15	21	2	7	4	10
All sub-Saharan African countries	-	-	4	12	8	17
Developing East Asian and Pacific countries	6	8	2	3	5	8
Developing Latin American and Caribbean countries	15	20	2	6	4	10
Developing sub-Saharan African countries	-	-	4	12	8	16
Heavily indebted countries	18	22	1	6	7	12

Source: Adapted from The World Bank (2014).

also highly dependent on natural resources as a main source of export income. Heavily indebted countries that usually face civil war also are highly dependent on natural resources as a main source of export income. The table also portrays that developing countries (with the exception of Latin America) are far more dependent on natural resources than high income countries. Developing countries are the venues for the bulk of the civil wars.

OIL, DIAMONDS, ILLICIT DRUGS, AND TIMBER

Oil, gold, diamonds, and illicit drugs are the key commodities in resource-related civil wars (Ross 2006). Wars that have been fueled by gold and other precious minerals have taken millions of lives in sub-Saharan Africa alone (Winer and Roule 2003). This section looks more closely at the key natural resources linked to civil war. These have already been referenced above, but they warrant individual attention given their potentially significant role in causing and prolonging many civil wars. It also allows a better explanation of dynamics involved in the conflicts linked to particular resources along with discussion of relevant case studies. Finally, the resources vary in how they affect civil war dynamics.

Oil

Oil is a non-lootable resource. Because of the technology needed to extract oil and gas, rebels do not usually undertake looting of oil. Oil is still related to civil war as a potential cause because it heightens the value (or prize) of victory (see Fearon 2005). There is reasonable agreement that oil can enhance the probability of civil war (see, e.g., de Soysa 2002; Fearon and Laitin 2003a). Fearon and Laitin (2003a) report that a country whose economy depends on oil exports is twice as likely to have war compared to a non-oil exporting state. de Soysa and Neumayer (2007) showed that oil is linked only to less intense civil wars. There are certain caveats to each study. For instance, the de Soysa and Neumayer (2007) study did not consider diamonds and other gems. Collier and Hoeffler's greed model on the other hand has a high relevance to non-lootable resources like oil. Making conclusions confirming the power of one model over the other in the absence of lootable resources in the data may prove premature.

As mentioned previously, oil can be a blessing as well as a curse. Oil-related civil wars have occurred in some countries (Nigeria) but not in others (Malaysia). A lot has to do with how elites manage the economy and how they manipulate economic policies to deter war. Indonesia was able to carry this out successfully, but Nigeria failed (Nafziger 2006). While Nafziger (2006) did not see any connection between oil and conflict in Indonesia, Ross (2005) found that in Aceh, Indonesia, natural gas was an indirect grievance-forming factor stirring rebellion. He highlighted that grievances were related to under-represented Acehnese employees in oil and gas projects, exclusion of local business participation in oil and gas projects, and the province not enjoying its "fair share" of oil and gas revenues.

Oil-exporting states derive good incomes from the sale of oil and gas. If oil-exporting states derive considerable revenue from oil, then these states should also be expected to have high per capita income. This is only true in some cases. In fact in some oil-exporting states, per capita incomes are still low, for example, in Angola, Indonesia, and Nigeria. The rents derived may not be channeled back to the citizens or to institution building. This leads to weakening of the state (Fearon and Laitin 2003a; Snyder and Bhavnani 2005), which can lead to civil war.

de Soysa (2002) linked oil to grievance-related conflicts thereby diverging from Fearon and Laitin's state capacity model and Collier and Hoeffler's greed model of resource-related conflicts. States can also be weakened due to sudden oil price drops. When the price of oil drops, the state's ability to fight rebels declines.

Collier and Hoeffler (2002a) write that poor countries with resources have the highest risk of experiencing civil war. However, it is hard to ascertain whether it is the low per capita income or the resource(s) that is driving the onset of war. A poorer country may be able to extract resources more easily than richer countries because of the indifference toward environmental degradation and the availability of cheap labor. At the same time, these poor countries may not possess the necessary capital, equipment, and infrastructure to extract the resources (Ross 2006). Ross advises exercising care when researching the resource-income-level-war connection because of conflicting relationships as shown above.

The importance of oil is vividly reflected in the Angolan civil war. Oil revenues were crucial for the Angolan Popular Movement for the Liberation of Angola (MPLA) regime's war against the National Union for the Total Independence of Angola (UNITA) rebel force. Three mechanisms were at play that linked oil to this war:

First a low-income country that is dependent on resource exports is prone to war because its institutions are weak and its tax systems are either incomplete or inefficient. Between 1993 and 1998, 87 percent of Angola's revenues came from oil rents (Reno 2000b). It is therefore not surprising to find Angola having weak institutions and a poor tax system at that time.

Second, there was major foreign investment in Angola during the war. Reno (2000b) reported that there existed symbiotic relationships between foreign MNCs and the Angolan government at that time. Firms prefer a stable environment to conduct business. Reno (2000b) noted that financial aid to the government was forthcoming from MNCs during the war. The UNITA rebels exploited diamonds sales.

Third, the ruling MPLA government pursued a strategy of state ownership of oil resource with foreign rather than domestic partners. While the MNCs preferred an open government in terms of accountability and transparency, the state preferred a nontransparent structure it could exploit (Ross 2006). Therefore, institutions remained weak, and the tax system was undeveloped. Ross (2006) states that oil-rich states should pursue an arrangement whereby the government oversees oil exports and private companies run the export process. Further, the chance of averting wars is higher if these private businessmen are locals instead of foreigners because local businesses will eventually force state leaders into consensus-forming arrangements and create a sense of belief in the citizenry that they are stakeholders in the government.

War can ensue even before oil enters the market. This was the case in Chad before 2003 where the potential to reap future benefits sparked conflict (Humphreys 2005). Outside government intervention and MNCs exacerbated the problem. How did the absence of physical sale of oil make this problem so complex? The answer lies with a peculiar practice of rebels and governments accepting funds in return for the promise to deliver the product sometime in the future— that is, "booty futures." Rebels and the government assure MNCs and other foreign parties that oil will be available once conflict issues are settled. In such a scenario, some parties would support the government while others support rebels.

Humphreys (2005) found that the state capacity model explains oil-related civil wars much more convincingly than the greed model. In one of Humphrey's statistical tests, a slight increase in oil production was connected to a proportionally larger chance of conflict. In addition, he observed that only the state capacity model explains African resource-related wars. This suggests that the mere presence of oil reserves is not a strong predictor of war as previously thought.

The evidence presented here indicates that the association between oil and conflict is based on political rather than economic mechanisms, in line with Ron's (2005) analysis of the literature.

Diamonds

Diamonds, a highly valued resource, are linked in several ways to civil war onset, but they are especially clearly linked to civil war duration. In addition to their use in jewelry, diamonds perform important nonornamental functions. They are exceptionally hard; hence, industrial diamonds are used for cutting, grinding, drilling, and polishing. In fact, only diamonds can cut other diamonds. Their value is increased by their rarity. They are found in abundance only in countries such as Botswana, Russia, Angola, Canada, DRC, South Africa, Australia, and Namibia (U.S. Department of Interior 2012). They are ideal as lootable commodities because they are easy to conceal during smuggling and have an extremely high value-to-weight ratio. Until recently, it was relatively easy to conceal the origin of diamonds to importers, and processers usually were not aware when they were dealing with conflict diamonds.

Primary diamonds, located in kimberlite shafts, are hard to access and are therefore mined by established mining companies. Secondary diamonds on the other hand are dispersed in alluvial plains or fields and are easier to mine. Since it requires a minimal capital outlay to collect secondary diamonds, these are the diamonds that are exploited by rebels. Reno (2000b) showed that the UNITA rebels in Angola made a few billion dollars in about ten years through diamond sales. Lujala et al. (2005) further observe that secondary diamonds are lootable because they are generally widely dispersed within a country. If they were concentrated in one place, the government could likely control the area.

The mechanism by which diamonds might cause civil war depends on three factors. First, it depends on which type (lootable or non-lootable) of diamonds is available. Second, it depends on the method used to mine the diamonds. Third, it depends on how elites spend the profits received from diamond rents (Snyder and Bhavnani 2005).

Three sub-Saharan African states were chosen by Snyder and Bhavnani (2005) to demonstrate the three mechanisms described in the preceding paragraph. Ghana, Guinea, and Sierra Leone stood out as countries similar in terms of conflict risk. All three countries had an abundance of lootable diamonds (secondary diamonds). Two of these countries escaped the diamond curse, but Sierra Leone became a war-torn country, which gave rise to the *blood diamond* phrase. In Guinea, both non-lootable and lootable resources were extracted industrially with the help of established companies. Therefore, lootable diamonds were under the control of the government. In Sierra Leone, there was no conflict when lootable diamonds were under the control of the government. When the control was interrupted and altered, the government's income was drastically reduced. The government's power weakened. This provided a motivation for the RUF to stage a rebellion. In Ghana, the non-lootable resource was extracted industrially, but the lootable diamonds were not. Even though lootable diamonds extracted by nonindustrial methods posed a higher risk of conflict, Ghana was able to avoid violence as the government spent considerable amounts of money received from lootable resource rents on security (Snyder and Bhavnani 2005).

The relationship between diamonds and civil war is complicated. Lujala et al. (2005) argued that previous research failed to arrive at concrete results because it failed to distinguish how primary and secondary diamonds explain the onset of war differently. In addition, they argued that older datasets did not provide comprehensive information on the exact location of diamonds, when they were found, and the year of production. Lujala et al. used a new dataset which covered 70 countries with diamonds. Upon splitting into primary and secondary diamonds, the dataset contained 25 primary diamond-abundant countries and 32 secondary diamond-abundant countries. This was also done for post-Cold War onset. Their findings showed that neither presence nor production type of either type of diamonds led to civil war during the Cold War.

There was a positive effect of diamonds on war for the post-Cold War era. During this era, the production of diamonds triggered civil war but simply availability of diamonds did not (Lujala et al. 2005).

The importance of disaggregating the different diamond types was also presented by Ross (2006), who did not find any link between aggregated diamonds and civil war. The findings were different for primary and secondary diamonds, though Ross's (2006) findings were the opposite of those of Lujala, Gleditsch, and Gilmore (2005). He found that civil war stems from primary diamonds and that secondary diamonds caused secessionist civil wars. Oil was a more prominent cause of civil war. However, Ross's (2006) conclusion that primary diamonds caused civil war failed to hold when the DRC data was removed from the data. Recall that Chapter 1 stressed that differences in data can lead to different conclusions.

Rebels conceivably fight either because of political differences, disagreements over strategy and aims, or economic reasons. In the case of the latter, rebel leaders must assure the group that there are sufficient funds to compensate combatants. Regan and Norton (2005) observe that the literature states diamonds make recruitment and maintenance of combatants easier. In this sense, diamonds are an indirect cause of civil war.

Other studies have also shown that civil wars do not necessarily stem from the presence or exports of diamonds. Using formal theory to arrive at the conclusion that diamonds did not spark conflict, Dunning's (2005) three-country case study highlighted that whether resources are a curse or a blessing is contingent upon a complex array of factors. Using Botswana as a case, Dunning (2005) illustrates how the complex mix of variables mentioned above made Botswana escape the resource curse. At independence, Botswana had an abundance of diamonds but was the second poorest country in the world, a perfect recipe for rebellion. Through skillful negotiations, Botswanian elites were able to secure excellent terms with De Beers, its main diamond trader. This included some guarantees on price stability. This avoided state economic instability caused by a sudden fall in prices.

Dunning demonstrated that the lack of political opposition and price stability of diamonds alleviated conflict risk for Botswana. The peaceful environment of Botswana at independence helped Botswana maintain peace compared with many other resource-rich but poor countries, such as DRC.

It would appear that diamonds are not a sufficient cause of war. Australia and Canada are wealthy countries with abundant diamonds but these countries never experienced civil war. This is likely because the countries have high income and are established democracies. Ross (2006) pointed out that when a country's discovery of primary diamonds is accompanied by an increase in its GDP per capita, the probability of civil war decreases. More broadly, Addison, Le Billon, and Murshed (2001) argue that not all resources cause civil wars. Minerals have a higher chance of spurring conflict than resources such as water or soil. This is because minerals are not renewable and are easily mined.

Several studies have looked specifically at diamonds with respect to conflict duration. Regan and Norton (2005) concluded if war breaks out in a diamond-producing country, a contest for diamonds between government and rebels can ensue. Both parties are tempted to exploit and profit from this resource to maintain their forces. This change causes civil wars relating to diamonds to last longer. Secondary diamonds make post-Cold War ethno-religious wars longer according to Lujala et al. (2005). This is in line with Fearon (2004), who showed that gems, like secondary diamonds, made sons-of-the-soil civil wars last longer.

Gold

The illegal extraction of gold is synonymous with civil wars in Sierra Leone, Liberia, and the DRC. Ross (2003) observed gold has been extracted by both rebels and government-funded militias in these wars. Gold located in deep mines or the ocean requires large amounts of capital to retrieve. This gold is typically not available to rebels. However, gold can also be collected with minimal investment by panning in rivers.

Warring parties commonly smuggled gold during the Liberian civil war (Reno 1998:97). The organized illegal extraction of gold allowed warring parties to make a fortune during the civil war in Sierra Leone. The youth working in illegal gold mines in Sierra Leone eventually became a pool for RUF recruitment (Keen 2005:59). In the DRC, a most peculiar phenomenon was taking place with regard to illegal gold exploitation. The DRC government was funding opposing warring ethnic groups. Odd as it may seem, the idea was to lengthen the war so that the government military could remain in the region to continue illegal mining (Keen 2012).

Illicit Drugs

The main drugs rebels exploit are opiates (from poppy plants) and cocaine (from coca plants). Some rebels also cultivate marijuana.

The world's largest producer of illicit opium is Afghanistan. In 2011, Afghanistan was home to 131,000 hectares of opium poppy, which produced 5,800 metric tons of opium. The world's largest producers of opiates are Afghanistan, Laos, Burma, Colombia, Mexico, and Guatemala. Afghanistan alone grows 63 percent of opium poppy. Laos and Burma account for 20 percent while Colombia and Mexico grow 7 percent of opium poppy (UN Office on Drugs and Crime [UNODC] 2012). Colombia is a world leader in cocaine production and also generates heroin (U.S. Department of State 2012). Europe is the largest market for heroin and the United States for cocaine (UNODC 2012).

The link between drugs and civil war is evident in Colombian civil war. Cocaine production and trafficking has generated millions of dollars for the Revolutionary Armed Forces (FARC) and Autodefensas Unidas de Colombia (AUC) of Colombia. Cocaine trafficking has also been linked to the Irish Republican Army (IRA) in Northern Ireland. Opium has been linked to the Shan rebellion in Burma and heroin to the Kurdistan Workers Party (PKK) in Turkey and the Tamil Tigers in Sri Lanka. The Taliban group in Afghanistan has been linked to both opium and heroin (UNODC 2012). These groups use the proceeds from illegal drug rents to finance their rebel groups. Over the years, the FARC has become so formidable the Colombian government has been unable to defeat it. FARC raises approximately US$500 million a year from illegal drugs (Collier et al. 2003) and has been able to maintain a de facto "state-within-a-state."

Goodhand (2005) studied the link between opium and civil war in the Afghan provinces bordering Pakistan and Tajkistan. Between 1979 and 1992 the border provinces became increasingly important because of the war involving mujahideen freedom fighters and the Soviet occupiers. The mujahids saw opium as a concrete source of finance for the maintenance of their army. About one third of the world's opium production was in Afghanistan during this war. Chaos ensued in the 3 years following the Soviet withdrawal. UCDP/PRIO recorded over ten warring factions during this time. The chaos allowed the opium trade to increase and Afghanistan surpassed Burma as the world's largest source of raw opium (see UNODC 2012).

The only time that opium production and trafficking were substantially reduced was after the Taliban administration's surprising ban on opium in 2000. When the Taliban regime was ousted by the United States and its allies, the Taliban took on the role of a rebel group. The change of role from being a government to a rebel group forced the Taliban to produce and trade opium to finance its army (UNODC 2012). Opium production increased in the post-Taliban period (after 2001), and illicit opium exports eventually became the main sector of the economy (Goodhand 2005). In 2004, Afghanistan generated a whopping US$2.2 billion from opium, with more than 3 million Afghans involved in that illegal economy (UNODC 2004). The opium trade continues to this day. In the absence of lootable resources, potential rebels will have to find alternative means of providing remuneration to combatants. When such means are unavailable, the risk of civil war decreases drastically, especially if the country does not have a low GDP per capita.

Goodhand (2005:211) describes the Afghan civil war environment:

> For a resource-poor farmer poppy is part of the coping or survival economy; for the landowner leasing his land or for the opium trader it is part of the shadow economy; and for the commanders who tax poppy it is part of the combat economy. Opium is simultaneously a conflict good.

Using the Colombian example, Sanchez et al. (2005) argued that the war in Colombia bred drug-related activities which in turn extended the conflict, intensified it, and increased its coverage. This dreadful scenario might not have been had drugs not been available to finance FARC and AUC.

The literature on illicit drugs is as mixed as the overall literature on resource-related civil wars. Snyder and Duran-Martinez (2009) showed that illicit drugs do not necessarily increase the risk of civil war onset. They found that in Burma, an increase in production and trafficking of opium did not lead to civil war. In fact, the onset and prevalence of war decreased sharply as the production and distribution of opium increased in the 1990s. They attributed the decrease in rebellions as a result of a change in the structure of the relationship between rebels and government. Prior to the 1990s, war-torn Burma had numerous rebel groups operating, using finances raised from opium trade. In the 1990s, the government offered to allow these groups to continue prospering in the opium trade if the groups agreed to lay down arms. This led to a symbiotic relationship in which rebel groups saw a partnership in the lucrative opium trade while the government saw peace and stability. Snyder and Duran-Martinez (2009:267) call such a cooperative, or profit-sharing, arrangement, an "exit option" for rebel groups in a "state-sponsored protection racket" system. Such an arrangement actually worked. Burma saw a sharp decrease in rebellion in the 1990s. The Burmese government, which also traded in opium, saw its opium revenues flourishing.

Snyder (2006) showed that during this cooperative era, illegal drugs were the number one export for Burma. Snyder (2006:960) showed how "joint extraction with former insurgents" in illegal drugs "helped make political order possible in Burma" during this era. He also observed a similar dynamic in Sierra Leone. Byrd and Ward (2004:6) provided a similar example in Afghanistan: Afghan warlords and the Taliban practiced a cooperative relationship even at a time when the Taliban was just beginning to hold its grip on Afghan politics. The warlords promised support for the Taliban if the Taliban allowed the warlords to keep their opium rents.

Timber

Timber is a lootable resource similar to secondary diamonds. It is easy to identify and easy to exploit. Timber felling does not always require sophisticated equipment or great capital investment. Timber is also usually spread out over a country. Rebel groups can move around with trucks and chainsaws and harvest the timber.

Timber has been linked to civil war. The Khmer Rouge used illegal timber revenues to fund its army during the Cambodian civil war in the 1980s and 1990s. Likewise the RUF survived in part from timber sales as Liberia channeled aid to RUF from timber revenues. In Indonesia, Exxon-Mobil is reported to have engaged the services of the Indonesian military during the Aceh civil war. Indonesian soldiers took advantage of this situation to log timber illegally (Keen 2012). When China ceased funding for Khmer Rouge's operations, the group was forced to resort to illegal timber logging for finances. In Burma, another country where rebels finance their armies from illegal timber logging, forest cover saw reduction from 70 percent to 30 percent between 1948 and 2002 (Global Witness 2002). Rebels in the Kachin, Shan, and Wa regions exploited timber to sustain their armies to fight the Burmese government (Ross 2003). In 1999, about 70 percent of timber imported into the European Union came from illegal sources (Crossin, Hayman, and Taylor 2003).

In conclusion, state capacity determines the ability of the state to defend itself from rebels and prevent the recruiting and organizational activities of rebels. Capacity varies across resource-producing countries. Some resource-rich countries are strong while others range from fairly strong to weak. The stronger countries have a lower risk of civil war due to resources, and the opposite is true for low-capacity states. Thus, a key finding to take away from this section is that resources do not necessarily lead to civil war. This link requires other conditions such as low state capacity and low levels of development.

CONCLUSION

The issue of ownership of resources often arises when they are spread unevenly, and this can cause conflict. Much research has been undertaken on the role of natural resources in civil wars. There are a wide variety of natural resources found all over the world that include oil, gemstones, gold, timber, and agricultural products. In countries rich in lootable resources, the ability of rulers to establish and maintain political order can depend on three key factors. First, order depends on the economy's overall resource profile, specifically the amount of non-lootable wealth available as a revenue source. Second, the mode of extraction is relevant. Whether lootable resources are extracted by difficult-to-tax artisans or by large taxable industrial firms are especially important. Finally, patterns of state expenditure impact on order. Of particular importance is whether rulers consume revenue frivolously or invest it in strengthening the military, providing social welfare, and improving their capacity to earn future revenue (Snyder and Bhavnani 2005:588).

Lootable resources are much easier than non-lootable resources to extract, transport, and distribute. An example of lootable resource is secondary diamonds. Secondary diamonds have been known to fuel civil conflicts, mainly in sub-Saharan Africa. Both lootable and non-lootable (oil, for instance) resources have been shown to have caused and prolonged civil war. However, these findings show more consistent support for oil as a cause of onset. The literature on diamonds and drugs as reasons for onset are more divided.

According to a review of research on the link between natural resources and war by Ross (2004), the weight of evidence suggests four regularities:

- Oil dependence appears to be linked to the start of conflict, but not to its duration. There is some evidence that oil dependence (and potentially mineral dependence) is more strongly linked with separatist conflicts than other conflict types.
- Gemstones, opium, coca, and cannabis do not seem to be linked to conflict initiation, but they do seem to lengthen preexisting wars. Timber's role remains untested.
- There is no statistical evidence, and very little case study evidence, linking agricultural commodities to either the initiation of civil wars or their duration.
- The claim that primary commodities are associated with civil war onset does not appear to be robust (Ross 2004:352).

The leading models of resource-related civil wars are presented in the chapter. The greed model is based on the premise that natural resources are a target for greedy rebels. The profits from the sale of such resources are used to set up and maintain a rebel army. The greed model portrays civil war as arising from the desire for private gain. War is a business enterprise, and war breeds war economies. The policy guidance provided by Collier and Hoeffler is for countries to diversify their economies as dependence on resources alone can be perilous.

The state capacity model argues that a weakened state creates an opportunity for potential rebels to fight the government. States in decline and states that are economically, politically, and militarily weak become targets of rebellion. The resource curse adds to this problem. In countries with abundant natural resources, a large portion of state revenues come from resource exports. Hence, there is less a necessity for the government to derive revenues from income tax. Lack of a solid taxation system makes for disengaged citizens that are more likely to see the government as illegitimate as under this arrangement elites tend to neglect the masses. This also implies developing resource-rich states will not have adequate strong political institutions.

The grievance model also has relevance for resource-related wars. Countries with low levels of resources are unlikely to generate enough resource rents to be able to evenly distribute economic benefits to all groups. This can cause feelings of envy and anger toward economically well-to-do groups, as in the case of the 1998 massacre of Indonesian Chinese. Highly resource-dependent states face threats of drastic drops in commodity prices that can devastate their economies. The poor are the most directly impacted by these drops and might direct grievances toward others not suffering the economic problems. Environmental degradation caused by natural resource exploitation can also lead to grievances as in the Bougainville copper mine case in Papua New Guinea. Addison, Le Billon, and Murshed (2001:13) observe that the Niger Delta region is an example of conflict arising from grievances about receipt of oil revenue and environmental degradation. The Aceh civil war broke out in part over grievances related to the sharing of revenue from natural gas deposits in the region (Ross 2005).

Oil is also associated with civil war. Statistically, secessionist rebellions are significantly more likely if the country has resources, particularly oil (World Bank 2003:60). Clear examples are provided by wars in Angola, Chad, and Nigeria. Oil can also act as a driver of conflict when rebel groups use illegal tactics, such as kidnapping, threat, and sabotage, to finance their armies. Various arguments have been presented for how oil is linked to resource-based civil wars. The majority of them fall within either the greed or the state capacity models.

The link between diamonds and civil wars has been studied by many scholars. First, diamonds have been found to influence the incidence of civil wars but generally not the risk of their onset. The effect of diamonds depends on the level of ethnic fractionalization, and they mainly affect ethnic war. Second, the geological form of diamond deposits is important. For example, easily exploited resources, such as secondary diamonds, can be used to finance prolonged fighting. Third, the impact of secondary diamonds on the start of fighting has been significantly higher since the Cold War's conclusion. Fourth, research suggests that diamonds are dangerous only after production has started. Therefore, the discovery of a diamond deposit in a country does not appear to affect the risk of civil war by itself (Lujala et al. 2005:559–560).

There are various mechanisms by which diamonds cause civil wars. These mechanisms broadly fit within the greed or state capacity models. The mode of extraction can determine if a country observes the onset of diamond-based wars. The likelihood of onset of civil war is decreased if diamonds are extracted industrially, by few businessmen, or by large established companies. Under such an arrangement, the government is likely to control diamonds and deny rebels the opportunity to loot these diamonds. Other studies have shown that primary and secondary diamonds connect differently with the onset and duration of civil war. Additionally, these different categories of diamonds connect differently to war during the cold war and post-Cold War eras. Aggregating the different categories of diamonds and disaggregating them produced different results. Studies have also shown that the onset of war is dependent on how elites spend diamond rents. If elites channel resource profits into their own coffers, war is likely to occur. However, if profits are channeled into building strong institutions, or distributed fairly among citizens, war may be deterred. Other studies have shown a combination of a myriad of factors that linked diamonds to civil war. In these studies, a mix of history, elite support, elite economic policies, and the state of nonresource sectors collectively explain civil war.

Illicit drugs have caused untold misery. The most common drugs related to conflict are opium and cocaine. Afghanistan, Burma, and Colombia have been plagued with drug-related civil wars. Studies showed that in Afghanistan, drugs were directly related to conflict. The situation in Afghanistan is so serious that sometimes the size of an illegal opium economy exceeds the size of the country's legal economy. Surprisingly, Snyder and Duran-Martinez (2009) argued that an increase in opium cultivation and other drug trade is likely to reduce civil wars within a country. They illustrated the Burmese case of the "win-win" collaboration between the corrupt government and rebel leaders in which the government successfully made rebels give up armed struggle in exchange for a share in the lucrative drug trade. The end result was a sharp drop in the onsets of civil wars.

SUGGESTED READING

Addison, Tony, Philippe Le Billon, and S. Mansoob Murshed. 2001. "Conflict in Africa: The Cost of Peaceful Behaviour." UNU-WIDER Discussion Paper 2001/51. United Nations University World Institute for Development Economic Research, Helsinki, Finland.

Collier, Paul. 2000. "Doing Well Out of War: An Economic Perspective." Pp. 91–112 in *Greed and Grievance, Economic Agendas in Civil Wars*, edited by M. Berdal and D. M. Malone. Boulder, CO: Lynne Rienner.

Collier, Paul and Anke Hoeffler. 2004a. "Greed and Grievance in Civil War." *Oxford Economic Papers* 56(4):563–595.

de Soysa, Indra and Eric Neumayer. 2007. "Resource Wealth and the Risk of Civil War Onset: Results from a New Dataset of Natural Resource Rents, 1970–1999." *Conflict Management and Peace Science* 24:201–218.

Fearon, James D. 2005. "Primary Commodity Exports and Civil War." *Journal of Conflict Resolution* 49(4):483–507.

Humphreys, Macartan. 2005. "Natural Resources, Conflict, and Conflict Resolution: Uncovering the Mechanisms." *Journal of Conflict Resolution* 49(4):508–537.

Lujala, Paivi. 2010. "Cursed by Resources? High Value Natural Resource and Armed Civil Conflict." In *War: An Introduction to Theories and Research on Collective Violence*, edited by T. G. Jacobsen. New York: Nova Science.

Lujala, Paivi and Nils Petter Gleditsch, and Elisabeth Gilmore. 2005. "A Diamond Curse? Civil War and a Lootable Resource." *Journal of Conflict Resolution* 49(4):538–562.

Regan, Patrick M. and Daniel Norton. 2005. "Greed, Grievance and Mobilization in Civil Wars." *Journal of Conflict Resolution* 49(3):319–336.

Reno, William. 2000a. "Clandestine Economies, Violence and States in Africa." *Journal of International Affairs* 53(2):433–460.

Ron, James. 2005. "Paradigm in Distress? Primary Commodities and Civil War." *Journal of Conflict Resolution* 49(4):443–450.

Ross, Michael. 2001. "Does Oil Hinder Democracy?" *World Politics* 53(3):325–361.

Ross, Michael. 2003. "The Natural Resource Curse: How Wealth Can Make You Poor." In *Natural Resources and Violent Conflict: Options and Actions*, edited by I. Bannon and P. Collier. Washington, DC: World Bank.

Ross, Michael. 2004. "What Do We Know about Natural Resources and Civil War?" *Journal of Peace Research* 41(3):337–356.

Ross, Michael. 2006. "A Closer Look at Oil, Diamonds, and Civil War." *Annual Review of Political Science* 9:265–300.

Snyder, Richard. 2006. "Does Lootable Wealth Breed Disorder?: A Political Economy of Extraction Framework." *Comparative Political Studies* 39(8):943–968.

Snyder, Richard and Ravi Bhavnani. 2005. "Diamonds, Blood, and Taxes. A Revenue-Centered Framework for Explaining Political Order." *Journal of Conflict Resolution* 49(4):563–597.

CHAPTER 6

The Termination of Civil War and Post-Conflict Issues

How wars end has much to do with how, and for how long, they are fought. In this chapter, we will find that wars can resolve political conflicts and lead to peace when all belligerents become exhausted or when one wins decisively (Luttwak 1999). War brings peace only after passing a culminating phase of violence, as hopes of military success must have declined for accommodation to be more attractive than continued fighting (Luttwak 1999). Some research indicates that the longer the war's duration, the less likely it will lead to one faction's victory and the more likely there will be a negotiated settlement. Indeed, rebel victories (the least likely outcome) usually occur in the first few years of the war and government victories typically within the war's first 5 years. After about ten years, a decisive victory by either group is rare (Brandt et al. 2008).

This chapter first examines the outcome of conflicts and the peace agreements that can be signed to cease hostilities before focusing on the nature of such agreements. Here, power sharing, territorial autonomy, and electoral and amnesty agreement provisions, along with their impact on the successful implementation of a peace agreement, are outlined. Finally, major post-conflict issues are identified. More specifically, state formation, democratization, and peace-building are outlined in this section.

TYPES AND TRENDS IN CIVIL WAR OUTCOMES

Theories of war termination rarely conceptualize or explain war termination as the obverse of war initiation. This is because of two key reasons. First, unlike decisions to initiate or join wars, which often are made unilaterally, war termination is not always the result of unilateral action because in many cases both sides must cooperate to end conflict. Wars can be terminated through unilateral action if one side defeats the other militarily. Second, war initiation and termination do not necessarily share the same causes (Wolf 2011:1756).

Scholars classify war outcomes according to several different types, and they often use UCDP data in their research. The UCDP's figures on major armed conflicts are published in the annual Stockholm International Peace Research Institute (SIPRI) *Yearbook*. (For more on SIPRI, see Box 6.1.) Among the types of outcomes, a cease-fire agreement with conflict regulation is an agreement between the main parties active in the last year of conflict, regarding the ending of military operations, along with some sort of mutual conflict regulatory steps. The agreement is signed and/or accepted either during the last year of active conflict or during the first year of inactivity.

BOX 6.1   Stockholm International Peace Research Institute (SIPRI)

The SIPRI is an independent international institute that undertakes research into conflict, armaments, arms control, and disarmament. The Institute provides data, analysis, and recommendations, based on open sources, to policy makers, researchers, the media, and interested members of the public. Although based in Stockholm, Sweden, the SIPRI has a presence in China and the United States. The institute cooperates closely with intergovernmental organizations, such as the United Nations and the European Union (EU). It was established in 1966 on the basis of a decision by the Swedish Parliament, and a significant part of its funding is via an annual Swedish government grant. The institute seeks additional financial support from other organizations to assist with its broad research program. The SIPRI is currently directed by Tilman Brück with staff numbering approximately 50 to 60 (SIPRI 2013a).

A cease-fire agreement is an agreement between all, or the main, parties active in the last year of conflict on the ending of military operations. The agreement is signed and/or accepted either during the last year of active conflict or during the first year of inactivity. The *victory* outcome means one side active in the last year of conflict is either defeated or eliminated, or otherwise succumbs to the power of the other through capitulation or public announcement. The *low activity* outcome obtains when conflict activity continues but does not reach the UCDP threshold for fatalities. Finally, *other* simply means the conflict does not fulfill the UCDP criteria for organization or incompatibility.

A useful way to evaluate how civil wars end is through using the comprehensive UCDP dataset of conflict terminations from 1946 to 2009. The dataset provides outcomes for 332 civil war episodes (see Table 6.1). An armed conflict was counted as having terminated each time the conflict or the warring party failed to reach UCDP's threshold for inclusion in one calendar year. This occurred when the incompatibility was solved either by an agreement or by a victory, when a party ceased to exist, or when the use of armed force did not meet the 25 battle-related deaths criteria (UCDP 2014b).

The most common termination outcome was the continuation of low activity fighting whereby fatalities did not meet the UCDP threshold for armed conflict (142 cases), followed by the victory of one faction over the other (102 cases) and peace agreements (42 cases). These were concerned with resolving or regulating the incompatibility—completely or a central part, which is signed and/or accepted by all or the main parties either during the last year of active conflict or during the first year of inactivity. The government was victorious over the rebels the majority of times (71 to 31 victories). The aggregate data on termination shown in Table 6.1 obscure some important historical context that distinguishes conflicts fought during the Cold War versus those fought after the Cold War, for reasons we will elaborate below.

During the Cold War, one party often was able to secure its victory. If analysts isolate the 141 Cold War civil wars that took place from 1946 to 1989, they find that victory for one party was the most common way conflicts were terminated (82 terminations or 58.2 percent). A high-profile example of this was the defeat of South Vietnam by North Vietnamese forces in April 1975. The second most common way conflicts were terminated—45 (31.9 percent)—involved neither a victory nor any type of agreement (an *other* outcome). For instance, conflict might have continued but not have reached the threshold of 25 battle-related deaths per year, or a party might have withdrawn from the fighting. A peace agreement, an agreement concerned with the resolution of the incompatibility signed and/or publicly accepted by all or the main conflict

TABLE 6.1
Outcomes of Civil Wars Terminated 1946–2009

Low or no activity	Victory	Peace Agreement	Cease-fire Agreement with Conflict Regulation	Cease-fire Agreement	Other
142	102	42	25	13	8

Source: UCDP Conflict Termination dataset v.2010–1, 1946–2009 and Codebook (2010) (see http://www.pcr.uu.se/research/ucdp/)

actors, was the third most common outcome (12, or 8.5 percent). The least number of conflicts—two, or 1.4 percent—were ended by a cease-fire whereby an agreement between all the main conflict actors terminated military operations, though the incompatibility between them was not addressed (Kreutz 2010:245–246). Luttwak has written that cease-fires allow factions to regroup and rearm. Thus, cease-fires can intensify and prolong conflict once they end, which usually occurs (Luttwak 1999).

In the years during and after the decline of Cold War tensions (1990–2005), the dataset indicates that changes occurred with how conflicts ended. Here, more conflicts ended through peace agreements and cease-fires. This was potentially influenced by many of the Cold War conflicts being proxy wars where the superpowers assisted the fighting parties. After the Cold War, the most common end of a conflict was via an *other* outcome (71 terminations, or 48.3 percent) and cease-fires (29, or 19.7 percent). These were followed by peace agreements (27, or 18.4 percent) and victory (20, or 13.6 percent). Research indicates that such outcomes might have been facilitated by the post-Cold War international community becoming more willing and capable at mediating conflict and by increased third-party peacekeeping abilities (Kreutz 2010:246). As already noted in Chapter 3, approximately 25 percent of post-World War II insurgencies were won by the government, and 11 percent were won by insurgents (Jones 2008:10, 14).

More recently, other conflicts have been classified as no longer active by the UCDP, though their conclusion is not necessarily permanent. The Russian conflict over Chechnya technically ended with the Chechen insurgent leader proclaiming the independent "Caucasus Emirate" including most of Russia's North Caucasus region. This created a more far-reaching territorial incompatibility, and there were fewer than 400 battle-related deaths during 2008. The Party for the Liberation of the Hutu People—National Liberation Forces signed a peace agreement in December, 2008 and the Tamil Tigers were defeated militarily the following May. After negotiations, a cease-fire officially declared in 2003 between the Philippine government and Moro Islamic Liberation Front was also reaffirmed in July 2009 (SIPRI 2005–2013, *Yearbook* 2009:73–74; *Yearbook* 2010:66; *Yearbook* 2011:65).

Eleven conflicts registered for 2011 by the UCDP, including 10 civil wars, were no longer active in 2012. The civil wars involved Iran, Cote d'Ivoire, Libya, Mauritania, Myanmar (Karen), Myanmar (Shan), Senegal (Casamance), Sudan (Abyei), Tajikistan, and Uganda. The Iranian and Tajikistan governments successfully targeted the insurgents, whereas Cote d'Ivoire and Libyan insurgents were victorious. Peace negotiations occurred in Myanmar and Senegal, with fighting deescalating in Mauritania and Uganda. Conflict over the Abyei area became an intrastate war with South Sudan's independence (Themnér and Wallensteen 2013:514–515).

TYPES OF PEACE AGREEMENTS

As peace agreements can be an effective tool for ending and resolving civil wars, they require study. This is reinforced by the use of such agreements changing over time and by their various types along with levels of effectiveness. As mentioned, overall, the UCDP conflict termination dataset 1946–2009 identified 42 observations of intrastate conflicts terminated by peace agreements (see Table 6.1). A peace agreement is a formal agreement between warring parties, which addresses their disputed incompatibility. This is either by settling all or part of it, or by clearly outlining a process for how the warring parties plan to regulate the incompatibility.

All agreements that concern, manage, or regulate the stated incompatibility are considered peace agreements, including peace process agreements. A full agreement occurs when two armed and opposing actors (dyads) agree to settle the whole incompatibility, while a partial peace agreement involves one or more dyad agreeing to settle part of the incompatibility. A peace process agreement is an agreement where one or more dyad agrees to initiate a process that aims to settle the incompatibility. Agreements are also categorized between comprehensive, which include all conflict dyads, and dyadic agreements where at least one of the conflict parties is excluded (UCDP 2012c). Although there was a high annual occurrence of signed peace agreements during the 1990s and early 2000s, the number dropped significantly from 10 to one between 2008 and 2009. The figure increased slightly to two the following year before falling to one in 2011, the lowest figure since 1987 (Themnér and Wallensteen 2012:571). Agreements increased to four in 2012, with three seeking to address civil wars (the Central African Republic, the Philippines, and South Sudan). These agreements illustrate the importance of taking into account the multiparty nature of many conflicts (Themnér and Wallensteen 2013:515–516). Such conflicts are particularly difficult to address via agreements given the challenge of negotiating between many parties. Given that many recent civil wars have involved multiple parties, this might help explain the decline of agreements.

Using the UCDP dataset on peace agreements from 1989 to 2005, 144 accords between warring parties, which cover one third of 121 armed conflicts, were identified. Of these accords, 142 were for intrastate conflicts and two for interstate conflicts. Three groups of agreements were distinguished. The most clear-cut was a full agreement where at least one dyad agreed to settle the whole incompatibility, with 43 such agreements recorded. Another 79 partial agreements, whereby the parties in at least one dyad agreed to settle part of the incompatibility, were made. Finally, there were 22 peace process agreements. These agreements involved at least one conflict dyad agreeing to initiate a process to settle the incompatibility, such as through peace talks (Harbom, Högbladh, and Wallensteen 2006:622–624).

Further information is provided by the "Peace Accords Matrix" (Kroc Institute 2012) developed by the Kroc Institute for International Peace Studies and UCDP to study comprehensive peace agreements (CPAs). A CPA is defined as a written document produced through negotiations. It is comprehensive in two dimensions. First, the major conflict parties are involved in the negotiations process. Second, the negotiation process includes substantive issues underlying the conflict. A CPA is defined by the process and product of negotiations, not the written document's implementation or impact. An agreement can still be comprehensive even if it does not lead to a comprehensive peace. The matrix outlines 35 such agreements from 1989 to 2004 in countries including Lebanon, Cambodia, and Bosnia and Herzegovina (see Table 6.2).

Various factors can influence the likelihood of a peace agreement being signed and its outcome. Here, a model developed by Mason, Weingarten, and Fett (1999) is particularly relevant. This implies that a settlement becomes more likely as estimates of the probability of victory decline, conflict costs increase, the estimated time required to win increases, or the utility from a settlement increases relative to that of victory. Contrasting this, factors that increase one faction's

TABLE 6.2

Selected Comprehensive Peace Agreements (CPAs)

Country	Agreement and Date
Lebanon	Taif Accord, October 22, 1989
Cambodia	Framework for a Comprehensive Political Settlement of the Cambodia Conflict, October 23, 1991
Bosnia and Herzegovina	General Framework Agreement for Peace in Bosnia and Herzegovina, November 21, 1995
East Timor (Timor-Leste)	Agreement between the Republic of Indonesia and the Portuguese Republic on the question of East Timor, May 5, 1999
Angola	Luena Memorandum of Understanding, April 4, 2002
Sudan	Sudan Comprehensive Peace Agreement, January 9, 2005

Source: Kroc Institute for International Peace Studies, University of Notre Dame (2012).

probability of victory, increase its payoffs from victory, reduce conflict costs, and/ or reduce the time required to win increase that faction's probability of victory and reduce the likelihood of a settlement. The scholars tested these propositions with a model that correctly predicted the outcome in 86 percent of the cases (Mason et al. 1999:239). With regard to the settlement's actual outcome, a statistical analysis of peace agreement concessions since 1989 indicated that rebels received substantially greater concessions when there was a mediator biased in their favor, while measures of relative strength and the costliness of combat were not associated with benefit distribution. The analysis also showed that rebel groups with an ethnic identity obtained greater concessions than those without (Cunningham 2012).

The U.S. Institute of Peace (USIP), an independent, nonpartisan conflict management center established by Congress to prevent and mitigate international conflict without resorting to violence, has identified common provisions included in agreements. This list includes security guarantees, human rights protections, elections, implementation strategies, timetables, return of displaced peoples, and disarmament/demobilization and reintegration (DDR) (see Smith and Smock 2008, Table 6.3). Here power sharing, territorial autonomy, and electoral and amnesty provisions are outlined along with their impact on the successful implementation of a peace agreement.

POWER-SHARING PROVISIONS

Relinquishing control over conquered territory and creating a new central government is important for groups seeking to end civil war through negotiation. Research has identified dangers of concentrating power with a single party or individual, and various scholars agree that deeply divided societies can best be governed via sharing power. Divided societies can be more stable and peaceful: Power is decentralized in a federal system; power is dispersed via a parliamentary rather than presidential system; individuals are elected through the proportion of votes cast rather than a strict majority; and proportional systems tend to be more consensual (Walter 1999:138–139). The importance of former enemies working together has been noted. For instance, successfully ending ethnic war requires faction leaders changing their nationalist discourses to justify peace and reconciliation, while reducing hostile discourses. Simultaneously, the societies themselves must rebuild their relationship into one cooperative enough to facilitate the resolving of mutual problems and compatible with positive images and attitudes toward the other group (Kaufman 2006a:215). Other scholars have also written that a stable postwar peace is helped by preventing either side from permanently excluding others from the political process (Fortna 2008).

Four types of power-sharing arrangements are typically identified: political, territorial, military, and economic. Political power-sharing rules stipulate that a new executive, legislative, and civil service be established so that factions share power. Territorial power sharing gives the rebel group autonomy to control local politics in a specific region or mandates a federal state where subunits have power relative to the central government. Military power sharing often allows both parties' troops in a new joint defense force and/or the appointment of rebels to high military ranks. Economic power sharing seeks a more balanced distribution of economic resources via redistributive policies (Mattes and Savun 2009:741). Walter (2002) writes that political power sharing involving a guaranteed share of cabinet posts or specific quotas in a main government branch along with military and territorial power sharing are important. Her research indicates that both political and territorial power sharing make it more likely that opponents sign a peace deal and that peace is maintained for at least 5 years (Mattes and Savun 2009:741). The Centre for the Study of Civil War (CSCW) has identified three key policy components often included in power-sharing negotiations: (a) recognition of ethnic and religious group rights, (b) inclusion of a "sunset" date (a limitation on the duration of power sharing), and (c) wealth sharing (formulas that distribute the state's resources or economic product among different regions or social groups) (Gates 2006–2011).

Settlements often include power-sharing provisions. The UCDP dataset on peace agreements 1989 to 2005 identified 48 percent of all agreements addressing intrastate conflict over government as including provisions on elections. Another 30 percent had provisions on the composition of an interim government, 28 percent on integration into the government civil service, and 15 percent on power sharing. The integration of former combatants into the army was provided for in 43 percent of agreements relating to intrastate conflicts over government and 27 percent over territory (Harbom et al. 2006:624).

Of 48 negotiated civil war settlements from 1945 to 2005, 14 (30 percent) included political power-sharing provisions. These were any of the following: legislative elections based on proportional or equal representation, each group being guaranteed cabinet and ministerial posts, and representation in the civil service. Ten (22 percent) had two of these provisions, and another 10 (22 percent) had only one provision. Military power sharing involved the military forces of factions being integrated into the new state's defense force, along with rebel representatives appointed to leadership positions. Seven cases (15 percent) had both these military provisions with 22 (48 percent) having one. Economic power-sharing provisions included resource redistribution to favor disadvantaged groups and specific redistributive policies, such as a percentage share of oil revenues. Three cases (7 percent) had both these provisions with 13 cases (28 percent) having one. Finally, territorial power-sharing provisions involved the group exercising control over local issues in a particular region (autonomy) and all subunits being given powers separate from the central government (federalism). No agreements had both of these provisions, but 16 cases (35 percent) included one (Mattes and Savun 2009:747–749, 756). Of the CPAs identified in the "Peace Accords Matrix," 17 included power sharing via a transitional government and three territorial power sharing (Kroc Institute 2012).

According to Hartzell and Hoddie (2007), civil war settlements including power-sharing and power-dividing institutions were most likely to provide enduring peace. First, institutions can be designed to address group concerns over the state's postwar control of political, economic, territorial, and military power. Second, creating institutions can signal a credible commitment to build long-term peace. The scholars' study of civil wars concluded through negotiations from 1945 to 1999, and they found that the durability of peace was strengthened by creating more power-sharing and power-dividing institutions. They suggested that implementing peace agreements including power-sharing institutions provided an opportunity for former combatants autonomously to overcome mutual distrust (Hartzell and Hoddie 2007). The nature of the war's conclusion can influence the success of political power-sharing agreements too. For example, if the war ended in a military stalemate, the government may exploit its offer of political power sharing to insurgents to misrepresent information about its military capacity and then defeat the insurgency. This can exacerbate commitment problems, increase support for insurgent leaders from civilian supporters, and ultimately increase the likelihood of renewed fighting (Mukherjee 2006). Civil war may lead to more inclusive polities if it serves to even the balance of power between contending groups. A balance is more likely to bring about more democratic polities, especially where power sharing is formalized in a negotiated settlement (Gurses and Mason 2008).

The difficulty of implementing power-sharing agreements impacts their durability. DeRouen, Lea, and Wallensteen (2009) write that power-sharing provisions that are costlier to the government and more difficult to implement decrease the agreement's life span. This is because of the government's motivations to renegotiate politically costly terms and rebel incentives to strike preemptively before the government does, or out of frustration with delays in implementing costly provisions. Hence, governments abandon the agreement because it concedes too much, or rebels abandon the agreement because of implementation delays and/or to act preemptively. The authors examined three forms of power-sharing provisions: military (integration of rebels into the army), territorial (autonomy), and political (shared government). The results indicated that the less costly concessions by government of military integration and autonomy increased the duration of peace agreements, while political power-sharing provisions had a negative but insignificant impact on duration (DeRouen et al. 2009).

The difficulties of ensuring stable peace through power sharing are illustrated by various conflicts. Major ethnic conflicts settled by compromise deals among the fighting factions often ultimately collapse. Peace agreements in Lebanon (1958 and 1976) failed with further fighting. Moreover, international efforts to promote power sharing can have major negative consequences. The 1994 Rwanda genocide was staged by Hutu extremists attempting to prevent implementation of a UN-sponsored power-sharing deal with a minority Tutsi-led rebel group. Likewise, when East Timorese voted for independence from Indonesia in a 1999 UN-sponsored deal, militia groups supported by the Indonesian military undertook massacres. More recently, moves to ensure fairer political power sharing in Iraq have not ended the violence. In February 2013, about 35 people were killed in two attacks in Kirkuk, a city in northern Iraq with many Kurds. This was despite the country formally being a parliamentary democracy with a 325-seat unicameral Council of Representatives. The council has 317 members elected by an optional open list and representing a specific governorate, proportional representation system and eight seats reserved for minorities (Central Intelligence Agency [CIA] 2013b). Furthermore, the country is classified as *not free* by Freedom House, the later section on democratization providing more coverage of freedoms.

Electoral Provisions

Over one third of civil war peace treaties signed between 1989 and 2005 included a provision for elections or electoral reforms. These elections became increasingly likely shortly after the civil war ended, the average time to the first post-civil war election falling from 5.5 years to 2.7 years (Brancati and Snyder 2011:470, 474). The actual timing of the first post-conflict election was primarily influenced by the balance of power between governments and rebels at the war's conclusion and the level of international involvement in post-conflict countries. Early elections were most likely when peace was tenuous and incumbents and rebels evenly matched, as frequently occurred when wars ended in settlements and truces. In this context, rebels were strong enough militarily to insist on elections, while international actors are capable of using their leverage to encourage early elections. When wars concluded in settlements and truces, rebels were likely to demand elections to win power and politically achieve their goals. For instance, this encouraged Nepal's Maoist rebels to make elections a central part of negotiations to end that country's civil war in 2006 (Brancati and Snyder 2011:473).

However, research indicates that holding elections soon after a civil war ends might increase the possibility of renewed fighting. Quick elections may increase the likelihood that one faction will reject the results and have the ability to resume fighting. Furthermore, early postwar elections can increase the prospect that the newly elected government consists of antireform elites who adopt policies likely to renew conflict. Elections involving evenly balanced armed parties without institutionalized guarantees of group security are especially dangerous. Thus, elections can lead back to war when they follow negotiated settlements or truces rather than decisive military victories, occur without power-sharing agreements, and precede the rebel army's demobilization and creation of strong governmental institutions (Brancati and Snyder 2011:470). Iraq again is a relevant case study as fighting has continued despite elections. Iraqis voted in December 2005 for the first full-term government and parliament since the U.S.-led invasion, with the most recent election in March 2010.

Territorial Provisions

Territorial autonomy can allow one (or more) subunits of a country to exercise control over local issues, without extending those powers to other subunits (Hartzell et al. 2001:205). Although groups may demand independence or sovereignty while the government seeks to strengthen its central control, autonomy may be acceptable to both. This is because it can allow each group to promote its interests and ensure that the other does not gain predominance on certain matters. Autonomy can reassure groups that state power will not be seized by one group and used to threaten them. By increasing policy-making influence at the subnational level while reducing central powers, groups can feel better protected from the central authority. Similarly, autonomy can be used to divide or balance power, such as through including groups in the central government. Autonomy can help to reduce competition among rival groups in a divided society, perhaps via addressing group disparities by enabling a minority people to advance within their own state bureaucracies and education systems. Providing resources and opportunities available at the subunit level can diffuse some of the economic power controlled by the political center too (Hartzell et al. 2001:191–192).

The frequency and effectiveness of this provision has been included in a study of 103 conflicts from 1945 to 1998. These conflicts had at least 1,000 battle deaths per year, the government was one of the fighting factions, there was effective resistance by both the national government and its adversaries during the conflict, and fighting occurred within a defined political unit (Hartzell et al. 2001:193–194). Of these conflicts, 13 were still unresolved at the end of 1998, and 49 ended in a military victory for one side. However, 41 were concluded through negotiated settlement with factional representatives holding direct talks. Of 38 peace agreements examined, 18 had territorial autonomy provisions. These included agreements to end conflicts in India (1946–1949), Sudan (1963–1972), the Philippines (1972–1996), Nicaragua (1981–1989), and Bosnia (1992–1995) (Hartzell et al. 2001:194, 204–205).

Research indicates that autonomy provisions can enhance peace agreement durability. The above study found that only 44 percent of agreements without a territorial arrangement were still in force after 5 years compared with a survival rate of 65 percent among those providing for regional autonomy. Territorial autonomy has the advantage of being a relatively flexible provision that can be designed for specific conflicts and by its nature suggests a compromise between factions (Hartzell et al. 2001:191, 200). Moreover, statistical modeling indicates increasing representativeness encouraged public participation by the potentially secessionist, regionally concentrated minority and decreased secessionist activity. This especially occurred when semiautonomous governing structures were created (Lustick, Miodownik, and Eidelson 2004:223).

However, regional autonomy deals may be unreachable when fluctuations in state strength undermine the government's ability to commit. According to Fearon (2004), commitment to an autonomy agreement becomes harder when the center has an enduring political or economic interest in expansion into the periphery. This can occur during sons-of-the-soil wars and when either the government or rebels are able to earn some income while fighting despite the conflict's costs, as might be generated through contraband funding (Fearon 2004:275). Autonomy does not necessarily establish long-term peace. Sudan's first civil war settled via a 1972 deal giving autonomy to the South collapsed with renewed fighting in 1983. Nor has the 2003 granting of more autonomy to Chechnya while enshrining its position within the Russian Federation prevented violence from occurring there. Similarly, violence plagues the southern island of Mindanao in the Philippines where insurgents have been fighting for decades to establish a separate Islamic state. This conflict has continued despite controversial moves to address the issue that have included the prospect of autonomy. There is also debate over the effectiveness of autonomy in producing long-term peace when conflict is based on ethnicity (Downes 2004:246).

Taking autonomy further, an agreement might seek to address secessionist movements by partitioning them or breaking them apart, as in Ethiopia-Eritrea. *Partitioning* is a process whereby a group of people defined by features such as their ethnicity or ideology extracts itself, together with the land it inhabits, from an existing state (Tir 2005:548). An internally motivated partition results in the division of a country's homeland territory with the creation of at least one new independent secessionist state (for instance, Eritrea in 1991). This leaves behind the now territorially smaller *rump state* (Ethiopia). Partitioning might occur to prevent tensions escalating into conflict (Yugoslavia-Macedonia), or to end conflict that has already started (Yugoslavia-Slovenia) (Tir 2005:545). Researchers in a study of partitions from 1900 to 1996 involving 19 rump states concluded that peaceful partitions were more beneficial than their violent counterparts, secessionist states were less likely to experience conflict than rump states, and partitioning for ethnic reasons did not increase the likelihood of future conflict (Tir 2005:545). The establishment of secessionist states though does not necessarily ensure peace. East Timor (Timor-Leste) became independent from Indonesia during May 2002 and South Sudan from Sudan in July 2011 after conflict, but both continue to face serious challenges such as violence.

Amnesty Provisions

The UCDP data from 1989 to 2005 on peace agreements showed that 30 percent of all agreements for intrastate conflicts over government and 27 percent over territory included amnesty provisions (Harbom et al. 2006:624). Of the CPAs identified in the "Peace Accords Matrix" (Kroc Institute 2012), 20 referred to amnesties. These agreements include the 1992 General Peace Agreement for Mozambique and the 2005 Memorandum of Understanding between the Government of the Republic of Indonesia and the Free Aceh Movement (Kroc Institute 2012). The coexistence of former enemies within one state generally involves new and increased vulnerabilities for the combatants and faction leaders. Individuals who have survived a conflict by hiding from and fighting their enemy must in a peace process often disarm, disband their units, and leave the relative protection of defensive positions or hiding places. To encourage this, combatants must be desperate for peace or strongly think that their increased vulnerability will not be exploited. Amnesties can help build this thinking (Melander 2009:7).

A study of peace agreements from 1989 to 2005 showed that only 26 percent of the agreements with amnesty provisions ended in renewed fighting within 2 years, while the failure rate for those agreements without these was 48 percent. However, the impact of amnesty provisions depended on the regime. They significantly reduced the risk of agreement failure only if the political institutions were authoritarian. This was because within democratic societies, the amnesties were more likely to be questioned with the fundamental clash between impunity for war crimes and the principles of human rights and the rule of law (Melander 2009:8, 13, 15). Amnesties can be very controversial as those wanted for serious human rights violations might escape justice. For instance, the 1999 Lomé Peace Accord's amnesty provision for human rights violations by warring factions in Sierra Leone was widely criticized because of post-accord violence, and the notorious crimes committed by the Foday Sankoh-led Revolutionary United Front faction. Sankoh was ultimately arrested in 2000 but died in 2003 during his trial for war crimes.

Agreement Implementation

The successful implementation of peace agreements is important. Indeed, the implementation of an intrastate peace agreement may actually be a much greater challenge for the parties than the initial agreement negotiations (Boltjes 2007). This is graphically shown by the two worst outbreaks of mass violence in the 1990s (Angola in 1993 and Rwanda in 1994) following the failure of peace agreements to end these wars. They cost an estimated 350,000 lives in Angola and 800,000 in Rwanda (Stedman 2001:4). The period immediately after the signing of an agreement is particularly important. The study of agreements from 1989 to 2005 mentioned above indicated that since the Cold War's end, the first two years are vital for durable peace. An agreement that held over these initial years had a 94 percent chance of averting renewed fighting in later years (Melander 2009:4).

The U.S. Institute of Peace identifies factors that can increase the likelihood of successful agreement implementation (see Table 6.3). These factors (apart from external parties covered in Chapter 7) are briefly outlined below:

Incorporate strategies for implementation and monitoring. A key factor is the inclusion of strategies for implementation and for monitoring, and (if possible) enforcing compliance with the agreement's terms. Clarity is needed over who does what by when, how performance is measured and by whom, and what happens if targets are not met.

TABLE 6.3
Selected Features That Can Assist Implementation of Agreements

- Incorporating in agreements strategies for implementation and monitoring
- Planning for implementation
- Making the local population stakeholders and agreement guarantors
- Using metrics to gauge progress
- Designing dispute resolution mechanisms
- Using external parties to support implementation

Source: Smith and Smock (2008).

Plan for implementation. Overly ambitious agreements without the resources, skills, and commitment to enforce them can cause damage by disillusioning the parties and encouraging the view that fighting is the only feasible way to achieving their goals. Thus, the conflict parties, affected societies, and external partners must be mobilized to assist implementation, from planning and managing to monitoring and enforcing. Plans should take into account the immediate transitions from violence and long-term post-conflict issues.

Make the local population stakeholders and agreement guarantors. Agreements should include the local community as planners, agents, managers, and implementation monitors. Utilizing local knowledge, networks, and leadership provides more resources for implementation, builds social capital, and strengthens local ownership, raising civil society's stake in the implementation. A successful and durable peace will be more likely with the society's full mobilization to implement agreement benchmarks. Local business community members can be directly involved in the economic reintegration of fighters, and traditional justice mechanisms or religious practices can be used to facilitate reconciliation, while local materials and labor can be utilized in reconstruction. Furthermore, local human rights monitors can help safeguard returning refugees, local stewards can keep watch to prevent corruption and waste, and local media can inform the community of developments. Ultimately, societal actors should be involved in ways that make them stakeholders and agreement guarantors rather than passive onlookers.

Use metrics to gauge progress. *Metrics* (measurable indicators of progress) can contribute to agreement formulation and implementation. More specifically, metrics help ensure the mediator and parties establish realistic goals, provide adequate resources and authorities to bear, strategically focus their efforts, and increase the likelihood of a stable peace. It is vital during the peace process to obtain baseline data to help diagnose potential challenges prior to an agreement. Likewise, during implementation, it is important to track progress from the point of the settlement through to sustained peace. The most important metrics must measure results and impact rather than level of effort as these are essential to agreement implementation. For example, the UN mission in Kosovo developed a set of metrics to evaluate progress toward meeting standards in core areas of governance and human rights. These had to be met before the international community would initiate a diplomatic process aimed at resolving the issue of Kosovo's political status.

Design dispute resolution mechanisms. During the transition from conflict, agreements often falter. Implementation designs should include mechanisms to review progress and address problems. Roundtables, implementation councils, or joint committees should be present to hear grievances, mediate disputes, and make implementation adjustments. The establishment of a monitoring and conflict resolution mechanism by the parties to the agreement may be sufficient (Smith and Smock 2008).

As already noted, research indicates that various factors can influence the durability of negotiated agreements. Success may lie in using various measures appropriate for the situation and the political regime—and not only by principal parties to the main peace process but also by other relevant actors (Boltjes 2007:2). The most durable agreements are often those concerning states where the previous stable regime was democratic and are concluding extended low-intensity conflicts. They also provide security assurances to former fighters by third-party states or regional or international organizations and provide territorial autonomy to threatened groups. Contrasting this, negotiated agreements where the states lack experience with democracy and have just concluded brief, highly intense wars can be more likely to fail in the short term. This is particularly when the negotiating parties do not include territorial autonomy and third-party security assurances in their agreements (Hartzell et al. 2001:202). An analysis of the numerous peace agreements of Liberia's first civil war (1989–1996) indicates that agreement implementation progresses if the level of vulnerability during the implementation period is equally balanced among the faction leaders. Thus, as agreement concessions will bring some change in military, economic, or political vulnerability among the factions, the implementation process proceeds when faction leaders feel mutually vulnerable (Bekoe 2003). Research has indicated that the demobilization of fighters and their reintegration into civilian life is vital for peace implementation (Stedman 2001:16).

POST-CONFLICT ISSUES

Civil wars have devastating consequences (see Chapter 2), and in their aftermath, many issues need to be addressed to increase the prospect of sustainable peace. After fighting ends, there is normally extensive damage to the state's institutions and infrastructure that can hinder the provision of security and basic services to citizens. Likewise, there is a need to improve the poor political rights and freedoms that often exist at the end of civil wars where factions have determinedly sought to exercise and hold power at any price. Hence, both statebuilding and democratization efforts are important, particularly given that strong democratic states should experience fewer civil wars. Peacebuilding, the overall consolidation of peace through tools that can include addressing underlying sources of conflict and strengthening respect for human rights, is another important tool. The next sections outline these three key concepts—statebuilding, democratization, and peacebuilding—within the context of post-civil war society.

Statebuilding

Statebuilding refers to the strengthening of state capacity by building institutions (e.g., judicial system), enhancing state legitimacy and responsiveness of the state, and enhancing overall service delivery of the government. Statebuilding is obviously most relevant in the case of failed states—those states which have ceased to function in terms of providing security and basic services for the citizens. Statebuilding is tied to civil war termination in cases where the conflict occurs in a failed, failing or weak, or new or fragile state. These types of wars have taken place in Timor-Leste (new, fragile state), Somalia (failed state), South Sudan (new, fragile state), Democratic Republic of Congo (fragile state), and others. In these situations, peacebuilding is a vital step in the progress toward building a strong state able to meet the needs of its people and deter further rebellion. Goldfinch and DeRouen (2014) note that post-termination settings in these states are notoriously unstable. Third-party actors and the state faced with building a stable state must first establish peace. In other words, once a war in a low-capacity state terminates, peace must take root before adequate state mechanisms can be established and more war headed off.

The Failed States Index is a useful indicator of the overall impact of conflict on the state and subsequent challenges faced in state rebuilding. This annual index is by *Foreign Policy Magazine* and The Fund for Peace, a research and educational organization working to prevent war and promote sustainable peace. The index examines 12 indicators divided into social, economic, and political categories. The social indicators are increasing demographic pressures, the mass movement of refugees or internally displaced persons creating complex humanitarian emergencies, the legacy of vengeance-seeking group or group paranoia, and chronic and sustained human flight. The economic indicators are uneven economic development along group lines and sharp and/or severe economic decline. The third category consists of political indicators. These are the state's criminalization and/or delegitimization, the progressive deterioration of public services, the suspension or arbitrary application of the rule of law, and widespread violation of human rights, the security apparatus operating as a state within a state, the rise of factionalized elites, and the intervention of other states or external political actors.

A failing state has various attributes. One of the most common is lost physical control of territory or of a monopoly on the legitimate use of force. Others include the erosion of legitimate authority to make collective decisions, an inability to provide reasonable public services, and the failure to interact with other states as a full member of the international community (Fund for Peace 2011). The 2012 index surveyed 178 states and listed the top failed states as Somalia, the

Democratic Republic of the Congo (DRC), and Sudan (see Table 6.4). This was the fifth time in a row that Somalia led the rankings. All of the top-10 failed states have witnessed conflict in recent years. The impact of conflict is further shown by the significant worsening of ratings for Libya and Syria because of fighting. Libya's decline was the most remarkable, the country registering the worst year-on-year change in the index's history. It fell from to 111th to 50th as a result of civil war, NATO-led air strikes, and the toppling of Muammar Gaddafi's regime. Similarly, Syria registered the fourth-greatest year-on-year negative change in history as escalated fighting against the Assad government led it to fall from 48th to 23rd, the bloody costs of this fighting noted in Chapter 2 (Fund for Peace 2012:13, 15, 25).

Many factors contribute to the failure of states. Acemoglu and Robinson (2012a) have outlined 10 main reasons for states collapsing with conflict included. According to the scholars, most countries collapse because they have what they term *extractive* economic institutions that seek to benefit the elite who then gain significantly. The extraction can take the form of forced labor, valuable minerals, or protected monopolies. Such extraction erodes incentives,

TABLE 6.4
Ten Worst Ranked Failed States in 2013 and Their 2012 Ranking

Country	2013 Ranking	2012 Ranking
Somalia	1	1
Democratic Republic of Congo	2	4
Sudan	3	3
South Sudan*	4	N/R
Chad	5	4
Yemen	6	8
Afghanistan	7	6
Haiti	8	7
Central African Republic	9	10
Zimbabwe	10	5

Source: Fund for Peace, "Failed States Index" (2011–2013).

* Although South Sudan was included for the first time as the 2012 Index's 178th country, it did not receive a formal rank for that Index as the data available since independence did not constitute a full year and, thus, could not be accurately compared to the other 177 countries.

discourages innovation, and wastes the talents of citizens, with states built on exploitation ultimately failing. The scholars identify 10 more specific reasons behind state collapses. These are the lack of property rights, forced labor, an unfair economy for most, the economic dominance of an elite few, elites blocking new technologies, no law and order, a weak central government, bad public services, political exploitation, and fighting over power (Acemoglu and Robinson 2012:89–91).

With the presence of such failed states, there have been international statebuilding efforts. This involves the complex and multidimensional set of activities aimed at promoting the creation of functioning and functional states. The main objective of statebuilding is to move a state from fragile or failed status to one where the organs of state operate and the state has full administrative control of all of its territory, effective rule of law, and stability. The importance of constructing institutional foundations for functioning governments and markets, and of identifying potential outcomes if those tasks are not undertaken, has been identified by Paris and Sisk (2009:2). For instance, the absence of mechanisms such as pre-election power-sharing pacts and institutions to uphold election results initially served as a catalyst for renewed conflict in Angola during 1992. Without arrangements ensuring that newly elected officials would themselves respect the rule of law, autocratic elites returned to undemocratic rule in Cambodia during the 1990s. Economic reforms were also blocked by black marketers in Bosnia after the 1995 Dayton Peace Accord as there were no institutions to govern the market (Paris and Sisk 2009:2). More recent moves have been made at statebuilding in Afghanistan (outlined below) and Iraq with mixed results.

There have been major recent efforts at statebuilding, with one of the largest being in Afghanistan, the 2012 sixth-ranked failed state. Both the UN Assistance Mission in Afghanistan (UNAMA) and ISAF are mandated by the UN Security Council to operate in Afghanistan, and they are there at the request of the Afghan Government. ISAF, which has been deployed since the end of 2001, has a peace-enforcement mandate and operates primarily in support of Afghanistan's National Security Forces. As an *integrated* Mission, UNAMA has two main operational areas: development and humanitarian issues, and political affairs. Both organizations have an integrated approach: coordinating governance, development, and security efforts to help the Afghan government promote peace and stability. UNAMA is mandated to support the government in its moves to improve critical areas. These include security, governance and economic development, and regional cooperation, along with the full implementation of commitments made at both 2010 London and Kabul Conferences (UNAMA, no date).

With the major international statebuilding efforts in Afghanistan, there have been positive developments, but serious challenges remain. From 2000 to 2011, life expectancy at birth increased from 45.3 years to 48.7 years, the expected years of schooling increased from 2.2 years to 9.1 years, and the standard of living measured by gross national income per capita rose from $435 to $1,416 (in constant 2005 purchasing price parity; UN Development Program 2011:2). The economy has improved since the 2001 fall of the Taliban regime primarily due to international assistance, the agricultural sector's recovery, and service sector growth. Indeed, the international community pledged over $67 billion at nine donors' conferences between 2003 and 2010. More recently, at a 2012 Tokyo donor conference, $16 billion in civilian aid was pledged up to 2016 (CIA 2013a). However, Afghanistan is extremely poor and very dependent on foreign aid. Many people continue to face shortages of housing, clean water, electricity, medical care, and paid work. Criminality, insecurity, weak governance, and the government's difficulty in extending rule of law throughout the country discourage future economic growth. Economic growth is further hindered by low revenue collection, limited job creation, widespread corruption, weak government capacity, and poor public infrastructure (CIA 2013a).

Democratization

Democratization is a process whereby the government comes to be more transparent, executive power becomes more constrained, unfettered public participation input into the election of governments becomes consolidated, and the right to be a candidate for public office is nearly universal. Democracy is associated with the peaceful resolution of conflict. All things being equal, democracies should have fewer civil wars.

In 2012, there were 47 countries identified, or ranked as *not free* by Freedom House, an independent organization supporting democratic change, monitoring freedom, and advocating for democracy and human rights internationally. In these countries, basic political rights were absent, and basic civil liberties were widely and systematically denied. Another 58 countries were *partly free* with limited respect of political rights and civil liberties (Freedom House 2013:4). More specifically, of the 11 countries experiencing conflict over government in 2010, only two were defined as *free* by Freedom House in 2012. Another five were *not free* and the others were only *partly free*. Countries were ranked from one (*the most free*) to seven (*the least free*) with both Somalia and Sudan receiving the worst possible rankings for both political rights and civil liberties. Countries experiencing conflict over territory in 2010 were better ranked, but half of the four countries were still ranked as either *not free* or *partly free* (see Table 6.5).

TABLE 6.5
Most Costly Civil Wars and Freedom of Country in 2012

Location	Freedom status	Political rights	Civil liberties
Countries with five most costly civil wars over government			
Syria	Not free	7	7
Afghanistan	Not free	6	6
Pakistan	Partly free	4	5
Somalia	Not free	7	7
Yemen	Not free	6	6
Countries with five most costly civil wars over territory			
Turkey	Partly free	3	4
Myanmar/Burma	Not free	6	5
Russia	Not free	6	5
India	Free	2	3
Thailand	Partly free	4	4

Source: Freedom House (2013:14–18) and Themnér and Wallensteen (2013:517–519).

The actual success of democratization in many post-civil war countries is debatable. In Cambodia, the civil war was ended by the 1991 Paris Peace Agreement that set a liberal democratic state as Cambodia's political goal. Elections have been held since 1993, and officially the country is a multiparty democracy under a constitutional monarchy. However, Prime Minister Hun Sen has held power since 1985 and staged a coup in 1997 to strengthen his position. There have been concerns that his rule is becoming increasingly authoritarian with Cambodia labeled *not free* by Freedom House. It scores poorly for both political representations (6) and civil liberties (5). Corruption and government unaccountability are issues, even though comparative peace has been maintained (Freedom House 2013). Moreover, although those countries still experiencing conflict might witness moves toward democracy, they still face major challenges. For example, Afghan presidential elections were staged in 2004 and 2009 and the first parliamentary elections in over 30 years occurred during 2005, with further elections taking place in 2010. However, as shown by Table 6.5, the country is termed *not free* by Freedom House, and it rates very poorly in both political rights and civil liberties.

With regard to a country's experiences with democracy, actors that have had a democratic or semidemocratic regime prior to a civil war appear more likely to have experience with the accommodation of competing interests than actors in countries whose former political regime was authoritarian. A history of inclusion at the political center, or at least the ability to compete for inclusion in central political institutions, can help address opponents' fears regarding potentially aggressive intentions by an adversary. This in turn should help reduce concerns regarding the potential for an antagonist's violations of or defections from a negotiated settlement (Hartzell et al. 2001:189). Civil wars that end in negotiated settlements are more likely to experience higher levels of democratization than civil wars that conclude in military victory by either side. Identity-based conflicts often lead to lower levels of democratization, while the impact of democratic experience on post-civil war democratization has been debated (Gurses and Mason 2008).

Post-civil war democratization helps to build sustainable post-civil war peace. However, studies of democratic transition and survival suggest that the post-civil war environment is not hospitable to either the transition toward or the survival of democracy. This inhospitality may be because post-civil war environments are contentious. After fighting, the former combatants might fear for their security and want to protect their political and economic interests. Former rivals can agree to a transition toward democracy to the extent that a stable balance of power exists between the government and rebels, a balance that eliminates the sort of security dilemma encouraging parties to resume fighting. Such a balance should ensure access to political power and economic resources (Joshi 2010). The victorious group in the postwar elections may use its democratically won power to dismantle the institutions of democracy, and repress the opposition. The fear of constant political marginalization, along with the fear of repression, might create incentives for the defeated party to reinitiate hostilities. Joshi (2013) suggests that former rivals would support democratic transition if they were confident that inclusive institutions ensured they could achieve their political interests through democracy. After analyzing data on 1946 to 2005 post-civil war transitions toward democracy, Joshi found that the proportional representation system and parliamentary system are the most important institutions helping sustain post-civil war democratic transitions (Joshi forthcoming).

Research by Joshi and Mason (2012) indicates that a larger governing coalition is more likely to emerge following negotiated settlements and government victories, compared to insurgent victories. Their findings also supported the proposition that enlarging the size of the governing coalition creates stronger incentives for former rivals to sustain the peace. This is because they can pursue their political objectives through institutional means that are less costly than a return to fighting.

Peacebuilding

Peacebuilding is a concept and practice that developed after the Cold War. The term first appeared in the 1992 report *An Agenda for Peace*. Here, UN Secretary-General Boutros Boutros-Ghali defined it broadly as "action to identify and support structures which tend to strengthen and solidify peace to avoid a relapse into conflict" (Boutros-Ghali 1992). Newman, Paris, and Richmond (2009:8) provide a slightly more expansive definition. They refer to peacebuilding as preventing a resumption or escalation of violent conflict in conflict-prone societies and establishing durable and self-sustaining peace; addressing underlying sources of conflict; building or rebuilding peaceful social institutions and values, including the respect for human rights; and building or rebuilding institutions of governance and rule of law. They then outlined peacebuilding activities. These targeted challenges that in their most acute form could weaken overall peacebuilding objectives. The definitions agree that peacebuilding means the consolidation of peace after war.

There has been debate over what constitutes the success of such operations. Doyle and Sambanis (2006) wrote that successful multilateral peacebuilding built functioning states that could defend their own interests. Indeed, such peacebuilding when well-designed and managed could produce sustainable peace from which neighbors and the wider international community would benefit, and did so while sharing costs fairly. They believed that *sustainable peace* was the measure of successful peacebuilding. This was influenced by three key factors characterizing the post-civil war peace environment. First, the degree of factional hostility measured by human cost (deaths and displacements), the type of war, and number of factions were influential. Added to this was the extent of local capacities remaining after the war, such as per capita GDP. The level of international assistance represented the final factor. This could be measured by economic assistance or the type of mandate given to a UN peace operation and number of personnel tasked with its undertaking (Doyle and Sambanis 2006:3–4).

Based on SIPRI data, a total of 52 peace operations were conducted in 2011. This was the same number as operations the previous year. The number of personnel involved in these operations was 262,129; international involvement in efforts to terminate conflict is noted in greater detail in the following chapter (SIPRI 2005–2013, *Yearbook* 2012:91). Kaufman's (2001) study of contemporary ethnic wars in the Caucasus and southeastern Europe indicated that diplomacy and economic incentives were not enough to prevent or end ethnic wars. He believed that the key to conflict resolution was peacebuilding, whereby nongovernmental organizations changed hostile attitudes at both the elite and local levels (Kaufman 2001).

Various key aspects of successful peacebuilding have been identified. Peacebuilding activities are wide-ranging. Newman et al. (2009:8–9) list a number of peacebuilding activities including the following: supporting cease-fires, demobilizing fighters, destroying weapons, resolving land ownership disputes, and protecting natural resources.

The extent of challenges facing post-conflict societies necessitates the prioritizing of peacebuilding efforts based on the importance of state functions. The state's first and primary function is to provide security and thus is the initial priority of post-conflict peacebuilding. This involves maintaining cease-fires and group disarmament, the creation of secure borders, "renationalization" of the use of force, and prevention of violence within the society. Interlinked with this is the second priority of establishing law and order. The third and fourth priorities are social and economic reconstruction, governance, and participation. Here, a basic degree of economic restructuring is important for building post-conflict confidence.

A key goal is rebuilding economies. Berdal and Wennmann (2010) have considered economic factors, such as harnessing the private sector, along with using taxes and natural-resource revenues, to provide a financial base for sustainable peace. Short-term demands for security and stability may require engagement with informal, often illiberal, power structures toward peaceful, legitimate economic activity. There is also a need to focus on significant actors and their economic interests in post-conflict countries. Resistance to strong central government does not preclude interest in and commitment to local governance systems, including law and order. Thus, external parties could target aid, encourage entrepreneurial initiative, and promote economic activity, including employment programs and direct support for businesses, at the local level. Ultimately, economic challenges facing countries emerging from conflicts, once contextualized and understood, need to be viewed as positive opportunities (Berdal and Wennmann 2010:9–13). The importance of extensive programs to rebuild economies in facilitating sustainable peace is acknowledged by others too (Doyle and Sambanis 2006:5).

IMPLICATIONS FOR CONFLICT MANAGEMENT

This chapter focuses on post-conflict issues. At first blush, there may not seem to be any conflict management issues if the war is over. However, many wars recur, and the probability of recurrence is usually highest just after a war ends. The conflict management implications of this are quite important. How a war ends can help predict whether the war will recur, for example, civil wars terminating with a military victory having lower probabilities of recurring. As discussed above, many wars end—that is, there are few or no battle-related deaths—with no clear explanation. Many others end with negotiated settlements that falter.

This chapter also considers peace agreements that often accompany the termination of a war. Peace agreements often do not endure. There are sometimes problems with implementation or one disputant will renege for any number of reasons. This party mediation and peacekeeping mission can reduce the odds that peace agreements will fail. Power-sharing provision is politically costly to governments and may lead to the government reneging on a deal when it comes time to implement these provisions (see DeRouen et al. 2009). State capacity is an important requirement for implementation to obtain (see DeRouen et al. 2010).

The post-conflict phase often involves peacebuilding and statebuilding with the former being an antecedent to the latter. The general argument is that an end to violence is required before a weak, failed, or otherwise low-capacity state can develop and sustain institutions that can provide security, effective public administration, education, service delivery, justice, and rule of law. Some critics of this peacebuilding model see it as a liberal, Western-oriented system designed to control and stabilize the developing world with a top-down approach that stresses free markets. Richmond (2011), for example, attacks the liberal model for undervaluing local actors and understating the importance of cultural diversity and indigenous populations. Paris (2004) takes a more circumspect view of the liberal model but does criticize it for pushing elections before institutions are set up. He argues that elections can actually be stabilizing and should not be rushed. In any case, the connection between peacebuilding and statebuilding is ever tighter in the post-9/11 world. The failed state of Afghanistan allowed a safe haven for al-Qaeda to train, recruit, and plan terrorist strikes.

CONCLUSION

As noted in the introduction, the devastating consequences of civil wars necessitate a better understanding of their termination and postwar issues. Four major conflicts registered for 2010 by the UCDP in Chad, Peru, India (Assam), and India (Bodoland) were no longer active in 2011. The specific outcomes of wars vary with the most common outcomes identified sometimes differing in accordance to the study and its time period. However, it is clear that a stable and durable peace is the best outcome for the war-inflicted society, the region, and international community. Thus, the signing and implementing of effective peace agreements is vital. Here, various factors can influence the likelihood of an agreement being signed and its outcome. Such an agreement can be encouraged by estimates of the probability of victory declining, conflict costs rising, the estimated time required to win increasing, or the utility from a settlement increasing relative to that of victory.

Peace agreements frequently have common provisions. In this chapter, power sharing, territorial autonomy, electoral, and amnesty provisions were outlined. Power-sharing arrangements generally cover political, territorial, military, and economic areas. Research indicates that power sharing can help effectively end conflict, but there are major challenges that need to be overcome to facilitate this. Elections or electoral reforms are frequently included in agreements, but their success rate is mixed and influenced by their timing. Regional autonomy can enhance the durability of an agreement. Taking this further, an agreement might seek to address secessionist movements by partitioning them or breaking them apart. As with the other provisions, these can help resolve conflict but do not necessarily lead to a durable end of a conflict. The granting of amnesties for fighters after conflict can be particularly controversial, especially when there have been serious violations of human rights.

The successful implementation of peace agreements is vital for a durable peace. Indeed, the implementation of agreements may actually be more challenging for the fighting parties than the initial agreement negotiations. Selected features that can assist here include careful planning for implementation and monitoring, making the local population stakeholders and agreement guarantors, and designing dispute resolution mechanisms. Success may lie in utilizing various measures appropriate for the situation and the political regime—not only by principal parties to the main peace process but also by other relevant actors. Furthermore, the most durable agreements are often those concerning states where the previous stable regime was democratic and where they conclude extended low-intensity conflicts.

Finally, state formation, democratization, and peacebuilding after wars were outlined. Conflict is often associated with failed states, and there have been international state building efforts. Statebuilding involves the complex and multidimensional set of activities aimed at promoting the creation of functioning and functional states. There have been major recent efforts at statebuilding, with one of the largest being in Afghanistan. Democratization efforts frequently are supported by the international community in post-conflict countries. Such efforts can help build a peace, but the post-civil war environment can be inhospitable for democracy. Peacebuilding includes preventing the resumption or escalation of fighting and establishing a durable and self-sustaining peace, addressing the underlying sources of conflict, and building or rebuilding peaceful social institutions and values. As with other efforts to effectively address conflict, major challenges face such endeavors. Ultimately, it is more effective to prevent the initial outbreak of war than to attempt to find a durable peace once fighting plagues a society.

More specifically, the next chapter covers international intervention and the termination of civil wars.

SUGGESTED READING

Brandt, Patrick T., T. David Mason, Mehmet Gurses, Nicolai Petrovsky, and Dagmar Radin. 2008. "When and How the Fighting Stops: Explaining the Duration and Outcome of Civil Wars." *Defense and Peace Economics* 19(6):415–434.

DeRouen, Karl and Jacob Bercovitch. 2008. "Enduring Internal Rivalries: A New Framework for the Study of Civil War." *Journal of Peace Research* 45(1):55–74.

DeRouen, Karl, Jenna Lea, and Peter Wallensteen. 2009. "The Duration of Civil War Peace Agreements." *Conflict Management and Peace Science* 26(4):367–387.

DeRouen, Karl R., Jr. and David Sobek. 2004. "The Dynamics of Civil War Duration and Outcome." *Journal of Peace Research* 41(3):303–320.

Doyle, Michael W. and Nicholas Sambanis. 2000. "International Peacebuilding: A Theoretical and Quantitative Analysis." *American Political Science Review* 94(4):779–801.

Doyle, Michael W. and Nicholas Sambanis. 2006. *Making War & Building Peace: United Nations Peace Operations*. Princeton, New Jersey: Princeton University Press.

Harbom, Lotta, Stina Högbladh, and Peter Wallensteen. 2006. "Armed Conflict and Peace Agreements." *Journal of Peace Research* 43(5):617–631.

Hartzell, Caroline A., Matthew Hoddie, and Donald Rothchild. 2001. "Stabilizing the Peace after Civil War: An Investigation of Some Key Variables." *International Organization* 55(1):183–208.

Kreutz, Joakim. 2010. "How and When Armed Conflicts End: Introducing the UCDP Conflict Termination Dataset." *Journal of Peace Research* 47(2):243–250.

Paris R. 2004. *At War's End: Building Peace after Civil Conflict.* Cambridge, UK: Cambridge University Press.

Wolf, Albert B. 2011. "War Termination." P. 1756 in *The Encyclopedia of Political Science*, edited by G. T. Kurian. Washington, DC: CQ Press.

CHAPTER 7

International Intervention

S ince the end of the Cold War, the international community has mounted a major effort to address civil wars, and in this chapter, we will focus on the role international actors play in terminating these conflicts. Though we will discuss several actors, we pay special attention to the United Nations given that the organization has played such a significant role in international interventions since its creation. We will consider the United Nations' historical and current peacekeeping operations, along with those conducted by other key actors, and will also assess their effectiveness. The use of mediation, the process of conflict management related to but distinct from the parties' own negotiations, is then noted. The mediators themselves—again, the United Nations is a major actor—are identified along with various mediation types and the likelihood of success. Although we have previously examined peace agreements and international military intervention (see Chapters 3 and 6), we will discuss military interventions that are more specifically associated with peace agreements. Finally, we look briefly at humanitarian law, emphasizing the role of international instruments in preventing and addressing the violation of human rights.

TYPES OF INTERNATIONAL INTERVENTIONS

International interventions occur when external actors become actively involved in civil wars. As noted in Chapter 3, internationalized conflicts have become increasingly common. Those since 2001 can be divided into two general groups: conflicts linked to the U.S. "global war against terrorism" and those where governments intervene in neighboring domestic conflicts (SIPRI 2005-2013, *Yearbook* 2012:67). Internationalized civil wars from 2002 to 2012 were at their lowest number in 2003 (two) and peaked at nine in 2010 and 2011. They declined to eight during 2012 (SIPRI 2005-2013, *Yearbook* 2013:47; UCDP 2014b). External actors can become active in civil wars in different ways, ranging from the deployment of their own forces to indirectly helping finance and equip those they support.

Various scholars have studied international interventions. Evidence indicates that states are most likely to intervene when they have the greatest impact on a civil war's outcome (Gent 2008). According to De Nevers (2007), when great powers seek to promote new norms, they coerce the weak and use persuasion with the strong. The international standing of a target state and its power relative to the great power helps explain whether force is used to promote norms. Power appears to be the best defense against being targeted by a great power, with good standing in the international community another key deterrent (De Nevers 2007:53). Saideman (2002) has identified approaches to address the challenge of encouraging states with different and often contrasting preferences to support a common intervention policy. Motivated actors should cooperate with states sharing similar preferences or converging goals rather than trying to bring into the intervention those with opposing interests. As this may anger excluded states, the trade-offs between intervention and good relations with countries supporting a different conflict party need to be appreciated.

When countries are unwilling to intervene, the act can be subcontracted to those who are more willing. However, major problems include how the international community holds intervening states accountable, especially as those states may not be its best agents. Furthermore, there is the question of whether the international community subsidizes or assists the intervening countries. Particular definitions of a conflict may encourage a greater consensus among outsiders, leading to more intervention support. A critical obstacle to conflict management is sovereignty. Given the current international system, one country cannot simply decide that another country does not enjoy sovereignty, even if that country is not behaving responsibly toward its citizens, because there is no universal international consensus that sovereignty is abrogated by such actions. Syria provides a pertinent example here. If the international community wanted respect for sovereignty to be conditional based on responsible treatment of citizens, then that would need to be negotiated among states, thus, encouraging common consensus. A single intervention is insufficient to change the meaning and impact of sovereignty, but efforts by different groups of countries may eventually produce a new norm that outsiders can, and should, assist groups at risk. This would not legitimate all interventions but only those satisfying the shared interpretation (Saideman 2002:85–86).

Regan's (2002a:141) analysis of post-World War II international interventions in civil war to 1994 found that the likelihood of successful intervention was less than 20 percent. However, interventions were more likely to be successful when conflicts were quite intense. Given a set of base conditions, intervention into an intense conflict had about a 70 percent chance of successfully ending the fighting.

Supporting the government rather than opposition increased the likelihood of success, while the type of conflict also influenced the outcome. Interventions into intense ideological conflicts had a 47 percent lower probability of success than the same interventions into religious conflicts. Those into ethnically orientated conflicts were 30 percent less likely to be successful. In another study, Regan (2002b:55) examined 150 conflicts from 1945 to 1999. His results suggested that interventions tended to extend civil war durations rather than shorten them. A study of interventions in low-intensity intrastate conflicts from 1993 to 2004 found that the Middle East had the most involvement relative to the number of active conflict dyads, whereas Asia was relatively neglected. International third-party efforts were relatively constant with the exception of a major increase linked to the Israeli-Palestinian conflict from 2000 to 2002. The most active third parties included major powers, intergovernmental organizations, and a few middle powers (Melander, Möller, and Öberg 2009).

International peacekeeping works to create the conditions for lasting peace in a country experiencing conflict (UN 2013). These interventions can have a positive impact on addressing conflict by reducing the risk of fighting. The effectiveness of peacekeeping is influenced by the operation's nature. Unarmed or lightly armed peacekeepers with strictly limited mandates can be less effective, while strong mandates seem particularly helpful in reducing violence when fighting has yet to cease. Well-resourced operations can be more effective as a robust mandate requires a larger budget to be implemented. A study covering 1970 to 2009 reported that peacekeeping operations reduced conflict. This effect was largely limited to preventing major armed conflicts. However, there was a discernible indirect impact as a reduction in conflict intensity tended to reduce the risk of minor conflict in following years. Operations appeared to have the strongest effect in regions with more major conflicts, such as West Asia and North Africa (Hegre, Hultman, and Nygård 2010:24).

UN peacekeeping began during 1948 with military observers deployed in the Middle East to monitor the Armistice Agreement between Israel and its Arab neighbors (this became known as the UN Truce Supervision Organization [UNTSO] and continues to operate). Early peacekeeping (sometimes called first-generation peacekeeping) was primarily limited to maintaining cease-fires between countries, stabilizing situations on the ground, and providing vital support for political efforts to peacefully resolve conflict. The earliest armed peacekeeping operation was the first UN Emergency Force deployed in 1956 to address the Suez Crisis (this ended in 1967). The UN Operation in the Congo launched in 1960 was the first large-scale mission with nearly 20,000 military personnel at its peak and was active until 1964. During the 1960s and 1970s, the United Nations established short-term missions including those in the Dominican Republic (1965–1966) along with longer-term deployments, as in Cyprus (1964 to present) and Lebanon (1978 to present). Five missions started during the 1980s (see Table 7.1), including the Iran-Iraq Military Observation Group from 1988 to 1991. UN peacekeepers were awarded the 1988 Nobel Peace Prize.

With the Cold War concluding, the UN operations shifted and expanded, moving from generally observational tasks by military personnel to complex "multidimensional" missions. Post-Cold War peacekeeping operations are often referred to as *second generation* while those during the Cold War are called *first generation*. These second-generation peacekeeping missions aimed to ensure comprehensive peace agreements were implemented and to help provide foundations for sustainable peace. A total of 20 new operations were authorized between 1989 and 1994, as in El Salvador (1991 to 1995) and Mozambique (1992 to 1994). Such operations increased the number of peacekeepers from 11,000 to 75,000. Peacekeeping operations were deployed to assist with implementing complex peace agreements, stabilize the security situation, reorganize the military and police, elect new governments, and construct democratic institutions. Some operations were controversial, especially during the mid-1990s as noted below, but with continuing crises occurring internationally, the fundamental role of UN peacekeeping was reaffirmed. In the second half of the 1990s, the UN Security Council authorized new operations. These ranged from short-term (Guatemala 1997) to long-term operations (Kosovo 1999 to present). With the 21st century's arrival, peacekeeping challenges were examined. This led to the introduction of reform aimed at strengthening the UN's capability to effectively manage and sustain field operations (UN Peacekeeping 2013). Numerous operations have started during the new century, as in Haiti (2004 to present) (see Table 7.1).

The UN and Other Actors

SIPRI provides data on peace operations carried out under UN authority and operations by regional organizations or by ad hoc coalitions of states that were

TABLE 7.1
Number of UN Peacekeeping Operations 1948 to 2013 by Decade

Years*	1940s	1950s	1960s	1970s	1980s	1990s	2000–2013
Operations	2	2	6	3	5	35	15

Source: UN (2014b).

* Period in which peacekeeping operations started.

UN-sanctioned or authorized by a UN Security Council resolution. They have the stated intention to (a) serve as an instrument to facilitate the implementation of peace agreements already in place, (b) support a peace process, or (c) assist conflict prevention and/or peacebuilding efforts. The SIPRI utilizes the UN Department of Peacekeeping Operations description of peacekeeping as a mechanism to help conflict-inflicted countries to create conditions for sustainable peace. As it is a key player in civil war conflict management, the United Nations is explored in greater detail in Box 7.1. This might include monitoring and observing cease-fire agreements; serving as confidence-building measures; protecting the delivery of humanitarian aid; helping with the demobilization and reintegration process; building institutional capacities in the areas of judiciary and the rule of law (including penal institutions), policing, and human rights; electoral support; and economic and social development (SIPRI 2013b).

BOX 7.1 The United Nations

The United Nations is an international organization founded by 51 countries in 1945 after WWII. It has four main purposes: to keep peace internationally; to develop friendly relations among nations; to help nations work together to improve the lives of poor people, to defeat hunger, disease, and illiteracy and to encourage respect for each other's rights and freedoms; and to be a center for harmonizing the actions of nations to achieve these goals. The General Assembly is the United Nation's primary deliberative body and has representatives from all 193 member states. The United Nations is headed by the Secretary-General, currently Ban Ki-moon of the Republic of Korea (South Korea), who took office in 2007 (UN 2013).

Of particular relevance in addressing civil wars is the Security Council. This has the main responsibility under the UN Charter for maintaining international peace and security. It is composed of five permanent members (China, France, Russia, the United Kingdom, and the United States) who have veto powers. Along with them are 10 nonpermanent members elected by the General Assembly for 2-year terms. These countries presently are Argentina (its term ends in 2014); Azerbaijan (2013); Australia (2014); Guatemala (2013); Luxembourg (2014); Morocco (2013); Pakistan (2013); the Republic of Korea (2014); Rwanda (2014); and Togo (2013). The council's presidency is held by each of the members in turn for one month. This follows the English alphabetical order of the member state names. Meetings are called whenever the need arises (UN Security Council 2013). Reform of the Council, including its membership, is being considered.

According to the SIPRI, there were 53 peace operations conducted in 2012, one more than in 2011, (see Figure 7.1). There were 233,642 personnel deployed on operations in 2012 compared to 262,129 the previous year. This decline occurred because of reductions in the International Security Assistance Force (ISAF) in Afghanistan. The ISAF with 102,052 troops was the largest operation for the fourth consecutive year. Excluding the ISAF, deployments increased by 847 personnel. This was the first increase in total personnel figures excluding the ISAF since 2008. The second and third largest were the African Union-UN Hybrid Operation in Darfur and the UN Organization Stabilization Mission in the Democratic Republic of the Congo (DRC), both of which are outlined below. The total known cost of peace operations in 2012 was $9 billion (SIPRI 2005-2013, *Yearbook* 2013:63–65).

The highest numbers of peace operations in 2011 were conducted in Africa and Europe. However, with the ISAF deployed in Afghanistan, the most personnel were deployed in Asia (see Table 7.2). There were four new operations launched

FIGURE 7.1
Peace Missions Conducted by
the United Nations, Regional Organizations or
Alliances and Non-standing Coalitions/Ad Hoc Coalitions 1996–2012

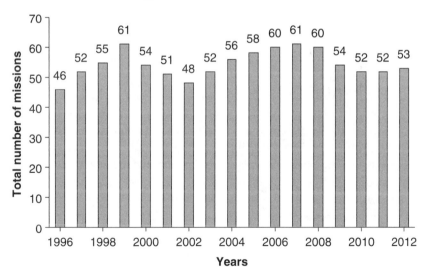

Sources: SIPRI (2005-2013, *Yearbook* 2007:134; 2009:118; *Yearbook* 2010:107; 2011:110; *Yearbook* 2012:91; and *Yearbook* 2013:63).

Note: Peace missions are defined as operations included in the SIPRI peacekeeping mission database. The complete definition of this appears above.

TABLE 7.2
Number of Peace Operations and
Personnel Deployed, by Region and Organization Type, 2011

Conducting organization	Africa	Americas	Asia	Europe	Mid-East	World
UN	10	1	3	2	4	20
Regional organization or alliance	5	1	2	13	5	26
Ad hoc coalition	1	0	3	0	2	6
Total operations	16	2	8	15	11	52
Total personnel	86,642	12,201	134,727*	11,932	16,627	262,129*

Source: SIPRI (2005–2013, *Yearbook* 2012:108).

Note: UN figures include peace operations led by the UN Department of Peacekeeping Operations, and those led by the UN Department of Political Affairs and the African Union-UN Hybrid Operation in Darfur.

* Figures also include the International Security Assistance Force in Afghanistan.

in 2012: the Economic Community of West African States (ECOWAS) Mission in Guinea-Bissau (ECOMIB), the European Union (EU) Capacity Building Mission in Niger (EUCAP Sahel Niger), and the United Nations Supervision Mission in Syria (UNSMIS). Four missions closed during the year. These were the EU Police Mission in Bosnia and Herzegovina (EUPM), the UN Integrated Mission in Timor-Leste (UNMIT), and two missions in Syria, the League of Arab States Observer Mission to Syria and UNSMIS. The Syrian missions both ended because significant violence hampered the ability to implement their mandates (SIPRI 2005–2013, *Yearbook* 2013:63).

UN peacekeeping operations play a vital role in the international community's recent interventions to address conflict. The United Nations was the main organization conducting peace operations in 2012. It was responsible for 20 of the 53 peace operations (38 percent) along with $7.2 billion (80 percent) of total known operational costs. However, the reported costs of most non-UN operations exclude personnel costs. Almost half of the personnel involved in peace operations internationally—107,186 (46 percent)—were deployed in NATO operations with the largest being the ISAF. Seven of the 10 peace operations with over 5,000 personnel were under UN command, two were under NATO control, and one came under African Union command. Including the ISAF, the largest contributor of troops to multilateral peace operations in 2012 was the United

States. However, when the ISAF was excluded, the largest contributors were Pakistan and Bangladesh (SIPRI 2005–2013, *Yearbook* 2013:64–65).

According to the United Nations, its peacekeepers provide security along with political and peacebuilding support to help conflict-inflicted countries make the challenging early transition toward peace. They are guided by three basic principles: consent of the parties; impartiality; and the nonuse of force except in self-defense and defense of the mandate (UN, no date-f). As of December 31, 2013, the United Nations had undertaken 68 peacekeeping operations since 1948 with 15 currently active; some are described below (see Mission list). The United Nations had approved resources for the period from July 1, 2013, to June 30, 2014, of about $7.83 billion (UN 2014d). From 1948 to January 31, 2014, an estimated 3,199 UN peacekeepers died in operations, the number peaking at 252 during 1993. The main causes of fatalities were accidents (1,215), illness (977), malicious acts (819), and other (188) (UN 2014e).

Selected UN peacekeeping operations active in December 2013 were as follows:

UN Mission for the Referendum in Western Sahara (MINURSO): In Western Sahara since April 1991, it comprised 502 personnel (this includes volunteers

Peacekeepers in Kivu

A schoolboy watches a MONUSCO vehicle on peacekeeping patrol in the Democratic Republic of Congo.

Credit: UN Photo/Sylvain Liechti

while all civilian personnel data here are from August 2013) and had suffered 15 fatalities. MINURSO had an approved budget from July 2013 to June 2014 of $60,475,700 (unless noted, budgets are for this period).

UN Stabilization Mission in Haiti (MINUSTAH): In Haiti since June 2004 with total personnel numbering 10,408. There have been 175 fatalities. The Mission's approved budget was $576,619,000.

UN Organization Stabilization Mission in the Democratic Republic of the Congo (MONUSCO): In the country since July 2010 with total personnel strength of 25,739, the UN Mission's fatalities have numbered 69. The approved budget for MONUSCO was $1,456,378,300.

African Union-UN Hybrid Operation in Darfur (UNAMID): In Darfur since July 2007 with 23,866 personnel. UNAMID has suffered 188 fatalities, and its approved budget was $1,335,248,000.

UN Interim Force in Lebanon (UNIFIL): Deployed within Lebanon since March 1978, this Force has 11,380 personnel, and there have been 299 fatalities. The approved budget was $492,622,000.

UN Interim Security Force for Abyei (UNISFA): The UNISFA was first stationed in Abyei, Sudan, during June 2011. It has comprised 4,287 personnel (12 fatalities have occurred), and its approved budget was $329,108,600.

UN Mission in the Republic of South Sudan (UNMISS): Deployed in South Sudan since July 2011, personnel numbered 10,294. There have been 20 fatalities, and the approved budget was $924,426,000.

UN Operation in Côte d'Ivoire (UNOCI): First stationed in Côte d'Ivoire during April 2004, the UNOCI has 11,290 personnel. Fatalities have numbered 115, and the approved budget was $584,487,000.

UN Interim Administration Mission in Kosovo (UNMIK): In Kosovo since June 1999 and totaling 362 personnel. The UNMIK has suffered 55 fatalities and has an approved budget of $44,953,000.

UN Mission in Liberia (UNMIL): From September 2003 in Liberia, the UNMIL has 8,970 personnel (178 fatalities have been recorded). The approved budget was $476,329,800 (UN 2014d).

There is much debate over the effectiveness of such interventions. The United Nations has referred to its peacekeeping as a central element of international conflict response that provides essential security and support to millions of people along with fragile institutions emerging from conflict. The United Nations has attributed a high success rate to its peacekeeping efforts. Since 1948, operations had enabled people in dozens of countries to participate in free and fair elections, and helped disarm more than 400,000 ex-combatants in the past decade alone. UN peace operations cost significantly less than other forms of international intervention, and their costs are shared more equitably among UN member states. Supporting research includes a survey by Oxford University economists who concluded international military intervention under Chapter VII of the UN Charter was the most cost-effective method of preventing a return to war in post-conflict societies. More specifically, a study by the U.S. Government Accountability Office estimated that it would cost the United States approximately twice as much as the United Nations to conduct a peacekeeping operation similar to the UN Stabilization Mission in Haiti (MINUSTAH)—$876 million compared to the UN-budgeted $428 million for the first 14 months of the mission (UN, no date-a).

However, the UN has recognized that the general success of earlier missions raised peacekeeping expectations beyond its capacity to deliver. This was particularly evident during the mid-1990s. Three missions were particularly controversial: the UN Protection Force (UNPROFOR) deployed between 1992 and 1995 in the former Yugoslavia, the UN Assistance Mission for Rwanda (UNAMIR) from 1993 to 1996, and the UN Operation in Somalia II (UNOSOM II) from 1993 to 1995. The operations were criticized as peacekeepers faced parties not adhering to peace agreements, while the peacekeepers themselves had inadequate resources or political support. As civilian casualties rose and hostilities continued, the reputation of UN peacekeeping declined. These setbacks led to a limit on the number of new peacekeeping missions and a review of operations (UN Peacekeeping 2013).

Beardsley (2012) found that UN military involvement reduced the likelihood of one side achieving victory, and diplomatic engagement increased the ability of parties to compromise in the long term. Furthermore, diplomatic engagement accompanied by military involvement significantly hastened the pace of stalemate outcomes. However, both tools had disadvantages. Military involvement could decrease the sense of urgency for compromise, while diplomatic engagement could be used for insincere motives and ultimately increased risk of one-sided victory (Beardsley 2012:335). After examining data on UN conflict management efforts in over 270 international crises between 1945 and 2002, measures of conflict severity and potential escalation appeared to be much better predictors of the extent of UN involvement than variables measuring the interests of the Security Council's veto-holding members that did not align with the UN's organizational mission of acting as a global peacemaker. This suggested that the United Nations adhered more closely to the humanitarian and security mission contained in its charter than critics often suggested (Beardsley and Schmidt 2012:33).

MEDIATION

According to the U.S. Institute of Peace, external partners can provide resources, assurance, expertise, and experience supporting peace agreement implementation. Third parties, such as allies or neighboring states, can assist in ensuring that promises are kept, timetables respected, and matching commitments fulfilled. Third-party tasks might include overseeing and monitoring cease-fires, weapon stockpiles, prisoner releases, and the return of refugees. These guarantors as part of an implementation plan increase confidence in the settlement and encourage parties to take risks associated with moving toward peace. A network of donors, including governments, aid organizations, and reconstruction agencies, can help pay for implementation, such as reconstruction bills. External experts can provide counsel. This might involve giving guidance on authoring a constitution, drafting election rules, selecting transitional justice mechanisms, vetting and training civilian police, undertaking a census, and managing natural resources and organizing revenue sharing (U.S. Institute of Peace 2013).

Mediators are third parties working to change disputant perceptions and/or behavior. This is done without using physical force or invoking the authority of law. The third party can be an individual, organization, group, or state (Bercovitch 2006:290). Some scholars believe that mediation is the most common and effective tool of conflict management. Although the relative success of mediation is not high, evidence indicates that certain types of mediation attempts are more successful than others. The key element of mediation is an explicit attempt to transform a conflict from hostility to cooperation. Furthermore, mediation involves the voluntary agreement by all parties, which then agree to the format, the location, and the range of issues. Mediation ultimately links the motivation to intervene explicitly to efforts at conflict management (Regan and Aydin 2006:741). Melin and Svensson (2009) write that mediation in civil wars transfers legitimacy to the nonstate actor and can encourage a precedent of exceptions to the norm of sovereignty. Therefore, the political cost associated with accepting international mediation will be significantly higher in civil wars compared to international conflicts. Hence, states should only accept mediation in the most serious disputes, or when the costs of legitimizing an opponent are outweighed by conflict resolution benefits.

Regan and Aydin (2006) have written that the role of an "outside" actor is central to peaceful settlement given two major problems confronting the civil war parties. These are: (a) the difficulty in signaling one's own strength, resolve, and preferences to the opponent, and (b) the inability to identify a mutually acceptable solution to their disagreements and make a credible commitment to this position without post-conflict vulnerability. Third parties can transmit information on the preferences of adversaries and provide inducements that enhance the attractiveness of a negotiated outcome compared to other solutions. Here, diplomatic initiatives can help parties find a cooperative solution that both sides can agree to and allows the parties to make credible commitments that negotiating the civil war's end require. Therefore, the reduction of the asymmetry of information about capabilities and incentives, and resultant help to parties seeking a peaceful solution that benefits both sides, is vital to successful interventions (Regan and Aydin 2006:739–741).

Regan and Aydin (2006; Regan, Frank, and Aydin 2009) studied the historical nature of diplomatic interventions (see also the civil war mediation dataset [DeRouen, Bercovitch and Pospieszna 2011]; DeRouen and Bercovitch 2012). Diplomatic interventions were defined as attempts by outside parties to transform a conflict by enhancing communication between the fighting groups and providing information about the conflict that might help encourage movement toward negotiated outcomes. Third parties can convey information about costs, prospects for victory, settlement benefits, or the subjective estimates of each held by the adversary. In addition, the outside party (or parties) could tie information to explicit "carrots" or "sticks" by linking diplomacy with possible economic or military interventions. Diplomatic interventions occurred in 68 of the 153 civil wars recorded from 1945 to 1999. Data on four specific forms of diplomatic interventions were coded: (a) mediation, (b) international forums, (c) the recall of ambassadors, and (d) explicit offers to mediate by third parties not accepted by both sides. Mediation involved noncoercive, nonviolent, and nonbinding intervention where mediators entered a conflict to affect, change, modify, or influence the outcome. The mediator could represent a state or a nonstate actor. There were minimal diplomatic interventions during the 1940s and 1950s before a gradual increase to the mid-1980s when they increased significantly. Overall, mediation represented the majority of post-WWII external diplomatic efforts recorded (see Table 7.3). Diplomatic interventions outnumbered military and economic interventions. They were highest in the Americas and sub-Saharan Africa (see Table 7.4) (Regan and Aydin 2006:744–746; Regan et al. 2009:138–143).

Mediators

Greig and Regan (2008) examined the questions of under what conditions third parties provide, and warring parties accept, offers of mediation. Their analysis suggested that third-party offers were closely associated with the interests a third

TABLE 7.3
Forms of Diplomatic Intervention in Conflicts 1945 to 1999

Mediations	Offers to mediate rejected by one or all parties	Multilateral forums	Mediation requests by one of the parties not undertaken by third-party states	Recalls of diplomatic representation	Total number of diplomatic interventions
352	44	23	12	5	438

Source: Regan et al. (2009:139).

TABLE 7.4
Average Number of Interventions per Conflict by Region 1945 to 1999

Diplomatic interventions by region				
Americas	Europe	Sub-Saharan Africa	Middle East	Asia
8.25	5.9	8	5	5.1
Military interventions by region				
3.3	4	8.3	5.3	9.8
Economic interventions by region				
1.6	1.75	2.5	3	2.5

Source: Regan et al. (2009:139).

party had in a civil war state, together with the historical ties between the third party and civil war state (Greig and Regan 2008:759). Böhmelt (2010) has noted that mediation is not only conducted by official actors, such as states or international organizations. Nonofficial parties including individuals and nongovernmental organizations increasingly intervene as third-party mediators. Both official and unofficial interventions were conceptualized as tracks of diplomacy (ToDs). A study of mediation from 1946 to 2004 indicated that it was a function of war type (territorial and internationalized wars were more likely to be mediated), war duration (the longer the war, the greater the probability of mediation), supply-side factors (the number of democracies internationally and the global polity average), and stratum (subsequent wars were less likely to be mediated). Battle-related deaths also seemed to increase the chances of mediation, but the relationship was not very significant (DeRouen, Bercovitch, and Pospieszna 2011:663).

According to "ripeness" theory, parties resolve their conflict only when they are ready to do so. This occurs when alternative, usually unilateral, means of achieving a satisfactory outcome are blocked, and the parties believe that they are in an uncomfortable and costly predicament. At that "ripe moment," they accept proposals that generally have been present for a long time and only now appear attractive. The concept of a ripe moment is based on the parties' perception of a mutually hurting stalemate (MHS), optimally associated with an impending, past, or recently avoided catastrophe. The founding notion is that when the parties identify themselves as locked in a conflict from which they cannot escalate to victory and this deadlock is painful to both of them, they look for an alternative policy or exit. The catastrophe provides a deadline or a lesson showing that pain can be significantly increased if something is not urgently done about it. The MHS assumes that a party will select the alternative that it prefers and that a decision to change is encouraged by raising pain associated with the present actions. If the parties fail to recognize "clear evidence" that they face an impasse, a MHS has not (yet) occurred. When they do perceive themselves to be in such a situation, regardless of the evidence's strength, the MHS has arrived. Parties need not be able to identify a specific solution, only a sense that a negotiated solution is possible for the searching and that the other party shares that sense and the willingness too. Ripeness itself is not enough for the initiation of negotiations. It must be seized, either directly by the parties or, if not, through a mediator's encouragement (Zartman 2001).

Ripeness theory seeks to explain why, and thus when, fighting parties are more likely on their own efforts to de-escalate conflict and attempt to seek a negotiated solution. Heraclides (1997) has summarized factors associated with ripe moments to end conflicts. In a study of civil wars that experienced significant stalemates but did not conclude in military victories, he found that, first, both parties must realize that they have more to gain and less to lose in a peace agreement than via continued fighting. The second factor associated with a ripe moment occurred when both parties reached economic, military, and moral exhaustion. This has been called "capability exhaustion" (Heraclides 1997:687). There are various challenges raised by ripeness theory. One complication with the notion of a hurting stalemate arises when increased pain increases resistance rather than reducing it. Although this might be considered "bad," irrational, or even adolescent behavior, it is a frequent reaction and one that may be natural and functional (Zartman 2001).

Historically, the United Nations has dominated diplomatic interventions aimed at encouraging warring groups to move toward negotiated outcomes. Regan and Aydin (2006) and Regan et al (2009) provide a useful breakdown of the most frequent diplomatic interveners from 1945 to 1999. The United

Nations undertook 89 diplomatic interventions to lead the top five interveners. Those outside of the top five included the European Commission (15 interventions) and Tanzania (15) (see Table 7.5). Groups of states like the United Nations that were inherently multilateral were likely to intervene alone (75 percent of UN interventions), as was the United States (again 75 percent). With regard to the rank of the mediator, private citizens undertook the most interventions (138) with 114 undertaken by heads of state and 100 by ambassadors (Regan et al. 2009:141–142). The most frequent individual mediators were Kenyan President Daniel arap Moi and former U.S. President Jimmy Carter (see Table 7.6).

TABLE 7.5
*Most Frequent Diplomatic Interveners and
Number of Interventions in Conflicts 1945 to 1999*

UN	US	Catholic Church	UK	Organization of African Unity
89	56	30	21	17

Source: Regan et al. (2009:140).

TABLE 7.6
*Most Frequent Individual Mediators and
Number of Mediations (and Conflicts) 1945–1999*

Kenyan President Moi	Former US President Jimmy Carter	UK Lord Owen	UN Representative Arnault
21 (5)	12 (5)	11 (2)	11 (1)

Source: Regan et al. (2009:143).

More recent data are provided by DeRouen et al. (2011). Their study of civil war mediation found that representatives of international organizations were the most frequent mediators, followed by representatives of large and small governments (see Table 7.7). The United Nations was the leading entity engaged in mediation, it being involved in 32 percent of all cases mediated by organizations (DeRouen et al. 2011:665).

The United Nations is active in conflict mediation with the Mediation Support Unit (MSU) established in 2006. This operates closely with the UN's Department of Political Affairs regional divisions to plan and assist mediation efforts. The MSU provides advisory, financial, and logistical assistance to peace processes; works to strengthen the mediation capacity of regional and

TABLE 7.7
Most Frequent Five Mediators by Rank 1946 to 2004

International Organization Representative	Large Government Representative	Small Government Representative	Regional Organization Representative	Small Government Leader
25%	20%	16%	15%	10%

Source: DeRouen et al. (2011:665).

subregional organizations; and is a repository of mediation knowledge, policy and guidance, lessons learned, and best practices. The Department manages a rapid response fund to quickly initiate mediation processes (UN Department of Political Affairs 2013a). The Standby Team of Mediation Experts is an "on call" group of experts established in 2008 whose members can be deployed to assist mediators. Members are appointed for 1-year terms and have expertise on issues including power sharing, peace processes, and constitution making (see Table 7.8).

According to the United Nations, demand for the MSU has increased annually. The members of the 2012 team were deployed on more than 70 occasions to over 30 countries. These ranged from the Central African Republic to Yemen and the Maldives, and from Kyrgyzstan to Libya and Somalia. For instance, one expert helped a Yemeni technical committee tasked with convening Yemen's forthcoming national dialogue process. In the Central African Republic, two experts assisted peace negotiations through providing expertise in power sharing, gender, security arrangements, and cease-fires (UN Department of Political Affairs 2013d).

Mediation Types and Success

Domestic and international politics can influence the choice of mediation to manage conflict in international crises. According to Beardsley (2010), combatants in conflicts often seek mediation as political cover for concessions made that could be viewed as unpalatable to their respective constituencies' domestic pressures. Thus, intermediaries might obscure responsibility for disappointing outcomes or signal the prudence of compromise. With regard to international audiences, affected third parties seeking to influence the resolution outcome might lobby to act as a mediator. Potential domestic audience costs for seeking peace, and the propensity for concessions, positively affected the likelihood of mediation. Less clear was the role of third-party incentives. Here, results indicated that a higher potential for neighboring-state intervention actually decreased

TABLE 7.8
Members of UN Standby Team of Mediation Experts in 2013

Name and Country	Area of Expertise	Background
John Packer (Canada)	Process Design	Conflict resolution expert and academic.
Rina Amiri (Afghanistan)	Gender and Social Inclusion	Expert on women and peace. Experienced working in Asia and the Middle East.
Michael Brown (Canada)	Natural Resources	Expert on mediation, conflict, and peacebuilding.
Hassen Ebrahim (South Africa)	Constitutions	Expertise in constitution making, popular consultation processes, power sharing, religion, and peacemaking.
Antje Herrberg (Germany)	Process Design	Expertise in mediation, process design, gender, civil society, coaching, and capacity building.
Sven Koopmans (The Netherlands)	Process Design	Expert in peace negotiations, process design, and international law.
Jeffrey Mapendere (Zimbabwe)	Security Arrangements	Experience and expertise in peace processes, cease-fires, process design, and gender and mediation.
Marie-Joëlle Zahar (Lebanon)	Power Sharing	Academic with a focus on the dynamics of power sharing.

Source: UN Department of Political Affairs (2013d).

the likelihood of mediation. Conflict costs increased mediation incidence, and with high conflict costs, states did not appear to need political cover when making concessions (Beardsley 2010:395).

According to Bercovitch and Lee (2003), mediation strategy denoted an overall plan of mediators resolving and managing conflicts. Within this, there were three categories of strategic behavior. These ranged from low to high intervention: *communication-facilitation*; *procedural-formulative*; and *directive*. The first strategy was characterized by the mediator's generally fairly passive role. The mediator channeled information to the parties and facilitated cooperation with minimal control over the more formal process or substance of mediation. Tactics included arranging interactions between parties, identifying issues and interests, establishing a rapport with the parties, and developing a framework for understanding. Procedural-formulative strategies facilitated a mediator's more formal control over mediation. A mediator might control the location of mediation, frequency and formality of meetings, the agenda's structure, and the distribution of information about progress. The mediator might also create protocols, suggest procedures, and highlight common interests.

Directive strategies were the most powerful form of intervention. These dealt with, and sought to change, the motivation and behavior of conflict parties by providing incentives for them or issuing ultimatums. Tactics included changing the parties' expectations, making significant suggestions and proposals, ensuring parties knew the nonagreement costs, supplying and filtering information, suggesting and rewarding concessions, assisting with the formulation of a framework for acceptable outcomes, encouraging flexibility, promising resources or threatening withdrawal, and offering to verify agreement compliance. Overall, Bercovitch and Lee (2003) found these strategies were much more effective than nondirective strategies. This was especially the case with tangible issues, parties from different blocs, and trust in a mediator. Böhmelt (2010) found that tracks of diplomacy leverage and resources determined their effectiveness. Track one diplomacy (efforts by official actors) tended to be the most effective form of intervention as it had greater leverage and more resources. Mediation efforts combining both official and unofficial tracks could be more effective than independent tracks actions too.

The Regan and Aydin (2006) study indicated that diplomatic interventions were effective conflict management strategies that dramatically changed the course of civil war events. Intervention strategies that combined different approaches were potentially more effective than individual components alone, and the right timing of intervention efforts was vital for terminating and settling a war. Thus, effective conflict management required the manipulations of information held by parties about their opponent, expectations regarding losses and gains, and benefits from a negotiated settlement (Regan and Aydin 2006:754). Regan (2002b) classified interventions generally as unilateral (when one state acted) or multilateral (if multiple states or an organization such as the United Nations or NATO intervened). His analysis suggested that the mutual consent of parties involved, impartial interveners, and a coherent intervention strategy increased the likelihood of successful multilateral interventions.

The role of impartial intervention has been questioned. Svensson (2009) examined the impact of biased versus neutral mediation on peace agreement content. Neutral mediators engaged primarily because of their interest to end fighting had incentives to hasten the conclusion of an agreement at the expense of its quality. By contrast, biased mediators aiming to protect their protégés took care to ensure that the agreement had stipulations guaranteeing the interest of "their" side, or they utilized their access and leverage to make their side agree to costly concessions. Thus, biased mediation processes were more likely than neutral processes to lead to institutional arrangements supporting democracy and durable peace. These included power-sharing, third-party security guarantees, and justice provisions. Analysis of 124 peace agreements from 1989 to 2004 supported these claims (Svensson 2009:446). Likewise, Krain (2005) examined the effectiveness of overt military intervention in reducing or stopping genocide or politicide. An analysis of all ongoing genocides or politicides from 1995 to 1997 suggested that interventions directly challenging the perpetrator or helping victims were the only effective type of military responses. Impartial interventions seemed to be ineffective, and interventions to challenge the perpetrator did not make matters worse for genocide or politicide targets. The findings were consistent with other arguments that attempts aimed at preventing or alleviating mass killings should focus on opposing, restraining, or disarming perpetrators and/or removing them from power (Krain 2005:363).

Beardsley (2011) has identified long-term limitations of conflict mediation. With a third-party mediator's intervention, fighting parties might formally agree to concessions insupportable in the long term. Thus, renewed conflict can soon occur. Based on data and historical cases, Beardsley concluded that a reliance on mediation risked greater likelihood of conflict reoccurring in the future, whereas the rejection of mediation threatened additional casualties as war continued. The trade-off between mediation's short-term and long-term effects was stark when the mediator adopted "heavy-handed" forms of leverage, while multiple mediators and intergovernmental organizations also did relatively poorly in creating long-term peace. He found that mediation had the greatest opportunity to foster both short-term and long-term peace when a single third party mediated among belligerents that could afford to wait for a self-enforcing arrangement to be reached (Beardsley 2011).

PEACE AGREEMENTS AND MILITARY PROVISIONS

The Uppsala Conflict Data Program (UCDP) defines peace agreements and collects data on the signing of such agreements within the context of armed conflicts (see Chapter 6). A peace agreement is a formal agreement between warring parties, which addresses the disputed incompatibility. This is either by settling all or part of it, or by clearly outlining a process for how the warring parties plan to regulate the incompatibility. Agreements frequently involve mediation by international figures and organizations. International resources, such as peacekeeping forces, are likewise often used to help establish and consolidate a long-term peace.

Peace agreements often include military provisions. According to Hartzell and Hoddie (2007), settlements with institutions designed to address the question of who controls the levers of state power better provided an enduring peace. Settlements including power-sharing institutions, such as the military, were more effective; a military could be shared, or an integrated national military could be established via disarmament and demobilization. The UCDP dataset on peace agreements from 1989 to 2005 identified 144 accords covering one third of 121 armed conflicts. Formal cease-fires were included in 60 percent of the 144 agreements. As already noted, civil wars often become internationalized with various parties becoming involved in the fighting (see Chapter 3). However, peace agreements themselves often include international involvement with both their crafting and implementation. In 25 percent of civil wars over government and 20 percent over territory, there were agreement provisions for peacekeeping operations (Harbom et al. 2006:617, 624).

There are various examples of agreements which stipulate the deployment of international forces. For instance, in October 1991, the Paris Peace Agreements were signed to provide a comprehensive political settlement aimed at ending ongoing fighting in Cambodia. Under the terms of the Accords, the United Nations sent a mission to Cambodia (UN Transitional Authority in Cambodia, or UNTAC) until 1993 to supervise the cease-fire and prepare the country for a new constitution and for free and fair elections. The UN mission was explicitly mandated to foster "an environment in which respect for human rights shall be ensured" so that past policies and practices would not return. The military component peaked in June 1993 at 15,991 with another 3,359 civilian police (UN OHCHR October 2011; UN, no date-b).

With regard to the impact of external peacekeeping forces on the success of agreements, research findings have been mixed. Hartzell, Hoddie, and Rothchild (2001) found that third-party involvement, including peacekeeping missions, significantly and substantially increased the duration of peace. Contrasting this, Dubey (2002) said that third-party peacekeeping interventions, including those by the United Nations, did not significantly impact upon the duration of peace. Fortna (2004:269), having examined previous research and controlling as much as possible for factors that might influence the likelihood of peacekeeper deployment and the degree of difficulty of maintaining peace, concluded that international intervention made an important contribution to peace stability. Such findings contribute to other research on peace agreements, such as that by DeRouen, Lea, and Wallensteen (2009) indicating the less costly concessions by government of military integration and autonomy increase the duration of agreements.

PEACEBUILDING

As noted in the previous chapter, UN Secretary-General Boutros Boutros-Ghali in 1992 defined peacebuilding broadly as the act of enhancing structures to consolidate the post-conflict peace and reduce the probability of civil war recurrence. Doyle and Sambanis (2006) further noted that peacebuilding sought to build the social, economic, and political institutions and attitudes preventing conflict (2006:23). Major efforts at peacebuilding include the United Nations assuming responsibility for the post-conflict administration of Kosovo and East Timor during 1999, both of which continue to face serious challenges to their stability (SIPRI 2005–2013, *Yearbook* 2005:142). Doyle and Sambanis (2000) studied the success of peacebuilding in post-WWII civil wars. They found that multilateral UN peace operations made a positive difference, such as on post-civil war democratization processes.

There has been discussion over international peacebuilders promoting liberal democratic and market-oriented economic principles. Paris (2002) has written that peacebuilders have "transmitted" Western-liberal standards of appropriate behavior to failed states. Thus, peacebuilding resembled "an updated (and more benign) version of the *mission civilisatrice*, or the colonial-era belief that the European imperial powers had a duty to 'civilize' dependent populations and territories" (Paris 2002:637). According to Pugh (2005), the promotion of liberal peace has been hindered by its contradictions, and because it ignored socio-economic challenges post-conflict societies faced. Indeed, challenges were even aggravated such as through the vulnerability of populations to poverty increasing. There have been pragmatic shifts to some degree toward pro-poor and emancipating engagement with local populations. However, the vital question remained as to who peacebuilding was for and what purposes it served (Pugh 2005:23, 37–38).

Peacebuilding success is made more difficult by the limited duration of most international operations. For example, Haiti relapsed into conflict in 2004 after multiple missions over a decade (SIPRI 2005–2013, *Yearbook* 2005:146). A further complication is a lack of international mechanisms to objectively assess when the state's structure is stable enough that peacebuilding is self-sustaining. Peacebuilding places further demands on the personnel involved. Many personnel are from less developed countries, such as Bangladesh, and hold military positions. These can place strains on forces not necessarily well-equipped or trained for their roles. The challenge can be exacerbated by inadequate operational funding. World Bank research has indicated that under the protection of military peacekeeping, a large and well-timed aid program, combined with rapid and well-selected policy reforms was vital for at least the first decade after a con-flict. Indeed, the optimal capacity to manage aid occurred only in the fourth or fifth year (World Bank 2003:157–159, 166–169). Another challenge facing the personnel is the legitimacy of their operation, both as perceived by the interna-tional community and the local population. Here, the operations in Afghanistan and Iraq have been particularly sensitive given that they resulted from the over-throw of regimes by U.S.-led forces (SIPRI 2005–2013, *Yearbook* 2005:148–150).

HUMANITARIAN LAW

War crimes can be defined as violations of the laws and customs of war entailing individual criminal responsibility directly under international law (Bellamy 2011d:1751). As noted in Chapter 2, civil war crimes cause numerous deaths and injuries. Human rights are often violated—as social mores against these crimes are eroded along with law and order collapsing. Such developments provide fertile ground for historical animosities to arise, for leaders to exploit tensions, and for factions to seek revenge for perceived past injustices. This, in turn, can start a cycle of violence that magnifies the level of hatred and the risk of war crimes. Human rights may also be systematically violated, as terror and brutality are used to win dominance and ensure a population's compliance. Furthermore, a breakdown of law and order can provide the opportunity for numerous violations to occur unhindered without fear of punishment (Bellamy 2013).

External actors have frequently intervened in civil wars for humanitarian pur-poses. For instance, UN involvement started in Bosnia during 1992 when the mandate of UNPROFOR, deployed to Croatia the previous year, was expanded to include ensuring the safety and functioning of the Sarajevo airport, along with the delivery of humanitarian assistance to the Bosnian capital. Later in 1992, the mandate was further expanded to allow UNPROFOR to support humanitarian efforts throughout Bosnia. UNPROFOR would eventually also monitor safe areas, the no-fly zone over Bosnia, and several cease-fires that were negotiated. The UN's performance has been strongly criticized, especially the failure of peace-keepers to prevent Bosnian Serb forces from killing more than 8,000 Muslim men and boys during July 1995. This massacre, the worst atrocity in Europe since the end of WWII, occurred within Srebrenica, despite the enclave having been desig-nated a UN safe haven (BBC 2012b). Another example of humanitarian interven-tion occurred after the 1991 Gulf War and impetus of UN Security Council Resolution 688, which condemned Iraqi repression in the Kurdish areas of Iraq. A multinational force was deployed to establish safe havens for refugees (Bellamy 2007b:47, 66).

There have been various legal moves to address the stark violations of human rights associated with civil wars. International human rights' treaties and other instruments adopted since the end of WWII have conferred legal form on inherent human rights and developed the body of international human rights. Other regional instruments have been used that reflect specific regional human rights concerns and provide for specific mechanisms of protection. Most states have adopted constitutions and other laws whereby basic human rights are formally protected too. While international treaties and customary law form the "backbone" of international human rights law, other instruments contribute to its understanding, implementation, and development. These include internationally adopted declarations, guidelines, and principles. Respect for human rights requires the establishment of the rule of law at the national and international levels (UN OHCHR 2012). As already noted, such rule of law is often absent when societies experience civil wars.

International human rights law provides obligations that states are bound to respect. By becoming parties to international treaties, states assume obligations and duties under international law to respect, protect, and fulfill human rights. Respect means that states do not interfere with or curtail the enjoyment of human rights, while protection requires states to protect individuals and groups against human rights abuses. The obligation to fulfill entails the states taking positive action to facilitate the enjoyment of basic human rights. Through ratification of international human rights treaties, governments undertake to implement domestic measures and legislation compatible with their treaty obligations and duties. Where domestic legal proceedings do not address human rights abuses, mechanisms and procedures for individual complaints or communications are available at the regional and international levels. These should help ensure that international human rights standards are locally respected, implemented, and enforced (UN OHCHR 2012).

However, international human rights agreements have often been violated. This is illustrated by the frequent violation of the Convention against Torture and Other Cruel, Inhuman or Degrading Treatment or Punishment (the Convention). The Convention was adopted by UN General Assembly Resolution 39/46 of December 10, 1984. It then entered into force in June 1987 (UN 2008). According to Powell and Staton (2007), the average yearly percentage of states that had ratified and at least minimally violated the Convention from 1987 to 2004 was 83. Moreover, 42 percent of states were systematic violators with at least 50 reported incidents of state-sponsored torture. It was not only autocracies that recorded violations. The average yearly percentage of democracies that had at least minimally violated their commitment was 77; 30 percent did this systematically.

Indeed, 81 percent of ratifying states violated the Convention during the year of ratification, including 78 percent of democratic ratifiers (Powell and Staton 2007:1, 42).

Based on research by Powell and Staton (2007), common arguments regarding the ratification of and compliance with international human rights agreements anticipate either subsequent compliance or universal ratification. In reality, the agreements are often violated, though not all states ratify without reservation. Understanding this empirical pattern requires an argument explicitly considering the link between a state's ratification and compliance choices. In their opinion, these choices involve a trade-off between alleviating pressure to accept international human rights norms and managing regime authority. Here, the effectiveness of the domestic judiciary influences the way states resolve this trade-off. Utilizing data on the ratification status of states under the Convention and states' torture practices, the scholars found that the joint probability of being ratified under the Convention and violating its terms decreased in the effectiveness of a state's judiciary. They also noted that the joint probability of not being ratified and engaging in behavior proscribed by the Convention increased in the effectiveness of a state's judiciary (Powell and Staton 2007).

The International Court of Justice (ICJ) is the UN's principal judicial organ. It was established in June 1945 by the Charter of the United Nations and started work during April 1946. The ICJ's role is to settle, in accordance with international law, legal disputes submitted to it by states and to give advisory opinions on legal questions referred to it by authorized UN organs and specialized agencies (International Court of Justice [ICJ] 2013). Powell and Mitchell (2007) found that civil law states were more likely to accept the ICJ jurisdiction than common law or Islamic law states. Common law states also placed the highest number of restrictions on their ICJ commitments, and Islamic law states had the most durable commitments (Powell and Mitchell 2007:397).

The Rome Statute of the International Criminal Court (ICC) entered into force on July 1, 2002, and established the ICC to help end the impunity and gross violations of international humanitarian law. It is an independent, permanent court that tries persons accused of the most serious crimes of international concern, namely, genocide, crimes against humanity, and war crimes (ICC 2013a, 2013b). From August 1, 2011 to July 31, 2012, there were seven situations under investigation. These were in the Democratic Republic of the Congo, Uganda, the Central African Republic, Darfur, Kenya, Libya, and Côte d'Ivoire. These countries all have experienced violent conflict involving frequent human rights violations. The ICC also issued its first judgment and sentence. Here, Thomas Lubanga Dyilo in 2012 was found criminally responsible, as a co-perpetrator, for the crimes of enlistment, conscription, and use of children under the age of 15 to participate actively in hostilities in the context of an armed conflict, not of an international character, in Ituri between September 2002 and August 2003 (ICC 2012:4, 7).

Other courts have been established to focus on war crimes during specific conflicts. Of particular relevance is the UN International Criminal Tribunal for the former Yugoslavia (ICTY) established during 1993 to address the 1990s atrocities in Croatia, Bosnia, and Herzegovina during the former Yugoslavia's devastating civil war. The ICTY was the first war crimes court created by the United Nations and the first international war crimes tribunal since the Nuremberg and Tokyo tribunals established to address WWII crimes. Under the ICTY statute, the tribunal has the power to prosecute persons violating the laws or customs of war. These violations include using poisonous weapons or other weapons designed to cause unnecessary suffering, the wanton destruction of cities or devastation not justified by military necessity, and the plunder of public or private property (International Criminal Tribunal for the Former Yugoslavia [ICTY] 2013a; Bellamy 2011d:1752).

The ICTY has actively sought to bring war criminals to justice. By March 2013, the tribunal had indicted 161 persons. According to the ICTY, those indicted included heads of state, prime ministers, army chiefs-of-staff, interior ministers, and numerous other high- to mid-level political, military, and police leaders from various parties involved with the Yugoslav conflicts. The indictments addressed crimes committed from 1991 to 2001 against members of ethnic groups in Croatia, Bosnia and Herzegovina, Serbia, Kosovo, and the former Yugoslav Republic of Macedonia. There were ongoing proceedings against 25 accused, and by 2013, the ICTY had concluded proceedings against 136 accused, 69 of whom were sentenced (ICTY 2013a; ICTY 2013b).

High-profile cases include the former president of Serbia and the Federal Republic of Yugoslavia Slobodan Milošević and former commander of the Bosnian Serb Army's main staff Ratko Mladić. Milošević was indicted on serious charges including genocide, complicity in genocide, deportation, murder, extermination, imprisonment, torture, willful killing, and unlawful confinement. Milošević had been arrested by Serbian authorities in April 2001 and transferred to the ICTY in June that year. His trial started the following February but was terminated in March 2006 after his death. By the time of his death, the prosecution had completed its case, but the defense was continuing, interrupted by Milošević's frequently poor health (ICTY, no date; BBC 2006). During May 2011, the tribunal welcomed the arrest in Serbia of Mladić. Mladić had evaded arrest for 16 years on charges of genocide, crimes against humanity, and war crimes (ICTY 2011).

IMPLICATIONS FOR CONFLICT MANAGEMENT

This chapter has perhaps the clearest implications for conflict management as external intervention is often undertaken with the explicit goal of managing the civil war. Intervention often occurs in the nastiest and most intractable of conflicts in part because neither side can gain a clear military victory. Military intervention can take place to favor one side (e.g., the U.S. involvement in Vietnam), or intervening states can become involved on both sides (e.g., the Soviet Union and Cuba supporting the government and the United States and South Africa supporting the rebels in the Angola civil war).

Intervention might actually decrease the chances of a negotiated settlement if the side with external support believes the intervention will increase the chances for military victory. In this event, the side receiving external help might be less likely to enter into negotiations, thinking it might have a better chance at battlefield success. In other words, foreign intervention could make some civil wars last even longer. The Angolan civil war that lasted from 1975 to 2002 could well have been shorter were it not for foreign intervention. Thus, the conflict management policy implication is that foreign intervention could have a counterintuitive effect. However, there are certain moral and ethical considerations that one must consider if considering nonintervention in a deadly civil war.

Many peacekeeping operations have proven successful (see Doyle and Sambanis 2000). These operations have the potential to prevent recurrence of war, oversee disarmament and reintegration of former rebels, aid in the implementation of peace agreements, and assist with statebuilding (e.g., in Timor-Leste). Each of these processes is vitally important in the post-conflict phase—especially in the early, more fragile stages of the peace. Peacekeepers are tasked with peacebuilding, which is often portrayed as a step in statebuilding after civil war. It is difficult to build a state if the peace has not been consolidated. Again, Timor-Leste provides a perfect example.

Mediation leading toward a negotiated settlement has often proven successful despite claims that its effects are often short term (see Beardsley 2011). Mediation is more likely to work in very costly wars in which the sides have reached a mutually hurting stalemate. If the war is low-cost, the disputants will often prefer to continue fighting over years or even decades.

Humanitarian law is a nonviolent form of intervention that can aid in the reconciliation process. It can also have a deterrence effect if world leaders know they might be held criminally responsible for their actions.

CONCLUSION

Because civil wars have a such a significant and major impact, the international community has actively sought to intervene in civil wars with the hope of ending, or at least reducing, the costly fighting.

The potentially complex and resource-demanding nature of intervening to end civil wars enhances the utility of countries and organizations adopting a collaborative approach. Here, intervention via respected international organizations with access to relevant expertise and resources provides a useful tool. The United Nations has been a particularly major actor, both in peacekeeping and mediation, in the post-Cold War period, witnessing an increase in its activities. Early peacekeeping was essentially restricted to ensuring that cease-fires were maintained, situations on the ground were stabilized, and important support for political efforts aimed at peaceful conflict resolution was provided. However, the Cold War's conclusion led to changes in peacekeeping operations with a transition to complex multidimensional missions. These entailed ensuring comprehensive peace agreements were implemented and assisting in the provision of foundations for sustainable peace. Despite challenges to peacekeeping during the mid-1990s, the importance of UN peacekeeping was reaffirmed with the mounting of new operations. With the 21st century, a review of peacekeeping led to reforms aimed at increasing the UN's ability to effectively manage and sustain field operations. Furthermore, peacebuilding operations that involve identifying and supporting structures which tend to strengthen and solidify peace to avoid a relapse into conflict have been staged.

The international community needs to consider intervening in low-intensity civil wars before they escalate. This might involve encouraging negotiations and dialogue between the aggrieved factions, such as through indirect, bilateral, and direct talks. Mediation is a common and potentially effective tool for resolving conflicts. Mediation involves conflict management related to, but distinct from, the parties' own negotiations. Here, conflict actors seek help or accept assistance from an outsider to transform a conflict from hostility to cooperation. This does not involve physical force or invoking the authority of law. Outsiders range from an individual to a state. Representatives of international organizations followed by representatives of large and small governments have been particularly active here. Directive strategies can also be more likely to succeed. These deal with, and seek to change, the motivation and behavior of conflict parties by providing incentives for them or issuing ultimatums. As already noted, tactics might include changing the parties' expectations, making substantive suggestions and proposals, and ensuring parties were aware of nonagreement costs.

The signing and effective implementation of agreements warrants particular attention given that their number has declined in recent years. This is a worrying trend, perhaps influenced by the increasing complexity of civil wars with the involvement of multiple factions. Peace agreements often include international involvement with both their crafting and implementation. Here, major case studies of such agreements and related military intervention indicate that success can be achieved in ending, or at least reducing, conflict. The international community has undertaken various moves to address graphic violations of human rights that occur during civil wars. Particularly relevant here is the International Criminal Court's establishment to help end the impunity and gross violations of international humanitarian law. Individual courts have also been established to address violations associated with specific civil wars, such as the ICTY.

Ultimately, civil wars can be very difficult to stop. This is graphically shown by the inability of the international community to unite and effectively intervene in Syria. However, there are ways to increase the likelihood of success. The effectiveness of intervention is enhanced through utilizing a combination of flexible engagement methods rather than depending on one method. A combination of military engagement, such as via peacekeeping and humanitarian operations and aid provision, can be more effective than intervention limited to one or the other. The likelihood of successful peacekeeping operations is enhanced with a strong mandate, adequate resources, and deployment. There is also a need for the international community to commit adequate resources after the cessation of the civil war to encourage an enduring peace. This may involve peacebuilding and democratization efforts, along with reconstructing damaged infrastructure and re-establishing law and order.

SUGGESTED READING

Beardsley, Kyle C. 2011. *The Mediation Dilemma*. Ithaca, NY: Cornell University Press.

Beardsley, Kyle C. and Holger Schmidt. 2012. "Following the Flag or Following the Charter? Examining the Determinants of United Nations Involvement in International Crises, 1945–2002." *International Studies Quarterly* 56(1):33–49.

DeRouen, Karl, Jr., Jacob Bercovitch, and Paulina Pospieszna. 2011. "Introducing the Civil Wars Mediation (CWM) Dataset." *Journal of Peace Research* 48(5):663–672.

Doyle, Michael W. and Nicholas Sambanis. 2000. "International Peacebuilding: A Theoretical and Quantitative Analysis." *American Political Science Review* 94(4):779–801.

Doyle, Michael W. and Nicholas Sambanis. 2006. *Making War & Building Peace: United Nations Peace Operations.* Princeton, NJ: Princeton University Press.

Paris, Roland. 2002. "International Peacebuilding and the 'Mission Civilisatrice.'" *Review of International Studies* 28(4):637–656.

Powell, Emilia J. and Sara M. Mitchell. 2007. "The International Court of Justice and the World's Three Legal Systems." *Journal of Politics* 69(2):397–415.

Pugh, Michael. 2005. "The Political Economy of Peacebuilding: A Critical Theory Perspective." *International Journal of Peace Studies* 10(2):23–42.

Regan, Patrick M. 2002a. *Civil Wars and Foreign Powers: Outside Intervention in Intrastate Conflict.* Ann Arbor: University of Michigan Press.

Regan, Patrick M. 2002b. "Third-Party Interventions and the Duration of Intrastate Conflicts." *Journal of Conflict Resolution* 46(1):55–73.

Regan, Patrick M. and Aysegul Aydin. 2006. "Diplomacy and Other Forms of Intervention in Civil Wars." *Journal of Conflict Resolution* 50(5):736–756.

CHAPTER 8

Terrorism and Civil War

The growth of terrorist groups has been facilitated by the link between civil war and terrorism. The state's inability to control territory, along with the general absence of law and order, can aid terrorist groups. In these areas, terrorists can operate with little or no interference from state authorities, and often the international community. Terrorists can establish organizational structures, recruit, and train supporters along with the development of international networks for intelligence and supplies. Moreover, terrorist organizations often constitute a militant faction of a significantly larger political opposition group, the majority of whom remain noncombatants. The traumatic nature of civil wars can make people more receptive to supporting terrorists or at least accept their presence. This is especially the case when people suffer because of atrocities committed by factions. Here, the loss of family, relatives, and friends along with their livelihoods can be influential. Those who do not willingly support factions might be pressured to do so or feel there is no alternative. Finally, terrorist attacks have the capability of derailing peace talks and preventing a durable peace.

State-sponsored terrorism represents the reciprocal situation. Here, terrorist methods are employed by a regime to promote its agenda and strengthen its power while avoiding public scrutiny. Well-known examples include the 20th-century military dictatorships in Latin America, Saddam Hussein's Iraq, and other Middle East autocracies. A problematic variant of state-sponsored terrorism can occur in the form of radical and sweeping counterterrorist policies that are implemented by a regime responding to attacks by civil war factions. In such cases, the general populace can be caught between the brutality of both the regime and its opponents. The actions of such regimes can motivate more people to bear arms against them, leading to escalating violence and ultimately civil war. In line with this, terrorists often exploit the strong emotions arising with death and destruction, for instance, by serving as a channel for retribution (Bellamy 2013:78–79).

WHAT IS TERRORISM?

On May 1, 2011, U.S. Navy Seals stormed a residential building to take on one of history's most notorious terrorists. Moments later, Osama bin Laden lay dead in the mansion where he was hiding in Abbottabad, Pakistan. In May 2009, after decades of bloody civil war, Sri Lankan forces managed to kill Velupillai Prabhakaran, leader of Liberation Tigers of Tamil Eelam (LTTE), the group responsible for numerous suicide bombings in Sri Lanka. Whereas there is broad international consensus that these two men were clearly terrorists, there is not similarly strong consensus about the definition of the term *terrorism*. Because the word has different connotations, it would be useful to have a universal definition of terrorism. Compare the following definitions:

According to the U.S. Patriot Act, terrorism refers to

> activities that involve acts dangerous to human life . . . appear to be intended to intimidate or coerce a civilian population . . . influence the policy of a government by intimidation or coercion . . . affect the conduct of a government by mass destruction, assassination, or kidnapping. (U.S. Patriot Act 2001)

The RAND Corporation has been using the following definition for more than 25 years:

> Terrorism is violence, or the threat of violence, calculated to create an atmosphere of fear and alarm, through acts designed to coerce others into actions they otherwise would not undertake or into refraining from actions that they desired to take. (RAND 2000:171)

The U.S. State Department defines terrorism with a focus on distinguishing it from other forms of violence and one that stresses attacks on civilians: "premeditated, politically motivated violence perpetrated against non-combatant targets by sub-national groups or clandestine agents" (U.S. Department of State, Bureau of Counterterrorism [CT] 2013:269).

During the 60th General Assembly in 2005, member states expressed concern that the United Nations had not arrived at an agreeable definition of terrorism (UN General Assembly [UN G.A.] Resolution 2005). Later, in a high-level panel meeting, the body promulgated an indirect definition by expressing that a world definition for terrorism should be based upon previous antiterrorism conventions and

> any action that is intended to cause death or serious bodily harm to civilians or non-combatants, when the purpose of such an act, by its nature or

context, is to intimidate a population, or to compel a Government, or an international organization to do or to abstain from doing any act.

Surprisingly, even as late as March 2007, there was no internationally accepted definition of terrorism. This prompted the British government to undertake the task of assembling and comparing the various definitions of terrorism found worldwide so as to ascertain if a universal definition is necessary.

Lord Carlile, an independent reviewer of terrorism legislation, was assigned to carry out this painstaking task. Aside from finding that there is no universal definition of terrorism, Carlile (2007) found that of the 60 countries that are signatories of a range of treaties relating to terrorism, 42 had national definitions of terrorism and 18 did not. Toward the goal of advancing a set of common criteria defining terrorism, Carlile urged the following:

- If an action by the perpetrator is only for the purpose of influencing and not intimidating the target, such acts should not be classified as terrorist acts.

- Even though terror is targeted at only property not involving humans, such acts should be considered acts of terror because of the negative psychological impacts they have on people.

- Religious or ethnic reasons should not be an excuse for committing acts of terror even though religion and ethnicity are difficult concepts to define.

- The employment of terrorist tactics by freedom fighters fighting authoritarian regimes should be treated on a case-by-case basis. This is because sometimes freedom fighters have no choice but to use terrorist methods, while at the same time, condoning terrorism for a special group and condemning its use for others would be hypocritical.

- Finally, the search for a universal definition of terrorism should not touch on diplomatic immunity currently enjoyed by diplomats and heads of states. The historical and practical aspects of immunity for these statesmen should not be disrupted because of the issue of terrorism.

Some of Carlile's suggestions are consistent with the U.S. Patriot Act and the British Terrorism Act of 2000. For instance, the third suggestion he made clarifies that a mere suggestion or an attempt to influence does not amount to acts of terror. If a suggestion or recommendation is treated as terrorism, it will curtail freedom of speech.

On September 8, 2006, the United Nations adopted its global counterterrorism strategy designed to provide a unified international effort to fight terrorism in member states (UN G.A. Resolution 2008). Recently, the UN declared that some form of terrorist activity is going on every week somewhere in the world (UN 2012b).

There are two types of terrorism. Domestic terrorism is carried out within a country by local actors and generally impacts that country alone. In contrast, acts that involve two or more countries are referred to as transnational terrorism (Enders and Sandler 2006). For example, 9/11 attacks were transnational. An attack on an intergovernmental organization like the United Nations or International Monetary Fund (IMF) is transnational terrorism (Sandler 2010).

Sandler (2010:205) distinguishes terrorism from crime. He states that terrorism comes with a political or social agenda and is aimed at a large target, usually the general public. Criminals target mainly individuals and do not have a political or social agenda. He provides two examples of the connection between terrorism and political agenda. Spain reacted to the commuter train attacks of Madrid in 2004 by withdrawing its troops from the western coalition in Iraq per al-Qaeda's political demand. In the 1980s, Israel was faced with citizen demands to withdraw its troops from Lebanon following Hezbollah suicide attacks on Israelis.

More specifically, Sambanis (2008:183–184) has analyzed the two phenomena and identified major differences between terrorism and civil war. He suggests these: Violent groups in civil wars are on average less unequal in their capabilities; they are organized in more coherent, hierarchical structures; they have broader political goals and public support; and they can inflict more destruction than violent groups engaged in terrorism.

With terrorism defined, this chapter examines its incidence and nature before outlining key causes, the nature of terrorism, and links with civil wars. Here, violence against civilians during civil wars, the occurrence of terrorism within this context, and conflict termination and terrorism spoilers are noted. Specific attention is given to Afghanistan and Iraq, both countries graphically illustrating how countries at war can become terrorist havens.

INCIDENCE OF TERRORISM

Terrorism has often occurred in those regions that have experienced civil wars. The incidence of terrorism varies according to the coding organization. The RAND Corporation lists about 39,000 incidents of terrorism from 1972 to 2009. During this period, there were 1,486 incidents of terrorist incidents in Africa; 251 in East and Central Asia; 1,650 in Eastern Europe; 3,640 in Latin America; 16,878 in the Middle East; 516 in North America; 6,450 in South Asia; 3,023 in Southeast Asia and Oceania; and 5,696 in Western Europe. Based on an annual average, there have been more attacks during the post-9/11 period than during the pre-9/11 period. Within a span of 8 years in the post-9/11 period (compared to 20 years in the pre-9/11 period) there were more than 27,000 incidents. During this 8-year period, Africa encountered 634 attacks; East and Central Asia endured 76; Eastern Europe had 1,050; Latin America had 1,330; Middle East had 14,100; North America had 86; South Asia had 5,744; Southeast Asia and Oceania had 2,532; and Western Europe faced 1,848 attacks (RAND 2012b). The figures above included attempted terrorist attacks.

The statistics above clearly show that the Middle East and Asia, both of which have witnessed deadly civil wars, faced the greatest threats of terror attacks both pre- and post-9/11. The Global Terrorism Database also lists these parts of the world as the most prone to terrorist strikes (START 2012). In terms of the comparison between the pre-9/11 and post-9/11 periods, the RAND Database of Worldwide Terrorism Incidents (RDWTI) statistics in the preceding paragraph indicate that all regions except North America have faced more attacks in the post-9/11 period based on an annual average basis. Again, the Middle East and Asia recorded the highest per capita jump during the post-9/11 period. Within Asia, both South Asia and Southeast Asia recorded high numbers of attacks during the post-9/11 period. These regions have become hot spots for terrorists. This is not surprising because since September 11, 2001, groups like Jemaah Islamiyah (JE) and the Abu Sayyaf Group (ASG) have been operating extensively in Southeast Asia. Other al-Qaeda-sponsored groups and Taliban-sponsored groups have been actively functioning in India and Pakistan. Table 8.1 shows the frequency of terrorist attacks across regions for the two periods.

The Global Terrorism Database shows that the highest number of terrorist incidents occurred in the early 1990s and the late 2000s (START 2012).

Enders and Sandler (2006) found that after 9/11, attacks on U.S. facilities and installations have increased immaterial of a country's economic levels. They also found that attacks have moved from Europe and Africa to Asia and the Middle East. This is especially true with regards to attacks on U.S. targets in these regions. These regions are perfect for terrorists to easily blend with locals, making it easier for them to hide and plan attacks. Since the end of the Cold War, and also after 9/11, the bulk of Islamic terror attacks took place in low-income countries. However, radical Islamic attacks did not increase in low-income countries after 9/11. It is just that such attacks have always been higher in such countries. Islamic terror has replaced left-wing terror widely practiced during the Cold War. With large Muslim population in these countries, recruitment becomes easier.

TABLE 8.1
Comparing Incidence of Terrorism Across Regions for Two Eras

Region	Total, 1972-2009	Post 9/11 Era: 9/12/2001 to 2009
Africa	1,486	634
East and Central Asia	251	76
Eastern Europe	1,650	1,050
Latin America	3,640	1,330
Middle East	16,878	14,100
North America	516	86
South Asia	6,450	5,744
Southeast Asia and Oceania	3,023	2,532
Western Europe	5,696	1,848
Total	39,590	27,400

Source: RAND (2012b).

TACTICS, TARGETS, AND MEANS

There are myriad tactics terrorists use to enhance or achieve their goals. Targets are often carefully chosen to reflect the objectives of the terrorist group during civil wars, with an aim to force the regime to surrender power or territory. Terrorists use various weapons to achieve their goals.

Common tactics used by terrorists and terrorist groups to inflict damage upon the enemy include the use of armed attack, arson, assassination, barricades and hostage-taking, bombings, hijackings, and kidnappings. These tactics are often associated with the guerilla tactics witnessed during civil wars. The usual targets of terrorist groups are airports, corporate offices, schools and universities, government buildings and embassies, food or water supply, military, non-governmental organizations (NGOs), police, religious figures or institutions, telecommunications, transportation, and private citizens including tourists and journalists and their property. Targets are therefore not just governmental or diplomatic settings but also business, educational, and religious settings. The methods of attack, as described in the RAND (2012a) Database definitions page, are remote-detonated explosive, fire or firebomb, explosive, firearm, knives or sharp object, biological agent, chemical agent, and radiological agent (RAND 2012b). The type of terrorism employed may depend on whether the group has an established territory or not and the size of the group. Groups operating from territories usually employ attacks on important facilities, raids, and actual battles with the government whereas underground groups without territories usually employ explosions (on people, not facilities), assassinations, and kidnappings. Larger groups tend to employ facility attacks whereas smaller groups employ bomb explosions (on people) and kidnappings.

According to the RAND (2000) Corporation report prepared for the then newly elected George W. Bush administration, a terrorist attack within U.S. borders is inevitable and is a grave threat. The organization also alerted the administration to be prepared for such an attack and noted that was becoming more and more likely. RAND also advised that to be able to deal with such an attack, the government must make sure that all levels—federal, state, and local—must communicate well and at the same time have coherent, coordinated interaction with all relevant agencies (RAND 2000).

Interestingly, less than one year later, on September 11, 2001, the worst-ever terrorist attack inside the United States took place. The federal government was ill-prepared to face the 9/11 attack. It is obvious that the federal government did not heed RAND's advice for effective communication between the various federal agencies. The 9/11 Islamic terrorist attack destroyed both World Trade Center buildings, resulting in thousands of casualties, and damaged the Pentagon. The incident had a profound impact on civil war studies. An added consequence of the 9/11 attacks is increased state budgets for counterterrorism. Enders and Sandler (2005:260) stated that since 2002, the budget supporting the activities of the U.S. Department of Homeland Security (DHS) grew by over 60 percent to $36.2 billion for fiscal year 2004. They added that before the 9/11 incident, no terrorist incident, domestic or transnational, resulted in more than 500 casualties and more than $90 billion in losses, as was caused by the 9/11 incident. Not only were a great number of lives lost arising out of Islamic militancy, but money expended to counter Islamic militancy by states also increased tremendously.

Scholars and policy makers began to wonder if the 9/11 incident acted as a motivation for other groups to stage similar attacks in the future. There have been about 2,500 Islamic terrorist attacks since September 11, 2001, made by various Islamic groups, such as Hamas and other Jihadist groups in Israel; Moro Islamic Liberation Front (MILF) and Abu Sayyaf Group (ASG) in the Philippines; Barisan Revolusi Nasional (BRN) and Runda Kumpulan Kecil (RKK) in Thailand; Jemaah Islamiyah (JI) in Indonesia; the three Sunni groups in Iraq, Ansar-al Sunna, Islamic Army, and Islamic State of Iraq; Jamiat ul-Mujahedin (JuM) and the Jammu and Kashmir Islamic Front in India; the Taliban in Afghanistan; Islamic Jihad Group (IJG) in Uzbekistan; Islamic Brigade of Ramzan Ahmadov and Black Widows in Russia; Mujahideen Youth Movement in Somalia; and al-Qaeda all over the world (RAND 2012b). The Fort Hood incident in Texas in 2009 may also be classified as an Islamic-related terrorist attack. The majority of Islamic-related terrorist attacks occurred in the Middle East and Asia (RAND 2012b). Victoroff (2005:3) argues that such fast-evolving trends constitute a clear and present danger to the security of civilization.

Violence Against Civilians in Civil Wars

Rebels sometimes use indiscriminate rampaging and killing. This is intended to serve as a lesson for those who defect to the government side. Fear forces civilians to lend support to the rebel group. Kalyvas (1999) mentions that the side that is more effective in instilling fear gets the civilian support because it is human nature to try to stay alive. The second strategy the rebel group employs to gain civilian support is the use of terrorism against the government. The rebel group hopes that the attack will result in a government indiscriminate counterattack. An indiscriminate attack is not accurately targeted, is unrestrained, and is nonselective and therefore can result in killing innocent civilians. Governments also use terror against civilians, which Azam and Hoeffler (2002) argue acts as a substitute for deploying the military. The authors argue that such acts by the government reduce or displace civilians making civilian population sparse. Once the population becomes sparse, it becomes more difficult for rebels to hide among people.

Usually, the government uses indiscriminate violence. However, when the insurgents are strong, indiscriminate violence by government can backfire (Kalyvas 2004:134–135). Azam and Hoeffler (2002) argue that when government has high capacity, it will resort to terrorism because it has the resources to pay for the terrorism. At the same time, a weak government that faces a poor rebel group will also choose to terrorize civilians because a head-on clash with rebels provides no guarantee of victory. For the government, driving out civilians from their villages or reducing rural population is a rational strategy because the smaller the rural base, the lesser the availability of support for the rebel group. Kalyvas (2004) provides three other possible reasons for indiscriminate violence: ignorance from weak army discipline and strong military emotions (individual level analysis), indiscriminate violence being easier than higher risk policies that could fail because of bureaucratic problems or inept advisors, and competition between military officials. However, Kalyvas argues selective violence is definitely better than indiscriminate because it is more effective and cheaper in the long run. He also stated that a major reason why wars of occupation turn into civil wars is because the occupiers use indiscriminate violence that is counterproductive. Lack of targeting information leads to the use of indiscriminate violence by governments, but insurgents have more targeting information because they are aware of local conditions and identities.

TERRORISM DURING CIVIL WAR

The preceding chapters illustrated how civil wars differ in many respects. Some civil wars are more severe. Others are more extended or cover a wider area. The tactics used by rebels and governments also differ. Acts of terror are common in civil wars. Usually when the perpetrator of the act carries out the attack on behalf of a terrorist group, he or she does it with great confidence because he or she has a group to lean back on. In contrast, the staging of terrorist-like attacks solely by individuals will lack repeat acts or sustainability. Kalyvas (2004) notes that when there is no organization to back the attack, or if the organization is weak, terrorist-like violence will likely fail.

Many studies note the lack of attention given to terrorism in civil wars (e.g., Boulden 2009; Findley and Young 2012; Moore 2011). Moore (2011) argues that terrorism should not be separated as a different form of violence but treated as a strategy in civil wars.

Findley and Young (2012) mention that terrorism is part of many civil wars. Terrorism occurs during, before, and after civil wars. For instance, in Latin American civil wars, acts of terror usually occur before the onset of civil wars while acts of terror occur after civil wars in other parts of the world. The relationship between civil war and terrorism has also been shown by Sambanis (2008). Sambanis examined conditions where terrorism outside of civil war was likely. His empirical analysis identified some similarities: the more people, the more terrorism or the more likely civil war was to occur. However, there were some differences. For instance, ethnic fractionalization seemed to increase the probability of civil war, but no relationship could be discerned between terrorism and ethnic fractionalization. GDP influenced civil war but not terrorism, while the average level of democracy was higher for terrorism (Sambanis 2008:183–184; Findley and Young 2012).

Why Do Rebels Use Terrorist Tactics in Civil War?

Not all rebel groups are fortunate enough to have territories to control. Some rebels with no territorial control employ terrorism to achieve their objectives. De la Calle and Sanchez-Cuenca (2012:581) provide the state capacity explanation of why some groups choose terrorism while others do not. They argue that in weak states, rebels have the advantage of controlling a territory to fight from. In stronger states, the government is able to easily wrest rebel territory from rebels or is able to easily defend itself from rebels operating from rural territories. This leaves rebels with no alternative but to use terrorist tactics, such as exploding bombs in large cities.

Rebels use terrorism to gain support for the group. When terrorists stage an attack, the government responds with counterterrorism. But counterterrorism can have adverse effects on the government (Arce and Sandler 2010; Sanchez-Cuenca and de la Calle 2009) because it can be construed as repression. Because of miscalculations or wrong strategies countering perpetrators, counterterrorism efforts sometimes wrongly take innocent lives. Therefore, the strategy can backfire. For the government, it is hard not to be indiscriminate when conducting counterattacks. Rebel groups count on this to garner sympathy from the public. The majority of MILF's terror tactics were employed during the late 1990s and early 2000s (RAND 2012b) during the time of its original demand for full independence from the Philippines. MILF staged the attacks to force the Philippines government to accept its demand for full independence of Muslim territories in Mindanao. From MILF's decision to drop the full independence demand to a demand for autonomy clearly indicates that it was a "P-type" (politically motivated type) organization. According to Arce and Sandler (2010) a P-type terrorist organization stages terrorist attacks hoping to force the government to at least agree to some of its demands. In contrast, an "M-type" (militantly motivated type) terrorist organization will not sway from its original demands. A P-type organization uses terror to achieve its political goal whereas the M-type uses it for purely religious or unwavering reasons. For the M-type organization, a successful attack produces satisfaction even if the act brings no benefit for the organization and even if the government makes absolutely no accommodation. Kalyvas (2004:112–113) provides experiences by the Portuguese-controlled colonial Mozambique government (against the FRELIMO fighters) and the Vietnam War to illustrate the backfire effect of indiscriminate acts.

Like individuals, governments are faced with the problem of distinguishing between correct and incorrect information. The wrong information can lead to the staging of counterproductive indiscriminate repressions by governments. Terrorist groups wait for governments to show excessive suppression because of past evidence of support derived from such instances. For example the IRA received heightened support as a result of the Bloody Sunday incident in which government troops took 14 civilian lives (Sanchez-Cuenca and de la Calle 2009). The change of heart is mainly an emotional response to government action, for when targeting "people independently of what they both did or could have done, it is perceived as deeply unfair" (Kalyvas 2004:115).

Western counterterrorism efforts are sometimes viewed as an attack on Muslims in general. This leads to greater support for Islamic groups. The more extreme case of such a backlash is in situations in which Western forces intervene to save Muslim lives—for example, in Kosovo and in the Desert Storm operation. The backlash happens when Muslims view these interventions as being conducted for selfish reasons (Mousseau 2011). Kalyvas (1999) provides the Algerian example: In the 1990s, the Algerian government killed seven civilians as a counterattack against the Islamic Salvation Movement (FIS) rebel group's earlier attack. Even though the government response took only seven lives while the rebel attack killed many more policeman and civilians, citizen sympathy and support for the rebel group was buttressed. The Armed Islamic Group of Algeria (Groupe Islamique Arme, or GIA), whose ideology was based on the goal of installing an Islamic government, was reported to have carried out similar tactics to garner local support. In this case, the group massacred civilians suspected of being informants and those suspected of turning to the enemies.

The Salafist Group for Preaching and Combat (GSPC) in Algeria used terrorism to spark the citizen uprising against the state similar to how al-Qaeda mustered huge support and recruitment after the 9/11 attacks (Sanchez-Cuenca and de la Calle 2009). Citizens who previously provided lackluster support or were only considering supporting the group that staged the terrorist act now will be more willing to join and fight for the rebel group. A successful attack makes the group look more powerful. This is partly caused by citizen perception. Victories by underdogs in battles give the impression that the government is not as indispensible as was previously thought. Similarly, many people who thought that the United States was invincible changed their minds after the 9/11 attacks.

A third reason for terrorism is that it is effective. Terrorist attacks receive huge media attention. The use of terrorism is so effective that the IRA staged 171 attacks within Great Britain between 1968 and 1977 (de la Calle and Sanchez-Cuenca 2012). The Tamil Tigers in Sri Lanka staged numerous attacks from the time the civil war started to its end in 2009. If a group knows it has little chance of military victory, then terrorism is a good alternative (Sambanis 2008:197). Robinson (2007) provides similar argument stating lack of resources, money, and skills for this. Terrorism is a form of asymmetrical warfare which is defined as "armed conflict between belligerents of vastly unequal military strength, in which the weaker side is often a non-state actor that relies on unconventional tactics" (Kegley 2010:387). Al-Qaeda has no chance of defeating the United States, yet the group uses terror as a means of inflicting political and human costs. Robinson (2007) asserts that the fear terrorism inflicts is an effective form of violence.

Rational selfish reasons mark another reason for terrorism. At the individual level of analysis, individuals who are concretely promised that upon death their families will be well taken care of may sacrifice their lives to ensure a bright future for the family. Such an arrangement, however, will only convince a potential suicide attempt if there is previous evidence that the group has in fact kept its promise. This is the case with the Sri Lankan Tigers.

The Algerian (discussed in the section on Islamic terrorism), Vietnamese, Peruvian, and Sierra Leonean cases indicate that terror is not a random act. Terrorist acts are carefully planned with specific goals in mind. The Shining Path rebel group in Peru performed specific killings on informants. During the Vietnam War, the Viet Cong strategically changed its strategy to mass killings of civilians to instill fear so that citizens did not become turncoats who switched support to the American side. The Sierra Leonean rebels did the same when they began to lose their grip on local support (Kalyvas 1999). Extending this argument to suicide terrorism provides interesting findings. Pape (2003) gathered details of all suicide attacks occurring between 1980 and 2001. He showed that terrorist attacks are aimed at fulfilling groups' basic goals such as self-determination. Suicide attacks are effective because of their destructive power, and that is perhaps the most important factor for terrorist groups. Groups calculate the timing and location of attacks, and in many occasions, the result is a concession from the government the group is fighting against (six out of the 11 suicide campaigns led to important concessions from the government that the terror group was fighting). Past concessions give terrorist groups greater motivation to stage further attacks, showing that suicide terrorism is a well-designed, strategic move. Pape also notes that suicide terror is strategically aimed at getting foreign, or outside, powers out of certain territory. Suicide terror is meant to mobilize domestic audiences in democratic regimes (e.g., Sri Lanka, United States, Israel, France) toward compelling the government to leave the territory in question (e.g., Palestine, Jaffna, Saudi Arabia).

The Algerian civil war illustrates a case in which terror seemed to defy rationality. The pillage of villages, the killing of women and children in different areas, and massacres of supporters painted this picture of randomness. However, careful analysis points to a different picture altogether. The killings, carried out by the GIA, were more systematic than random. Eyewitness accounts showed that perpetrators targeted specific individuals and families and spared the lives of friends and sympathizers of these individuals and families. The group specifically targeted government soldiers and security personnel, supporters of opposing rebel groups, and informants. Additionally, they specifically targeted individuals and families that refused to provide help for the GIA. Second, the terrorist-styled killings were initiated to instill fear on those considering leaving the group or on those who were supporting the government, and this was done systematically as a signaling tool. Third, terrorist-like attacks were more rampant during a time of uncertain territorial control and uncertain times. This is to say, more massacres occurred when a territory was neither completely ruled by rebels nor the government and in times when it was uncertain who was winning the war. Fourth, terrorist-like attacks were more rampant during a time when rebels were losing their grip on territory (Kalyvas 1999).

CAUSES OF TERRORISM

In this section, we explore what causes terrorism in general, looking at all forms of terrorism, including transnational terrorism, and beyond the employment of terror during civil wars. We do so because of the links between civil wars and terrorism noted earlier. Hassan (2001) found, from interviews with Hamas leaders, that the group did not have a preference for recruiting the uneducated poor.

A European case study criticized previous studies on poverty and terror. Using the Northern Ireland case, Honaker (2008) argued that researchers in previous studies considered aggregate measures of unemployment in Northern Ireland. The aggregate measure counted as a single measure of unemployment that included both Protestant and Catholic group unemployment. This, according to Honaker (2008), would not accurately and specifically measure just the Catholic grievances. As a result, those studies did not show a link between unemployment and civil war involving terrorism as was the case in Northern Ireland. He found that terrorist attacks increased as unemployment increased. In Northern Ireland, the level of autocracy (measured by state military size) mattered too. He found that as the state military size increased, rebel group frequency of attacks on civilians increased.

Some scholars have found that terrorism is more likely in richer states (see Choi 2010; Krueger and Laitin 2008). A low GDP per capita does not necessarily breed terror (Piazza 2006, 2011). Krueger and Laitin (2008) concluded that terrorism is a political and not an economic agenda. The political rather than economics explanation of terrorism within a state may be explained by political diversity. A higher number of political parties can increase the likelihood of terrorism. In line with political conflict theories like the social cleavage theory, socially and culturally divided states manifest themselves in political divisions, for instance, in a high number of political parties (Piazza 2006). Li and Schaub's (2004) conclusion that richer states mitigate terrorism may be because wealthier individuals do not need to resort to life-threatening actions. Educational achievement also may act as a mitigator of terrorism because higher education usually leads to higher incomes and makes the individual more satisfied with the status quo. Shafiq and Sinno (2010) found both of these factors—higher income and higher educational attainment—to directly reduce a person's likelihood of involvement in terrorist acts. First, higher income provides a satisfactory life. Second, formal education teaches a person to be more tolerant and accept that people have different ideas. However, the authors also state that higher income and education tend to make a person more politically dissatisfied. Political dissatisfaction brings about sympathy for terrorist acts. Thus, income and education directly deters terrorism but indirectly causes it. Their argument applies only to suicide terrorism specifically in countries with predominantly Muslim populations. The study also found that between suicide attacks on civilians and on foreign occupation, there is clear evidence that individuals in Muslim countries sympathize with attacks on foreign occupation, such as the case of Iraq.

The mixed results in the academic literature on the relationship between GDP per capita and terrorism may be caused by emphasis on overall state economy or state poverty instead of analyzing group poverty. Piazza (2011) attributed terrorism within a country to economic discrimination of minorities. He argued that GDP per capita of the country will not explain terrorism because it is an aggregate measure. A richer country is more prone to terrorism by minority groups because of the opportunities available for such endeavors in richer states. Minorities who feel left out and isolated in the system lose faith in leaders and the institutions that they administer. This is the root of terror according to him. All forms of economic discriminations (in the form of jobs, health care, education, social, and housing) can contribute to minority terrorism as observed in the Northern Ireland Basque region in Spain and in Sri Lanka.

Li and Schaub (2004) found that globalization had no effect in reducing international terrorist attacks within a country. They argued that what really mattered was the country's economic development. This study showed that a country with a higher GDP per capita is less likely to face international terrorists.

Burgoon (2006) finds a clear link between socioeconomic factors and terrorism. An analysis of the socioeconomic policies of countries for the period 1968 to 2003 enabled him to conclude that the more a country spends on social welfare for its citizens, the less prone that country is to terrorist incidences. The reasons for this are that the higher spending in the social sector fights poverty and reduces religiosity and income inequality that in turn reduces social grievances that can lead to joining terrorist groups. Even a slight increase in welfare spending significantly reduces terrorist incidences. These arguments may be useful to predict left wing and ethnic terrorism because social policies affect these types of terrorism more than purely religious terrorism. Western Europe is perhaps the best candidate to portray ethno-religious and ideological terrorism not involving purely religious terrorism. Krieger and Meierrieks (2010) extended the Burgoon (2006) study for the Western European sample. They argue that increased government expense on health care, housing, employment creation, senior citizens, and family welfare (collectively called social spending) should reduce terrorism because of the indirect influence of these disbursements. They indirectly create a sound socioeconomic status and citizen satisfaction. The reverse is true for low social spending.

In addition, a democratic state that incorporates both socialist and capitalist ideas (social democracies) are less prone to terrorism. In social democracies, unlike more capitalistic states, each of the main actors—the state, the market, and the family—play completely different roles. Because they are provided these differing roles, each actor's dependence on the market is different. Such an arrangement leads to differing grievances and levels of satisfaction between the different sectors of society. As a result of this, terrorist groups are unable to accurately calculate success and level of support from the masses. In addition to this, social democracies have a lower level of unemployment making the pool of disgruntled citizens (potential terrorists) narrower. The less market-dependent the state is, the more equal it is socially and the less likely it is to face terrorism. Their study proved all of the above arguments to be true except, surprisingly, for one area: The provision of unemployment insurance, health insurance, or pensions have no effect in controlling terrorism. Of the 15 western European countries considered in the study, United Kingdom, France, Greece, Italy, Spain, and Germany had more terrorist incidents than the rest.

Burgoon (2006) finds that a country with a higher population stands to be more prone to domestic terror. This is in accordance with findings by Choi (2010), Piazza (2006), and Krueger and Laitin (2008). This can be especially true in highly populated countries that are ethno-religiously diverse (Piazza 2006). Terrorists can use large populations to obscure their operations, escape detection, finance operations, and recruit members. With regard to diverse societies, the potential and opportunity for ethnic and religious communitarian violence is also greater. More diverse societies, in terms of ethnic and religious demography, and political systems with large, complex, multiparty systems were more likely to witness terrorism than more homogeneous states with few or no parties at the national level. Features of these systems that facilitate political violence include an inability to moderate and integrate the participation of newly mobilized political forces into legal political behavior and the empowerment and success of extremist political forces in government (Piazza 2006).

Burgoon (2006) reports a country with a strong military or economy is more likely to face terrorist attacks. Counter to Fearon and Laitin's (2003a) state capacity model of civil war, Piazza (2006) found that terrorism is very likely to take place in autocratic countries (see Choi 2010). Terrorist groups tend to target stronger countries because of wider media coverage, in order to appear more credible, and because these are the countries with which they have disputes.

As mentioned, Pape (2003) points to democracies as more prone to suicide terrorism. As mentioned before, it is easier in democracies to mobilize and organize groups. In addition, democratic leaders are constrained from quick and strong reactions to terrorist activities because democratic norms constrain leaders from brutal reactions. If they do react brutally, it is difficult to justify such an act. Because democracies are not prone to overreaction, they typically do not launch immediate counterterrorism attacks (Schmid 1992). Pape argues terrorists view democracies as manipulable because the public does not tolerate loss of lives and property. Since citizens in democracies have a say in how government is run, when they are tired of losses, they will conceivably demand the government concede to some terrorist demands. Additionally, witnessing other democracies conceding in the past to terrorist groups employing suicide attacks encouraged other terrorist groups to employ suicide attacks. Instances of concessions made to terrorist groups by Israel, Sri Lanka, and Lebanon illustrate the above argument. It is therefore not surprising when Pape (2003) stated that the target of all suicide campaigns between 1980 and 2001 were democracies. Some prior researchers (see e.g., Eubank and Weinberg 2001) have presented similar arguments, further solidifying the positive relationship between democracy and terrorism. The freedoms accorded by democracies may be abused by setting up terrorist networks. The ease of movement and mobilization allows terrorists to carry out their tasks more easily in democracies. While autocracies are better equipped to control acts of terror, they can also breed terrorism but via a different mechanism than democracies. In autocracies, citizens are politically so restricted that they are left with no nonviolent channels to air their grievances. In such circumstances, they are forced to resort to speaking in violent terms, for instance, terrorism. Terrorism is not likely in autocratic states, but terrorists are likely to emerge in these autocratic countries (Krueger and Laitin 2008).

Choi (2010) presents a differing view. In his study of 131 states from 1984 to 2004, he found that there is a clear indication that democracies pacify terrorism. The author attributes this dampening effect to two important reasons. First, the rule of law (high-quality legal system) in democratic countries increases citizens' trust in the proper functioning of the legal system. Citizens recognize the system and therefore accept the government. Perception of a legitimate government deters uprisings in the form of terrorist attacks. Second, because of the existence of rule of law, grievances are dealt with amicably and peacefully. Aggrieved parties may take up challenges against leadership to the judiciary. The presence of a trusted legal system in turn creates trust in the courts.

Li and Schaub (2004) report findings from a study of 112 countries for the period 1975 to 1997. They reveal prior terrorist attacks raise a country's chance for future attacks. In line with Choi (2010), Honaker (2008) found a positive relationship between prior violence and rebellion.

Terrorist attacks can yield trouble for the perpetrator. Benmelech, Berrebi, and Klor (2009) used the Palestinian civil war to show that for every successful Palestinian terrorist attack on Israel, the home district of the individual(s) suffered economically after the attack. In addition to this, Palestinians in Israel generally faced negative effects following a Palestinian attack on Israel. For example, Palestinian job seekers in Israel faced a 6.7 percent drop in employment after a successful Palestinian attack on Israel.

This section illustrated that some factors are clear predictors of terrorism whereas others are not. Population size, state capacity, and prior terrorist acts are good predictors of terrorism. The lack of consensus in the literature for GDP per capita, education, and regime type indicates that these factors may not accurately predict terrorism.

CHARACTERISTICS AND STRUCTURE OF TERRORIST GROUPS

The ways terrorist groups are organized has important implications for their efficacy. Some terrorist groups are highly structured while others are more loosely structured. The former boasts strength and superior networking while the latter is more secure because they are more difficult to infiltrate (Enders and Jindapon 2010). Terrorist groups may also be classified based on frequency of attacks. The first category consists of groups that stage frequent attacks over time. The second category contains groups that stage sporadic attacks (Blomberg, Engel, and Sawyer 2010). The authors also found that the current trend is gravitating toward smaller but more deadly terrorist groups.

Al-Qaeda may be referred to as a terrorist organization made up of, among others, the Jamiat-i-Islami, the Abu Sayyaf, and the Hezbollah cells. Even though cells combine to form a larger terrorist organization, each individual cell can stage a terrorist attack (Clauset and Wiegel 2010). More cells means less control from central command (Enders and Jindapon 2010). For example, the Jamiat-i-Islami in Indonesia is affiliated with al-Qaeda but not all its attacks had al-Qaeda's blessing. Enders and Jindapon (2010) argue that in highly structured terror networks, information flow is good. This explains why highly structured groups can carry out more sophisticated and more frequent attacks and respond more robustly to state counterterrorism measures. Even though less rigidly structured terror groups lack the advantages mentioned above, they stand to benefit from greater secrecy.

Enders and Jindapon (2010) argue that terrorist organizations made up of cells change and adapt according to changing circumstances. For instance, terrorist organizations adapt to state policy changes. The trend these days is that terrorist cells have much more leeway to carry out operations. Information technology has enabled individual cells access to pertinent information necessary for decision making without having to rely on a central command. When the costs of keeping the cells under a strict structure (networking) rise, terrorist organization becomes more decentralized. Sometimes, a terrorist organization employs both top-down strict structure as well as the loose, decentralized structure. Enders and Jindapon (2010) provide the case of al-Qaeda network strategically practicing dual structures in different occasions.

Helfstein and Wright (2011) argue that neither structure nor network characteristics decide the effectiveness and severity of attacks. Groups do not portray a single structure or a single network style throughout their life span. Instead, they change. Additionally, the authors demonstrated that groups do not seek strategic structuring if they perceive they will not be located easily. Thus, they suggest that attempts by states to identify and kill individuals who are main information disseminators will prove futile. Rather, a good strategy would be to send false signals that the group is not easily identifiable.

Terror groups have the choice of staging large, well-planned, and long-term attacks or smaller, short-term ones. Groups will not choose large or sophisticated attacks unless they know they have grown to that level and are up to the task. Further, scarce finances and human resources force groups to forgo small attacks if they decide on large attacks (Feinstein and Kaplan 2010). This explains why MILF and Abu Sayyaf stage only small attacks in the Philippines civil war whereas al-Qaeda stages only large-scale attacks. Terror groups may therefore be considered rational.

The survival of terror groups depends on the type of organization. For groups that stage sporadic attacks, the older the group, the better its chance of survival. The exact opposite scenario is seen in groups conducting more frequent attacks—the older the group, the lesser its chance of future survival. Besides age, various other factors affect the survival rate of terror groups. Regional factors dictate that groups have a greater chance of survival in sub-Saharan Africa than in North America. We can also expect groups to have better survival rates in countries with higher GDP per capita and in countries that have a higher population size. Additionally, more deadly groups tend to live longer than their counterparts. Interestingly, ethno-religious factors, such as ethno-religious fractionalization, do not have any effect on the survival rate of terrorist groups (Blomberg et al. 2010).

ISLAM, CIVIL WAR, AND TERRORISM

Of the 42 religious civil wars between 1940 and 2000, 34 (81 percent) of the combatants identified themselves with Islam, a fact that had prompted many scholars to speculate about the reason for the connection. Toft (2007) asserts that Islam was involved in the most religious civil wars. She invokes the instrumentalist idea of leaders manipulating religion and masses for self-interest and political survival. Indra de Soysa (2002), on the other hand, reported that Catholicism was equally conflict prone. Scholars have debated over the reasons behind both Islamic international conflict as well as Islamic civil conflict.

The role of religion in civil war is illustrated by recent and current wars in Iraq and Kashmir in India; previously in Mindanao, Philippines, and in Kosovo in the former Yugoslavia. Islam is the second largest religion in the world and is the fastest growing (Young 1997). The Pew Research Center (2009) Report estimated that there are 1.57 billion Muslims in the world. About 100 countries in the world are at least 5 percent Muslim. Islamic militancy has been accused of causing internal strife in many countries. The subject of Islamic militancy therefore demands a scientific investigation.

Causes of Islamic Terrorism

There are four nuanced explanations of Islamic terrorism (Mousseau 2011). The first is based on the nature of Islam itself. This argument posits that the teachings of Islam may be propagating violence. The clash of civilization model foresees that the conflict between the West and Islam will be more severe in the future. This is caused by sharp ethno-religious or cultural differences between Islam and the West. The model disputes the proposition that the source of ethno-religious conflicts is economic or ideological (Huntington 1993, 1996). Venkatraman (2007) argues that the freedom accorded to Muslims to individually interpret the Holy Koran is another reason for Islamic terrorism. Because of this freedom, Islam has developed into four different Islamic practices, namely, modern Islam, pragmatic Islam, traditional Islam, and fundamental Islam. The modernists and the pragmatists practice tolerance and are more understanding of other religions. On the other hand, the traditionalists and fundamentalists aim to isolate themselves from non-Muslims and wish to impose Islamic principles. They can be expected to use religion to fight. Venkatratam (2007) argued that because Prophet Muhammad used violence to spread the word of God, traditionalists and fundamentalists can be expected to emulate his actions in the modern world. She expressed that because the Koran allows violence in specific circumstances and allows individual interpretations, adherents can be expected to legitimize political terrorism, as long as the act can be justified as having a firm Islamic basis. In short, traditionalists and fundamentalists aim to bring back the golden era of Muslim rule of yesteryears through crusades using the Prophet's style of a warrior. This explanation runs counter with Halliday (1996) who argues that a sound model connecting violence to the religion itself must be able to show that there is a common characteristic in all states or all Islamic militancy. Evidence shows that many Islamic societies can separate religion from politics. Different Islamic countries follow different policies, and there is really no single common idea connecting all Islamic states. Because different states portray different characteristics of Islamic militancy depending on the specific circumstances faced, and because there is an absence of a stateless or international Islamic movement, Halliday asserts that such a model fails to provide a concrete argument for the Islam-terror nexus.

Mousseau (2011) criticizes this explanation as shallow because Islamic militancy is a fairly new phenomenon (a product of the 1980s and 1990s). Radicals wish to bring back Islamic teachings that lay claim to the idea that Muslims have been corrupted and lead a non-Islamic life. Radicals argue that the solution to cleanse corrupted life is to return to the manner of the old days.

The second explanation for Islamic terrorism connects education to violence. Mousseau (2011) shows that low educational attainment is associated with Islamic terror. Even though Kavanagh (2011) and Hassan (2001) found that it is the individuals with higher educational levels who join terrorist groups, Kavanagh (2011) clearly indicated to the contrary that the educated poor are the ones specifically likely to join these groups.

The third explanation of Islamic terrorism is economic grievances. Some studies (see Enders and Sandler 2006; Honaker 2008) on terrorism in general have highlighted poverty or economic grievances (as in Gurr's relative deprivation theory) as drivers of terrorism. Survey respondents in 14 countries representing 62 percent of the world's Muslim population have indicated that approval of Islamist terror is not associated with religiosity, lack of education, poverty, or income dissatisfaction. Instead, it is associated with urban poverty. The rise of militant Islam can be attributed to high rates of urbanization in many Muslim countries in recent decades, which fosters violence as rising groups seek to dislodge prior groups entrenched in power (Mousseau 2011:35).

The fourth explanation posits that the root cause of Islamic terrorism lies in the politico-economic makeup of a country. In capitalistic states, ordinary citizens are inseparable economically from the business class because of the unique relationship that exists between these two groups. In such an arrangement, the masses purchase everyday goods produced by strangers (businessmen). A disruption such as a terrorist attack on the business elites will have negative effects on the masses because of the intertwined nature of the capitalist economy. This has been evidenced in the past, for instance, the sufferings of the average person from the recession created indirectly by the 9/11 incidents. For Mousseau (2011), among the four explanations, only this argument explains Islamic terrorism. He pointed out that because of such a politico-economic makeup in capitalist countries, citizens will be less inclined to use terror as means of achieving desired goals. In non-capitalist or semicapitalist states that lack the masses-businessman symbiotic relationship arrangement, groups compete with each other to receive government resources outside of the market. Group members are at the mercy of group leaders to bring in benefits. Group cohesion and loyalty tends to be strong in such a scenario. This allows leaders to drive members according to their wishes because members are at the mercy of leaders to bring in their benefits.

Mousseau presented this argument with reference to predominantly Muslim countries in which the imams (leaders of mosques) are able to influence Muslim followers into terrorist activities. New migrants to cities from rural areas have limited contacts in the urban areas. New migrants need help of various sorts upon arriving in the city because of unaccustomed lifestyle. These migrants typically depend on friends and relatives who introduce them to the imam or his representatives. Being new and in need of help, these migrants are easily influenced with anti-Western thoughts (some of these rural folks migrate to the city with existing anti-Western ideas). The imams and their representatives portray themselves as champions of the rural migrants in the city. The argument above is especially true, according to Mousseau, in noncapitalist or semicapitalist states that are undergoing political, economic, or social changes, such as globalization, urbanization, or foreign invasion. He found that the majority of terrorist incidents within predominantly Islamic countries were staged by urban individuals, many of whom migrated from rural areas to large cities. Sageman (2004) pointed out that a good number of individuals involved in terrorist activities only became religious after being affiliated with one of these urban groups. Different individuals from different places and countries meet in large cities, which become their new homes. The friendships that are fostered among them lead to the formation of hubs of potential terror cells. Therefore, collective identity is a key to Islamic terrorism.

CONFLICT TERMINATION AND TERRORIST SPOILERS

The end of fighting after a civil war does not always guarantee long-term peace. Much depends on the fairness and legitimacy of the peace agreement, whether it is actually implemented, and the disarming of the rebels. One party may suddenly decide to sabotage the agreement at a later time. Sometimes, outside parties sabotage agreements. A party that attempts to sabotage a peace process is referred to as a *spoiler*. Stedman (1997:5) characterized spoilers as "leaders and parties who believe that peace emerging from negotiations threatens their power, worldview, and interests." Spoilers are a critical problem faced by peacemakers as they are often willing to use violence to achieve their goals. They appear during peace talks or after a pact has been signed (Stedman 1997).

Terrorism has been shown to be an effective method to sabotage peace processes. Examples of spoiler effects have been witnessed in peace processes in Rwanda, Northern Ireland, and Bosnia (Findley 2011). In the most recent peace agreement, between the government of Philippines and the MILF, there is not yet an indication of a spoiler problem. However, the agreement was only recently signed on October 15, 2012. In January 2014, agreement was reached on the final section of a peace deal with the Muslim insurgents. The accord detailed how the insurgents would hand over their weapons in exchange for self-rule in parts of the south.

While Pape (2003) argued that suicide terrorism is an effective tool to bring the government to the negotiation table, Fortna (2008) found that terrorism in general makes it harder for civil wars to end. In fact, terrorist tactics do not really bring victory for rebel groups. Their chance of a victory is greater if they employ conventional tactics or if they decide to negotiate with the government. This is because evidence has shown that in civil wars in which the rebel groups use terrorism, the war usually ends with government victory (Fortna 2008).

Stedman (1997) notes spoilers may emerge from an actor that is party to the agreement or an outside party. He provided the Khmer Rouge and UNITA as examples of internal spoilers because both groups defaulted on the peace agreements that they signed because they subsequently felt the agreements were unfavorable to them. He provided the example of the Committee for the Defense of the Revolution (CDR) of Rwanda as an example of an external spoiler. This group was not a party to the Rwandan peace agreement. It was keen in seeing the agreement fall apart, hence, the spoiler staged violence to disrupt it.

Spoilers may be influential leaders. The leader of UNITA in Angola, Jonas Savimbi, acted to spoil a peace process (Findley 2011; Stedman 1997). Even though the United Nations monitored the 1992 Angolan elections, Savimbi refused to validate the results. This returned Angola to war. A radical group on the other hand may resort to terrorist tactics to stop peace agreements in which the parties are moderates (Findley 2011). The Real IRA in Northern Ireland is such an example.

Spoilers are so significant in the termination of war that even small-scale violence employed by a spoiler group can disrupt or delay peace. As mentioned previously, terrorism is the weapon of the weaker side. This explains why even a small spoiler group with little power causes big impacts on the success of peace processes.

To achieve a fair and desirable outcome of war, Stedman (1997) recommends peacekeeping organizations (such as the United Nations) analyze and manage spoilers effectively. Additionally, he argues that there is a greater chance to totally end a civil war if there is international consensus on peace agreements and the management of spoilers.

CASE STUDIES

Two cases that help illustrate terrorism-civil war links are Afghanistan and Iraq. The ongoing conflicts in both countries have led them to become terrorist havens. They have drawn the international community's attention and massive involvement while inflicting heavy costs on both of their civilian populations, rival factions, and coalition forces. The Soviet occupation of Afghanistan (1979–1989) was followed by internal fighting that ultimately led to the Taliban's 1996 seizure of power. They allowed al-Qaeda to establish bases, and Osama bin Laden, the terrorist group's leader, allegedly lived there. Despite the Taliban losing power in December 2001, conflict and lawlessness remain, as both Taliban and al-Qaeda elements operate within the country or near its borders. Nor has bin Laden's death in May 2011 ended al-Qaeda attacks. More recently, the 2003 U.S.-led coalition that overthrew Iraqi President Saddam Hussein occurred within the aftermath of 9/11. Despite coalition attempts to enforce its control and establish law and order, fighting continues.

Afghanistan

Post-World War II terrorism in Afghanistan may be divided into two stages: terrorism during the Soviet occupation and terrorism in the post-9/11 era. (The use of terrorism has been practiced even long before the Soviet occupation, but for the sake of space, that will not be discussed here.)

In 1979, the Soviet Union invaded Afghanistan and installed a puppet government headed by Babrak Karmal. Afghan freedom fighters who called themselves mujahideen opposed Kamal's puppet government from the time he took power. The mujahideen were later supported by the United States to fight the Soviet occupation and the Kamal administration. They forced the Soviets to give up and leave Afghanistan. The vacuum that the Soviets left behind led to civil war between the different Islamic rebel groups, such as between the Jamiat-i-Islami and the Herb-i-Islami. Numerous other rebel groups and warlords took sides with one of these two groups. A strong united extremist Islamic group sprang to its advantage amid this anarchy (U.S. Department of State 2011).

In 1996, Taliban militants opposing Soviet rule seized Kabul, Afghanistan's capital city. The Taliban installed extremist Islamic rule over the country (Juergensmeyer 2013). The Taliban fought alongside the mujahideen during Soviet occupation. These groups practiced terrorist tactics to fight the Soviets.

One would have expected that during the Taliban administration terrorism would end because the former terrorists themselves were now in power. Terrorism continued, however, but it took a different form. Under Taliban rule, Islamic extremists flocked to Afghanistan (for example, Egyptian Islamic radicals who were released from prison post-Anwar Sadat era and Indonesian, Malaysian, and Middle Eastern radicals). From here, they trained and planned terrorist attacks in other countries to achieve what the Taliban achieved in Afghanistan (Sageman 2013). The funding of these operations came from none other than bin Laden who was already domiciled in Afghanistan when the Taliban took power. Here, bin Laden and his combatants received a sort of a sanctuary from which to operate. Bin Laden converted former CIA-sponsored mujahideen camps into terrorist training facilities (Snow 2003). There were 41 terrorist attacks during the Soviet occupation of Afghanistan in addition to many other various nonterrorist insurgencies (RAND 2012b).

The case of terrorism in Afghanistan fits well with two academic arguments: Islamic extremism (see Juergensmeyer 1993, 2001, 2013; Venkatraman 2007) and state capacity (see Fearon and Laitin 2003a).

After the U.S.-led invasion of Afghanistan in 2001, terrorism continued. This time, the Karzai government installed by the United States faced attacks from two of his foes working together: bin Laden's al-Qaeda group and the Taliban led by Mullah Mohammed Omar (Council on Foreign Relations 2005). The Taliban was reported to have been practicing terrorism, including attacks on schools and hospitals, and was accused of terrible human rights violations (Keen 2012). There were 1,976 terrorist attacks (215 of these were suicide attacks) from the time of the U.S.-led invasion in October 2001 to the end of 2010 in Afghanistan (RAND

2012b). The nature of the war therefore changed dramatically between the Soviet occupation and the U.S.-backed Karzai government. The number of terrorist attacks from October 2001 to the end of 2010 is about 50 times higher than the number of attacks during the Soviet rule from December 1979 to December 1998. This trend illustrates a clear departure from the traditional method of warfare to a style focused on terrorism. Similarly, Combs (2011:156) provides instances of children handling explosives and of a Taliban commander boasting to a *Newsweek* reporter that he was responsible for training 1,800 suicide bombers. The post-9/11 war in Afghanistan has become brutal and asymmetrical. For example, in July 2009, extremist Muslims killed 20 civilians including children on the way to school in the Logar province. The most depressing news of terror is that within a span of 2 months in 2009, rebels initiated 98 attacks on schools (UN News Centre 2009). Many of these attacks are directed on Americans and other Westerners, but some of them have been staged on Afghans by Taliban and other rebel groups. This may be explained by the freedom that Muslims have in interpreting the Holy Koran, the Islamic holy book.

Venkatraman (2007) opines that sometimes Muslims use religion as an excuse for violence with the justification that the Koran allows adherents to decide on the use of violence. Therefore, it is not surprising to see the Taliban and other Afghan rebel groups use violence because the Koran allows them to fight to defend the preservation of the principles contained in the Koran.

Additionally, the Koran specifically allows violence against nonbelievers. Radical Muslims therefore interpret this as an approval of violence against non-Muslim Soviet occupiers and Americans and the American-backed Karzai administration. The groups do not hesitate to use brutal force on fellow Muslims because the Koran allows this as well when Muslims prevent the fundamental preservation of the general Islamic society. Venkatraman (2007) argues that Islamic militancy is used as a remedy for solving long-term problems including political problems, such as in Kashmir, India. The same argument may be applied to Afghanistan.

Keen (2012) notes that in Afghanistan, when American forces kill rebel soldiers, the rebel group receives more support because locals view death of rebel soldiers as death of one of them. The counterterrorism strategy backfires. This connection is not new as scholars have noticed on many occasions that counterattacks result in increased support for rebel groups.

In the case of Afghanistan, there is a direct connection between terrorism and natural resources. Three groups—Hizb-i-Islami, Taliban, and al-Qaeda—have been found to have a clear link to drug trade, and one other, the Islamic Movement of Uzbekistan (IMU), has been shown to have a probable link (U.S. Congress 2004).

Keen (2012) points to opium trade as a huge funding source for the Afghan rebels. Piazza (2012) found that opium is a significant cause of terrorism in Afghanistan. Those provinces that produce more opium are at a higher risk of facing terrorist attacks. The author however did not provide convincing evidence as to why this is the case. Nevertheless, he was able to provide some superficial explanation for the connection. One of the reasons for this connection is rebels are found where opium is found. Opium is used to raise revenue to maintain rebel force. The routes of illegal opium trade coincide with the location of opium fields, and rebels maintain these routes. Areas with opium cultivation draw other illegal trade, such as illegal weapons trade. Hence, terrorists are guaranteed access to cheap weapons. This shows that drug trade is directly related to terrorism. Goodhand (2005) provides a detailed case study of how Afghanistan's opium trade is related to the civil war there. He shows how both the Mujahideens (during Soviet occupation) and the Taliban (currently) reaped opium profits to fund their militaries. The Goodhand (2005) study will be discussed in more detail in the next chapter.

Recent attacks on U.S. forces by friendly Afghan security trained by Americans are another obvious example of terrorist-like warfare. In August 2012, an Afghan National Police commander opened fire on three American soldiers during a friendly discussion over dinner. The killing was preplanned. There were more than 40 such attacks in 2011 and 2012 combined, which caused more than 60 deaths (Taylor 2012).

Iraq

Since 1958, Iraq has experienced both ethno-religious and non-ethno-religious civil wars. All the civil wars fought between 1958 and 1963 were non-ethno-religious. During this time, military factions staged coups d'etat to take control of the Iraqi government. Since 1982, ethno-religious civil wars became the predominant form of civil war. The Kurdish minority group has been fighting the Iraqi government since the 1960s. However, the rise of Islamic extremism in Iraq is a fairly new phenomenon. UCDP/PRIO lists the 1980s as the earliest Islamic civil wars in Iraq.

The reasons for the use of terror by Kurdish groups in Iraq is, as mentioned before, that it is effective against a much stronger enemy, successful attacks provide recruitment boost for the group, and counterterrorism brings support for the rebel group because of sympathy. Dekmejian (2007) provides a historical account of the Kurdish civil war against the Saddam Hussein administration. In 1974 Saddam Hussein, then Iraqi vice-president, ordered implementation of the Kurdish autonomy measures which had earlier been rejected by the Kurds. This angered the Kurds who staged a rebellion against Iraq. Strategic manipulations by Hussein removed support for the Kurds from their allies. Hussein took advantage of this to kill thousands of Kurds. Hundreds of thousands of Kurds fled or sought refuge in Iran. During the Iran-Iraq war in the 1980s, Hussein massacred thousands more Kurds because of the impression that Iran was an ally of the Kurds.

One Iraqi Kurdish group, Ansar-al-Islam, decided to follow the Islamic extremist path. Founded in the 1990s, the group became affiliated with al-Qaeda in the early 2000s. Since then, the group has been staging suicide bombings against American forces. Originally, the group operated from Kurdish territories in northern Iraq but since September 11, 2001, has infiltrated farther south. The group uses various terrorist methods. They have assassinated Iraqi government officials, educators, and judges who have ties with the Americans and journalists. They have used suicide attacks and car bomb explosions on American interests (Gregory 2008). In 2012, a new group, al-Qaeda Kurdish battalions (AQKB), has been designated by the United States as a terrorist organization (U.S. Department of State, CT 2012).

Bin Laden was able to persuade thousands of Arabs to flock to Iraq to face the impending American invasion right before the 2003 U.S.-led invasion. The post-9/11 civil war in Iraq has seen a major use of terrorist tactics by Islamic groups to win the war against U.S. forces, and the new Iraqi government installed by the U.S. Islamic groups, such as the Ansar-al-Islam and al-Qaeda, have been reported to use terrorist tactics against U.S. forces occupying Iraq (Nacos 2008:121).

Various Islamic extremist groups have been in civil war against American forces and the American-installed government in Iraq. Almost all of them are Sunni groups. Sunnis are fighting the Iraqi government because, first, the government that the United States ousted in 2003 was a Sunni-led government headed by Saddam Hussein. Second, the United States installed a new government based on a coalition between Shi'ites and Kurds. Third, al-Qaeda comprises mostly Sunnis.

The Tanzim Qa'idat al Jihad fi Bilad al Rafidayn (TQBR), or al-Qaeda Organization in the Land of Two Rivers, was formed by al-Zarqawi. Its goal is to force Americans out of Iraq and to install an Islamic Iraq. It is obvious that this civil war is ethno-religious but at the same time it is also for the control of government. Its brutality is obvious because of its use of terrorism on a daily basis. The group stages terrorist attacks using a myriad of ways ranging from suicide attacks to kidnappings and actual guerilla warfare. Further, beheading of enemies is not an uncommon strategy for this group (START 2012).

The Al Mahdi Army also uses terror. This is a Shi'ite group formed to fight the foreign control of Iraq and its allies in Iraq. This group uses guerilla warfare, extortion, unsophisticated rockets, and execution of enemies (UCDP 2012a).

Among the numerous Sunni groups is al-Qaeda. Al-Qaeda is perhaps the most significant rebel group in Iraq with regards to the use of terror. It is responsible for the expansion of the size, training, and extremism of Sunni radicals in Iraq (Dekmejian 2007:303). It employs not only various terrorist techniques, but also high-profile ones. Most of the suicide attacks in Iraq have been carried out by al-Qaeda. This group has brutally videotaped the beheading of Americans in Iraq (U.S. Department of State, CT 2012). The group's primary goal is to force the United States and all Western powers to leave the Middle East alone (Snow 2003:304–305). To achieve this, it attacks both military and civilians. It attacks major infrastructures (residents, businesses, and government), civil servants, women, and children, using car bombs, roadside bombs, and rockets. Al-Qaeda's operations are not confined to the capital city, Baghdad, alone but all over the country (U.S. Department of State, CT 2013). Al-Qaeda was responsible for 165 terrorist incidents in Iraq from the day of the U.S. invasion in 2003 to the end of 2010. Out of this, 72 were suicide attacks (RAND 2012a).

The situation in Iraq is not confined to civil war between rebel groups and the government. There are cases of sectarian violence between Sunnis and Shi'ites to the extent of destroying each other's mosques, unquestionably sacred sites for Muslims. For instance in 2006, the Sunni destruction of one of Shi'ite's holiest shrines was returned with Shi'ite attacks on many Sunni mosques and the murder of Sunnis (Dekmejian 2007:305).

IMPLICATIONS FOR CONFLICT MANAGEMENT

Terrorism is common in many civil wars. It is often a strategy of the weaker rebels who realize they cannot prevail in conventional warfare or who want the attention of citizens in a democratic occupying state. The IRA and RIRA versus Britain and Israel versus Palestinian groups are classic examples of civil wars involving terrorism.

A common challenge for conflict management in civil wars is that peace processes can lead to spoilers who do not agree with the negotiations or who fear loss of status. These spoilers often turn to terrorism that can, in turn, hamper the peace effort. When mediators accompany these processes, special care must be made to reach out to potential spoilers so they do not feel excluded in the process. Of course, it is not always possible to prevent spoilers, so the negotiators (and mediator if applicable) must be prepared to deal with the fallout if spoilers emerge. In addition to loss of lives, terrorism by spoilers can reduce public support for the peace process. This is, in fact, what the spoilers hope to achieve. If the negotiating teams are calm and each side is credibly committed to the peace process, there is a better chance the talks will survive terrorism by spoilers.

If a peace agreement is signed, provisions should address all potential user groups. The agreement should be as fair as possible to disgruntled rebels who might otherwise see terrorist violence as the only solution. For example, the agreement can contain language reintegrating former rebels, amnesties, special cultural and/or religious concessions for the rebels (e.g., the 2005 Aceh Accord), power sharing, and reconciliation.

CONCLUSION

The threat of terrorism has been internationally acknowledged, particularly in the aftermath of the 9/11 attacks. Civil wars have facilitated the growth of terrorist groups, especially when unpopular regimes lose control over territory and cannot maintain law and order despite aggressively seeking to retain power. Here, terrorists can operate with little or no interference from the state, and it is difficult for the international community to prevent the violation of basic human rights. Civil wars can make people more receptive to supporting terrorists, or at least accept their presence. Indeed, terrorists might be helped by some combatants who share the same beliefs. The decline of living standards along with regime atrocities can make promises of support from terrorists and their propaganda more attractive. Ultimately, terrorists exploit the death and destruction commonly associated with civil wars, such as through providing an avenue for retribution.

The RAND Corporation lists 36,000 terrorist attacks over the period 1972–2009. Taken together, these incidents, as with civil wars, have cost hundreds of thousands of lives. Moreover, many of the casualties are innocent civilians. The Middle East and Asia have become favorite spots for terror. Terrorist groups, such as Hamas and Hezbollah in the Middle East and JI and ASG in Southeast Asia, execute bombings and suicide attacks on airports, embassies, religious institutions, individuals, and other targets. Such incidents increase instability and, particularly with the likelihood for brutal responses from authoritarian regimes, the prospect of ongoing violence. The cycle of retribution between factions and the regime can ultimately escalate into civil war.

Rebel groups use terror for various reasons. Terrorism might be a useful tool to gain support from the masses. Previously uninformed or indifferent citizens have been shown to sympathize with terrorists after a successful attack. Additionally, rebel groups that have staged successful attacks can be perceived as reliable or powerful. Rebel groups that employ terror are faced with counterterrorism measures from the government. Counterterrorism measures are sometimes indiscriminate, killing innocent citizens. This might actually help the rebels through generating sympathy and the perception of counterterrorism as repression. Groups employ terror because it is a potentially very effective tool for weak groups fighting a more powerful force. Terrorists are often not easily identified. They rarely wear uniforms and often hide among ordinary citizens, carry light arms, and are flexible. This is a huge disadvantage for the government, which is used to fighting in symmetrical ways.

An effective method of terrorism often involves suicide attacks, these being very difficult to effectively counter. Groups such as the LTTE in Sri Lanka have taken advantage of this and have staged numerous suicide attacks to achieve their goals. Pape (2003) showed that suicide attacks are not random acts but are well-calculated rational actions. Economic and religious considerations mark additional reasons for terrorism. Individual terrorists generally have narrow motives ranging from economic security for the family upon his or her death or the ambition to reach heaven as a martyr. However, terrorists also risk losing support and any legitimacy they might have by staging indiscriminate attacks.

The academic literature on Islamic terrorism outlines various explanations for Islamic terrorism. In Islamic terrorism, instrumentalism serves as an important reason why terrorism takes place. Radical Muslims of traditionalist and funda-mentalist Islam are sometimes successful in persuading followers to stage vio-lence especially on Western targets. For them the West, democracy, and secularism are traditional enemies. The religiosity argument states that the religion itself acts as a motivation of conflict. The argument illustrates radical Muslims emu-lating violent acts that the Prophet staged during his time. The Koran permits some self-interpretation which has allowed radicals to justify acts of terror as not religiously immoral. Interestingly, studies have shown that a highly educated person is more likely to be recruited as an Islamic terrorist especially if he or she is economically disadvantaged.

Mousseau (2011) posited the structural argument that states Islamic terror-ism is more likely in noncapitalist states. The political-economic structure in capitalist states situates citizens within a mutually beneficial arrangement with the capitalist elites. This prevents citizens from staging attacks which will only disrupt the system. According to Mousseau (2011: 35), the best political strategy to limit support and recruits for Islamist terrorist groups is to enhance the eco-nomic opportunities available for the urban poor and to provide them the needed services that many currently obtain from Islamist groups. These services include access to health care and education.

Terror in civil wars may also be explained by macro-level variables, such as GDP per capita, democracy, population size, state capacity, social divisions, education level, and prior attacks. Of these, only population size, state capacity, and prior terrorist attacks meaningfully explain why terrorism occurs. Among these factors, high population size is the most robust indicator of potential use of terror.

Both governments and rebels are known to have employed terror on noncombatants. Contrary to popular belief, both parties often perform cost-benefit calculations before embarking on terror.

In civil wars, certain parties play the role of spoilers. These are either outsiders or an inside party to the war. Individuals can also be spoilers. A spoiler gains from disrupting potential peace or a peace agreement taking place. One way of spoiling peace is by staging terrorist attacks.

In general, terrorist organizations have some common characteristics. Members join terrorist organizations because of beliefs, not because of selfish reasons. The presence of more cells that are disciplined is an advantage for any terrorist group. There are two types of terrorist groups, highly structured groups and more loosely structured groups. Groups may also be classified based on attack frequency. A scientific analysis of the structure of terrorist organizations allows policy makers and scholars to forecast more accurately where and when terrorists will strike.

Fortunately, evidence suggests that international efforts to counter terrorism have experienced some success. According to the U.S. Department of State, al-Qaeda's core has been significantly degraded by continuing worldwide efforts. The loss of leaders has degraded the group's ability to direct the activities and attacks of affiliates with senior figures increasingly focused on survival. This has driven affiliates to become more independent. They have increasingly set their own goals and specified their own targets. As previous avenues for receiving and sending funds have become more difficult to access, several affiliates have staged kidnappings for ransom. Through these operations and other criminal activities, the affiliates have increased their financial independence. Ultimately, affiliates have seemed to be more focused on smaller scale attacks closer to their home base (U.S. Department of State, CT 2013:5).

SUGGESTED READING

Arce, Daniel G. and Todd Sandler. 2010. "Terrorist Spectaculars: Backlash Attacks and the Focus of Intelligence." *Journal of Conflict Resolution* 54(2):354–373.

Azam, Jean-Paul and Anke Hoeffler. 2002. "Violence against Civilians in Civil Wars: Looting or Terror?" *Journal of Peace Research* 39(4):461–485.

Enders, Walter and Paan Jindapon. 2010. "Network Externalities and Structure of Terror Networks." *Journal of Conflict Resolution* 54(2):262–280.

Enders, Walter and Todd Sandler. 2005. "After 9/11: Is It All Different Now?" *Journal of Conflict Resolution* 49(2):259–277.

Enders, Walter and Todd Sandler. 2006. "Distribution of Transnational Terrorism among Countries by Income Class and Geography after 9/11." *International Studies Quarterly* 49(2):259–277.

Feinstein, Jonathan S. and Edward H. Kaplan. 2010. "Analysis of Strategic Organizations." *Journal of Conflict Resolution* 54(2):281–302.

Findley, Michael G. and Joseph K. Young. 2012. "Terrorism and Civil War: A Spatial and Temporal Approach to a Conceptual Problem." *Perspective on Politics* 10(2):285–305.

Kalyvas, Stathis. 2004. "The Paradox of Terrorism in Civil War." *The Journal of Ethics* 8:97–138.

Mousseau, Michael. 2011. "Urban Poverty and Support for Islamist Terror: Survey Results of Muslims in Fourteen Countries." *Journal of Peace Research* 48(1):34–47.

Piazza, James A. 2011. "Poverty, Minority Economic Discrimination, and Domestic Terrorism." *Journal of Peace Research* 48(3):339–353.

Piazza, James A. 2012. "The Opium Trade and Patterns of Terrorism in the Provinces of Afghanistan: An Empirical Analysis." *Terrorism and Political Violence* 24(2):213–234.

Sandler, Todd. 2010. "Terrorism and Policy: Introduction." *Journal of Conflict Resolution* 54(2):203–213.

Weinstein, Jeremy M. 2005. "Resources and the Information Problem in Rebel Recruitment." *Journal of Conflict Resolution* 49(4):598–624.

CHAPTER 9

Conclusion

As shown throughout this book, civil wars cause widespread death, devastation, disease, and economic hardship, and given their frequency and the extent of their impact, it is imperative that we continue to improve our understanding of their diverse causes as well as the factors that facilitate a durable peace. The competing models of civil war onset that we explored—greed, grievances, and state capacity— contribute to that goal as they usefully explain (or disprove) what causes civil wars under certain conditions. An understanding of the types of civil war (those fought over control of government or territory, extra-systemic civil wars with fighting outside the government's territory, internationalized conflicts involving external actors, and nonstate actor conflicts) likewise helps us further to understand how the form of conflict shapes causes and outcomes. We also saw how major datasets like the SIPRI, UCDP, PRIO, and others help test and extend established theories of conflict and formulate, develop, and refine new ones.

Conflict management, as defined here, refers to a set of practices encompassing negotiation, mediation, conflict prevention, peace agreements, and peacebuilding and peacekeeping operations that are designed to ameliorate, resolve, and hopefully prevent future conflict. The demanding nature of successful conflict resolution requires the prioritization of collaborative action to address the civil war, while mediation and peacebuilding efforts are enhanced through flexibility and innovation. Signing and implementing effective peace agreements is vital, as is the long-term commitment of adequate resources.

This chapter brings the study of civil war to a conclusion by identifying trends, summarizing findings, and relating these directly to policy formation. First, we will remind readers of the costs of civil wars given their magnitude and centrality to the debates before we turn to key trends in the occurrence, duration, and nature of conflict. For further insight, I provide brief regional summaries and supporting statistics to connect these cases to the studies we have discussed. Finally, the study's major conclusions are linked with policy formulation and conflict management. Three key themes are understanding the nature and causes of civil wars, intervening to end fighting, and establishing a durable peace.

CIVIL WAR COSTS AND TRENDS

Costs

It is vital to study the incidence of civil wars given they pose a major threat to life and well-being. Their costs have already been detailed (see Chapter 2) but warrant summarizing here given their wide-ranging and devastating nature. The widespread loss of life and sustaining of injuries is shown by international data on civil wars and in ongoing conflicts in countries such as Afghanistan and Iraq. Casualties are especially common among those most vulnerable. The indiscriminate use of weapons and violence by combatants contribute to losses. Moreover, those fleeing the devastation are likely to become refugees struggling to survive.

Human rights are frequently violated as general law and order, along with social norms, disintegrate. Of serious concern is the likely cycle of violence whereby factions commit violence against each other that provokes retaliation. Human rights may be systematically violated, as terror and brutality are employed by factions to win dominance and force the population's compliance. Moreover, collapsing law and order provide an opportunity for abuses, such as rape and human trafficking, without fear of punishment.

Casualties continue to be sustained long after combat has subsided or concluded. Deaths occur with the severe social and health hazards emerging from chaos and the destruction of vital infrastructure, war remnants such as mines, and the disastrous economic impact of fighting. The negative long-term impact is made worse by detrimental effects on educational attainment. Lost educational opportunities impact the health outcomes and career opportunities of future generations. Nor is the destructive impact confined to human life but rather encompasses the natural environment and ecosystems. Indeed, the natural environment can be targeted by combatants, and environmental protection is rarely prioritized in countries experiencing conflict. Ultimately, the magnitude and range of civil war costs make it critical to better understand them and attempt to prevent their occurrence, or at least improve the ability to establish a sustainable peace. A starting point for this better understanding is a review of post-WWII trends.

Trends

As is graphically evident, conflict poses a major threat worldwide and thus warrants the attention along with active commitment of policy makers. (See the Appendix, which contains a list of civil wars from 1946 to 2009.) Civil wars were ignited during post-WWII years, and they inflicted heavy costs against the background of Cold War tensions. This meant that civil wars frequently involved conflict between forces identified as Communist or non-Communist. In turn, the United States and the Soviet Union commonly became involved, raising the threat of conflict escalation and casualties. This blight was felt internationally but especially in developing Asia.

Costs are exacerbated by the frequency of civil war. Internationally, evidence indicates that an overall increase in both the number of ongoing civil wars and percentage of countries experiencing such wars occurred after WWII until a peak during the early 1990s was followed by a decline (see Chapter 1). UCDP data provide a useful overview of armed conflict; a contested incompatibility that concerns government and/or territory where the use of armed force between two parties, of which at least one is the government of a state, results in at least 25 battle-related deaths in one calendar year. Civil wars and internationalized civil wars dominated the 2002–2012 period, representing about 97 percent of wars in 2012. Civil wars over governmental power are more common (18 of the 31 civil wars) and costly than those over territory (see Chapter 3).

The civil war in Syria has been particularly costly. In January 2014, the UN's Office of the High Commissioner for Human Rights (UN OHCHR) said it had ceased updating the death toll as it could no longer verify information sources for which it based its last count of at least 100,000 in late July 2013. The United Nations said this was due to its lack of access on the ground in Syria and inability to verify "source material" from others (Associated Press 2014). However, other organizations continue to provide estimates. For instance, the Syrian Observatory for Human Rights in February 2014 estimated over 140,000 had died since the conflict started (Syrian Observatory for Human Rights 2014).

Other data support the notion that civil wars have dominated recent conflicts. The SIPRI, using UCDP data, identified 15 major armed conflicts active internationally during 2010; all were civil wars. Major armed conflicts involve a contested incompatibility concerning government and/or territory witnessing the use of armed force between the military forces of two parties. At least one of these is a state government, and there are at least 1,000 battle-related deaths in a single calendar year (SIPRI 2005–2013, *Yearbook* 2011:61). Fighting over power has been more common than conflict over territory. During the 21st century, major conflicts have overwhelmingly been civil wars with no interstate major conflicts recorded from 2004 to 2010 (see Table 9.1).

Fighting over power has frequently occurred. A study covering 1946 to 2001 identified 225 armed conflicts. Of these, 163 were internal conflicts involving the state government and internal opposition groups without other states intervening (Bellamy 2007a:2). Conflicts over territory have been particularly common relative to those over government in recent years. Except for the year 2007, incompatibilities over government outnumbered those over territory for major conflicts from 2004 to 2010, all being civil wars. Civil wars over government were particularly prevalent

TABLE 9.1

Major Armed Conflicts—Intrastate and Interstate 2001 to 2010

Number of Intrastate Major Armed Conflicts Per Year

2001	2002	2003	2004	2005	2006	2007	2008	2009	2010
19	18	18	14	17	15	14	17	17	15

Number of Interstate Major Armed Conflicts Per Same Year

1	2	0	0	0	0	0	0	0	0

Source: SIPRI (2005–2013, *Yearbook* 2011:61–62).

in Africa and the Americas. During 2010, there were four major conflicts over territory; these occurred in the Middle East and Asia (see Table 9.2).

With fighting over territory, civil wars can occur as factions seek the secession and autonomy of state territory. Territory is often associated with ethnic conflicts given its importance to both ethnic groups and states. A common feature of secessionist wars is the promotion of a separate identity of those people in a particular area. Ethnic groups frequently closely link territory to their identity, its control ensuring a secure identity. State territorial control is directly associated with their survival. Various conditions are associated with the violent escalation of ethnic fighting. Conflict can occur between members of a minority ethnic group concentrated in a region that perceives itself the indigenous "sons of the soil" and relatively recent ethnically distinct migrants from other parts of the country. This conflict arises with competition and disputes over scarce resources and work (see Chapter 3). Asia and the Middle East have experienced major armed conflicts—civil wars, especially over territory in recent years (see Table 9.2). In 2012, civil wars over governmental power were more costly in fatalities than those over territory (see Chapter 3).

Given the above distribution of civil wars, it is useful to briefly identify key features that face policy makers according to their region.

Africa: Many African countries have been ravaged by civil wars with widespread brutality. The genocide in Rwanda is graphic evidence of this brutality. Key advantages for insurgents include the presence of natural resources that can be exploited to finance activities and terrain suiting guerilla tactics (see Chapter 3). However, disadvantages are also evident, such as that afforded government forces by Ethiopia's terrain. Ethnic tensions have often been a major factor. The duration of wars in the Congo, Uganda, and Somalia demonstrate the difficulties of ending conflict.

TABLE 9.2
Major Armed Conflicts—Civil Wars, Incompatibility, and Region 2004 to 2010

Number of Major Armed Conflicts Per Year and Type of Incompatibility
(G: government; T: territory)

Region	Years						
	2004	2005	2006	2007	2008	2009	2010
Africa	G: 3	G: 3	G: 3	G: 1	G: 4	G: 4	G: 4
	T: 0	T: 0	T: 0	T: 0	T: 0	T: 0	T: 0
Americas	G: 2	G: 2	G: 2	G: 3	G: 3	G: 3	G: 3
	T: 0	T: 0	T: 0	T: 0	T: 0	T: 0	T: 0
Asia	G: 3	G: 3	G: 3	G: 2	G: 3	G: 3	G: 3
	T: 2	T: 4	T: 3	T: 4	T: 4	T: 4	T: 2
Europe	G: 0	G: 0	G: 0	G: 0	G: 0	G: 0	G: 0
	T: 1	T: 2	T: 1	T: 1	T: 0	T: 0	T: 0
Middle East	G: 1	G: 1	G: 1	G: 1	G: 1	G: 1	G: 1
	T: 2	T: 2	T: 2	T: 2	T: 2	T: 2	T: 2
Totals	G: 9	G: 9	G: 9	G: 7	G: 11	G: 11	G: 11
	T: 5	T: 8	T: 6	T: 7	T: 6	T: 6	T: 4

Source: SIPRI (2005–2013, *Yearbook* 2011:62).

Americas: The Americas are comparatively peaceful. Where civil wars have occurred, guerilla tactics taking advantage of regional geography are common. Insurgents here, like those in other regions, have exploited natural resources. However, cocaine is a greater revenue source and controlling this revenue a stronger incentive to fight, as shown by Colombia's conflict. Grievances against the government, especially those over land rights, and economic turmoil have also been major factors encouraging civil wars.

Asia: Civil wars have involved groups varying widely in terms of their tactics, goals, and size. However, some commonalities are apparent. Insurgencies have been affected by the region's geography, especially its mountains and forests. Ideological struggles have inflamed tensions, as in Afghanistan, and are a common feature of grievances that groups believe can only be addressed forcibly. Grievances have been particularly related to rights and land.

Europe: Europe has witnessed fewer civil wars than other regions since WWII but has not been immune. Heavy weaponry has been prominent in wars; the brutality and magnitude of fighting in Bosnia-Herzegovina and Chechnya reinforce the importance of a durable peace. Funding for insurgents has come from diverse avenues, with illegal sources often being important. Causes of war range from ethnic tensions through competition for resources but have especially involved secessionist desires.

Middle East: The region illustrates the complicated nature of civil wars. For instance, the Lebanese war involved numerous groups, while the tribes in Yemen often changed sides. The struggle for power against the backdrop of conflicting ideologies and international intervention were key factors behind the wars and intensified fighting. Insurgents have exploited geographical features, but conflicts demonstrate that terrain can both help and hinder insurgencies. The difficulty of ending conflicts is clearly shown by continued violence in Iraq. Moreover, the Syrian civil war is a particular concern given its costs, the threat to regional peace, and the international community's inability to strongly intervene.

Conflict episodes lasting five or more years have become less common in recent decades. As figures show strong annual fluctuations, the moving average helps uncover the broad underlying trend. Conflict relapse has become characteristic of recent civil wars. Onsets of new conflicts—conflicts previously unrecorded—were less frequent between 2000 and 2009 than in any other decade after WWII (see Table 9.3). These outbreaks peaked in the 1990s, with 46 new conflicts, and dropped to 13 in the first years of the 21st century. Although old conflicts erupting into new fighting dropped by about one third over the same period, their number remained very high. The share of recurrences from 2000 to 2009 exceeded that during the Cold War by a factor of roughly two or more. Recurrences of earlier civil wars now represent a majority of conflict episode outbreaks (see UCDP 2013). Sons-of-the-soil wars are generally longer than others with an estimated median length of 15.1 years, over twice the median length of other civil wars (Fearon and Laitin 2011).

Signing and implementing successful peace agreements is most desirable. Here, UCDP data covering agreements and conflicts from 1975 to 2011 are useful. The dataset defines an armed conflict as a contested incompatibility concerning government and/or territory with the use of armed force between two parties including the state government. This incompatibility causes at least 25 battle-related deaths in one calendar year. A peace agreement is an agreement between two or more primary warring parties addressing the disputed incompatibility, either by settling all or part of it, or by clearly outlining a process for the parties regulating the incompatibility. The dataset includes 216 agreements in 60 conflicts. Thus, 34 percent of the conflicts have had at least one agreement (Högbladh 2012:42–43).

TABLE 9.3
New Versus Recurring Intrastate Conflicts, 1950–2009

Years	New Conflict Onsets	Recurring Conflict Onsets
1950–59	15	7
1960–69	29	16
1970–79	29	21
1980–89	22	27
1990–99	46	69
2000–09	13	48

Source: UCDP (2013).

Civil wars have dominated the 1975 to 2011 period, and the vast majority of agreements have been signed in such conflicts. Only 23 of 173 conflicts were interstate, and 20 of 216 agreements were signed here. Of all the agreements, 72 percent were concluded in intrastate governmental conflicts. Forty seven accords were concluded in conflicts over territory, seven in interstate conflicts, and 40 in intrastate conflicts. A few conflicts involved both conflict issues. These were all interstate conflicts and had 13 agreements.

The number of agreements in recent years has declined. In general, relatively few agreements, zero to two per year, were concluded between 1975 and 1989, although there were exceptions, as during 1975 when 12 agreements were concluded. The number then rose dramatically in the 1990s. In 1991 alone there were 19 agreements, more than the total for the 1976–1989 years. The trend continued through much of the early 2000s, not one single year from 1990 to 2008 recorded less than five agreements. After 2008, the number declined, reverting to the Cold War level. In 2011, only one agreement was concluded, in Sudan, and this failed. Of the 216 agreements signed, 141 were signed in active years of the conflict with the remainder signed after the conflicts reached a lower level of violence than 25 battle-related deaths, or where violence had ended.

Turning to the actual success of agreements, this is often measured by whether violence ends. Many researchers have used a 5-year period as a measure of successful termination. Of all the dataset's agreements, 125 were followed by the termination of violence for at least five years in the dyads signing the agreement. Sixty-six of the 156 agreements that concluded in conflicts over government restarted involving the same parties within five years. More agreements over territory managed to end violence. In territory conflicts, violence recurred after only 12 of 47 agreements involving the same parties within five years. Seventy-seven of the 216 agreements were never implemented; in 19, the violence with the same parties did not restart despite the agreement's nonimplementation (Högbladh 2012:43, 49, 50–53).

OVERVIEW OF CONCLUSIONS AND POLICY IMPLICATIONS

The world in the 21st century poses major challenges to policy makers. According to the IISS, the year to mid-2012 was "one of uncertain transitions and hectic crisis-management diplomacy. Weakness and fragility have been the greatest threats to stability and growth; the diffusion of power and lack of leadership the greatest barriers to diplomatic or economic problem-solving" (IISS 2012: para. 4). It further listed fundamental questions facing the international community. These included the following:

- What will be the power balance in the Middle East with Egypt's resurgent Muslim Brotherhood and Syria's escalating conflict?
- Can China's new generation of leaders cope with the contradictions of their country's polity and a potential slowdown in growth?
- While rising Asian and South American powers are apparently approaching the top of the global power hierarchy, do they know what to do when they arrive?
- On what issues is American power still crucial? (IISS 2012).

The IISS noted that upheaval in the Arab world was a prominent feature of international affairs in the year to mid-2013, with Syria's ongoing civil war and Egyptian protesters toppling their government for a second time. The United States and European countries were faced with defining their interests and developing policies in a fast-changing and uncertain world. Spontaneous protests occurred in Brazil and Turkey, while new leaders entered office in China, Japan, and South Korea. The possibility of conflict over Iran's nuclear program continued, and terrorist attacks in various countries illustrated the ongoing global threat posed by jihadist violence (IISS 2013). Moreover, after the February 2014 revolution in Ukraine where pro-Western and nationalist Ukrainians seized power following President Viktor Yanukovych's fall, there was concern that the southern region of Crimea could witness fighting between forces loyal to Ukraine and Russia. Turning to conflict and civil wars, this section looks at key themes for policy makers, starting with the need to understand such brutal events.

Understanding the Nature and Causes of Civil Wars

In general, wars are based on two major classifications—interstate and intrastate (civil war). Since the Cold War, fewer interstate wars have occurred, but the frequency of civil wars has increased. This threatens the entire international community with states increasingly interconnected, as through trade, treaties, and migration. The threat is worsened by the presence of conflict-vulnerable fragile and failed states, and the widespread availability of weapons. Thus, there is a shared interest in actively addressing issues before they spark conflict and helping to resolve those already initiated. This is especially the case for policy makers whose countries are close to conflicts. They can face the real threat of fighting and its repercussions crossing their borders. For instance, precautions might need to be taken to cope with a massive influx of refugees from the conflict zone.

Policy makers and those providing close support, such as diplomats, should be well-briefed on civil wars that pose a threat to national interests. This necessitates accurate and ample knowledge of the conflict's origins, nature, and relevant conflict management tools. Ideally, decisions should be evidence based, and be made in an environment which encourages *free and frank* discussions where a range of tools can be critically evaluated. Diplomacy is an important tool, and thus, the diplomatic service requires adequate resources, experience, and support. The constructive engagement of policy makers with relevant academia, and other independent groups, to enhance their knowledge can be useful here. This might involve providing an appropriate process whereby academia and the wider public can have an input into policy formulation. The active support of research on civil wars and datasets also helps increase the understanding of conflicts.

Findings about causes and durational aspects of civil wars are based on different data, measures, and definitions. As we have seen, there are various types of civil wars. An extra-systemic war involves insurgents and the government, but it occurs outside the government's territory. When an external actor intervenes for or against a faction, it can become internationalized, and nonstate wars are fought between or among nonstate groups. Colonial wars are those between locals and colonial authorities, while irredentist wars involve a group rebelling to unite its territory with a neighboring country (see Chapter 1).

Analysis by policy makers and their advisors is helped by the presence of more or less uniform civil war definitions founded on two measures: the number of casualties and nature of the conflict parties. Regardless of the type, widespread suffering is closely related to civil wars, especially when internationalized. Another common feature is fighting over governmental power. Revolutions and coups often have a major impact on the control of power and increase the potential for civil wars. Thus, their occurrence warrants close attention (see Chapter 3).

To better address and resolve civil wars peacefully, an accurate understanding of key factors causing and facilitating the conflict is important (see Chapter 4). Two major models focus on greed and grievances. According to the first model, greed fuels war as leaders raise forces for their own personal gain. Greed basically follows a calculation maximizing benefit to cost. Civil wars can be driven by greed for natural resources, such as oil, diamonds, and drugs, that can be looted; war essentially is a business enterprise. Turning to the second model, factions are motivated by grievances including political, economic, social, and cultural and ethnic demands. A common grievance is the government's restriction of certain groups from equal participation or its failure to provide equal rights, opportunities, and services. For instance, certain religious or cultural practices may be restricted. A third model focuses on the rationality of actors. Here, potential rebels study the cost of war and the probability of success. Important factors considered by rebel leaders are the state's capacity to defeat a rebellion and physical bases for them to hide.

Economic grievances can also be powerful. Many countries have been severely hit by global economic problems that inflame grievances and degrade economic development. Economic uncertainty impacts upon living standards and thus can increase the appeal of extremists. It was reported in mid-2009 that hunger in South Asia had reached its highest level in 40 years because of food and fuel price increases and the global economic downturn (BBC 2009). The threat of conflict is worsened by the region's large supplies of weapons that can be legally or illegally obtained by extremists and criminal activities, such as drug trafficking. Economic development, as measured by the country's gross domestic product per capita, is a key factor reducing the likelihood of war. According to the state capacity model, declining and weak states are vulnerable to rebellion. The "resource curse" adds to this challenge as less taxation due to the abundance of resources that isolates people; they are no longer "shareholders" in the country. Under this arrangement, elites often neglect the masses, while resource-rich states commonly have weak political structures with the masses disconnected from the government. In addition, abundant resources increase a country's worth and make its capture more desirable (see Chapter 4).

Associated with the importance of better understanding causes is greater knowledge on conflict duration and recurrence (see Chapters 1 and 6). This needs to be accessible in an easily understood form that facilitates its effective use in policy formulation and conflict management. Time spent fighting is measured by duration, while recurrence is by renewed fighting. Duration is not necessarily dependent on a faction's decision, as when one is defeated. Recurrence involves a decision, often by insurgents, to resume fighting. Duration generally increases when fighting is ethnic and peripheral, insurgents can loot natural resources, and external intervention occurs. Such factors can make recurrence more likely too, as can incentives to join insurgents, valuable natural resources in rebel territory, and ineffective conflict mediation or peacekeeping. There are important policy implications here. Policy makers can work to overcome a weak commitment to peace and work toward further curtailing the exploitation of resources that can be looted during war. For example, the UN-coordinated Kimberley Process established in 2003 has made it harder to deal in black market diamonds.

Intervening to End Civil Wars

As already established, civil wars pose a major international threat that warrants attention by policy makers. With their ongoing occurrence, there is the potential for more attempts to practice conflict management. Indeed, despite the frequency of fighting, data on third-party attempts to provide conflict management in Southeast Asian civil wars from 1993 to 2004 found it received the lowest level of attention from the international community relative to other regions. Only 7 percent of third-party efforts occurred in Southeast Asia whereas 37 percent were in the Middle East and 28 percent in Africa. A third party was defined as a party involved in either helping the warring parties to reframe issues defining their conflict, to reduce overt conflict behavior, or to regulate other matters relating to the interaction between the adversaries. This lack of involvement might have been influenced by the difficulty of effectively ending the civil wars. Many conflicts included a party, invariably the rebel group, that was small and usually well out-gunned and outmanned. Likewise, fighting was often over contraband and resources. Such conflicts can be difficult to effectively address via outside intervention (Möller et al. 2007:375–389).

Early and active intervention by policy makers is preferable. This might entail promoting good governance and transparency, social services, democracy, economic development, and the acceptance of human rights. The United Nations in 2009 identified five recurring priority areas for international assistance to build peace in the aftermath of conflict. These areas were support to basic safety and security, political processes, provision of basic services, restoration of core government functions, and economic revitalization. Three years later the United Nations reported more was needed to ensure those countries emerging from conflict were able to contain and manage conflict themselves and develop a sustainable peace. Inclusivity, institution building, and sustained international support were identified as critical in preventing a relapse into conflict and producing more resilient societies. Furthermore, successful peacebuilding processes needed to be transformative. These created space for a wider set of actors—including women, youth, marginalized groups, civil society, and the private sector—to participate in national post-conflict decision making. With respect to institution building, public administration and social services delivering equitably and accountably could help address grievances and rebuilding a country's legitimacy (UN, no date-e).

Constructive processes that can address possible "triggers" for civil wars should also be considered. This can involve the impartial monitoring and verifying of elections and disarmament processes. Where there are easily accessible resources, policy makers can develop strategies to counter their exploitation by fighting factions, given such resources can increase the duration and intensity of fighting. For instance, security around natural resources might be enhanced and efforts be made to police border crosses. Moreover, constructive communication between factions needs to be supported and facilitated. Policy makers can make concentrated efforts to solidify any lull in fighting through supporting indirect, bilateral, or direct talks (Bellamy 2011b:308). Holding both track one (official) and track two (unofficial) talks can enhance this communication. Simultaneously, policy makers need the capacity to accurately assess the environment within which conflict management is undertaken. Of particular importance are the motives, intentions, and capabilities of the peace parties and spoilers.

Effective conflict management is assisted by policy makers having access to, and the ability to swiftly utilize, diverse multilevel tools. Strong international condemnation of fighting and active support for peacekeeping through international organizations, such as the United Nations, is one such tool. Policy makers need to carefully take into account and support those factors often associated with successful peacekeeping. These are the need for peacekeeping to be guided by the principles of consent, impartiality, and the nonuse of force except in self-defense and defense of the mandate; perceived as legitimate and credible, especially among the local population; and aimed at promoting national and local ownership of the peace process in the host country. There are also other key factors that policy makers can promote to increase the effectiveness of peacekeeping. They might work to ensure there is genuine commitment to a political process by the parties in working toward peace (there must be a peace to keep), and there are clear, credible, and achievable mandates. Likewise, suitable personnel, logistic, and financial resources are required (UN, no date-d).

Direct military intervention is another possible tool, though such intervention can be controversial and inflame the conflict if the deployment of forces is not accepted by the fighting factions and the international community (see Chapter 7). Once the decision to intervene is made, careful planning and preparations, the identification of measureable and realistic objectives, and the effective use of forces are necessary. It is important to maximize resources and to use them most effectively. Depending on the approach taken by policy makers, this might be via strong interstate and intrastate coordination, cooperation between government agencies and with civil society, and determining the priority of conflict management efforts. Prioritization might be based on the civil war's severity, longevity, and proximity, the engagement of other actors, intervention costs, and forecast success. Examples of military intervention include the French during January 2013 deploying military force in Mali, the improvised country that had gained independence from Paris in 1960. The intervention occurred as instability increased and radical Islamist insurgents seized towns after President Amadou Toumani Touré's overthrow via a March 2012 coup (BBC 2013d).

So-called smart sanctions might also be available. These aim to put pressure on selected persons and in targeted areas rather than general society to encourage them to engage constructively to end a conflict. They might include travel bans, bans on high-level contact, a reduction in contacts, the realignment of aid away from a regime to alternative providers such as non-governmental organizations (NGOs), and the cessation of military cooperation. The sanctions can be better than general sanctions that have a wider negative impact on the general community, but their effectiveness is debatable.

Ultimately, successfully ending civil wars is enhanced through a combination of appropriate, flexible, and innovative engagement methods rather than by utilizing a single method. This is especially the case given the need to achieve a range of goals such as democracy, good governance, and respect for human rights; the effective provision of social services; and economic development. Combining military engagement, such as peacekeeping with aid provision, can be more successful than just one or the other. For example, financial aid can be misused without effective monitoring and enforcement of best practice. The sudden inflow of aid can also encourage disagreements over its allocation and use, disrupt traditional norms, motivate corruption, and ultimately cause inflation. Thus, a mix of "soft" and "hard" power can equate with effective "smart power." Regardless of the actual conflict management tools utilized, there should be contingency plans in place to help counter unanticipated developments, such as a renewal of fighting.

The commitment of adequate and appropriate resources after the cessation of conflict to encourage an enduring peace is needed. This may involve rebuilding damaged infrastructure and reestablishing law and order. The success of future engagement will thus be influenced by the presence of multirole and flexible forces that can be deployed rapidly, if and when requested. These forces need to provide security for peacebuilding efforts. Furthermore, their performance is enhanced when they can operate effectively within different social and cultural contexts and engage positively with local peoples. As shown by New Zealand's successful South Pacific conflict-resolution and peacekeeping efforts, military strength is not necessarily required to resolve conflict. Indeed, a low-key approach can be more readily acceptable to factions and more effective in sensitively addressing grievances. The likelihood of successful peacekeeping is enhanced with a strong mandate, adequate resources, and deployment when fighting has ceased (Bellamy 2011b:309, 312–313).

With such a significant and major impact, the international community has actively sought to intervene in civil wars with the hope of ending, or at least reducing, the costly fighting. Constructive cooperation and engagement at regional and international levels is beneficial. This can include promoting and supporting good governance and transparency, democracy, the acceptance of international law, development, and human rights. Policy makers need to consider intervening in low-intensity conflicts before they escalate. Encouraging and facilitating negotiations and dialogue between factions via indirect, bilateral, and direct talks can help settle grievances, or at least de-escalate them. Mediation can be an effective conflict resolution tool. Directive strategies can also be successful. These address, and seek to change, factional motives and behavior by providing incentives for them or issuing ultimatums. Tactics might include changing expectations, making substantive suggestions and proposals, and ensuring factions are aware of nonagreement costs (see Chapter 6). The UN Security Council's disunity over Syria illustrates the difficulties for policy makers to initiate peace processes, despite an often explicit and outspoken will to work for peace. The Syrian civil war is detailed in Box 9.1. When different interests clash, the chances of reaching a peaceful solution to conflicts decline. Moreover, the placement of many rebel groups on the U.S. list of terrorist organizations makes negotiations politically difficult. This further reinforces concern that the negative trend in the number of peace agreements will continue (UCDP 2013, see December 2012 data at http://pcr.uu.se/research/ucdp/datasets/).

BOX 9.1 Syria

France acquired a mandate over the northern portion of the former Ottoman Empire's province of Syria after World War I. This was administered as Syria until its 1946 independence. Syria then experienced instability with coups and changes in its composition; it united with Egypt in February 1958 to form the United Arab Republic which ended in

September 1961 with the Syrian Arab Republic's reestablishment. Hafiz al-Assad, a member of the socialist Ba'th Party and the minority Alawi sect, seized power in a November 1970 coup and headed an authoritarian regime until his 2000 death. His son, Bashar al-Assad, was then approved as president via referendum in July 2000, and a second term was approved by a May 2007 referendum. Within the context of regional uprisings (see Chapter 3 and Box 3.1) antiregime protests started in the southern province of Dar'a during March 2011. Here, protesters sought the repeal of the Emergency Law allowing arrests without charge, the legalization of political parties, and the removal of corrupt officials. Demonstrations and unrest spread with the regime's response including some concessions, such as the repeal of the Emergency Law and approving laws permitting new political parties and liberalizing local and national elections. However, brute force was increasingly used, and heavy casualties occurred (CIA 2013d).

The regime's response failed to address opposition demands for Assad's removal, and its brutal operations to counter unrest have sparked a prolonged conflict with insurgents. International pressure on the regime has intensified since late 2011. The Arab League, European Union, Turkey, and the United States have extended economic sanctions. Lakhdar Brahimi, the Joint Special Representative of the United Nations and the League of Arab States on the Syrian crisis, in October 2012 started meeting with regional state heads to help establish a cease-fire. In December 2012, the National Coalition of Syrian Revolution and Opposition Forces was recognized by over 130 countries as the population's sole legitimate representative (CIA 2013d). The regime is increasingly isolated, the Arab League in March 2013 allowing the main opposition coalition to take the country's official seat at its summit. Unrest persists in 2014; the conflict appears likely to continue with the international community's unified intervention hindered by disagreements, especially between the United States and Russia. There has been some international cooperation to remove the regime's chemical weapons but Assad has failed to meet deadlines.

Policy goals need to be in line with the resources available and permissible strategies, while efforts that seek to limit unrealistic expectations are commendable. The demanding nature of conflict resolution emphasizes the need for its prioritization and usefulness of collaborative action. As policy makers have finite resources, it is important to prioritize conflict resolution efforts. This can be based on the war's severity and duration, the engagement of other actors, intervention costs, threat of recurrence, and the likelihood of success. Once the decision to engage is made, careful planning and preparations along with the effective use of resources are required. The potentially demanding nature of resolution highlights the importance of interoperability and multilateral efforts, particularly via credible organizations like the United Nations. This is apparent in various cases—studies beyond the largest and well-known operations in countries like Afghanistan and Iraq. For instance, within the comparatively peaceful South Pacific, these attributes have been vital for operations addressing conflicts in Bougainville (an autonomous region of Papua New Guinea), Timor Leste, and the Solomon Islands.

Whether a multilateral approach of a regional or international nature is most appropriate depends on various factors. The resources required to successfully engage is another fundamental factor—conflict management might require resources beyond the scope of those regional powers seeking to intervene. Another factor is the conflict parties—the presence of a powerful faction can necessitate a stronger international component rather than a purely regional approach.The success of peace efforts is enhanced by effective cooperation, thereby, reinforcing the importance of positive relations between policy makers, especially those directly involved in efforts. Effective resolution is interlinked with broader foreign policy successfully ensuring strong high-value relations and cultivating friends and allies, particularly among existing and emerging regional powers. This can increase the likelihood of a request to mediate being accepted. Likewise, policy makers need to work toward putting aside or resolving issues where there are disagreements when conflict necessitates cooperation.

A capably led, well-resourced foreign service with experience and expertise facilitates effective engagement (Bellamy 2011b:308–309, 315). This is especially important for U.S. Secretary of State John Kerry's Department of State given the international influence of the United States. More information on Secretary Kerry is provided in Box 9.2. Moreover, active support for major organizations such as the United Nations is vital. While every member state is legally obligated to pay their respective share toward peacekeeping, as of January 31, 2014, member states owed approximately $2.51 billion in current and back peacekeeping dues. Thus, moves by U.S. President Barack Obama (president 2009–present) to reduce UN arrears should be applauded. This is particularly the case given the United States is the United Nations' single biggest contributor, responsible for 28.38 percent of the 2013 peacekeeping budget (UN Peacekeeping 2014; Reuters 2011).

BOX 9.2   U.S. Secretary of State John Kerry

The U.S. secretary of state is appointed by the president with the advice and consent of the Senate. The secretary is the president's chief foreign affairs adviser. The secretary carries out the president's foreign policies through the State Department. On February 1, 2013, John Kerry was sworn in as the 68th Secretary of State, his appointment making him the first sitting Senate Foreign Relations Committee chairman to become secretary in over a century. Kerry joined the State Department after 28 years in the Senate, the last four as chairman of the Senate Foreign Relations Committee. He also was the unsuccessful Democratic presidential nominee in 2004. Kerry followed Hillary Rodham Clinton (secretary of state 2009–2013). She was previously a U.S. senator for New York, and the first lady (U.S. Department of State 2013).

With policy makers recognizing the effectiveness of multilateralism and the rule of international law, opportunities for involvement in resolving civil wars may increase. Peace agreements often include international involvement with both their crafting and implementation. The international community has undertaken various constructive moves to address violations of human rights. Particularly relevant here is the ICC's establishment to help end impunity for the perpetrators of the most serious crimes of concern to the international community, along with violations of international humanitarian law (ICC 2013a, 2013b). Individual courts have also been established to address acts associated with specific wars, such as the UN International Criminal Tribunal for the former Yugoslavia (ICTY 2013b). This is funded by regular contributions from member states, plus donations, equipment, and gratis personnel (ICTY 2013c). Active support for such bodies from policy makers is commendable.

Closely associated with the utility of a multilateral approach is the need for policy makers to recognize the potentially effective role of nonstate actors. Civil society organizations are diverse and include NGOs, voluntary organizations, faith-based groups, and media organizations. Relevant legitimate and reputable organizations warrant consideration such as in aid distribution. They often have a good understanding of local social and cultural intricacies along with knowledge of grievances and appropriate methods to address these. They also can be better positioned to rapidly respond. The IISS notes that policy responsibilities cannot fall only on government shoulders. International companies need to go beyond corporate social responsibility and to develop virtual foreign policies protecting their interests and environments. The media and NGOs need to assume greater responsibility for the impact of their actions too (IISS 2012).

Establishing and Building a Lasting Peace

The consequences of civil wars necessitate a better understanding of their termination and postwar issues; a stable and durable peace is the best outcome for the war-inflicted society, the region, and international community. Thus, policy makers must recognize that the signing and implementing of effective peace agreements is vital (see Chapter 6). It is useful to take into account factors influencing the likelihood of agreements being signed, and their outcomes, when intervening. An agreement can be encouraged by estimates of the probability of victory falling, conflict costs escalating, the estimated time required to win increasing, or the utility from a settlement increasing relative to that of victory. Policy makers can help ensure that factions are aware of such factors and stress the need for constructive negotiations.

Incentives to cease fighting might include the provision of aid for rebuilding. However, much care is needed to ensure that aid reaches its intended recipients and is not lost to corruption. Thus, the effective enforcement of best practice procedures, transparency, and the careful monitoring and recording of disbursements are vital. Respected organizations such as the Red Cross can be used to distribute aid. This is particularly important given restraints on aid budgets but wide breadth of demands and often their costly nature. Monetary assistance alone might not be the best option available. Apart from its possible misuse—factions might even use the funding to continue fighting—the sudden influx of monetary assistance can cause disagreements over its allotment and use, disrupt traditional norms, increase the potential for corruption, and ultimately cause inflation. There might also be no lack of money present in the strife-torn area but rather its misdirection or ineffective use. Hence, helping to supply the skills to establish greater transparency and good governance that helps address civil war grievances can be more beneficial than purely financial assistance. Skills as in construction and medicine can be most needed in conflict areas. The supply and transfer of these can help reduce casualties and maintain long-term peace.

Peace agreements often share common provisions. Power-sharing arrangements frequently cover political, territorial, military, and economic areas. Research indicates that power sharing can help effectively end fighting, but major challenges need to be addressed. Elections or electoral reforms are commonly included in agreements, but their success rate is mixed and influenced by their timing. Regional autonomy can strengthen agreement durability.

Furthermore, an agreement might seek to address secessionist movements by partitioning them or breaking them apart. As with other provisions, these can help end fighting but do not necessarily ensure a durable peace. Granting amnesties for combatants can be controversial, especially when human rights were seriously violated.

Successfully implementing agreements is vital for a durable peace but can be more challenging for factions than initial negotiations. Policy makers need to be aware that effective implementation is helped by careful planning and monitoring, making local people stakeholders and agreement guarantors, and designing dispute resolution mechanisms. Success may involve utilizing various measures appropriate for the situation and the regime, not only principal parties to the main peace process but also other relevant actors. The most durable agreements are frequently those concerning states where the previous stable regime was democratic, and they conclude extended low-intensity conflicts.

Key lessons for policy makers can be derived from Walter's study of 41 civil wars from 1940 to 1990. First, even the most promising negotiations often require external enforcement for success; factions commonly proceed with a peace plan when a third party has the political will to verify or enforce demobilization. Second, relying on the promise of free and fair elections to introduce democracy to states appears to be self-defeating. If factions fear that the victor of the first post-civil war elections will establish an authoritarian state, outlaw the opposition, and punish its members, they will probably refuse to participate in negotiations. Policy makers should refrain from promoting "quick and easy" democratization and understand that they cannot simultaneously end fighting and establish a fully liberal democracy without a democratic transition in between. Third, because factions commonly become fearful and insecure as they demobilize, safety can be provided by not forcing them to disarm fully, particularly prior to an agreement's political terms being fulfilled. Allowing factions to retain some arms in the open can reassure them and deter one faction from attempting to take dictatorial powers. Outsiders can also provide factions "escape hatches," such as territorial autonomy, open borders, and generous asylum provisions (Walter 1999:154–155).

Finally, conflict is often associated with failed states, and statebuilding efforts warrant policy discussion. Statebuilding involves complex and diverse activities to promote the creation of functioning and functional states, as in Afghanistan. Democratization efforts often are supported by the international community in postwar countries. Such efforts can help build a peace, but the postwar environment can be inhospitable for democracy. Effective peacebuilding involves policy makers preventing the escalation or recurrence of fighting and establishing a durable and self-sustaining peace, addressing the underlying causes of war, and building or rebuilding peaceful social institutions and values.

Terrorism is a major threat to establishing long-term peace and stability that needs to be taken into account in the policy process. Conflict can make people more receptive to supporting terrorists or at least accepting their presence. The decline in living standards and economic opportunities associated with conflict can make promises of support from terrorists more attractive. Effective conflict resolution and counterterrorism strategies need to address such issues. This can involve the effective provision of humanitarian aid, long-term assistance aimed at rebuilding the infrastructure, and employment creation. Ultimately, giving people, especially former combatants and youth, the means to make an adequate and legitimate living, and to voice their views through appropriate avenues such as free and fair elections, can reduce the likelihood of them turning to violence. The initiation of broad and fundamental political and economic reforms to address grievances, along with restructuring military and law enforcement agencies to better combat factions is also vital (see Chapters 3 and 8).

FINAL WORD

With the 21st century's second decade, the international community faces a major threat to peace and stability in the form of civil wars but also opportunities for effective conflict management and resolution. Challenges include ongoing and potential civil wars along with their repercussions and the threat of terrorism. More positively, the value of multilateral engagement and strong constructive relations between policy makers appears to be better acknowledged now by some international actors. Civil wars have increasingly dominated post-WWII conflicts with fighting over territory and government. Although conflict episodes lasting five or more years are less common, the magnitude of civil war costs and fewer peace agreements make it vital to better understand them to try and prevent their occurrence or at least enhance the ability to establish peace.

There is a clear need for more and better regional conflict mediation. The disproportionate number of conflicts that are civil wars, along with the complexity and unique nature of particular conflicts, requires the careful analysis of methods managing conflict constructively and reducing their destructive consequences. The need for greater knowledge of effective management is reinforced by the mixed performance of regional conflict management to date. In line with this, analyzing their causes, dynamics, and conclusions to provide practical advice for policy makers is important. The greed and grievances of combatants are often influential causes, while weak or ill-prepared governments provide opportunities for challenges. There are various types of civil wars. Extra-systemic civil wars involve insurgents and the government, but they occur outside the government's territory. When an external actor intervenes, it can become internationalized, and nonstate civil wars are between or among nonstate groups. Colonial wars are fought between locals and colonial authorities, while irredentist wars involve a group rebelling to unite its territory with a neighboring country. Regardless of the type, a stable and durable peace is vital.

Three key themes warranting attention by policy makers are understanding the nature and causes of civil wars, intervening to end such wars, and establishing a lasting peace. Ultimately, a better understanding of civil wars taking into account their diverse causes along with factors that facilitate a durable peace is required. The demanding nature of successful resolution emphasizes the need for collaborative action and their prioritization. Resolution efforts are enhanced through utilizing a combination of flexible and innovative engagement methods rather than a single method. The signing and implementing of effective peace agreements is vital, as is the long-term commitment of adequate and appropriate resources.

Ultimately, one hopes that a better understanding of civil wars will facilitate the development of more effective tools to reduce their occurrence and their terrible consequences that blight so many societies. For the sake of the world's people and environment, I hope that such an understanding will emerge and will effectively be practiced.

UCDP Civil Wars Involving at
Least 25 Battle-Related Deaths per Year, 1946–2009

Government	Rebels	Years Active
USSR	Forest Brothers	1946–1948
USSR	LTS(p)A, LNPA	1946
USSR	UPA	1946–1950
China	PLA	1946–1949
Iran	Republic of Azerbaijan	1946
Greece	DSE	1946–1949
Iran	KDPI	1946
Bolivia	Popular Revolutionary Movement	1946
USSR	BDPS	1946–1948
Philippines	HUK	1946–1954
China	Taiwanese insurgents	1947
Paraguay	Opposition coalition (Febreristas, Liberals, and Communists)	1947
Hyderabad	CPI	1947–1948
Myanmar	APLP, Mujahid Party	1948–1961
Myanmar	CPB-RF, CPB, PVO—"White Band" faction	1948–1988
North Yemen	Opposition coalition	1948
Costa Rica	National Liberation Army	1948
India	CPI	1948–1951

Government	Rebels	Years Active
Myanmar	PNDF	1949–1950
Israel	Palestinian insurgents, PLO groups, Non-PLO groups, Rejectionist Front, PFLP, PFLP-GC, Fatah, Hamas, PIJ, PNA	1949–1996
Myanmar	KNUP, KNU	1949–1992
Myanmar	MFL-MUF, MPSG/MPF, NMSP	1949–1963
Guatemala	Military faction	1949
Indonesia	Republic of South Moluccas	1950
China	Tibet	1950
Thailand	Military faction (navy)	1951
Bolivia	MNR	1952
Indonesia	Darul Islam	1953
Cuba	M-26–7	1953
Paraguay	Military faction (forces of Alfredo Stroessner)	1954
Guatemala	Forces of Carlos Castillo Armas	1954
South Vietnam	FNL	1955–1964
Argentina	Military faction (forces of Eduardo A. Lonardi Doucet)	1955
India	NNC	1956–1959
China	Tibet	1956
Cuba	M-26–7	1956–1958
Myanmar	KNPP	1957
Oman	State of Oman/Free Oman	1957
Indonesia	Darul Islam, PRRI, Permesta	1958–1961
Malaysia	CPM	1958–1960
Lebanon	Independent Nasserite Movement/Mourabitoun militia	1958
Iraq	Military faction (Free Officers Movement), Military faction (forces of Colonel Abdul Wahab al-Shawaf)	1958–1959

(Continued)

(Continued)

Government	Rebels	Years Active
China	Tibet	1959
Laos	Pathet Lao, Neutralists	1959–1961
Myanmar	NSH, SSIA, SNUF, SSA, SURA, SSNLO	1959–1970
Cameroon	UPC	1960–1961
Nepal	Nepali Congress	1960–1962
Dem. Rep. of Congo (Zaire)	Katanga	1960–1962
Dem. Rep. of Congo (Zaire)	Independent Mining State of South Kasai	1960–1962
Ethiopia	Military faction (forces of Mengistu Neway)	1960
India	NNC	1961–1968
Myanmar	KIO	1961–1992
Cuba	Cuban Revolutionary Council	1961
France	OAS	1961–1962
Iraq	KDP	1961–1970
Venezuela	Military faction (navy)	1962
North Yemen	Royalists	1962–1970
Laos	Pathet Lao	1963–1973
Malaysia	CCO	1963–1966
Sudan	Anya Nya/SSLM	1963–1972
Iraq	NCRC, Military faction (forces of Brigadier Arif)	1963
Argentina	Military faction (Colorados)	1963
Guatemala	FAR I	1963
Myanmar	ANLP, CPA, RPF, ALP	1964–1978
Colombia	FARC, ELN, M-19, EPL	1964–2009*
Ethiopia	Ogaden Liberation Front	1964
Dem. Rep. of Congo (Zaire)	CNL	1964–1965

Government	Rebels	Years Active
Gabon	Military faction (forces loyal to Léon M'Ba)	1964
Ethiopia	ELF, EPLF, ELF-PLF	1964–1991
Guatemala	FAR I, FAR II, EGP, ORPA, URNG	1965–1995
Dominican Republic	Military faction (Constitutionalists)	1965
Indonesia	OPM	1965
Peru	MIR, ELN	1965
Burundi	Military faction (forces loyal to Gervais Nyangoma)	1965
Iran	KDPI	1966–1968
Nigeria	Military faction (forces of Patrick Nzeogwu)	1966
Syria	Military faction (forces loyal to Nureddin Atassi and Youssef Zeayen)	1966
Ghana	NLC	1966
Chad	Frolinat, First Liberation Army, Second Liberation Army	1966–1972
India	MNF	1966–1968
South Africa	SWAPO	1966–1988
Indonesia	OPM	1967–1969
Bolivia	ELN	1967
Cambodia	Khmer Rouge/FUNK	1967–1975
Dem. Rep. of Congo (Zaire)	Opposition militias	1967
Nigeria	Republic of Biafra	1967–1970
Zimbabwe (Rhodesia)	ZAPU	1967–1968
Oman	PFLO	1969–1975
India	CPI—ML	1969–1971
Philippines	CPP, Military Faction (forces of Honasan, Abenina, and Zumel)	1969–1995

(Continued)

(Continued)

Government	Rebels	Years Active
Philippines	MIM, MNLF, MILF	1970–1990
Madagascar	Monima	1971
Uganda	Military faction (forces of Idi Amin), Kikosi Maalum	1971–1972
Pakistan	Mukti Bahini	1971
Sri Lanka (Ceylon)	JVP	1971
Morocco	Military faction (forces of Mohamed Madbouh)	1971
Sudan	Sudanese Communist Party	1971
United Kingdom	PIRA	1971–1991
Myanmar	SSA	1972–1973
Uruguay	MLN/Tupamaros	1972
Zimbabwe (Rhodesia)	ZANU, ZAPU, PF	1973–1979
Myanmar	LNUP	1973–1981
Iraq	KDP, PUK, KDP-QM	1973–1992
Chile	Military faction (forces of Augusto Pinochet, Toribio Merino, and Leigh Guzman)	1973
Pakistan	Baluchi separatists	1974–1977
Malaysia	CPM	1974–1975
Uganda	Military faction (forces of Charles Arube)	1974
Argentina	ERP, Monteneros	1974–1977
Thailand	CPT	1974–1982
Bangladesh	JSS/SB	1975–1992
Ethiopia	ALF	1975–1976
Lebanon	LNM, LAA	1975–1976
Morocco	POLISARIO	1975–1989
Angola	FNLA, UNITA	1975–1995
Indonesia	Fretilin	1975–1989

Government	Rebels	Years Active
Mauritania	POLISARIO	1975–1978
Myanmar	SURA, SSRA, TRC, MTA	1976–1988
Indonesia	OPM	1976–1978
Chad	FAN, FAP, FAT, GUNT	1976–1984
Ethiopia	TPLF, EPRP, EDU, EPDM, Military faction (forces of Amsha Desta and Merid Negusie), EPRDF	1976–1991
Sudan	Islamic Charter Front	1976
Ethiopia	WSLF	1976–1983
Mozambique	Renamo	1977–1992
Ethiopia	OLF	1977–1978
Ethiopia	SALF	1977–1980
Dem. Rep. of Congo (Zaire)	FLNC	1977–1978
Nicaragua	FSLN	1977–1979
Afghanistan	PDPA, Jam'iyyat-i Islami-yi Afghanistan, Harakat-i Inqilab-i Islami-yi Afghanistan, Jabha-yi Nijat-i Milli-yi Afghanistan, Mahaz-i Milli-yi Islami-yi Afghanistan, Hizb-i Islami-yi Afghanistan—Khalis faction, Afghanistan, Harakat-i Islami-yi Afghanistan, Hizb-i Wahdat, Military faction (forces of Shahnawaz Tanay), Junbish-i Milli-yi Islami, Taliban, UIFSA, Hizb-i Islami-yi Afghanistan—Hekmatyar faction, Ittihad-i Islami Bara-yi Azadi-yi	1978–2001
Spain	ETA	1978–1982
Cambodia	KNUFNS, Khmer Rouge, KPNLF, FUNCINPEC	1978–1998
El Salvador	ERP, FPL, FMLN	1979–1991
India	TNV	1979–1988
Iran	MEK	1979–1982
Iran	KDPI	1979–1988
Uganda	Kikosi Maalum, Fronasa, UNLF, FUNA, UNRF, NRA, UFM, UPDA, HSM, UPA, LRA, Lord's Army	1979–1992

(Continued)

(Continued)

Government	Rebels	Years Active
North Yemen	National Democratic Front	1979–1982
Iran	APCO	1979–1980
Syria	Muslim Brotherhood	1979–1982
Saudi Arabia	JSM	1979
Ethiopia	OLF	1980–1981
Tunisia	Résistance Armée Tunisienne	1980
Liberia	Military faction (forces of Samuel Doe)	1980
Malaysia	CPM	1981
Indonesia	OPM	1981
Gambia	NRC	1981
South Africa	ANC	1981–1983
Ghana	Military faction (forces of Jerry John Rawlings)	1981
Somalia	SSDF, SNM	1982–1984
Venezuela	Bandera Roja	1982
Nicaragua	Contras/FDN	1982–1990
India	PLA	1982–1988
Kenya	Military faction (forces of Hezekiah Ochuka)	1982
Iraq	SCIRI	1982–1984
Peru	Sendero Luminoso, MRTA	1982–1999
Lebanon	LNM, Amal, NUF, Lebanese Forces—Hobeika faction	1982–1986
India	Sikh insurgents	1983–1993
Ethiopia	SLM	1983
Sudan	SPLM/A, NDA, SLM/A, JEM, SLM/A-MM, NRF, SLM/A-Unity	1983–2009*
Ghana	Military faction (forces of Ekow Dennis and Edward Adjei-Ampofo)	1983
Ethiopia	OLF	1983–1985

Government	Rebels	Years Active
Cameroon	Military faction (forces of Ibrahim Saleh)	1984
Turkey	PKK/Kadek/KONGRA-GEL	1984–2009*
Sri Lanka (Ceylon)	LTTE, TELO, EPRLF	1984–2001
South Africa	ANC	1985–1988
Spain	ETA	1985–1987
Iran	MEK	1986–1988
Chad	GUNT, CDR	1986–1987
South Yemen	Yemenite Socialist Party—Abdul Fattah Ismail faction	1986
Somalia	SNM, SPM, USC, USC/SNA	1986–1996
Togo	MTD	1986
Iraq	SCIRI	1987
Myanmar	KNPP	1987
Suriname	SLA	1987
Burkina Faso	Popular Front	1987
Ethiopia	OLF	1987–1992
Sri Lanka (Ceylon)	JVP	1989–1990
Paraguay	Military Faction (forces of Andres Rodriguez)	1989
Chad	MOSANAT, Revolutionary Forces of 1 April, Islamic Legion, MPS, Military faction (forces of Maldoum Bada Abbas), MDD, CNR, CSNPD, FNT	1989–1994
Lebanon	Lebanese Army (Aoun), Lebanese Forces	1989–1990
India	ABSU	1989–1990
Haiti	Military faction (forces of Himmler Rebu and Guy Francois)	1989
Panama	Military faction (forces of Moisés Giroldi)	1989
Papua New Guinea	BRA	1989–1990
Comoros	Presidential guard	1989
Laos	LRM	1989–1990

(Continued)

(Continued)

Government	Rebels	Years Active
India	Kashmir Insurgents	1989–2009*
Romania	NSF	1989
Liberia	NPFL, INPFL	1989–1990
India	PWG, MCC	1990–1994
Iran	KDPI	1990
Russia (Soviet Union)	APF	1990
Myanmar	ABSDF	1990–1992
Myanmar	NMSP	1990
India	ULFA	1990–1991
Pakistan	MQM	1990
Indonesia	GAM	1990–1991
Israel	Hezbollah	1990–1999
Mali	MPA	1990
Trinidad and Tobago	Jamaat al-Muslimeen	1990
Senegal	MFDC	1990
Russia (Soviet Union)	Republic of Armenia	1990–1991
Rwanda	FPR	1990–1994
Iran	MEK	1991–1993
Spain	ETA	1991–1992
Myanmar	ARIF, RSO	1991–1992
Iraq	SCIRI	1991–1996
Sierra Leone	RUF, AFRC, Kamajors, WSB	1991–2000
Angola	FLEC-R	1991
Serbia (Yugoslavia)	Republic of Slovenia	1991
Turkey	Devrimci Sol	1991–1992

Government	Rebels	Years Active
Serbia (Yugoslavia)	Republic of Croatia, Croatian irregulars	1991
Haiti	Military faction (forces of Raol Cedras)	1991
Djibouti	FRUD	1991–1994
Burundi	Palipehutu	1991–1992
Niger	FLAA	1991–1992
Algeria	Takfir wa'l Hijra, MIA/FIS/AIS, GIA, AQIM	1991–2009*
Georgia	National Guard and Mkhedrioni, Zviadists	1991–1993
Azerbaijan	Republic of Nagorno-Karabakh	1991–1994
Indonesia	Fretilin	1992
India	PLA, UNLF	1992–2000
Senegal	MFDC	1992–1993
Myanmar	KNPP	1992
Papua New Guinea	BRA	1992–1996
Venezuela	Military faction (forces of Hugo Chávez)	1992
Moldova	PMR	1992
Bosnia and Herzegovina	Serbian Republic of Bosnia and Herzegovina, Serbian irregulars	1992–1995
Tajikistan	UTO	1992–1996
Croatia	Serbian Republic of Krajina, Serbian irregulars	1992–1993
Georgia	Republic of South Ossetia	1992
India	NSCN—IM	1992–1997
Georgia	Republic of Abkhazia	1992–1993
India	ATTF	1992–1993
Philippines	MNLF, ASG, MILF, MNLF-NM, MNLF-HM	1993–2009*
India	NDFB	1993–2004
Iran	KDPI	1993
Bosnia and Herzegovina	Croatian Republic of Bosnia and Herzegovina, Croatian irregulars	1993–1994

(Continued)

(Continued)

Government	Rebels	Years Active
Egypt	Al-Gamaa al-Islamiyya	1993–1998
Myanmar	MTA, SSA-S	1993–2002
Azerbaijan	Military faction (Forces of Suret Husseinov)	1993
Russia	Parliamentary forces	1993
Bosnia and Herzegovina	Autonomous Province of Western Bosnia	1993–1995
Congo	Ninjas	1993–1994
India	ULFA	1994–2009*
Mexico	EZLN	1994
Ethiopia	OLF	1994–1995
Myanmar	ABSDF	1994
Myanmar	RSO	1994
Angola	FLEC-R, FLEC-FAC	1994
Uganda	LRA, WNBF, ADF, UNRF II	1994–2009*
Ethiopia	ONLF	1994
Yemen (Arab Rep. of Yemen)	Democratic Republic of Yemen	1994
Niger	CRA	1994
Mali	FIAA	1994
Burundi	CNDD, Frolina, Palipehutu-FNL, CNDD-FDD	1994–2006
Russia	Republic of Chechnya (Ichkeria)	1994–1996
Pakistan	MQM	1995–1996
Myanmar	KNU	1995
Iraq	PUK	1995–1996
Azerbaijan	OPON forces	1995
Croatia	Serbian Republic of Krajina	1995
Senegal	MFDC	1995
Ethiopia	Al-Itahad al-Islami	1995–1996

Government	Rebels	Years Active
Niger	FDR	1995
India	NLFT	1995
Ethiopia	ONLF	1996
India	PWG, MCC, CPI-M	1996–2009*
Myanmar	KNPP	1996
Angola	FLEC-FAC, FLEC-R	1996–1998
Ethiopia	ARDUF	1996
Nepal	CPN-M	1996–2006
Iran	KDPI	1996
Mexico	EPR	1996
Dem. Rep. of Congo (Zaire)	AFDL, RCD, RCD-ML, MLC	1996–2001
Myanmar	BMA	1996
Indonesia	Fretilin	1997–1998
India	NLFT, ATTF	1997–2004
Iran	MEK	1997
Senegal	MFDC	1997–1998
Myanmar	KNU	1997–1998
Myanmar	UWSA	1997
Eritrea	EIJM—AS	1997
Rwanda	FDLR	1997–2002
Rwanda	FDLR	2009*
Congo	Cobras, Cocoyes, Ninjas, Ntsiloulous	1997–1999
India	KNF	1997
Comoros	MPA/Republic of Anjouan	1997
Niger	FARS	1997
Niger	UFRA	1997

(Continued)

(Continued)

Government	Rebels	Years Active
Chad	FARF, MDD, MDJT	1997–2002
Philippines	CPP	1997
Ethiopia	OLF	1998–2009*
Serbia (Yugoslavia)	UCK	1998–1999
Angola	UNITA	1998–2002
Tajikistan	UTO, Movement for Peace in Tajikistan	1998
Guinea-Bissau	Military Junta for the Consolidation of Democracy, Peace and Justice	1998–1999
United Kingdom	RIRA	1998
Lesotho	Military faction	1998
Eritrea	EIJM—AS	1999
Ethiopia	ONLF	1999–2002
Iran	MEK	1999–2001
Ethiopia	Al-Itahad al-Islami	1999
Indonesia	GAM	1999–2005
Uzbekistan	IMU	1999–2000
Russia	Republic of Chechnya (Ichkeria)	1999–2007
Djibouti	FRUD—AD	1999
Russia	Wahhabi movement of the Buinaksk district	1999
Philippines	CPP	1999–2009*
Israel	PNA, Fatah, Hamas, PFLP, AMB, PIJ, PRC	2000–2009*
India	NSCN—IM	2000
Myanmar	God's Army, KNU	2000–2003
Senegal	MFDC	2000–2001
Liberia	LURD, MODEL	2000–2003
Guinea	RFDG	2000–2001
Macedonia	UCK	2001

Government	Rebels	Years Active
Somalia	SRRC	2001–2002
Central African Republic	Military faction (forces of André Kolingba), Forces of Francois Bozize	2001–2002
United States of America	Al-Qaeda (The Base)	2001–2002
Angola	FLEC-R, FLEC-FAC	2002
Congo	Ntsiloulous	2002
Cote D'Ivoire	MPCI, MPIGO, MJP, FN	2002–2004
Eritrea	EIJM—AS	2003
India	UNLF, PLA, PREPAK, KCP	2003–2009*
Senegal	MFDC	2003
Afghanistan	Taleban, Hizb-i Islami-yi Afghanistan—Hekmatyar faction	2003–2009*
Sri Lanka (Ceylon)	LTTE	2003
Thailand	Patani insurgents	2003–2009*
Ethiopia	ONLF	2004–2009*
Haiti	FLRN, OP Lavalas (Chimères)	2004
Angola	FLEC-FAC	2004
United States of America	Al-Qaida (The Base)	2004–2009*
Uzbekistan	JIG	2004
Iraq	Al Mahdi Army, ISI, Ansar al-Islam, RJF	2004–2009*
Nigeria	NDPVF	2004
Pakistan	BLA, Baluch Ittehad, BRA	2004–2009*
Georgia	Republic of South Ossetia	2004
Nigeria	Ahlul Sunnah Jamaa	2004
Myanmar	KNPP	2005
India	NSCN—K	2005–2007

(Continued)

(Continued)

Government	Rebels	Years Active
Myanmar	KNU	2005–2009*
Turkey	MKP	2005
Iran	PJAK, Jondullah	2005–2009*
Azerbaijan	Republic of Nagorno-Karabakh	2005
Sri Lanka (Ceylon)	LTTE	2005–2009*
Chad	FUCD, UFDD, RAFD, AN, UFR	2005–2009*
Myanmar	SSA-S	2005–2009*
Israel	Hezbollah	2006
Somalia	ARS/UIC, Harakat Ras Kamboni, al-Shabaab, Hizbul-Islam	2006–2009*
India	NLFT	2006
Dem. Rep. of Congo (Zaire)	CNDP	2006–2008
Central African Republic	UFDR	2006
Dem. Rep. of Congo (Zaire)	BDK	2007–2008
Angola	FLEC-FAC	2007
Niger	MNJ	2007–2008
Pakistan	TNSM, TTP	2007–2009*
Mali	ATNMC	2007–2009*
Peru	Sendero Luminoso	2007–2009*
Russia	Forces of the Caucasus Emirate	2007–2009*
Burundi	Palipehutu—FNL	2008
Georgia	Republic of South Ossetia	2008
India	NDFB—RD	2009—*
Angola	FLEC–FAC	2009—*
Nigeria	Boko Haram	2009—*

Government	Rebels	Years Active
Myanmar	MNDAA	2009—*
Central African Republic	CPJP	2009—*
Yemen	AQAP	2009—*

Note: These data are from the Uppsala Conflict Data Program's Conflict Termination Dataset (see Kreutz 2010; UCDP 2012). Years Active represents years of at least 25 battle-related deaths. Many of the episodes are recurrences of previous warring dyads. The Conflict Termination Dataset codebook is available at http://www.pcr.uu.se/digitalAssets/55/55056_UCDP_Conflict_Termination_Dataset_v_2010–1.pdf. The reader is urged to refer to the main UCDP data website at http://www.pcr.uu.se/research/ucdp/datasets/ for more information on civil wars, such as more precise start and end dates, type of termination, and type of war. This list does not include wars between colonial powers and insurgent groups.

* War was ongoing as of 12/31/2009.

ABC News. 2012. "Atrocities." April 26. Retrieved from http://abcnews.go.com/Blotter/ charles-taylor-african-warlord-convicted-sierra-leone-atrocities/story?id=16218011

Acemoglu, Daron and James A. Robinson. 2012. "Ten Reasons Countries Fall Apart." July/ August. *Foreign Policy*: 89–91.

Addison, Tony, Philippe Le Billon, and S. Mansoob Murshed. 2001. "Conflict in Africa: The Cost of Peaceful Behaviour." UNU-WIDER Discussion Paper 2001/51. United Nations University World Institute for Development Economic Research, Helsinki, Finland.

"Al-Assad's Fall Just 'Matter of Time.'" 2012, July 8. *Dominion.*

Alexseev, Mikhail A. 2003. "Economic Valuations and Interethnic Fears: Perceptions of Chinese Migration in the Russian Far East." *Journal of Peace Research* 40(1): 85–102.

Amnesty International. 2005. *Report 2005—Democratic Republic of the Congo.* May 25. Retrieved from http://www.unhcr.org/refworld/country,,AMNESTY,,COD,,429b27dc2,0.html.

Andersson, Neil, Cesar Palha da Sousa, and Sergio Paredes. 1995. "Social Cost of Land Mines in Four Countries: Afghanistan, Bosnia, Cambodia, and Mozambique." *British Medical Journal* 311:718–721.

Arce, Daniel G. and Todd Sandler. 2010. "Terrorist Spectaculars: Backlash Attacks and the Focus of Intelligence." *Journal of Conflict Resolution* 54(2):354–373.

Associated Press. 2014. "UN Decides to Stop Updating Syria Death Toll." January 7. Retrieved from http://bigstory.ap.org/article/un-decides-to-stop-updating-syria-death-toll.

Auvinen, Juha. 1997. "Political Conflict in Less Developed Countries 1981–1989." *Journal of Peace Research* 34(2): 177–195. Retrieved from http://www.reuters.com/article/2011/01/25/ us-un-usa-arrears-idUSTRE7007DW20110125.

Ayres, William R. 2000. "A World Flying Apart? Violent Nationalist Conflict and the End of the Cold War." *Journal of Peace Research* 37(1):107–117.

Azam, Jean-Paul and Anke Hoeffler. 2002. "Violence against Civilians in Civil Wars: Looting or Terror?" *Journal of Peace Research* 39(4): 461–485.

Balch-Lindsay, Dylan and Andrew J. Enterline. 2000. "Killing Time: The World Politics of Civil War Duration, 1820–1992." *International Studies Quarterly* 44:615–642.

Banton, Michael. 1983. *Racial and Ethnic Competition.* Cambridge, UK: Cambridge University Press.

Barbieri, Katherine and Rafael Reuveny. 2005. "Economic Globalization and Civil War." *The Journal of Politics* 67(4):1228–1247.

Baruah, Sanjib. 2003. "Confronting Constructionism: Ending India's Naga War." *Journal of Peace Research* 40(3):321–338.

Beardsley, Kyle C. 2010. "Pain, Pressure and Political Cover: Explaining Mediation Incidence." *Journal of Peace Research* 47(4):395–406.

Beardsley, Kyle C. 2011. *The Mediation Dilemma.* Ithaca, NY: Cornell University Press.

Beardsley, Kyle C. 2012. "United Nations Intervention and the Duration of International Crises." *Journal of Peace Research* 49(2):335-349.

Beardsley, Kyle C. and Holger Schmidt. 2012. "Following the Flag or Following the Charter? Examining the Determinants of United Nations Involvement in International Crises, 1945-2002." *International Studies Quarterly* 56(1):33-49.

Bekoe, Dorina A. 2003. "Toward a Theory of Peace Agreement Implementation: The Case of Liberia." *Journal of Asian and African Studies* 38(2-3):256-294.

Bellamy, Paul. 2005. "Cambodia: Remembering the Killing Fields." *New Zealand International Review* 30(2):17-20.

Bellamy, Paul. 2007a. "Introduction." Pp. 1-26 in *Civil Wars of the World—Major Conflicts since World War II,* edited by K. DeRouen and U. Heo. Santa Barbara, CA: ABC-CLIO.

Bellamy, Paul. 2007b. "Regional" chapters. Pp. 26-82 in *Civil Wars of the World—Major Conflicts since World War II,* edited by K. DeRouen and U. Heo. Santa Barbara, CA: ABC-CLIO.

Bellamy, Paul. 2008. "The 2006 Fiji Coup and Impact on Human Security." *Journal of Human Security* 4(2):4-18.

Bellamy, Paul. 2010. "The Last Cold War? Thoughts on Resolving Korea's Sixty Year-old Family Feud." *Journal of Human Security* 6(2). Retrieved from http://search.informit.com.au/documentSummary;dn=183703445248614;res=IELHSS.

Bellamy, Paul. 2011a. "Cold War." P. 261 in *The Encyclopedia of Political Science,* edited by G. T. Kurian (editor in chief). Washington, DC: Congressional Quarterly Press: 261.

Bellamy, Paul. 2011b. "Conclusion: Australian and New Zealand Policy-Making and Practical Implications for Internal Conflicts in Asia Pacific." Pp. 293-322 in *Unraveling Internal Conflicts in East Asia and the Pacific: Incidence, Consequences, and Resolutions,* edited by J. Bercovitch and K. DeRouen. Lanham, MD: Lexington Books.

Bellamy, Paul. 2011c. "Preparing for an Uncertain Korean Future." November/December. *New Zealand International Review* 36(6):17-20.

Bellamy, Paul. 2011d. "War Crimes." Pp. 1751-1752 in *The Encyclopedia of Political Science,* edited by G. T. Kurian (editor in chief). Washington, DC: Congressional Quarterly Press.

Bellamy, Paul. 2012. "A Reluctant Friend—New Zealand's Relationship with North Korea 1973-1989." *New Zealand Journal of Asian Studies* 14(1):30-48.

Bellamy. Paul. 2013. "Threats to Human Security—An Overview." Pp. 57-81 in *Human Security in World Affairs: Problems and Opportunities,* edited by A. K. Lautensach and S. W. Lautensach. Vienna, Austria: Caesar Press. Published electronically 2013: http://www.scribd.com/doc/123123994/Human-Security-in-World-Affairs-Problems-and-Opportunities-Preview-Alexander-K-Lautensach-Sabina-W-Lautensach-eds.

Benmelech, Efraim, Claude Berrebi, and Esteban F. Klor. 2009. "Economic Cost of Harboring Terrorism." *Journal of Conflict Resolution* 54(2):331-353.

Bercovitch, Jacob. 2006. "Mediation Success or Failure: A Search for the Elusive Criteria." *Cardozo Journal of Conflict Resolution* 7(2):289-302.

Bercovitch, Jacob and Scott Sigmund Gartner. 2006. "Is There Method in the Madness of Mediation? Some Lessons for Mediators from Quantitative Studies of Mediation." *International Interactions* 32(4):329-354.

Bercovitch, Jacob and Su-Mi Lee. 2003. "Mediating International Conflicts: Examining the Effectiveness of Directive Strategies." *International Journal of Peace Studies* 8(1):1-17.

Berdal, Mats and Achim Wennmann, eds. 2010. *Ending Wars, Consolidating Peace: Economic Perspectives.* Adelphi Series 50. Abingdon, UK: Routledge for the International Institute for Strategic Studies.

Berhe, Asmeret Asefaw. 2007. "The Contribution of Landmines to Land Degradation." *Land Degradation and Development* 18: 1–15.

Blomberg, Brock S., Rozlyn C. Engel, and Reid Sawyer. 2010. "On the Duration and Sustainability of Transnational Terrorist Organizations." *Journal of Conflict Resolution* 54(2):303–330.

Bodea, Cristina and Ibrahim A. Elbadawi. 2007. "Riots, Coups and Civil War: Revisiting the Greed and Grievance Debate." November. Policy Research Working Paper 4329. Washington, DC: World Bank.

Böhmelt, Tobias. 2010. "The Effectiveness of Tracks of Diplomacy Strategies in Third-Party Interventions." *Journal of Peace Research* 47(2):167–178.

Boltjes, Miek. 2007. "The Implementation Challenge in Intrastate Peace Processes: An Analysis." Pp. 1–48 in *Implementing Negotiated Agreements: The Real Challenge to Intrastate Peace*, edited by M. Boltjes. Cambridge, UK: Cambridge University Press.

Boucher, Alix J., William J. Durch, Margaret Midyette, Sarah Rose, and Jason Terry. 2007. March. *Mapping and Fighting Corruption in War-Torn States*. Stimson Center Report 61. Retrieved from http://www.stimson.org/images/uploads/research-pdfs/Mapping_and _Fighting_Corruption_in_War-Torn_States.pdf.

Boulden, Jane. 2009. "Terrorism and Civil Wars." *Civil Wars* 11(1):5–21.

Boutros-Ghali, Boutros. 1992. *An Agenda for Peace. Preventive Diplomacy, Peacemaking and Peace-keeping: Report of the Secretary-General Pursuant to the Statement Adopted by the Summit Meeting of the Security Council on 31 January*. New York: UN General Assembly.

Brancati, Dawn and Jack L. Snyder. 2011. "Rushing to the Polls: The Causes of Premature Postconflict Elections." *Journal of Conflict Resolution* 55(3):469–492.

Brandt, Patrick T., T. David Mason, Mehmet Gurses, Nicolai Petrovsky, and Dagmar Radin. 2008. "When and How the Fighting Stops: Explaining the Duration and Outcome of Civil Wars." *Defense and Peace Economics* 19(6):415–434.

British Broadcasting Corporation (BBC). 2005a. "1995: Serbs overrun UN 'Safe Haven.'" July 11. Retrieved from http://news.bbc.co.uk/onthisday/hi/dates/stories/july/11/ newsid_4080000/4080690.stm.

British Broadcasting Corporation (BBC). 2005b. "1996: Siege of Sarajevo is lifted." February 29. Retrieved from http://news.bbc.co.uk/onthisday/hi/dates/stories/february/29/ newsid_4667000/4667292.stm.

British Broadcasting Corporation (BBC). 2006. "Obituary: Slobodan Milošević." March 11. Retrieved from http://news.bbc.co.uk/2/hi/europe/655616.stm.

British Broadcasting Corporation (BBC). 2009. "S Asia Hunger 'at 40-Year High.'" June 2. Retrieved from http://news.bbc.co.uk/2/hi/south_asia/8079698.stm.

British Broadcasting Corporation (BBC). 2010. "Clinton Says Mexico Drug Crime Like an Insurgency." September 9. Retrieved from http://www.bbc.co.uk/news/world-us -canada-11234058.

British Broadcasting Corporation (BBC). 2012a. "Arab Uprisings." December 14. Retrieved from http://www.bbc.co.uk/news/world-middle-east-12813859.

British Broadcasting Corporation (BBC). 2012b. "Srebrenica: Mass Reburials on 1995 Massacre Anniversary." July 11. Retrieved from http://www.bbc.co.uk/news/world -europe-18795203.

British Broadcasting Corporation (BBC). 2012c. "Syria In Civil War, Red Cross Says." July 15. Retrieved from http://www.bbc.co.uk/news/world-middle-east-18849362.

British Broadcasting Corporation (BBC). 2012d. "Syria Intervention Is More Likely, Says UK Think Tank." July 25. Retrieved from http://www.bbc.co.uk/news/world-middle -east-18973997.

British Broadcasting Corporation (BBC). 2012e. "Traumatised Syrians Flee to Jordan." February 24. Retrieved from http://www.bbc.co.uk/news/world-middle-east-17151364.

British Broadcasting Corporation (BBC). 2013a. "Afghanistan Profile." February 25. Retrieved from http://www.bbc.co.uk/news/world-south-asia-12024253.

British Broadcasting Corporation (BBC). 2013b. "Arms treaty blocked by Iran, North Korea and Syria." March 29. Retrieved from http://www.bbc.co.uk/news/world-us -canada-21972700.

British Broadcasting Corporation (BBC). 2013c. "Iraq Profile." March 21. Retrieved from http://www.bbc.co.uk/news/world-middle-east-14546763.

British Broadcasting Corporation (BBC). 2013d. "Mali Profile." March 7. Retrieved from http://www.bbc.co.uk/news/world-africa-13881978.

British Broadcasting Corporation (BBC). 2013e. "Syria Fires Ballistic Missile at Rebels, NATO Says." January 10. Retrieved from http://www.bbc.co.uk/news/world-middle -east-20970866.

Buhaug, Halvard, Scott Gates, and Paivi Lujala. 2009. "Geography, Rebel Capability, and the Duration of Civil Conflict." *Journal of Conflict Resolution* 53:544–569.

Burgoon, Brian. 2006. "On Welfare and Terror: Social Welfare Policies and Political-Economic Roots of Terrorism." *Journal of Conflict Resolution* 50(2):176–203.

Bussman, Margit and Gerald Schneider. 2007. "When Globalization Discontent Turns Violent: Foreign Economic Liberalization and Internal War." *International Studies Quarterly* 51(1):79–97.

Byrd, William and Christopher Ward. 2004. *Afghanistan's Drug Economy. A Preliminary Overview and Analysis.* Washington, DC: World Bank.

Cable News Network (CNN). 2012. "US Sees Increased Iran Involvement in Syria." March 5. Retrieved from http://security.blogs.cnn.com/2012/03/05/u-s-sees-increased-iran -involvement-in-syria/.

Cable News Network (CNN). 2013a. "The Gruesome Toll of Deadly Cluster Bombs in Syria." January 21. Retrieved from http://edition.cnn.com/2013/01/16/opinion/syria -cluster-bombs-hrw/index.html?hpt=hp_c1.

Cable News Network (CNN). 2013b. "UN's Syria Death Toll Jumps Dramatically To 60,000-Plus." January 3. Retrieved from http://edition.cnn.com/2013/01/02/world/meast/ syria-civil-war/index.html.

Cable News Network (CNN). 2014. "Iraq and Afghanistan War Casualties." January 4. Retrieved from http://www.cnn.com/SPECIALS/war.casualties/index.html.

Carlile of Berriew, Lord. 2007. "The Definition of Terrorism: A Report by Lord Carlile of Berriew Q.C. Independent Reviewer of Terrorism Legislation. Cm 7052." Presented to Parliament by the Secretary of State for the Home Department, by Command of Her Majesty, March.

Canetti, Daphna, Sandro Galea, Brian J. Hall, Robert J. Johnson, Patrick A. Palmer, and Stevan E. Hobfoll. 2010. "Exposure to Prolonged Socio-Political Conflict and the Risk of PTSD and Depression among Palestinians." *Psychiatry* 73(3):219–231.

Carment, David and Dane Rowlands. 1998. "Evaluating Third-Party Intervention in Intrastate Conflict." *Journal of Conflict Resolution* 42(5):572–599.

Central Intelligence Agency (CIA). 2013a. "Afghanistan." The World Fact Book. February 12. Retrieved from https://www.cia.gov/library/publications/the-world-factbook/geos/af.html

Central Intelligence Agency (CIA). 2013b. "Iraq." The World Factbook. February 12. Retrieved from https://www.cia.gov/library/publications/the-world-factbook/geos/iz.html.

Central Intelligence Agency (CIA). 2013c. "The World Factbook—"Syria." February 20. Retrieved from https://www.cia.gov/library/publications/the-world-factbook/geos/sy.html.

Chen, Siyan, Norman V. Loayza, and Martha Reynal-Querol. 2007. "The Aftermath of Civil War." *World Bank Policy Research Working Paper 4190*. April. Washington, DC: World Bank.

Choi, Seung-Whan. 2010. "Fighting Terrorism Through the Rule of Law." *Journal of Conflict Resolution* 54 (6): 940–966.

Clauset, Aaron and Frederik W. Wiegel. 2010. "A Generalized Aggregation-Disintegration Model for the Frequency of Severe Terrorist Attacks." *Journal of Conflict Resolution* 54(1):179–197.

Cluster Munition Coalition. 2013. "113 states on board the convention on cluster munitions." September 13. Retrieved from http://www.stopclustermunitions.org/treatystatus/.

Collier, Paul. 2000. "Doing Well Out of War: An Economic Perspective." Pp. 91–112 in *Greed and Grievance, Economic Agendas in Civil Wars,* edited by M. Berdal and D. M. Malone. Boulder, CO: Lynne Rienner.

Collier, Paul, V. L. Elliot, H. Hegre, A. Hoeffler, M. R. Querol, and N. Sambanis. 2003. *Breaking the Conflict Trap: Civil War and Development Policy*. Washington, DC: World Bank and Oxford University Press.

Collier, Paul and Anke Hoeffler. 1998. "On Economic Causes of Civil War." *Oxford Economic Papers* 50(4):563–573.

Collier, Paul and Anke Hoeffler. 1999. "Justice Seeking and Loot Seeking in Civil War." The World Bank. Retrieved from http://econ.worldbank.org/programs/conflict/library.

Collier, Paul and Anke Hoeffler. 2000. "Greed and Grievance in Civil War." The Center for the Study of African Economic Working Paper Series (128).

Collier, Paul and Anke Hoeffler. 2001. "Greed and Grievance in Civil War." The World Bank. Retrieved from http://econ.worldbank.org/programs/library.

Collier, Paul and Anke Hoeffler. 2002a "Greed and Grievance in Civil War." The Center for the Study of African Economic Working Paper Series No. 2355. Oxford, UK: University of Oxford.

Collier, Paul and Anke Hoeffler. 2002b. "The Political Economy of Secession." Retrieved from http://users.ox.ac.uk/~ba110144/self-det.pdf.

Collier, Paul and Anke Hoeffler. 2004a. "Greed and Grievance in Civil War." *Oxford Economic Papers* 56 (4): 563–595.

Collier Paul and Anke Hoeffler. 2004b. "Military Expenditure in Post-conflict Societies." April 8. Oxford University Centre for the Study of African Economies, Department of Economics Working Paper. Oxford, UK: Oxford University.

Collier, Paul and Anke Hoeffler. 2006. "The Political Economy of Secession." In *Negotiating Self-Determination,* edited by H. Hannum and E. F. Babbitt. Lanham, MD: Lexington Books.

Collier, Paul and Anke Hoeffler. 2007. "Military Spending and the Risks of Coups d'état." Oxford, UK: Oxford University. Retrieved from http://users.ox.ac.uk/~econpco/research/pdfs/MilitarySpendingandRisksCoups.pdf.

Collier Paul, Anke Hoeffler, and Mats Soderbom. 2004. "On the Duration of Civil War. *Journal of Peace Research* 41(3):253–273.

Combs, Cindy C. 2011. *Terrorism in the Twenty-First Century.* Boston, MA: Longman.

Connable, Ben and Martin C. Libicki. 2010. *How Insurgencies End.* Santa Monica, CA: RAND Corporation.

Cooper, Neil. 2002. "State Collapse as Business: The Role of Conflict Trade and the Emerging control Agenda." *Development and Change* 33(5):935-955.

Cooper, Neil. 2008. "As Good As It Gets? Securing Peace and Diamonds in Sierra Leone." Paper Presented at the ISA Annual Convention, March 26-29, San Francisco, CA.

Cordesman, Anthony H. 2013. "The Human Cost of the Syrian Civil War." Center for Strategic and International Studies. September 3. Retrieved from http://csis.org/publication/human-cost-syrian-civil-war.

Council on Foreign Relations. 2005. "Terrorism Havens: Afghanistan." Retrieved from http://www.cfr.org/afghanistan/terrorism-havens-afghanistan/p9357.

Crossin, Corene, Gavin Hayman, and Simon Taylor. 2003. "Where Did It Come From?: Commodity Tracking Systems." Pp. 97-160 in *Natural Resources and Violent Conflict: Options and Actions,* edited by I. Bannon and P. Collier. Washington, DC: The World Bank.

Cunningham, David E. 2006. "Veto Players and Civil War Duration." *American Journal of Political Science* 50(4):875-892.

Cunningham, David E. 2012. "Who Gets What in Peace Agreements" Pp. 248-269 in *The Slippery Slope to Genocide: Reducing Identity Conflicts and Preventing Mass Murder,* edited by I. W. Zartman, M. Anstey, and P. Meerts. Oxford, UK: Oxford University Press.

Czaika, M. and K. Kis-Katos. 2009. "Civil Conflict and Displacement: Village-Level Determinants of Forced Migration in Aceh." *Journal of Peace Research* 46(3):399-418.

Dagne, Ted. 2011. "The Democratic Republic of Congo: Background and Current Developments." Congressional Research Service, Washington, DC. Retrieved from http://www.fas.org/sgp/crs/row/R40108.pdf.

Davies, Thomas M., Jr. 2001. "Guevara, Ernesto." P. 344 in *Oxford Companion to Politics of the World Second Edition,* edited by J. Krieger (editor in chief). Oxford, UK: Oxford University Press.

de la Calle, Luis and Ignacio Sanchez-Cuenca. 2012. "Rebels Without a Terriotry: An Analysis of Nonterritorial Conflicts in the World, 1970-1997." *Journal of Conflict Resolution* 56(4):580-603.

De Nevers, Renee. 2007. "Imposing International Norms: Great Powers and Norm Enforcement." *International Studies Review* 9(1):53-80.

Dekmejian, Hrair R. 2007. *Spectrum of Terror.* Washington, DC: CQ Press.

Delawala, Imitiyaz. 2001. "What is Coltan?" ABC Nightline News. September 7. Retrieved from http://abcnews.go.com/Nightline/story?id=128631&page=1.

DeRouen, Karl and Jacob Bercovitch. 2008. "Enduing Internal Rivalries: A New Framework for the Study of Civil War." *Journal of Peace Research* 45(1):55-74)

DeRouen, Karl, Jr., Jacob Bercovitch, and Paulina Pospieszna. 2011. "Introducing the Civil Wars Mediation (CWM) Dataset." *Journal of Peace Research* 48(5):663-672.

DeRouen, Karl, Mark Ferguson, Jenna Lea, Ashley Streat-Bartlett, Young Park, and Sam Norton. 2010. "Civil War Peace Agreement Implementation and State Capacity." *Journal of Peace Research* 47(3):333-346.

DeRouen, Karl and Shaun Goldfinch. 2005. "Putting the Numbers to Work: Implications for Violence Prevention." *Journal of Peace Research* 27(1):27-45.

DeRouen, Karl R., Jr. and Uk Heo, eds. 2007. *Civil Wars of the World—Major Conflicts since World War II.* Santa Barbara, CA: ABC-CLIO.

DeRouen, Karl Jr., Jenna Lea, and Peter Wallensteen. 2009. "The Duration of Civil War Peace Agreements." *Conflict Management and Peace Science* 26 (4): 367–387.

DeRouen, Karl R., Jr. and David Sobek. 2004. "The Dynamics of Civil War Duration and Outcome." *Journal of Peace Research* 41(3):303–320.

de Soysa, Indra. 2002. "Paradise Is a Bazaar? Greed, Creed, and Governance in Civil War, 1989–99." *Journal of Peace Research* 39(4):395–416.

de Soysa, Indra and Eric Neumayer. 2007. "Resource Wealth and the Risk of Civil War Onset: Results from a New Dataset of Natural Resource Rents, 1970–1999." *Conflict Management and Peace Science* 24:201–218.

Dixon, William. 1994. "Democracy and the Peaceful Settlement of International Conflict." *The American Political Science Review* 88(1):14–32.

Dougherty, James E. and Robert L. Pfaltzgraff, Jr. 2001. *Contending Theories of International Relations: A Comprehensive Survey*, 5th ed. New York: Longman.

Downes, Alexander B. 2004. "The Problem with Negotiated Settlements to Ethnic Civil Wars." *Security Studies* 13(4):230–279.

Doyle, Michael W. and Nicholas Sambanis. 2000. "International Peacebuilding: A Theoretical and Quantitative Analysis." *American Political Science Review* 94(4):779–801.

Doyle, Michael W. and Nicholas Sambanis. 2006. *Making War & Building Peace: United Nations Peace Operations*. Princeton, NJ: Princeton University Press.

Dubey, Amitabh. 2002. "Domestic Institutions and the Duration of Civil War Settlements." Paper presented at the Annual Meeting of the International Studies Association, March 24–27, New Orleans, LA.

Dunning, Thad. 2005. "Resource Dependence, Economic Performance, and Political Stability." *Journal of Conflict Resolution* 49(4):451–482.

Elbadawi, Ibrahim A. and Nicholas Sambanis. 2000. "External Interventions and the Duration of Civil Wars." World Bank Development Research Group, Policy Research Working Paper No. 2433. Washington, DC: Work Bank.

Ellingsen, T. 2000. "Colorful Community or Ethnic Witches Brew? Multiethnicity and Domestic Conflict after the Cold War." *Journal of Conflict Resolution* 44(2):228–249.

Enders, Walter and Paan Jindapon. 2010. "Network Externalities and Structure of Terror Networks." *Journal of Conflict Resolution* 54(2):262–280.

Enders, Walter and Todd Sandler. 2005. "After 9/11: Is It All Different Now?" *Journal of Conflict Resolution* 49(2):259–277.

Enders, Walter and Todd Sandler. 2006. "Distribution of Transnational Terrorism among Countries by Income Class and Geography after 9/11." *International Studies Quarterly* (June).

Eubank, William and Leonard Weinberg. 2001. "Terrorism and Democracy: Perpetrators and Victims." *Terrorism and Political Violence* 13(1):155–164.

Fearon, James D. 2004. "Why Do Some Civil Wars Last So Much Longer Than Others?" *Journal of Peace Research* 41(3):275–301.

Fearon, James D. 2005. "Primary Commodity Exports and Civil War." *Journal of Conflict Resolution* 49(4):483–507.

Fearon, James D. and David D. Laitin. 2003a. "Ethnicity, Insurgency, and Civil War." *American Political Science Review* 97(1):75–90.

Fearon, James D. and David D. Laitin. 2003b. "Additional Tables for 'Ethnicity, Insurgency, and Civil War.'" February. Stanford, California: Stanford University. Retrieved from http://www.academia.edu/156305/Additional_Tables_for_Ethnicity_Insurgency_and _Civil_War_.

Fearon, James D. and David D. Laitin. 2011. "Sons of the Soil, Migrants, and Civil War." *World Development* 39(2):199-211.

Feinstein, Jonathan S. and Edward H. Kaplan. 2010. "Analysis of Strategic Terror Organization." *Journal of Conflict Resolution* 54(2):281-302.

Findley, Michael G. 2013. "Terrorism, Spoiling, and Civil Wars." Paper presented at the Annual Meeting of the Midwest Political Science Association, Chicago, IL, April 11-14.

Findley, Michael G. and Joseph K. Young. 2012. "Terrorism and Civil War: A Spatial and Temporal Approach to a Conceptual Problem." *Perspective on Politics* 10(2):285-305.

Fortna, Page. 2008. "Terrorism, Civil War Outcomes, and Post-War Stability: Hypothesis and (Very) Preliminary Findings." Presented at the MIT Security Studies Program Seminar, Cambridge, MA.

Fortna, Virginia Page. 2004. "Does Peacekeeping Keep Peace? International Intervention and the Duration of Peace after Civil War." *International Studies Quarterly* 48(2):269-292.

Fox, Jonathan. 2002. *Ethnoreligious Conflict in the Late 20th Century: A General Theory*. Lamham, MD: Lexington Books.

Freedom House. 2013. *Freedom in the World 2013—Democratic Breakthroughs in the Balance.* Washington, DC. Retrieved from http://www.freedomhouse.org/sites/default/files/FIW%202013%20Booklet%20-%20for%20Web_0.pdf.

Fund for Peace. 2011. *Fragile States Index 2011.* Washington, DC. Retrieved from http://ffp .statesindex.org/rankings-2011-sortable.

Fund for Peace. 2012. *Failed States Index 2012.* Washington, DC. Retrieved from http://ffp .statesindex.org/rankings-2012-sortable

Fund for Peace. 2013. "Failed States Index 2013: The Troubled Ten." June 24. Washington, DC. Retrieved from http://library.fundforpeace.org/fsi13-troubled10.

Gall, Timothy L. and Susan B Gall, eds. 1999. *Worldmark Chronology of the Nations, Volume 4—Europe.* Detroit, IL: Gale Group.

Gates, Scott. 2006-2011. "Power Sharing Agreements, Negotiations and Peace Processes." Oslo, Norway: Peace Research Institute. Retrieved from http://www.prio.no/Projects/Project/?x=835.

Gent, Stephen E. 2008. "Going in When It Counts: Military Intervention and the Outcome of Civil Conflicts." *International Studies Quarterly* 52(4):713-736.

Ghobarah, Hazem Adam, Paul Huth, and Bruce Russett. 2004. "The Post-War Public Health Effects of Civil Conflict." *Social Science & Medicine* 59:869-884.

Gleditsch, Nils Petter. 2012. "Whither the Weather? Climate Change and Conflict." *Journal of Peace Research* 49(1):3-9.

Gleditsch, Nils Petter, Peter Wallensteen, Mikael Eriksson, Margareta Sollenberg, and Havard Strand. 2002. "Armed Conflict 1946-2001: A New Dataset." *Journal of Peace Research* 39(5):615-637.

Global Witness. 2002. "Resources, Conflict, and Corruption. A Case Study: The Ukranian Mafia and the Links Between Timber and Arms." Retrieved from http://www.globalwitness.org/sites/default/files/import/Global%20Witness%20profile.pdf.

Goldfinch, Shaun and Karl DeRouen, Jr. 2014. "In It for the Long Haul? Lessons from Post-Conflict Statebuilding, Peacebuilding and Good Governance in Timor-Leste." *Public Administration and Development* 34(2):96-108.

Goldstone, Jack A. 1993. "Revolution." Pp. 786-790 in *Oxford Companion to Politics of the World Second Edition*, edited by J. Krieger (editor in chief). Oxford, UK: Oxford University Press.

Goldstone, Jack A, Robert H Bates, David L Epstein, Ted Robert Gurr, Michael B Lustik, Monty G Marshall, Jay Ulfelder, and Mark Woodward. 2010. "A Global Model for Forecasting Political Instability." *American Journal of Political Science* 54(1):190-208.

Goodhand, Jonathan. 2005. "Frontiers and Wars: The Opium Economy in Afghanistan." *Journal of Agrarian Change* 5(2):191-216.

Greenwood, Gavin. 2012. "Deep Impact." *Jane's Intelligence Review* (02):56-57.

Gregory, Kathryn. 2008. "Ansar al-Islam (Iraq, Islamists/Kurdish Separatists), Ansar al-Sunnah." Council on Foreign Relations Backgrounder. Available at http://www.cfr.org/iraq/ansar-al-islam-iraq-islamistskurdish-separatists-ansar-al-sunnah/p9237.

Greig, Michael. 2005. "Stepping into the Fray: When Do Mediators Mediate?" *American Journal of Political Science* 49:249-266.

Greig, J. Michael and Patrick M. Regan. 2008. "When Do They Say Yes? An Analysis of the Willingness to Offer and Accept Mediation in Civil Wars." *International Studies Quarterly* 52(4):759-781.

Grossman, Herschel I. 1991. "A General Equilibrium Model of Insurrections." *American Economic Review* 81(4):912-921.

Grossman, Herschel I. 1995. "Insurrections." Chap. 8 in *Handbook of Defense Economics*, edited by K. Hartley and T. Sandler. New York: Elsevier.

Grossman, Herschel I. 1999. "Kleptocracy and Revolutions." *Oxford Economic Papers* 51:267-283.

Gurr, Ted R. 1970. *Why Men Rebel*. Princeton, NJ: Princeton University Press.

Gurr, Ted R. 1993. *Minorities at Risk: A Global View of Ethnopolitical Conflicts*. Washington, DC: U.S. Institute of Peace Press.

Gurr, Ted R. 1994. "Peoples Against States: Ethnopolitical Conflict and the Changing World System." *International Studies Quarterly* 38(3):347-377.

Gurr, Ted R. 2000. *People versus States: Minorities at Risk in the New Century*. Washington, DC: U.S. Institute of Peace Press.

Gurses, Mehmet and T. David Mason. 2008. "Democracy Out of Anarchy: The Prospects for Post-Civil-War Democracy." *Social Science Quarterly* 89(2):315-336.

Hall, John. 2003. "Religion and violence: social processes in comparative perspective," pp. 359-81 in Michele Dillon, ed., Handbook for the Sociology of Religion. Cambridge: Cambridge University Press.

Halliday, Fred. 1996. *Islam and the Myth of Confrontation: Religion and Politics in the Middle East*. London, UK: I. B. Tauris.

Hansenclever, Andreas and Volker Rittberger. 2000. "Does Religion Make a Difference? Theoretical Approaches to the Impact of Faith on Political Conflict." *Millennium Journal of International Studies* 29(3):641-674.

Harbom, Lotta and Peter Wallensteen. 2005. "Armed Conflicts, 1946-2004." *Journal of Peace Research* 42(5):623-635.

Harbom, Lotta and Peter Wallensteen. 2009. "Armed Conflicts, 1946-2008." *Journal of Peace Research* 46(4):577-587.

Harbom, Lotta, Stina Högbladh, and Peter Wallensteen. 2006. "Armed Conflict and Peace Agreements." *Journal of Peace Research* 43(5):617-631.

Hartzell, Caroline A. and Matthew Hoddie. 2007. *Crafting Peace: Power-Sharing Institutions and the Negotiated Settlement of Civil Wars*. University Park: Pennsylvania State University Press.

Hartzell, Caroline A., Matthew Hoddie, and Donald Rothchild. 2001. "Stabilizing the Peace after Civil War: An Investigation of Some Key Variables." *International Organization* 55(1):183-208.

Hassan, Nasra. 2001. "An Arsenal of Believers." *The New Yorker*, November 19, 36–41.

Hauge, Wenche and Tanja Ellingsen. 1998. "Beyond Environmental Scarcity: Casual Pathways to Conflict." *Journal of Peace Research* 35(3):299–317.

Hegre, Håvard, Lisa Hultman, and Håvard Mokleiv Nygård. 2011. "Simulating the effect of peacekeeping operations 2010-2035." Social Computing, Behavioral-Cultural Modeling and Prediction. Springer Berlin Heidelberg, pgs. 325-332.

Hegre, Håvard, Scott Gates, Nils Petter Gleditsch, and Tanja Ellingsen. 2001. "Toward a Democratic Civil Peace? Democracy, Political Change and Civil War 1816-1992." *American Political Science Review* 95(1):33-48.

Helfstein, Scott and Dominick Wright. 2011. "Covert or Convenient? Evolution of Terror Attack Networks." *Journal of Conflict Resolution* 55(5):785-813.

Henderson, Errol A. and David Singer. 2000. "Civil War in the Post-Colonial World, 1946-92." *Journal of Peace Research* 37(3):275-299.

Henderson, John and Paul Bellamy. 2002. "Prospects for Future Military Intervention in Melanesian Politics." *World Affairs* 164(3):124-133.

Heraclides, Alexis. 1997. "The Ending of Unending Conflicts: Separatist Wars." *Millennium: Journal of International Studies* 26(3):679-707.

Hoddie, Matthew and Jason Matthew Smith. 2009. "Forms of Civil War Violence and Their Consequences for Future Public Health." *International Studies Quarterly* 53(1):175-202.

Högbladh, Stina. 2012. "Peace Agreements 1975-2011—Updating the UCDP Peace Agreement Dataset." In *States in Armed Conflict 2011*, edited by P. Thérése and L. Themnér. Report 99. Uppsala University, Sweden: Department of Peace and Conflict Research Report 99. Retrieved from http://www.pcr.uu.se/digitalAssets/142/142371_peace-agreements-1975-2011final.pdf.

Homer-Dixon, Thomas F. 1994. "Environmental Scarcities and Violent Conflict: Evidence from Cases." *International Security* 19(1):5-40.

Honaker, James. 2008. "Unemployment and Violence in Northern Ireland: A Missing Data Model for Ecological Inference." Presented at the Summer Meetings of the Society for Political Methodology, Tallahassee, FL.

Hooglund, Eric. 2001. "Khomeini, Ruhollah." P. 467 in *Oxford Companion to Politics of the World Second Edition*, edited by J. Krieger (editor in chief). Oxford, UK: Oxford University Press.

Horowitz, Donald. 1981. "Patterns of Ethnic Separatism." *Comparative Studies in Society and History* 23(2):165-195.

Horowitz, Donald. 1985. *Ethnic Groups in Conflict*. Berkeley: University of California Press.

Human Rights Watch. 1995. *The Fall of Srebrenica and the Failure of UN Peacekeeping*. October. Vol. 7(13). Retrieved from http://www.hrw.org/sites/default/files/reports/bosnia1095web.pdf.

Human Rights Watch. 2000. *Civilian Deaths in the NATO Air Campaign*. February. Vol. 12(1). Retrieved from http://www.hrw.org/legacy/reports/2000/nato/index.htm#TopOfPage.

Human Rights Watch. 2002. *The War within the War—Sexual Violence against Women and Girls in Eastern Congo*. Retrieved from http://www.hrw.org/reports/2002/drc/Congo0602.pdf.

Human Rights Watch. 2013a. "About us." Retrieved from http://www.hrw.org/about.

Human Rights Watch. 2013b. "The Gruesome Toll of Deadly Cluster Bombs in Syria." January 16. Retrieved from http://www.hrw.org/news/2013/01/16/gruesome-toll-deadly-cluster-bombs-syria.

Human Security Report Project (HSRP). 2011a. *Human Security Report 2009/2010: The Causes of Peace and the Shrinking Costs of War*. New York: Oxford University Press.

Human Security Report Project (HSRP). 2011b. "Reported Battle Deaths per State-Based Armed Conflict: International Conflicts versus Intrastate Conflicts, 1946-2008."

Human Security Report 2009/2010: The Causes of Peace and the Shrinking Costs of War. New York: Oxford University Press.

Human Security Report Project (HSRP). 2012a. "Graphs and Tables: Report 2012." Vancouver, Canada: Human Security Press. Retrieved from http://www.hsrgroup.org/human-security-reports/2012/graphs-and-tables.aspx.

Human Security Report Project (HSRP). 2012b. *Human Security Report 2012: Sexual Violence, Education and War: Beyond the Mainstream Narrative.* Vancouver, Canada: Human Security Press.

Humphreys, Macartan. 2005. "Natural Resources, Conflict, and Conflict Resolution: Uncovering the Mechanisms." *Journal of Conflict Resolution* 49(4):508–537.

Huntington, Samuel. P. 1993. "The Clash of Civilizations?" *Foreign Affairs* 72(3):22–49.

Huntington, Samuel. P. 1996. *The Clash of Civilizations and the Remaking of World Order.* New York: Simon and Schuster.

International Court of Justice (ICJ). 2013. "The Court." Retrieved from http://www.icj-cij.org/court/index.php?p1=1.

International Criminal Court (ICC). 2012. *Report of the International Criminal Court to the United Nations for 2011/12.* Retrieved from http://www.icc-cpi.int/en_menus/icc/reports%20on%20activities/court%20reports%20and%20statements/Documents/A67308EN.pdf

International Criminal Court (ICC). 2013a. "About the Court." Retrieved from http://www.icc-cpi.int/en_menus/icc/about%20the%20court/Pages/about%20the%20court.aspx.

International Criminal Court (ICC). 2013b. "ICC at a Glance." Retrieved from http://www.icc-cpi.int/en_menus/icc/about%20the%20court/icc%20at%20a%20glance/Pages/icc%20at%20a%20glance.aspx.

International Criminal Tribunal for the Former Yugoslavia (ICTY). 2011. "Tribunal Welcomes the Arrest of Ratko Mladic." May 26. Retrieved from http://www.icty.org/sid/10671.

International Criminal Tribunal for the former Yugoslavia (ICTY). 2013a. "About the ICTY." Retrieved from http://icty.org/sections/AbouttheICTY.

International Criminal Tribunal for the Former Yugoslavia (ICTY). 2013b. "Key Figures of the Cases." March. Retrieved from http://www.icty.org/sections/TheCases/KeyFiguresoftheCases.

International Criminal Tribunal for the Former Yugoslavia (ICTY). 2013c. "Support and Donations." Retrieved from http://www.icty.org/sections/AbouttheICTY/SupportandDonations.

International Criminal Tribunal for the Former Yugoslavia (ICTY). No date. "Kosovo, Croatia and Bosnia (IT-02-54) Slobodan Miloševic, Case Information Sheet." Retrieved from http://www.icty.org/x/cases/slobodan_milosevic/cis/en/cis_milosevic_slobodan_en.pdf.

International Institute for Strategic Studies (IISS). 2011. *Strategic Survey 2011—The Annual Review of World Affairs.* London, UK: Routledge.

International Institute for Strategic Studies. (IISS) 2012. "Strategic Survey 2012—Press Statement." September. Retrieved from http://www.iiss.org/en/about%20us/press%20room/press%20releases/press%20releases/archive/2012-ebe1/september-ddc8/strategic-survey-2012-press-statement-a74a.

International Institute for Strategic Studies (IISS). 2013. "Strategic Survey 2013: The Annual Review of World Affairs." September. Retrieved from http://www.iiss.org/en/publications/strategicsurvey/issues/strategic-survey-2013—the-annual-review-of-world-affairs-7179.

Iraq Body Count. 2014. "Documented Civilian Deaths from Violence as of August 20, 2013." Retrieved from http://www.iraqbodycount.org/database/.

Jalali, Rita and Seymour Martin Lipset. 1992–1993. "Racial and Ethnic Conflicts: A Global Perspective." *Political Science Quarterly* 107(4):585–606.

Jean, Moise. 2006. "The Rwandan Genocide: The True Motivations for Mass Killings." Retrieved from http://history.emory.edu/home/assets/documents/endeavors/volume1/Moises.pdf.

Johnson, Joshua. 2006. "From Cuba to Bolivia: Guevara's *Foco* Theory in Practice." *Innovations: A Journal of Politics* 6:26–32.

Johnston, Patrick. 2008. "The Geography of Insurgent Organization and Its Consequences for Civil Wars: Evidence from Liberia and Sierra Leone." *Security Studies* 17(1):107–137.

Johnston, Patrick. No date. "The Effectiveness of Leadership Decapitation in Counterinsurgency." Retrieved from http://iis-db.stanford.edu/evnts/5724/Johnston_-_Decapitation_%28CISAC%29.pdf.

Jones, Seth G. 2008. "Counterinsurgency in Afghanistan." *RAND Counter-Insurgency Study 4.* Retrieved from http://www.rand.org/content/dam/rand/pubs/monographs/2008/RAND_MG595.pdf.

Joseph, William A. 2001. "Cultural Revolution." P. 188 in *Oxford Companion to Politics of the World Second Edition,* edited by J. Krieger (editor in chief). Oxford, UK: Oxford University Press.

Joshi, Madhav. 2010. "Post-Civil War Democratization: Promotion of Democracy in Post-Civil War States, 1946–2005." *Democratization* 17(5):826–855.

Joshi, Madhav. 2013. "Inclusive Institutions and Stability of Transition toward Democracy in Post-Civil War States." *Democratization* 20(4): 743–770.

Joshi, Madhav and T. David Mason. 2012. "Balance of Power, Size of Governing Coalition and Durability of Peace in the Post-Civil War States." *International Interactions* 37:388–413.

Juergensmeyer, Mark. 1993. *The New Cold War?: Religious Nationalism Confronts the Secular State.* Berkeley: University of California Press.

Juergensmeyer, Mark. 2001. *Terror in the Mind of God: The Global Rise of Religious Violence.* Berkeley: University of California Press.

Juergensmeyer, Mark. 2013. "Religious Radicalism and Political Violence." Pp. 525–540 in *Conflict After the Cold War: Arguments on Causes of War and Peace,* edited by R. K. Betts. Boston, MA: Pearson.

Kalyvas, Stathis. 1999. "Wanton Senseless? The Logic of Massacres in Algeria." *Rationality and Society* 11(3):243–285.

Kalyvas, Stathis. 2004. "The Paradox of Terrorism in Civil War." *The Journal of Ethics* 8:97–138.

Kan, Abdullar, Conflict Monitoring Centre. January 2012. "Significant Decline in Suicide Attacks in Pakistan." Retrieved from http://cmcpk.wordpress.com/2012/01/01/significant-decline-in-suicide-attacks-in-pakistan/.

Kang, Seonjou and James Meernik. 2005. "Civil War Destruction and the Prospects for Economic Growth." *Journal of Politics* 67(1):88–109.

Kaufman, Stuart J. 2001. *Modern Hatreds—The Symbolic Politics of Ethnic War.* New York: Cornell University Press.

Kaufman, Stuart J. 2006a. "Escaping the Symbolic Politics Trap: Reconciliation Initiatives and Conflict Resolution in Ethnic Wars." *Journal of Peace Research* 43(2):201–218.

Kaufman, Stuart J. 2006b. "Symbolic Politics or Rational Choice? Testing Theories of Extreme Ethnic Violence." *International Security* 30(4):45–86.

Kavanagh, Jennifer. 2011. "Selection, Availability, and Opportunity: The Conditional Effect of Poverty on Terrorist Group Participation." *Journal of Conflict Resolution* 55(1):106–132.

Kearney, Robert N. 1987–1988. "Territorial Elements of Tamil Separatism in Sri Lanka." *Pacific Affairs* 60(4):568.

Keen, David. 2005. *Conflict & Collusion in Sierra Leone*. New York: Palgrave.

Keen, David. 2012. *Useful Enemies: When Waging Wars Is More Useful Than Winning Them*. New Haven, CT: Yale University Press.

Kegley, Charles W. 2010. *World Politics: Trend and Transformation*. Boston, MA: Wadsworth Cengage.

Khan, Abdullah. 2012. "Decline in Suicide Attacks." Conflict Monitoring Center. Retrieved from http://www.cmcpk.net/wp-content/uploads/2012/05/annual-report-suicide -english-reviewed.pdf.

Kilcullen, David. 2006. "Counterinsurgency Redux." *Survival* 48(4):111–130.

Knight, Franklin W. 2001. "Cuba." P. 185 in *Oxford Companion to Politics of the World Second Edition*, edited by J. Krieger (editor in chief). Oxford, UK: Oxford University Press.

Krain, Matthew. 2005. "International Intervention and the Severity of Genocides and Politicides." *International Studies Quarterly* 49(3):363–387.

Kreutz, Joakim. 2010. "How and When Armed Conflicts End: Introducing the UCDP Conflict Termination Dataset." *Journal of Peace Research* 47(2):243–250.

Kreuzer, Peter. 2005. "Political Clans and Violence in the Southern Philippines." Peace Research Institute Frankfurt Report No. 71. Frankfurt, Germany: PRIF.

Krieger, Joel, editor in chief. 2001. *Oxford Companion to Politics of the World Second Edition*. Oxford, UK: Oxford University Press.

Krieger, Tim and Daniel Meierrieks. 2010. "Terrorism in the Worlds of Welfare Capitalism." *Journal of Conflict Resolution* 54(6):902–939.

Krippendorff, Ekkehart. 1979. "Minorities, Violence, and Peace Research." *Journal of Peace Research* 16 (1):27–40.

Kroc Institute for International Peace Studies, University of Notre Dame (Krock Institute). 2012. "Peace Accords Matrix." Retrieved from https://peaceaccords.nd.edu/.

Krueger, Alan B. and David D. Laitin. 2008. "Kto Kogo?: A Cross-Country Study of the Origins and Targets of Terrorism." In *Terrorism, Economic Development, and Political Openness*, ed. Philip Keefer and Norman Loayza. Cambridge, UK: Cambridge University Press, 148–173.

Kurian, George Thomas, editor in chief. 2011. *The Encyclopedia of Political Science*. Washington, DC: Congressional Quarterly Press.

Lacina, Bethany. 2006. "Explaining the Severity of Civil Wars." *Journal of Conflict Resolution* 50(2):276–289.

Lacina, Bethany and Nils Petter Gleditsch. 2005. "Monitoring Trends in Global Combat: A New Dataset of Battle Deaths." *European Journal of Population* 21(2–3):145–166.

Lai, Brian and Clayton Thyne. 2007. "The Effect of Civil War on Education, 1980–1997." *Journal of Peace Research* 44 (3):277–292.

Leaning, Jennifer. 2000. "Environment and Health: 5. Impact of War." *Canadian Medical Association Journal* 163(9):1157–1161.

Lenin, Vladimir Ilyich. 1917. "The Tasks of the Proletariat in the Present Revolution." *Pravda* No. 26. April 7. Retrieved from http://www.marxists.org/archive/lenin/works/1917/apr/04.htm.

Li, Quan and Drew Schaub. 2004. "Economic Globalization and Transnational Terrorism: A Pooled Time Series Analysis." *Journal of Conflict Resolution* 48(2):230–258.

Li, Quan and Ming Wen. 2005. "The Immediate and Lingering Effects of Armed Conflict on Adult Mortality: A Time-Series Cross-National Analysis." *Journal of Peace Research* 42(4):471–492.

Loveman, Brian. 2001. "Guerilla Warfare." Pp. 342–343 in *Oxford Companion to Politics of the World Second Edition*, edited by J. Krieger (editor in chief). Oxford, UK: Oxford University Press.

Lujala, Paivi. 2010. "Cursed by Resources? High Value Natural Resource and Armed Civil Conflict." In *War: An Introduction to Theories and Research on Collective Violence*, edited by T. G. Jacobsen. New York: Nova Science.

Lujala, Paivi. 2011. "Cursed by Resources? High-Value Natural Resources and Armed Civil Conflict." Pp. 145–166 in *War: An Introduction to Theories and Research on Collective Violence*, edited by T. G. Jakobsen. New York: Nova Science.

Lujala, Paivi, Nils Petter Gleditsch, and Elisabeth Gilmore. 2005. "A Diamond Curse? Civil War and a Lootable Resource." *Journal of Conflict Resolution* 49(4):538–562.

Lustick, Ian S., Dan Miodownik, and Roy J. Eidelson. 2004. "Secessionism in Multicultural States: Does Sharing Power Prevent or Encourage It?" *American Political Science Review* 98(2):209–229.

Luttwak, Edward N. 1999. "Give War a Chance." Foreign Affairs. July/August. Retrieved from http://www.foreignaffairs.com/articles/55210/edward-n-luttwak/give-war-a-chance.

Mansfield, Edward D. and Jack Snyder. 2005. *Electing to Fight: Why Emerging Democracies Go to War.* Cambridge, MA: MIT Press.

Maoz, Zeev and Bruce Russett. 1993. "Normative and Structural Causes of Democratic Peace." *American Political Science Review* 87(3):624–638.

Marinov, Nikolay and Hein Goemans. 2012. "Coups and Democracy." October 23. Retrieved from http://www.nikolaymarinov.com/wp-content/files/GoemansMarinovCoup.pdf.

Marques de Morais, Rafael. 2009. "How France Fuelled Angola's Civil War." *Guardian.* November 1. Retrieved from http://www.guardian.co.uk/commentisfree/2009/nov/01/angola-civil-war-falcone-conviction.

Mason, David T. 2003a. "Globalization, Democratization, and the Prospects for Civil War in the New Millennium." *International Studies Review* 5(4):24.

Mason, T. David, Joseph P. Weingarten Jr., and Patrick J. Fett. 1999. "Win, Lose, or Draw: Predicting the Outcome of Civil Wars." *Political Research Quarterly* 52(2):239–268.

Mattes, Michaela and Burcu Savun. 2009. "Fostering Peace after Civil War: Commitment Problems and Agreement Design." *International Studies Quarterly* 53(3):737–759.

McLaughlin, Abraham and Meera Selva. 2004. "Sudan's Refugees Wait and Hope." *Christian Science Monitor.* February 18. Retrieved from http://www.csmonitor.com/2004/0218/p06s01-woaf.html.

Melander, Erik. 2009. *Justice or Peace? A Statistical Study of the Relationship between Amnesties and Durable Peace.* JAD-PbP Working Paper Series 4. Retrieved from http://www.lu.se/upload/LUPDF/Samhallsvetenskap/Just_and_Durable_Peace/Workingpaper4.pdf.

Melander, Erik, Frida Möller, and Magnus Öberg. 2009. "Managing Intrastate Low-Intensity Armed Conflict 1993–2004: A New Dataset." *International Interactions* 35(1):58–85.

Melin, Molly M. and Isak Svensson. 2009. "Incentives for Talking: Accepting Mediation in International and Civil Wars." *International Interactions* 35(3):249–271.

Midlarsky, Manus. I. 1998. "Democracy and Islam: Implications for Civilizational Conflict and the Democratic Peace." *International Studies Quarterly* 42(3):485–511.

Minorities at Risk Project (MAR). 2005. College Park, MD: Center for International Development and Conflict Management. Retrieved from http://www.cidcm.umd.edu/mar/.

Möller, Frida, Karl DeRouen Jr., Jacob Bercovitch, and Peter Wallensteen. 2007. "The Limits of Peace: Third Parties in Civil Wars in Southeast Asia, 1993-2004." October. *Negotiation Journal* 23(4):373-391.

Moore, Matthew M. 2011. "Sparks to Kindling: Terrorism's Role in Civil War Onset, Recurrence, and Escalation." Ph.D. dissertation, University of Missouri, Columbia, MO.

Moore, Will H. and Stephen M. Shellman. 2004. "Fear of Persecution—Forced Migration, 1952-1995." *Journal of Conflict Resolution* 40(5):723-745.

Moore, Will H. and Stephen M. Shellman. 2006. "Refugee or Internally Displaced Person? To Where Should One Flee?" *Comparative Political Studies* 39(5):599-622.

Mousseau, Michael. 2011. "Urban Poverty and Support for Islamist Terror: Survey Results of Muslims in Fourteen Countries." *Journal of Peace Research* 48(1):34-47.

Mukherjee, Bumba. 2006. "Why Political Power-Sharing Agreements Lead to Enduring Peaceful Resolution of Some Civil Wars, but Not Others?" *International Studies Quarterly* 50(2):479-504.

Murdoch, James C. and Todd Sandler. 2002. "Economic Growth, Civil Wars, and Spatial Spillovers." *Journal of Conflict Resolution* 46(1):91-110.

Nacos, Brigitte L. 2008. *Terrorism and Counterterrorism: Understanding Threats and Responses in the Post-9/11 World.* New York: Pearson.

Nafziger, Wayne E. 2006. "Resource Wars in Africa-Roundtable." Presented at the African Studies Association, San Francisco, CA.

Narayanan, Sugumaran. 2008. "Islam and the Onset of Civil War, 1946-2004." Ph.D. dissertation, University of Alabama.

Newman, Edward, Roland Paris, and Oliver P. Richmond, eds. 2009. "Introduction." *New Perspectives on Liberal Peacebuilding.* Tokyo, Japan: United Nations University Press.

Nordas, Ragnhild. 2004. "State Religiosity and Civil War: How Religious Heterogeneity and the Degree of Separation between Religion and State Influence the Risk of Intrastate Armed Conflict." Master's thesis, Norwegian University of Science and Technology, Trondheim, Norway.

North Atlantic Treaty Organization (NATO). 2014. "International Security Assistance Force." Retrieved from http://www.isaf.nato.int/news/3.html.

Obermeyer, Ziad, Christopher J. L. Murray, and Emmanuela Gakidou. 2008. "Fifty Years of Violent War Deaths from Vietnam to Bosnia: Analysis of Data from the World Health Survey Programme." *British Medical Journal* 336:1482-1486.

Pape, Robert A. 2003. "The Strategic Logic of Suicide Terrorism." *American Political Science Review* 97(3):343-361.

Paris, Roland. 2002. "International Peacebuilding and the 'Mission civilisatrice.'" *Review of International Studies* 28(4):637-656.

Paris R. 2004. *At War's End: Building Peace after Civil Conflict.* Cambridge, UK: Cambridge University Press.

Paris, Roland and Timothy D. Sisk, eds. 2009. "Introduction—Understanding the Contradictions of Postwar Statebuilding." *The Dilemmas of Statebuilding—Confronting the Contradictions of Postwar Peace Operations.* London, UK: Routledge.

Patrick, Erin. 2011. "When War Stops, the Impact on the Environment Lives On." *Huffington Post.* November 4. Retrieved from http://www.huffingtonpost.com/erin-patrick/when -war-stops-the-impact_b_1076658.html.

Peace Pledge Union. No date. "War and the Environment." Retrieved from http://www.ppu .org.uk/learn/infodocs/st_environment.html.

Pearson, Frederick S. 1974. "Foreign Military Interventions and Domestic Disputes." *International Studies Quarterly* 18(3):259–289.

Petersen, Roger D. 2001. *Resistance and Rebellion, Lessons from Eastern Europe*. Cambridge, UK: Cambridge University Press.

Petersen, Roger D. 2002. *Understanding Ethnic Violence, Fear, Hatred, and Resentment in 20th-Century Eastern Europe*. Cambridge, UK: Cambridge University Press.

Pew Research Center. 2009. *Mapping the Global Muslim Population*. Washington, DC: Author

Piazza, James A. 2006. "Roots in Poverty?: Terrorism, Poor Economic Development, and Social Cleavages." *Terrorism and Political Violence* 18:159–177.

Piazza, James A. 2011. "Poverty, Minority Economic Discrimination, and Domestic Terrorism." *Journal of Peace Research* 48(3):339–353.

Piazza, James A. 2012. "The Opium Trade and Patterns of Terrorism in the Provinces of Afghanistan: An Empirical Analysis." *Terrorism and Political Violence* 24(2):213–234.

Powell, Emilia J. and Jeffrey K. Staton. 2007. "Domestic Judicial Institutions and Human Rights Treaty Violation." February 12. Retrieved from http://mailer.fsu.edu/~jstaton/ treatyviolation.pdf.

Powell, Emilia J. and Sara M. Mitchell. 2007. "The International Court of Justice and the World's Three Legal Systems." *Journal of Politics* 69(2):397–415.

Powell, Jonathan M. and Clayton L. Thyne. 2011. "Global Instances of Coups from 1950 to 2010: A New Dataset." *Journal of Peace Research* 48(2):249–259.

Powell, Jonathan M. and Clayton L. Thyne. 2012a. Appendix Table 1. University of Kentucky. Retrieved from http://www.uky.edu/~clthyn2/coup_data/appendix_T1.pdf.

Powell, Jonathan M. and Clayton L. Thyne. 2012b. Appendix Table 2. University of Kentucky. Retrieved from http://www.uky.edu/~clthyn2/coup_data/appendix_T2.pdf.

Powell, Jonathan M. and Clayton L. Thyne. 2012c. "Correspondence with Paul Bellamy." March 3.

Powell, Jonathan M. and Clayton L. Thyne. 2012d. "Coup Dataset 2, 2012". University of Kentucky. Retrieved from http://www.uky.edu/~clthyn2/coup_data/powell_thyne _coups_final.txt.

Pugh, Michael. 2005. "The Political Economy of Peacebuilding: A Critical Theory Perspective." *International Journal of Peace Studies* 10(2):23–42.

Quinn, J. Michael, David Mason, and Mehmet Gurses. 2007. "Sustaining the Peace: Determinants of Civil War Recurrence." *International Interactions* 33(2):167–193.

RAND. 2000. Second Annual Report to the President and the Congress of the Advisory Panel to Assess Domestic Response Capabilities for Terrorism Involving Weapons of Mass Destruction. Retrieved from http://www.rand.org/content/dam/rand/www/external/ nsrd/terrpanel/terror2.pdf.

RAND. 2012a. Rand Database of Worldwide Terrorism Incidents. Retrieved from http:// www.rand.org/nsrd/projects/terrorism-incidents.html.

RAND. 2012b. Rand Database of Worldwide Terrorism Incidents: Database Scope. Retrieved from http://www.rand.org/nsrd/projects/terrorism-incidents/about/ definitions.html.

Red Cross. 2013. "Rule 156: Definition of War Crimes." Retrieved from http://www.icrc .org/customary-ihl/eng/print/v1_cha_chapter44_rule156.

Regan, Patrick. 2000. *Civil Wars and Foreign Powers*. Ann Arbor: University of Michigan Press.

Regan, Patrick M. 2002a. *Civil Wars and Foreign Powers: Outside Intervention in Intrastate Conflict*. Ann Arbor: University of Michigan Press.

Regan, Patrick M. 2002b. "Third-Party Interventions and the Duration of Intrastate Conflicts." *Journal of Conflict Resolution* 46(1):55–73.

Regan, Patrick M. and Aysegul Aydin. 2006. "Diplomacy and Other Forms of Intervention in Civil Wars." *Journal of Conflict Resolution* 50(5):736–756.

Regan, Patrick M., Richard W. Frank, and Aysegul Aydin. 2009. "Diplomatic Interventions and Civil War: A New Dataset." *Journal of Peace Research* 46(1):135–146.

Regan, Patrick M. and Daniel Norton. 2005. "Greed, Grievance and Mobilization in Civil Wars." *Journal of Conflict Resolution* 49(3):319–336.

Religions for Peace—African Council of Religious Leaders. 2010. *Small Arms and Light Weapons: Africa. A Resource Guide for Religions for Peace*. Retrieved from http://www.un.org/disarmament/education/docs/SALW_Africa.pdf.

Reno, William. 1998. *Warlord Politics and African States*. Boulder: CO: Lynne Reinner.

Reno, William. 2000a. "Clandestine Economies, Violence and States in Africa." *Journal of International Affairs* 53 (2): 433–460.

Reno, William. 2000b. "The Real (War) Economy of Angola." Pp. 219–235 in *Angola's War Economy*, eds. Jakkie Cilliers and Christian Dietrich. Pretoria, South Africa: Institute for Security Studies.

Reuters. 2011. "US Pays off Much of UN Arrears, Now Owes $736 million." January 25.

Reynal-Querol, Marta. 2002. "Ethnicity, Political Systems, and Civil Wars." *Journal of Conflict Resolution* 46(1):29–54.

Richmond, Oliver. 2011. *A Post-Liberal Peace*. London, UK: Routledge.

Robinson, Kristopher K. 2007. "The Challenges of Political Terrorism: A Cross-National Analysis of the Downward Spiral of Terrorist Violence and Socio-Political Crisis." Ph.D. dissertation, Ohio State University.

Ron, James. 2005. "Paradigm in Distress? Primary Commodities and Civil War." *Journal of Conflict Resolution* 49 (4): 443–450.

Ross, Michael. 2001. "Does Oil Hinder Democracy?" *World Politics* 53(3):325–361.

Ross, Michael. 2003. "The Natural Resource Curse: How Wealth Can Make You Poor." In *Natural Resources and Violent Conflict: Options and Actions*, edited by I. Bannon and P. Collier. Washington, DC: World Bank.

Ross, Michael. 2004. "What Do We Know About Natural Resources and Civil War?" *Journal of Peace Research* 41(3):337–356.

Ross, Michael. 2005. "Resources and Rebellion in Aceh, Indonesia." Pp. 35–58 in *Understanding Civil War: Evidence and Analysis*, edited by P. Collier and N. Sambanis. Washington, DC: World Bank.

Ross, Michael. 2006. "A Closer Look at Oil, Diamonds, and Civil War." *Annual Review of Political Science* 9:265–300.

Russett, Bruce and John Oneal. 2001. *Triangulating Peace: Democracy, Interdependence, and International Organizations*. New York: W.W. Norton.

Rutagarama, Eugene. 2001. "A Conservation Triumph: The Mountain Gorillas of Rwanda." *Science in Africa*, July. Retrieved from http://www.scienceinafrica.co.za/2001/july/gorilla.htm.

Saab, Bilal Y. and Alexandra W. Taylor. 2009. "Criminality and Armed Groups: A Comparative Study of FARC and Paramilitary Groups in Colombia." *Studies in Conflict & Terrorism* 32:455–475.

Sageman, Marc. 2004. *Understanding Terror Networks*. Philadelphia: University of Pennsylvania Press.

Sageman, Mark. 2013. "Jihadi Networks of Terror." In *Conflict After the Cold War: Arguments on Causes of War and Peace*, edited by R. K. Betts. Boston, MA: Pearson.

Saideman, Stephen M. 2002. "Overlooking the Obvious: Bringing International Politics Back into Ethnic Conflict Management." *International Studies Review* 4(3):63–86 (Online see v2.2).

Saideman, Stephen M., Beth K. Dougherty, and Erin K. Jenne. 2005. "Dilemmas of Divorce—How Secessionist Identities Cut Both Ways." *Security Studies* 14(4):607–636.

Saideman, Stephen M., David J Lanoue, Michael Campenni, and Samuel Stanton. 2002. "Democratization, Political Institutions, and Ethnic Conflict: A Pooled Time-Series Analysis, 1985–1998." *Comparative Political Studies* 35(1):103–129.

Salehyan, Idean. 2007. "The Externalities of Civil Strife: Refugees as a Source of International Conflict." March. Paper presented at the conference on "Migration, International Relations, and the Evolution of World Politics." Retrieved from http://www.cas.unt.edu/~idean/RefugeesWar.pdf.

Salehyan, Idean and Kristian Skrede Gleditsch. 2006. "Refugees and the Spread of Civil Wars." *International Organization* 60:335–366.

Sambanis, Nicholas. 2001. "Do Ethnic and Non-ethnic Civil Wars Have the Same Causes?: A Theoretical and Empirical Inquiry (Part 1)." *Journal of Conflict Resolution* 45(3):259–282.

Sambanis, Nicholas. 2008. "Terrorism and Civil War." Pp. 174–201 in *Terrorism, Economic Development, and Political Openness*, edited by P. Keefer and N. Loayza. Cambridge, UK: Cambridge University Press.

Sanchez, Fabio, Andres Solimano, and Michel Formisano. 2005. "Conflict, Violence, and Crime in Colombia." Pp. 119–160 in *Understanding Civil War: Evidence and Analysis*, edited by P. Collier and N. Sambanis. Washington, DC: World Bank.

Sanchez-Cuenca, Ignacio and Luis de la Calle. 2009. "Domestic Terrorism: The Hidden Side of Political Violence." *Annual Review of Political Science* 12:31–49.

Sandler, Todd. 2010. "Terrorism and Policy: Introduction." *Journal of Conflict Resolution* 54(2): 203–213.

Schmid, Alex P. 1992. "Terrorism and Democracy." *Terrorism and Political Violence* 4(4): 14–25.

Shafiq, Najeeb M. and Abdulkader H. Sinno. 2010. "Education, Income, and Support for Suicide Bombings: Evidence from Six Muslim Countries." *Journal of Conflict Resolution* 54(1):146–178.

Skocpol, Theda. 1979. *States and Social Revolutions: A Comparative Analysis of France, Russia, and China*. Cambridge, UK: Cambridge University Press.

Smith, Amy L. and David R. Smock. 2008. *Managing a Mediation Process*. Washington, DC: U.S. Institute of Peace. Retrieved from http://www.usip.org/programs/projects/managing -mediation-process.

Smith, Gar. 2002. "It's Time to Restore Afghanistan—Afghanistan's Crying Needs." *Earth Island Journal*. Summer. Retrieved from http://www.earthisland.org/journal/index.php/eij/article/its_time_to_restore_afghanistan/.

Snow, Donald M. 2003. *Cases in International Relations: Portraits of the Future*. Washington, DC: Addison Wesley Longman.

Snyder, Richard. 2006. "Does Lootable Wealth Breed Disorder?: A Political Economy of Extraction Framework." *Comparative Political Studies* 39(8):943–968.

Snyder, Richard and Ravi Bhavnani. 2005. "Diamonds, Blood, and Taxes. A Revenue-Centered Framework for Explaining Political Order." *Journal of Conflict Resolution* 49(4):563–597.

Snyder, Richard and Angelica Duran-Martinez. 2009. "Does Illegality Breed Violence? Drug Trafficking and State Sponsored Protection Rackets." *Crime Law Social and Change* 52:253–273.

START. 2012. National Consortium for the Study of Terrorism and Responses to Terrorism. Global Terrorism Database [Data file]. Retrieved from http://www.start.umd.edu/gtd.

Stedman, Stephen J. 1997. "Spoiler Problems in Peace Processes." *International Security* 22(2):5–53.

Stedman, Stephen. 2000. "Spoiler Problems in Peace Processes." In National Research Council. *International Conflict Resolution after the Cold War*. Washington, DC: National Academies Press.

Stedman, Stephen John. 2001. *Implementing Peace Agreements in Civil Wars: Lessons and Recommendations for Policymakers, IPA Policy Paper Series on Peace Implementation*. New York: International Peace Academy. Retrieved from http://peacemaker.un.org/sites/peace maker.un.org/files/ImplementingPeaceAgreementsinCivilWars_IPI2001.pdf

Steele, A. 2009. "Seeking Safety: Avoiding Displacement and Choosing Destinations in Civil Wars." *Journal of Peace Research* 46(3):419–430.

Stockholm International Peace Research Institute (SIPRI). 2005–2013. *Yearbook—Armaments, Disarmament and International Security*. Oxford, UK: Oxford University Press.

Stockholm International Peace Research Institute (SIPRI). 2013a. "About." Retrieved from http://www.sipri.org/about.

Stockholm International Peace Research Institute (SIPRI). 2013b. "Definitions and Methodology." Retrieved from http://www.sipri.org/research/conflict/pko/multilateral/sipri-database-on-multilateral-peace-operations.

Stockholm International Peace Research Institute (SIPRI). 2013c. "SIPRI Military Expenditures Database." Retrieved at http://www.sipri.org/research/armaments/milex/milex_database.

Stockholm International Peace Research Institute (SIPRI). 2014. "Afghanistan and its Neighborhood: The Wider Central Asia Initiative." Retrieved from http://www.sipri.org/research/security/afghanistan.

Svensson, Isak. 2009. "Who Brings Which Peace? Neutral versus Biased Mediation and Institutional Peace Arrangements in Civil Wars." *Journal of Conflict Resolution* 53(3):446–469.

Syrian Observatory for Human Rights. 2014. Retrieved from http://syriahr.com/en/.

Taras, Raymond C. and Rajat Ganguly. 2008. *Understanding Ethnic Conflict: The International Dimension*, 3rd edition. New York: Pearson Longman.

Taylor, Rob. 2012. "Three U.S. soldiers killed by Afghan police in Helmand?" Reuters News. August 10. Retrieved from http://www.reuters.com/article/2012/08/10/us-afghanistan-shooting-idUSBRE87907Q20120810.

Teed, Peter. 1992. *A Dictionary of Twentieth-Century History 1914–1990*. Oxford, UK: Oxford University Press.

Thambiah, Stanley J. 1989. "Ethnic Conflict in the World Today." *American Ethnologist* 16(2):335–349.

Themnér, Lotta and Peter Wallensteen. 2011. "Armed Conflict, 1946–2010." *Journal of Peace Research* 48(4):525–536.

Themnér, Lotta and Peter Wallensteen. 2012. "Armed Conflicts, 1946–2011." *Journal of Peace Research* 49(4):565–575.

Themnér, Lotta and Peter Wallensteen. 2013. "Armed Conflicts, 1946–2012." *Journal of Peace Research* 50(4):509–521.

Tilly, Charles. 1978. *From Mobilization to Revolution*. New York: McGraw-Hill.

Tir, Jaroslav. 2005. "Dividing Countries to Promote Peace: Prospects for Long-Term Success of Partitions." *Journal of Peace Research* 42(5):545–562.

Toft, Monica D. 2007. "Getting Religion?: The Puzzling Case of Islam and Civil War." *International Security* 31(4):97–131.

Toft, Monica Duffy. 2001. "Indivisible Territory and Ethnic War." Paper 01-08. December. Retrieved from http://civicrm.wcfia.harvard.edu/node/546.

Toft, Monica Duffy. 2009. *Securing the Peace: The Durable Settlement of Civil War*. Princeton, NJ: Princeton University Press.

Transparency International. 2001–2013. "Corruption Perceptions Index (CPI)." Retrieved from http://www.transparency.org/research/cpi/overview.

UN Children's Fund. No date. *Factsheet: Child Soldiers*. Retrieved from http://www.unicef.org/emerg/files/childsoldiers.pdf.

UN Department of Political Affairs. 2013a. "Mediation Support." Retrieved from http://www.un.org/wcm/content/site/undpa/mediation_support.

UN Department of Political Affairs. 2013b. "Peacemaking and Conflict Prevention." Retrieved from http://www.un.org/wcm/content/site/undpa/lang/en/main/issues/peacemaking.

UN Department of Political Affairs. 2013c. "Promoting Peaceful, Political Solutions to Conflict." Retrieved from http://www.un.org/wcm/content/site/undpa/lang/en/main.

UN Department of Political Affairs. 2013d. "Standby Team of Mediation Experts." Retrieved from http://www.un.org/wcm/content/site/undpa/standby_team.

UN Development Program. 2011. "Human Development Report 2011—Afghanistan." New York. Retrieved from http://hdr.undp.org/en/countries/profiles/AFG.

UN Educational, Scientific and Cultural Organization (UNESCO). 2011a. *The Hidden Crisis: Armed Conflict and Education, Education for All Global Monitoring Report 2011*. Retrieved from http://unesdoc.unesco.org/images/0019/001907/190743e.pdf.

UN Educational, Scientific and Cultural Organization (UNESCO). 2011b. *How Does Violent Conflict Impact on Individual Educational Outcomes? The Evidence So Far, Background Paper Prepared for the Education for All Global Monitoring Report 2011*. Retrieved from http://unesdoc.unesco.org/images/0019/001907/190710e.pdf.

UN Environment Program. 2010. "The State of the Planet's Biodiversity." Retrieved from http://www.unep.org/wed/2010/english/biodiversity.asp#biodivloss.

UN General Assembly (UN G.A.) Resolution. 2005. Agreed Definition of Term 'Terrorism' Said to be Needed for Consensus on Completing Comprehensive Convention Against It. GA/L/3276.

UN General Assembly (UN G.A.) Resolution. 2008. The United Nations Global Counter-Terrorism Strategy. A/RES/62/272).

UN High Commissioner for Refugees (UNHCR). 2011a. "Asylum Applications in Industrialized Countries Rise in First Six Months in 2011." October 18. Retrieved from http://www.unhcr.org/4e9d33cc9.html.

UN High Commissioner for Refugees (UNHCR). 2011b. "Rainfall, Disease, Hitting Refugee Camps in Kenya, Ethiopia." November 15. Retrieved from http://www.unhcr.org/4ec2652b9.html.

UN High Commissioner for Refugees (UNHCR). 2011c. "UNHCR looks at the Economic Contribution of Afghan Refugees in Pakistan." January 10. Retrieved from http://www.unhcr.org/4d2b1dd96.html.

UN High Commissioner for Refugees (UNHCR). 2013. *2012 Statistical Yearbook.* Retrieved from http://www.unhcr.org/52a722559.html.

UN High Commissioner for Refugees (UNHCR). 2014a. "Internally Displaced People Figures." Retrieved from http://www.unhcr.org/pages/49c3646c23.html.

UN High Commissioner for Refugees (UNHCR). 2014b. "Refugee Facts and Figures." Retrieved at http://www.unhcr.org/pages/49c3646c1d.html.

UN News Centre. 2009. "Terrorism kills more Afghan civilians than any military action—UN mission." July 13, 2009. Retrieved from http://www.un.org/apps/news/story.asp?NewsID=31446.

UN News Centre. 2012. "Syria—UN Official Urges International Community to Boost Funds for Humanitarian Needs." August 22. Retrieved from http://www.un.org/apps/news/story.asp?NewsID=42725&Cr=Syria&Cr1.

UN News Centre. 2013. "Ban decries escalating violence in Syria, condemns use of 'barrel bombs.'" December 26. Retrieved from http://www.un.org/apps/news/story.asp?NewsID=46834&Cr=syria&Cr1=#.Ur0xRvsvnSc.

UN Office of the High Commissioner for Human Rights (UN OHCHR). 2007. "Convention against Torture and Other Cruel, Inhuman or Degrading Treatment or Punishment." Retrieved from http://www.ohchr.org/EN/ProfessionalInterest/Pages/CAT.aspx.

UN Office of the High Commissioner for Human Rights (UN OHCHR). 2011. "Cambodia—20 years on from the Paris Peace Agreements." October. Retrieved from http://www.ohchr.org/EN/NewsEvents/Pages/Cambodia-20yearsonfromtheParisPeace.aspx.

UN Office of the High Commissioner for Human Rights (UN OHCHR). 2012. "International Human Rights Law." Retrieved from http://www.ohchr.org/EN/ProfessionalInterest/Pages/InternationalLaw.aspx.

UN Office on Drugs and Crime (UNODC). 2004. "World Drug Report": Volume 2: Statistics. Retrieved from http://www.unodc.org/unodc/en/data-and-analysis/WDR-2004.html.

UN Office on Drugs and Crime (UNODC). 2012. World Drug Report. Retrieved from http://www.unodc.org/unodc/en/data-and-analysis/WDR-2012.html.

UN Office on Drugs and Crime (UNODC). 2013. "UNODC on human trafficking and migrant smuggling." Retrieved at http://www.unodc.org/unodc/human-trafficking/index.html?ref=menuside.

UN Office on Drugs and Crime (UNODC). 2014. "Human Trafficking FAQs." Retrieved from http://www.unodc.org/unodc/en/human-trafficking/faqs.html#How_widespread_is_human_trafficking.

UN Peacekeeping. 2013. "History of Peacekeeping." Retrieved from http://www.un.org/en/peacekeeping/operations/history.shtml.

UN Peacekeeping. 2014. "Financing Peacekeeping." Retrieved from http://www.un.org/en/peacekeeping/operations/financing.shtml.

UN Security Council. 2013. Retrieved from http://www.un.org/en/sc/.

United Nations (UN). 2000. The Role of the United Nations in the 21st Century. Millennium Report. Retrieved from http://www.un.org/millennium/sg/report/.

United Nations (UN). 2008. "Convention against Torture and Other Cruel, Inhuman or Degrading Treatment or Punishment." Retrieved from http://www.ohchr.org/EN/ProfessionalInterest/Pages/CAT.aspx

United Nations (UN). 2009. *Security Council Final Report of the Group of Experts on the Democratic Republic of Congo.* Reference no. S/2009/603. Retrieved from http://www.un.org/ga/search/view_doc.asp?symbol=S/2009/603.

United Nations (UN). 2010. *Security Council Report of the mission to the Democratic Republic of Congo* (May 13 to 16). Reference no. S/2010/288 Retrieved from http://www.un.org/en/ga/search/view_doc.asp?symbol=S/2010/288.

United Nations (UN). 2012a. "U.N. Action to Counter Terrorism." Retrieved from http://www.un.org/terrorism/.

United Nations (UN). 2012b. "U.N. High Level Panel Action to Counter Terrorism." Retrieved from http://www.un.org/en/terrorism/highlevelpanel.shtml

United Nations (UN). 2014a. Index. Retrieved from http://www.un.org/en/index.shtml.

United Nations (UN). 2014b. "List of Peacekeeping Operations 1948 to 2013." Retrieved from http://www.un.org/en/peacekeeping/documents/operationslist.pdf.

United Nations (UN). 2014c. "Peacekeeping." Retrieved from http://www.un.org/en/peacekeeping/.

United Nations (UN). 2014d. "Peacekeeping Factsheet." Retrieved from http://www.un.org/en/peacekeeping/resources/statistics/factsheet.shtml.

United Nations (UN). 2014e. "Peacekeeping—Fatalities." February 5. Retrieved from http://www.un.org/en/peacekeeping/resources/statistics/fatalities.shtml.

United Nations (UN). No date-a. "Background Note: UN Peacekeeping." Retrieved from http://www.un.org/en/peacekeeping/documents/backgroundnote.pdf.

United Nations (UN). No date-b. "Cambodia—UNTAC Facts and Figures." Retrieved from http://www.un.org/en/peacekeeping/missions/past/untacfacts.html.

United Nations (UN). No date-c. "Impact of Armed Conflict on Children." Retrieved from http://www.un.org/rights/concerns.htm.

United Nations (UN). No date-d. "Success of peacekeeping." Retrieved from http://www.un.org/en/peacekeeping/operations/success.shtml.

United Nations (UN). No date-e. "What is Peacebuilding?" Retrieved from http://www.unpbf.org/application-guidelines/what-is-peacebuilding/.

United Nations (UN). No date-f. "What is Peacekeeping?" Retrieved from http://www.un.org/en/peacekeeping/operations/peacekeeping.shtml.

United Nations Mission in Afghanistan (UNAMA). n.d. "Mandate." Available at http://unama.unmissions.org/Default.aspx?tabid=12255&language=en-US.

Uppsala Conflict Data Program (UCDP). 2012a. "Ongoing Conflicts 2010–2011." Uppsala University. Retrieved from http://www.pcr.uu.se/.

Uppsala Conflict Data Program (UCDP). 2012b. "Peace Researchers Worried over a Marked Decrease in the Number of Peace Agreements." December 27. Retrieved from http://www.pcr.uu.se/digitalAssets/142/142555_ucdp2012_english.pdf.

Uppsala Conflict Data Program (UCDP). 2012c. "UCDP Peace Agreement Dataset v. 2.0, 1975-2011." Retrieved from http://www.pcr.uu.se/research/ucdp/datasets/ucdp_peace_agreement_dataset/.

Uppsala Conflict Data Program (UCDP). 2013. "Uppsala University." Retrieved from http://www.pcr.uu.se/research/ucdp/.

Uppsala Conflict Data Program (UCDP). 2014a. "Definitions." Uppsala University. Retrieved from http://www.pcr.uu.se/research/ucdp/definitions/.

Uppsala Conflict Data Program (UCDP). 2014b. "Ongoing Armed Conflicts." Retrieved from http://www.pcr.uu.se/research/UCDP/.

Urdal, Henrik. 2005. "People Versus Malthus: Population Pressure, Environmental Degradation, and Armed Conflict Revisited." *Journal of Peace Research* 42(4):417–434.

U.S. Congress. House of Representatives. Committee on International Relations. 2004. *Afghanistan Drugs and Terrorism and U.S. Security Policy.* 108th Congress, 2nd session, 12 February.

U.S. Department of State. 2011. "Background Notes: Afghanistan." Retrieved from http://www.state.gov/outofdate/bgn/afghanistan/191350.htm.

U.S. Department of State. 2012. 2012 INSCR: Country Reports–Afghanistan through Costa Rica. Available at http://www.state.gov/j/inl/rls/nrcrpt/2012/vol1/184098.htm.

U.S. Department of State. 2013. "Secretary of State." Retrieved from http://www.state.gov/secretary/.

U.S. Department of State. 2014. "A-Z List of Country and Other Area Pages." Retrieved from http://www.state.gov/misc/list/index.htm.

U.S. Department of State, Bureau of Counterterrorism (CT). 2012. "Country Reports on Terrorism 2011." Retrieved from http://www.state.gov/documents/organization/195768.pdf.

U.S. Department of State, Bureau of Counterterrorism (CT). 2013. "Country Reports on Terrorism 2012." Retrieved from http://www.state.gov/documents/organization/210204.pdf.

U.S. Department of the Interior. 2012. "U.S. Geological Survey: Mineral Commodity Summaries 2012." 2012. Retrieved from http://minerals.usgs.gov/minerals/pubs/mcs/2012/mcs2012.pdf.

U.S. Institute of Peace. 2013. "Managing a Mediation Process." Retrieved from http://www.usip.org/managing-mediation-process/step-6-construct-peace-agreement.

U.S. Patriot Act. 2001. Public Law 107–56. Retrieved from http://www.gpo.gov/fdsys/pkg/PLAW-107publ56/pdf/PLAW-107publ56.pdf.

Vanhanen, Tatu. 1999. "Domestic Ethnic Conflict and Ethnic Nepotism: A Comparative Analysis." *Journal of Peace Research* 36(1):55–73.

Venkatraman, Amritha. 2007. "Religious Basis for Islamic Terrorism: The Quran and Its Interpretations." *Studies in Conflict & Terrorism* 30:229–248.

Victoroff, Jeff. 2005. "The Mind of the Terrorist: A Review and Critique of Psychological Approaches." *Journal of Conflict Resolution* 49(1):3–42.

Voice of America. 2010. "UN: Illegal Arms Trade Fuels Central African Conflicts." March 21. Retrieved from http://www.voanews.com/content/illegal-arms-trade-fuels-central-african-conflicts-88828077/153799.html.

Walter, Barbara F. 1999. "Designing Transitions from Civil Wars—Demobilization, Democratization, and Commitments to Peace." *International Security* 24(1):127–155.

Walter, Barbara F. 2002. *Committing to Peace: The Successful Settlement of Civil Wars.* Princeton, NJ: Princeton University Press.

Walter, Barbara F. 2003. "Explaining the Intractability of Territorial Conflict." *International Studies Review* 5(4):137–153.

Walter, Barbara F. 2004. "Does Conflict Beget Conflict? Explaining Recurring Civil War." *Journal of Peace Research* 41(3):371–388

Ware, Natalie D. 2001. "Congo War and the Role of Coltan." *American University ICE Case Studies.* December 2001. Retrieved from http://www1.american.edu/ted/ice/congo-coltan.htm

Weinstein, Jeremy M. 2005. "Resources and the Information Problem in Rebel Recruitment." *Journal of Conflict Resolution* 49(4):598–624.

Welch, Claude E., Jr. 2001. "Counterinsurgency." P. 181 in *Oxford Companion to Politics of the World Second Edition*, edited by J. Krieger (editor in chief). Oxford, UK: Oxford University Press.

Williams, Robin M., Jr. 1994. "The Sociology of Ethnic Conflicts: Comparative International Perspectives." *Annual Review of Sociology* 20:49–79.

Winer, Jonathan M. and Trifin J. Roule. 2003. "Follow the Money: The Finance of Illicit Resource Extraction." In *Natural Resources and Violent Conflict: Options and Actions*, edited by I. Bannon and P. Collier. Washington, DC: World Bank.

Wittman, Donald. 1979. "How a War Ends: A Rational Model Approach." *Journal of Conflict Resolution* 23(4):743–763).

Wolf, Albert B. 2011. "War Termination." P. 1756 in *The Encyclopedia of Political Science*, edited by G. T. Kurian (editor in chief). Washington, DC: Congressional Quarterly Press.

Wood, Reed M. 2010. "Rebel Capability and Strategic Violence against Civilians." *Journal of Peace Research* 47(5):601–614.

World Bank. 2003. *Breaking the Conflict Trap: Civil War and Development Policy, a World Bank Policy Research Report*. Washington, DC: World Bank and Oxford University Press.

World Bank. 2010. "The Impacts of Refugees on Neighbouring Countries: A Development Challenge." *World Development Report 2011 Background Note*. July. Retrieved from http://siteresources.worldbank.org/EXTSOCIALDEVELOPMENT/Resources/244362-1265299949041/6766328-1265299960363/WDR_Background_Paper_Refugees.pdf.

World Bank. 2013. "Poverty data." Retrieved from http://data.worldbank.org/topic/poverty.

Wucherpfennig, Julian. 2008. "Issue Indivisibility, Nationalism and Civil War Recurrence." Paper presented at SVPW Kongress, St. Gallen, Switzerland.

Young, Gale. 1997. "Fastest Growing Islam Winning Converts in the Western World." Retrieved from http://www.cnn.com/WORLD/9704/14/egypt.islam/.

Young, Joseph K. 2012. "Repression, Dissent and the Onset of Civil War." *Political Research Quarterly* 20(10):1–17.

Zartman, William. 1989. *Ripe for Resolution*. New York: Oxford University Press.

Zartman, I. William. 2001. "The Timing of Peace Initiatives: Hurting Stalemates and Ripe Moments." *The Global Review of Ethnopolitics* 1(1):8–18.

Zartman, I. William, Mark Anstey, and Paul Meerts. 2012. *The Slippery Slope to Genocide: Reducing Identity Conflicts and Preventing Mass Murder*. Oxford, UK: Oxford University Press.

Zedong, Mao. 1937. *On Guerrilla Warfare*. Translated with an Introduction by Brigadier General Samuel B. Griffith (retired), United States Marine Corps, 1989. Retrieved from http://www.marines.mil/Portals/59/Publications/FMFRP%2012-18%20%20Mao%20Tse-tung%20on%20Guerrilla%20Warfare.pdf.

Zenko, Micah and Emma Welch. 2012. "Where the Drones Are." *Foreign Policy* (Online article). May 29. Retrieved from http://www.foreignpolicy.com/articles/2012/05/29/where_the_drones_are.

Karl DeRouen, Jr. is Professor of Political Science and Director of the International Studies B.A. Program at the University of Alabama. He has authored or co-authored numerous articles and chapters on civil war, mediation, diversionary use of force, defense economics, and international political economy. His most recent books are *Routledge Handbook of Civil Wars* (2014, Routledge Press, co-edited with Edward Newman) and *Understanding Foreign Policy Decision Making* (2010, Cambridge University Press, with Alex Mintz).

CQ Press, an imprint of SAGE, is the leading publisher of books, periodicals, and electronic products on American government and international affairs. CQ Press consistently ranks among the top commercial publishers in terms of quality, as evidenced by the numerous awards its products have won over the years. CQ Press owes its existence to Nelson Poynter, former publisher of the *St. Petersburg Times*, and his wife Henrietta, with whom he founded Congressional Quarterly in 1945. Poynter established CQ with the mission of promoting democracy through education and in 1975 founded the Modern Media Institute, renamed The Poynter Institute for Media Studies after his death. The Poynter Institute (www.poynter.org) is a nonprofit organization dedicated to training journalists and media leaders.

In 2008, CQ Press was acquired by SAGE, a leading international publisher of journals, books, and electronic media for academic, educational, and professional markets. Since 1965, SAGE has helped inform and educate a global community of scholars, practitioners, researchers, and students spanning a wide range of subject areas, including business, humanities, social sciences, and science, technology, and medicine. A privately owned corporation, SAGE has offices in Los Angeles, London, New Delhi, and Singapore, in addition to the Washington, DC office of CQ Press.

®SAGE research**methods**

The essential online tool for researchers from the world's leading methods publisher

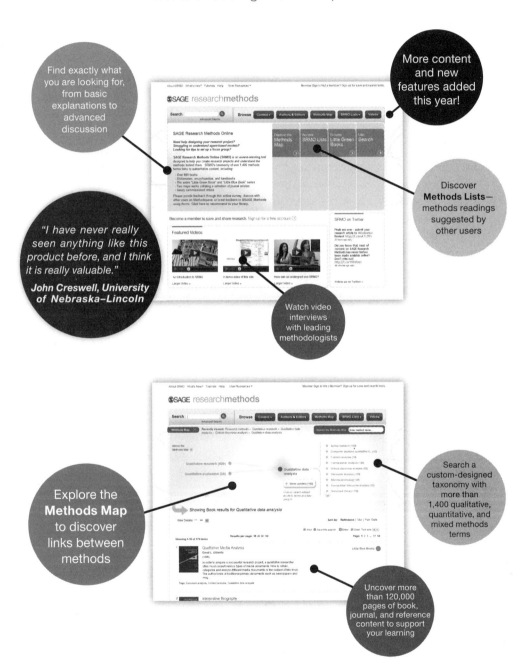

Find exactly what you are looking for, from basic explanations to advanced discussion

More content and new features added this year!

Discover **Methods Lists**— methods readings suggested by other users

"I have never really seen anything like this product before, and I think it is really valuable."

John Creswell, University of Nebraska–Lincoln

Watch video interviews with leading methodologists

Explore the **Methods Map** to discover links between methods

Search a custom-designed taxonomy with more than 1,400 qualitative, quantitative, and mixed methods terms

Uncover more than 120,000 pages of book, journal, and reference content to support your learning

Find out more at
www.sageresearchmethods.com